Danger in Kashmir

Danger
in Kashmir

by
JOSEF KORBEL

WITH A FOREWORD BY

C. W. NIMITZ, FLEET ADMIRAL, U.S. NAVY

Revised Edition

PRINCETON · NEW JERSEY

PRINCETON UNIVERSITY PRESS

To My Wife

Foreword

By C. W. Nimitz, Fleet Admiral, U.S. Navy

ONE hundred and seventy-three years ago on the North American continent, thirteen rebellious colonies won their independence from their mother country after six years of hard and desperate warfare. Seven years ago, on August 15, 1947, on another continent two great countries, India and Pakistan, had their independence thrust upon them by that same mother country in a somewhat urgent and not completely orderly manner.

It was not that the peoples of these two new-born countries had not been agitating for independence—as indeed they had for many years, sometimes with open violence, but mostly with passive resistance. When suddenly independence came with a rush, these new countries, whose combined numbers approximate one-fifth of the world's population, were ill-prepared for the peaceful settlement of the many knotty problems that such a hasty separation entailed. The existing situation, complicated by deep-seated antagonisms between the two most interested parties, called for a judicial procedure somewhat similar to that employed in a present-day settlement of an important estate. However, the mother country, instead of presiding as a probate court, left the two principal heirs more or less on their own to settle the division of the estate as best they could.

It was, of course, inevitable that there would be many matters on which the interested parties could reach no agreement without outside help. Among these residual problems, perhaps the most important that separates India and Pakistan today is their dispute over the ownership of the Princely State of Kashmir. This is the most important because it has flared into open, though undeclared, war, which has involved troops of both countries in fighting in Kashmir.

It is important also because a continuation of such fighting might develop into a world conflagration. To the casualties resulting from the fighting between the opposing troops must be added some ten million refugees and one million dead as a result of the disorderly rioting which accompanied or followed the inadequately prepared separation of the Indian subcontinent into two countries.

It was into this tense and dangerous situation that the youthful three-year-old United Nations moved in early 1948 to bring an end to the fighting, and to seek a peaceful solution to the basic dispute as to whether Kashmir should belong to India or to Pakistan. By January 1, 1949, a five-member United Nations Commission on India and Pakistan (UNCIP) had succeeded in stopping the fighting and had secured a cease-fire which became effective on January 1, 1949, and which to this date constitutes the high-water mark of agreement between the two contending countries. This cease-fire stands to the credit of the United Nations as one of its early and important successes. Then followed the long, patient (and to date, unsuccessful) efforts of the United Nations through its Commission, and later by employment of single mediators, to find a fair and peaceful settlement of the Kashmir dispute, a dispute which concerns not only India and Pakistan but the whole world as well.

The recording of this chapter of contemporary history has been undertaken by Dr. Josef Korbel, who is eminently qualified to present an accurate and impartial account of the Kashmir crisis down to the present. Dr. Korbel served as a member of the Commission (UNCIP) during its early and critical days, and in that capacity visited India, Pakistan, and Kashmir and conferred with their leaders and met their people. In the pages which follow, he makes a very important contribution to history. In our rapidly shrinking world there are very few people left unaffected by disturbances in other areas, even though such upheavals are remote or far removed. Certainly a dispute that involves one-fifth of the world's population, and that can erupt into a world war, bears careful watching. To all readers, then, I commend this authoritative account.

BERKELEY, CALIFORNIA
FEBRUARY 19, 1954

Preface

Over the vast Indo-Pakistan Subcontinent lies a shadow. It is a shadow cast from beyond the towering Himalayas and the Pamirs, from Sinkiang and Tibet and the Soviet Union. Four hundred and thirty million people, who so recently gained their independence, face the possible threat of its loss to those who, unlike the British, possess not even the doubtful asset of good intentions.

If such a tragedy should take place, it will be, however, the result not only of pressure from without but also, and more directly, by forfeiture from within. For today, as for the past seven years, under the awesome shadow of this possible disaster, the two great nations of the Subcontinent, India and Pakistan, continue to dissipate their wealth, their strength, and their energy on a near fratricidal struggle in which the hitherto almost unknown State of Kashmir has become the physical battleground.

It requires no thorough knowledge of political or military strategy to understand the interdependence of these two great nations. Geographically the Subcontinent is one entity of more than 1,500,000 square miles, almost devoid of natural inland barriers. In the north it is separated from the rest of Asia by the majestic peaks and tortuous defiles of the Himalayas and the Pamirs. Elsewhere the shores of India and Pakistan are watered in common by the waves of the Bay of Bengal and the Arabian Sea. Economically, their interdependence has been demonstrated over the years, the imports of one nation being in many instances the exportable products of the other.

But even as these factors point to the mutual advantages of close cooperation, so too do they indicate the compulsion of each to preserve the independence of the other. For should Pakistan, composed as it is of two geographically separated areas, succumb to Communism, two spearheads for invasion would be aimed at the heart of India. Should

India be communized, Pakistan would survive only so long as the Communists, for reasons of their own, wished to restrain their expansionist impulses.

Not only then for reasons of the Subcontinent's prosperity but also for deeply compelling reasons of its security, neither the nations immediately involved nor the rest of the free world can afford to see this animosity continue, an animosity of which the struggle for Kashmir is not only the principal external evidence but also the principal continuing source of infection.

And yet, since 1947, the conflict has continued. Although its original violence has given way to a prolonged and uneasy truce, the pressures of hatred and fear and frustration continue to exist under the thin crust of the cease-fire arrangement. If a satisfactory solution cannot be found, the danger of an explosion remains ever present. If it comes, there will come with it the moment which the Communist world alone eagerly awaits.

Should India and Pakistan consume themselves in war, surely the dark shadow would slide over the Himalayas and the Pamirs, and in its gloom there would have been found the unhappy solution to the problem of Kashmir.

J.K.

August 1954

Preface to the Second Edition

AS these words are being written, a tenuous cease-fire separates the armed forces of India and Pakistan along a fifteen-hundred-mile-long line. The cessation of hostilities was the result of a resolute demand from the Security Council addressed to India and Pakistan, who from August 5 to September 22, 1965, were engaged in bloody fighting over Kashmir. The Tashkent Agreement, signed by the President of Pakistan and the Prime Minister of India under the auspices of the Soviet Premier, Alexei N. Kosygin, on January 10, 1966, further provided for the withdrawal of the armed forces, not later than February 25, to the positions held before the outbreak of hostilities.

Every person acquainted with the complex aspects of the Kashmir dispute, dreaded the possibility of such large-scale hostilities between the two nations of the vast Subcontinent as for seventeen long years they failed to solve the future of Kashmir. Yet, after bloodshed and with the threat of continued bloodshed India and Pakistan seem as far away as ever from a solution to the Kashmir problem.

The first edition of this book was published in 1954 and covered the history of the Kashmir conflict up to that year. The second edition seemed to require no changes (although the tense of the last chapter reflects the year of its writing) except a final chapter to bring developments up to date. Lack of space and pressure of time imposed limitations on both the scope and research dimensions of this additional chapter. It could not have been accomplished without substantial help. My warm thanks go, therefore, to Mrs. Madeleine Albright (Russian Institute, Columbia University) and Mr. David M. Freeman (Graduate School of International Studies, University of Denver) for their research assistance, as well as to Miss Sue Ellen Markey (Graduate School of International Studies, University of Denver) and my friend, R. Russell Porter, for their editorial assistance.

J.K.

January 1966

Acknowledgments

I would like to express my sincere thanks to the Rockefeller Foundation, which facilitated the preparation of this book through a grant to the Social Science Foundation of the University of Denver. I am grateful to the governments of India and Pakistan for the source material they kindly sent me, and to the members of the Secretariat of the United Nations for their assistance in filling in the inevitable gaps in my documentation of the United Nations intervention in the Kashmir dispute. My profound gratitude goes also to Dr. Ben Cherrington, Dr. Raymond Dennett, Professor Rupert Emerson, Professor C. Dale Fuller, Professor Harold II. Fisher, Fleet Admiral Chester W. Nimitz, Professor David N. Rowe, and Professor Walter Sikes. Their generosity in reading my manuscript and their advice was of invaluable assistance to me. I owe special thanks to my colleague, Professor Russell Porter, for his patient and skilled work in editing the manuscript. I am indebted to the members of the secretarial staff of the Social Science Foundation, who gave freely of their time in typing it. It is perhaps needless to add that I am solely responsible for the contents of the book.

I gratefully acknowledge permission to quote from materials published by: Sh. Muhammad Ashraf, *Some Recent Speeches and Writings of Mr. Jinnah*, by Jamil-ud-Dinahmad; The John Day Company, *The Unity of India*, by Jawaharlal Nehru; *Civil and Military Gazette*; Doubleday & Company, Inc., *Beyond the High Himalayas*, by William O. Douglas, copyright 1952 by William O. Douglas; E. P. Dutton & Co., Inc., *Mission with Mountbatten*, copyright, 1951, by Alan Campbell-Johnson; Victor Gollancz, Ltd., *Betrayal in India*, by D. F. Karaka; *The Hindustan Times*; *Kashmir Affairs*; *New York Herald Tribune*; *The New York Times*; Nicholas Kaye, Ltd., *Time Only to Look Forward*,

Acknowledgments

by Rear Admiral The Earl Mountbatten of Burma; Oxford University Press, *The Indian Problem,* by R. Coupland; *The Pakistan Times*; People's Publishing House Ltd., *Kashmir and the Conspiracy against Peace,* by Rajbans Krishen; Princeton University Press, *The Soviets in World Affairs,* by Louis Fischer; Royal Asiatic Society, *The Tuzuk-I-Jahangiri or Memoirs of Jahangir,* translated by A. Rogers, edited by H. Beveridge; *The Statesman; The Times.*

Contents

Contents

MAPS OF THE AREA WILL BE FOUND ON PAGES 2 AND 51
DRAWN BY WALDO R. BARTON

Danger in Kashmir

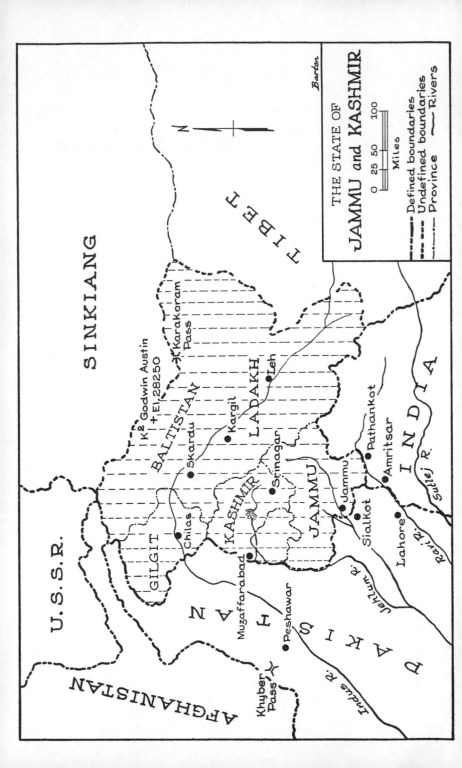

THE STATE OF
JAMMU and KASHMIR

Miles
0 25 50   100

— · — · — Defined boundaries
— · · — · · — Undefined boundaries
— · — · — Province
~~~~~~~ Rivers

Barton.

SINKIANG

TIBET

Karakoram
Pass

K² Godwin Austin
+ El, 28250

BALTISTAN

Skardu

Kargil

LADAKH

Leh

GILGIT

Chilas

KASHMIR

Srinagar

JAMMU

Muzaffarabad

Jammu

Pathankot

Amritsar

Sialkot

Lahore

INDIA

Sutlej R.

Ravi R.

Jhelum R.

U.S.S.R.

PAKISTAN

Peshawar

Indus R.

Khyber
Pass

AFGHANISTAN

N

1. The Forgotten Nation

"If one were to take to praise Kashmir, whole books would have to be written. . . . Kashmir is a garden of eternal spring, or an iron fort to a palace of kings—a delightful flower-bed, and a heart-expanding heritage for dervishes. Its pleasant meads and enchanting cascades are beyond all description. There are running streams and fountains beyond count. Wherever the eye reaches, there are verdure and running water. The red rose, the violet and the narcissus grow of themselves; in the fields, there are all kinds of flowers and all sorts of sweet-scented herbs more than can be calculated. In the soul-enchanting spring the hills and plains are filled with blossoms; the gates, the walls, the courts, the roofs, are lighted up by the torches of the banquet-adoring tulips. What shall we say of these things or the wide meadows and the fragrant trefoil?

> "The garden-nymphs were brilliant,
> Their cheeks shone like lamps;
> There were fragrant buds on their stems,
> Like dark amulets on the arms of the beloved;
> The wakeful, ode-rehearsing nightingales
> Whetted the desires of wine-drinkers;
> At each fountain the duck dipped his beak
> Like golden scissors cutting silk;
> There were flower-carpets and fresh rosebuds,
> The wind fanned the lamps of the roses,
> The violet braided her locks,
> The buds tied a knot in the heart."[1]

THUS in 1620 wrote Emperor Salim Jahangir of the beauties of Kashmir. Since that time many others have added their voices to the Emperor Salim's paean—but none more

[1] *The Tuzuk-I-Jahangiri or Memoirs of Jahangir*, translated by A. Rogers, edited by H. Beveridge. 2 volumes, Royal Asiatic Society, London, 1914, vol. II, p. 114.

eloquently than one of Kashmir's greatest descendants, Pandit Jawaharlal Nehru.

In 1940 Pandit Nehru revisited the beautiful land of his ancestors after an absence of twenty-three years, dedicated to his nation's frantic struggle for independence. And in the ripe years of his rich life he wrote with lyrical nostalgia:

". . . Like some supremely beautiful woman, whose beauty is almost impersonal and above human desire, such was Kashmir in all its feminine beauty of river and valley and lake and graceful trees. And then another aspect of this magic beauty would come to view, a masculine one, of hard mountains and precipices, and snow-capped peaks and glaciers, and cruel and fierce torrents rushing down to the valleys below. It had a hundred faces and innumerable aspects, ever-changing, sometimes smiling, sometimes sad and full of sorrow. The mist would creep up from the Dal Lake and, like a transparent veil, give glimpses of what was behind. The clouds would throw out their arms to embrace a mountaintop, or creep down stealthily like children at play. I watched this ever-changing spectacle, and sometimes the sheer loveliness of it was overpowering and I felt almost faint. I gazed at it, it seemed to me dreamlike and unreal, like the hopes and desires that fill us and so seldom find fulfillment. It was like the face of the beloved that one sees in a dream and that fades away on awakening. . . ."

Nehru saw Srinagar as "a fairy city of dreamlike beauty" which "is no fancy picture, for fairyland lies all around it; the magic is there already. . . ." And, "Kashmir calls [him] back, its pull is stronger than ever; it whispers its magic to the ears, and its memory disturbs the mind. How can they who have fallen under its spell release themselves from this enchantment?"[2]

What is this Kashmir that calls from a seventeenth-century emperor and a twentieth-century statesman such

[2] Jawaharlal Nehru, *The Unity of India*. The John Day Company. New York, 1942, pp. 223, 226, 240. Quoted by permission of The John Day Company, Inc.

ecstatic songs? The name itself is familiar through its wool, and the beauty of the Shalimar gardens is legend. But this is all the average man or woman can tell you of this forgotten corner of land, shrinking in the shadow of the majestic Himalayan colossus and the "roof of the world," the Pamirs.

The shy Kashmiri would look at you with gentle amazement if you told him that his case has been debated before the world forum, the United Nations, and that his plight has from time to time made headlines in the press of every country. Centuries of hard life have taught him to be reconciled to the strange role of living in a paradise that treats him poorly, forgotten by all, helped by none. Obediently and stolidly he accepts the status of the forgotten man in an undiscovered nation.

Only those who have visited Kashmir can see this cruel contrast between the nostalgic beauty and power of its scenery and the frightened dark eyes of its countless poor. Such visitors are few, and the country and its people have remained, to most of the world, obscure.

The Country

The term "Kashmir," as it is generally used, is actually not accurate. It applies only to one part of the entire territory, the official name of which is the State of Jammu and Kashmir. The state consists of several regions. Its heart is the famous Vale of Kashmir. South of it is the Jammu Province, to the east is Ladakh, and north of it, Baltistan; farther north are the regions of Hunza and Nagir, and west of them, the Gilgit Agency, composed of several political districts. West of the Vale are the districts of Muzaffarabad, Riasi, Poonch, and Mirpur.

Kashmir's irregular borders, many miles of which are as yet not internationally determined, touch a number of states. Beginning at its most northeasterly point, Kashmir borders upon Sinkiang, the line running south and east for some 400 miles; then for about 450 miles it finds itself neighbor to Tibet. Between India to the south and Kashmir to the north, the border continues for some 350 miles, then joins the boundary of Pakistan and turning northwest for about 700 miles finds Afghanistan. Here the border swings east for about 160 miles, where it ends in a somewhat unclear situation—on some maps it joins the Soviet Union for about 20 miles, while on others (including some Russian maps)[3] it ends at a common point with the borders of both Sinkiang and Russia.

The whole country is about the size of Minnesota—84,471 square miles—and its latitude is approximately that of North Carolina. The total population, according to the census of 1941, was 4,021,616 (in 1950 an executive statement declared the population to be 4,370,000). Of these, 77.11 per cent (3,101,247) were Muslims, 20.12 per cent Hindus, and 1.64 per cent Sikhs. The rate of increase of population has been estimated at 1 per cent a year.

As to the individual provinces, the Jammu Province has an area of 12,378 square miles and a population of 1,981,433. Of this number, 61 per cent are Muslims living mainly west and north of the Chenab River. The other 39 per cent, mostly Hindus, are concentrated predominantly south and east of the river. The Kashmir Province, 8,539 square miles in size, has a total population of 1,728,705, of which 93.7 per cent are Muslims. The other regions—Gilgit, Baltistan, and Ladakh—are almost entirely Muslim with the exception of the one region of Ladakh adjacent to Tibet, where 40,939 Buddhists live.

The political and economic life of the entire area is centered around the Vale of Kashmir, a rich strip of land about 85 miles long and 25 miles wide. Its principal city, the ancient Srinagar (Shri Nagar = City of Wealth of Knowledge), with 210,000 inhabitants, was the home of the Maharaja except for the winters, which he usually spent in

[3] *Bol'shoi Sovetskii Atlas Mira,* Moskva, 1937.

6

Jammu. The Vale, lying 5,000 feet above sea level, is rich in fruits of all kinds as well as in wheat, rice, maize, and wood.

Jammu, geographically, is a succession of mountain ranges and plateaus and is separated from Kashmir by Pir Panjal, which is accessible only during the snow-free period through Banihal Pass, 9,000 feet high. The southwestern part of Jammu is open to Pakistan, and its southeastern part to India. The only 16 miles of railroad built in Jammu run to Sialkot in Pakistan.

In the northern regions the rugged mountains are topped by the world's second highest peak, Mt. Goodwin Austen, unconquered until July 1954. The sparse population is scattered over vast distances and isolated almost entirely from their capital city of Srinagar.

Few roads connect the towns and provinces or open Kashmir to the outside world. One of these leads northwest from Srinagar through Baramula Pass, along the Jhelum River, to Pakistan. Another runs south from Srinagar to Jammu over the Banihal Pass and farther to Sialkot in Pakistan. A third was built in the fall of 1947 by the Indian army, a branch road from the town of Jammu to the Indian border village of Pathankot. The final one of any importance is the trade route running from Srinagar east to Kashgar in Chinese Turkestan and to Tibet over Zojila Pass.

Indeed, the principal highways were (and still largely are) three rivers: Jhelum, Chenab, and Indus, which flow from or through Kashmir to Pakistan. Over them floated the timbers from the Kashmir forests, the sale of which was once the most important source of Kashmir's total revenue. Upon these waters and over the roads running along their banks there went, towards Pakistan, the fruit, vegetables, wine, woolen and silk materials, carpets, and the pretty products of skilled Kashmiri artists and artisans.

On the other hand, coal and steel, metal and cotton

products, sugar, tea, oidseeds, and tobacco were imported to Kashmir from what is the Republic of India today; wheat, oils, salt and petrol came from Pakistan or from overseas, passing through the port of Karachi. According to rough estimates, 36 per cent of Kashmir imports came from Pakistan or from overseas; 64 per cent from India. It should be remembered, however, that Indian products were shipped westward through the present Pakistan, since Kashmir was not directly accessible from India. It mattered little in the old days, for British India and the Princely States formed one economic entity. No railroad was constructed in Kashmir because its rulers preferred their isolation. And, with the exception of its southwestern border, Kashmir was indeed isolated by its colossal mountains: from India, Tibet, and Sinkiang by the Himalayas; from the Soviet Union and Afghanistan by the Pamirs.

The People

The Kashmiris call their country Kasheer and the language they speak Koshur. Though technically under the central administration of one dynasty, the people of the State of Jammu and Kashmir have hardly any sense of cohesion. Wild mountains and primitive roads, most of them impassable for several months of every year, discourage any sense of unity.

Just as the country is broken into separate areas by geography, so are its people separated and divided by cultural differences. The Hindus of Kashmir remain apart from all other people; the 73,000 Kashmiri Pandits, members of the Brahmin caste, and the 155,000 Jammu Brahmins enjoyed until recently the privileged position of landowners, moneylenders, and state functionaries. The Muslims, though bound by the very strong tie of Islam, show little unity in temperament or attitude.

Kashmiris from the Vale of Kashmir reveal such individual traits that they are considered by some historians as a nation in their own right. They are docile and passive, whereas the Jammu Muslims resemble the Muslims of Pakistan's Punjab, renowned for their fearlessness as warriors. The Gilgit and Baltistan Muslims live in complete isolation from the rest of this divided country, administering themselves through their chieftains. Ladakh's Buddhists, living in what is also called Little Tibet, have spiritual affinity with the Chinese Tibetans, and their lamas offer allegiance to the Dalai Lama in Lhasa.

This, then, is Kashmir, a nation divided by its mountains, its gods, its traditions, its allegiances, and the temperament of its peoples.

The Past

Some historians have made of Kashmir the principal invasion route to India, including that of Alexander of Macedonia in 326 B.C. They explain the light complexion of Kashmiris by the fact that when Alexander withdrew he left behind a number of soldiers. They also find in Kashmir remnants of Hellenic sculpture and architecture. Others give little support to this location of the path of invasions and assert that the waves of intrusions—including the landing of Mohammed Bin Kasim on the shores of Sind—followed different roads and various passes leading to the Subcontinent from Persia, Baluchistan, and Afghanistan, or the northern passes between Central Asia and Kashmir. There is a common view, however, that some invasions of Central Asia tribes, including the Scythians, did pass through Kashmir. It would be difficult, at any rate, to exaggerate the strategic importance of the State of Jammu and Kashmir to the security of the Subcontinent, lying as it does so near the precarious borders of the Soviet Union and China.

The history of Kashmir is a sad story. As one scholar, Vincent H. Smith, wrote, "Few regions in the world can have had worse luck than Kashmir in the matter of government." And his explanation, which seems to be echoed by

9

most historians of this unfortunate country, ascribes their fate "partly to the cowardly character of the population, which invited oppression."[4]

Only one writer, G. M. D. Sufi, seems to disagree. In his monumental work[5] he pictures the Kashmiris as feared warriors of an ancient day who through centuries of oppression lost these fighting qualities. He quotes from a report, "Remonstrantie," written by Francisco Pelsaert, who was in India from 1621 to 1627 in the service of the Dutch East India Company. Pelsaert described the Kashmiris as "fanatical Muslims." Sufi further found them to be a people of superior intellect, intelligent and gay; emotional, hospitable, fond of singing, good cooking; good businessmen and excellent craftsmen; not drunkards, kind to their wives and children. He criticized them, however, for being envious, sometimes malicious and dirty; also, contrary to the spirit and philosophy of Islam, mystical and superstitious. "The Kashmiri is indeed made up of contradictions. He is timid, yet persistent, degraded yet intellectual, mystical yet adventurous, shrewd and businesslike."[6]

As the centuries passed, the people of Kashmir lived under a succession of foreign dynasties—Pandava, Maurya, Kushan, Gonandya, Karkota, Utpala and Lohara. Only one characteristic was held in common by these foreign rulers —the cruelty of their suppression and exploitation.

Reliable sources trace the history of Kashmir only to the beginning of the seventh century, although it is known that in the second century Kashmir was annexed by Emperor Kanishka and became part of the Kushan Empire, later a part of China. For a period of 600 years (from the eighth to the fourteenth century) the country, despite its exploita-

[4] Vincent H. Smith, *The Oxford History of India*. The Clarendon Press, Oxford, 1928, p. 176.

[5] G. M. D. Sufi, *Kashīr, Being a History of Kashmir*. 2 volumes, the University of Punjab, Lahore, 1948.

[6] G. M. D. Sufi, *Islamic Culture in Kashmir*. The Army Press, Simla, p. 13.

tion, was relatively independent and flourishing. Historians nevertheless have called its ruler for the second part of the eleventh century the "Nero of Kashmir."

In the fourteenth century Kashmir was invaded and conquered by Muslims, and the population, sometimes peacefully, sometimes forcibly and in masses, was converted from Hinduism to Islam. The period of the fifty-year rule of Zain-Ul-Abidin (1422-1474) was considered one of Kashmir greatness and has been called its Golden Age. Various Sultans continued in their rule over the country till 1587 (some sources name other dates, 1586 or 1588), when it was annexed by Emperor Akbar and made a part of the Moghul Empire.

For the first time in centuries the exhausted and exploited people enjoyed a short breathing spell under the rule of this enlightened monarch. One legend says, however, that even Akbar, when first taking refuge from the Indian summer heat in the ideal climate of Kashmir, was enraged by the docile character of the Kashmiris. "You Kashmiris have stomachs to eat but not to fight," he told them. "Men? Faint-hearts, not lion-hearts."[7] And to show his contempt, he ordered them to change their dress into a skirtlike costume as a symbol of their feminine behavior. There is another story, however, that attributes far different motives to the Emperor's command. This one insists that it was because of his fear of the Kashmiris' fighting spirit and ability that he ordered them to put on over their trousers a clumsy skirt which would make their movements, and therefore their fighting, more difficult.

Akbar's son and successor, Jahangir, followed his father's example as did the two last Moghul Emperors. And whatever the truth of their attitude toward the people may be, their devotion to its climate and its beauty may be seen in the monuments of architecture they erected on Dal Lake.

[7] Maud Diver, *Royal India*. Appleton-Century Co., New York, 1942, p. 274.

In 1752, with the declining power of the last Moghul, Kashmir was conquered by Ahmad Shah Abdali of Afghanistan, who established a brutally oppressive rule over the passive Kashmiris. When in 1819 the Sikhs, coming from their homeland in the adjacent Punjab, entered Kashmir to oust the Afghan tyrants, they were welcomed by the population as liberators. But the unhappy Kashmiris soon discovered that the liberators were nothing more than a new type of oppressor, this time religious fanatics seeking revenge upon the helpless Kashmiri Muslims whose forefathers had once been Hindus. "The penalty imposed on a Sikh for slaying a Muslim was only twenty rupees [seven dollars]."[8]

With the Sikh "protectorate" over Kashmir, forces were set in motion which eventually produced the modern State of Jammu and Kashmir.

Jammu had consisted for centuries of a number of small principalities whose uninterrupted pastime seems to have been warring upon one another. One principality in the southeast area, high in the hills, was populated by the Dogras. As a matter of fact, an expert on the history of the Princely States wrote, "The Jammu people are known generally as Dogras whatever their origin."[9] They consisted of Sikhs, Rajputs, other Hindus and Muslims, all of whom displayed extraordinary fighting qualities in contrast to the indolent Kashmiris.

When the Sikhs launched their expedition against the Afghan ruler in Kashmir, they were assisted by a member of the Dogra family, Raja Gulab Singh. Because of his assistance, the Sikhs rewarded him by establishing his control over the whole Province of Jammu. In 1837 and in 1839, he extended his rule by seizing from Tibet the northern areas, Ladakh and Baltistan.

[8] Sir William Barton, *The Princes of India*. Nisbet & Co., London, 1934, p. 121.
[9] *Ibid.*, p. 120.

Seven years later the British waged war against the re-bellious Sikhs. It was at this time that Raja Gulab Singh engineered his great coup. Any sense of obligation he may have felt toward the Sikhs for establishing his rule over Jammu vanished before his realistic appraisal of the even-tual outcome of the struggle. At first he remained strictly neutral; then he assumed the role of adviser and mediator for the British; and finally, according to some sources, he actively participated in fighting his one-time protectors. When, after their defeat, the Sikhs were ordered to re-linquish their hold over Kashmir, Raja Gulab Singh played his ace. He offered the British 7,5 mil rupees (750,000 pounds) for the possession of Kashmir, and the final re-sult was the Treaty of Amritsar, signed in 1846. Kashmir, by its terms, was to belong "forever, an independent pos-session, to Maharaja Gulab Singh and the heirs male of his body."

His purchase included Gilgit, but the Dogra dynasty never succeeded in establishing actual control over this re-mote and wild area. In 1889 the British, wary of increasing Russian pressure towards the Pamirs, instituted the Gilgit Agency under the direct rule of a British political agent, and from that time Gilgit paid even less allegiance to the Maharaja of Kashmir.

Thus began the modern history of Kashmir, united with Jammu under the rule of the Dogra dynasty. It was for the Kashmiris another tragic experience in a millennium of trag-edies. Though once Hindus, they had for 500 years been Muslims. Now, by the terms of the Treaty of Amritsar, the Hindu Dogras possessed the territory; they immediately set out upon a policy of unlimited cruelty that seemed to vent upon the hapless Kashmiris all the pent-up hatred of the Hindus for the five centuries of Muslim rule. The willing instruments of this policy became the Kashmiri Pandits, who shared with the Maharaja his contempt for his Muslim subjects. The land was mostly owned by the Maharaja or the Hindu landowners. The Muslims, toiling on their land, had to pay such high taxes that economic crises bordering on starvation became more or less a regular affair.

The State of Jammu and Kashmir was, among the Princely States of the Subcontinent, second in importance only to the State of Hyderabad. The "paramount power," the British Crown, had an exclusive responsibility, as in the case of other states, for the country's foreign affairs and defense, but according to Dr. K. M. Panikkar, it was until 1886 "a completely independent state maintaining its own limited diplomatic relations. It received no British residents in its courts."[10] The internal affairs were left to the authority of the Maharaja, and his oppressive measures were followed vigilantly, though benevolently, by the viceroy representative at his court, a resident. The Maharaja was flattered by the exalted title of His Highness. He was a major-general of the British Indian army and when paying a visit was saluted by 21 guns—one among five "twenty-one-gun" princes. His pleasures included gold, polo, tennis, and hunting; he delighted in extravagant parties, maintained expensive stables, and in all ways indulged himself with extravagant pomp and luxury. Not the least of his idle pleasures was his persecution of the Muslims, and to his underlings he gave his blessing for their slaughter.

At times this "amusement" took a bizarre turn. The story is told that on one of his tours, the Maharaja stopped at a river to watch the convicts working at the construction of a bridge. He was impressed by the skill of one of them and praised him, whereupon the convict asked for his release. "What was your offense?" asked the Maharaja. "Only a little matter," said the convict, and explained that he had killed a little girl for her ornaments. The Maharaja took a pen and "drew a line down and then across his trunk. Then a sawyer was ordered to saw the man in four pieces. 'One

[10] Sardar Dr. K. M. Panikkar, *Kashmir*. India League, London, p. 8.

piece shall be sent to North, one South, one East, and one West,' said the Maharaja. . . . 'For I want my people to know that I do not regard the murder of a girl for the sake of her ornaments as a little matter.' "[11]

In 1850 the Maharaja expressed the wish that the Kashmiris return to the faith of their forefathers and wanted to reconvert them en masse to Hinduism, but the high priests of Hinduism at Benares refused to give their blessing to the plan.

The first Maharaja, Gulab Singh, was succeeded in 1857 by Maharaja Ranbir Singh. Some sources describe him as a noble and just ruler, though in the hands of greedy and cruel Hindu administrators. His rule was followed by that of Major-General, His Highness Sir Partab Singh, G.C.I., G.C.I.E., in 1885. Because of court intrigue growing out of the fact that the Maharaja had no son to succeed him, and because of Russian activities on the Pamir border of Kashmir, the British Crown in 1889 replaced his rule temporarily by a council, and strengthened the garrisons on the northern roads. This temporary arrangement lasted till 1905. The Maharaja was then reinstalled, at least nominally. But there is evidence that the council, following the advice of Sir Walter Lawrence, somewhat alleviated the plight of the people by introducing many reforms. But despite such reforms (continuing down to the last few years) the life of the Kashmiris remained a saga of poverty and oppression. Everything and everybody was taxed. Production of silk, saffron, paper, tobacco, wine, and salt, as well as the sale of grain, was the monopoly of the state. The state police ruled mercilessly. For minor offenses people were thrown in jail, often without trial. As late as the 1920's it was a capital offense for a Muslim to kill a cow; later, the penalty was reduced to ten years of imprisonment and still later to seven years (Section 219 of the State Penal Code).

[11] Sir Walter R. Lawrence, *The India We Served.* Houghton Mifflin, New York, 1929, p. 125.

The Forgotten Nation

Little was done by the Dogra ruler for the health and welfare of the people. According to the 1941 census 93.4 per cent of the population was illiterate. In 1939 there was one boys' primary school for every 66 square miles and for every 3,850 people, and one girls' school for every 467 square miles and 25,670 persons. One state college existed in the whole country. About 60 per cent of the peasants had holdings of about 16 *kanals* (two acres) each. Their net annual income was 74-8-0 rupees (about $17) per family and 10-10-3 rupees (about $2.50) per head. The rest of the peasant population was landless. As late as 1944-1945 the per capita income was only 11 rupees (about $3.00). Out of this sum people had to pay taxes of around 21 cents per head. Although the Maharaja's court spent four million rupees, and five million rupees went to the army, only 3.6 million rupees were spent on public health, agriculture, industries, roads, irrigation, and education.

The First Awakening

In 1925 the nephew of the Dogra ruler, His Highness Maharaja Sir Hari Singh Bahadur, mounted the throne. It was with the beginning of his rule that the first signs of political awakening were seen among the oppressed peoples of his Princely State. The first tangible evidence was a proclamation in 1927, made in response to the protests of a small group of professional and white-collar workers, which theoretically opened the way for the participation of Muslims in government and military services. For some time the proclamation was meaningless, as only local Pandits and some Hindus and Sikhs continued to occupy all the profitable positions in government and to serve in the state armed forces.

In 1929, however, an All-India National Congress meeting was held in Lahore, the ancient city of India not far from the border of Jammu and Kashmir. The resolutions of this meeting found an echo in Kashmir. In the early

1930's the waves of the non-violence movement were sweeping India, and patriots in Kashmir, inspired by this spirit of revolt, renewed their claims for the admission of Muslims to the administrative and military services of their country. They formed first a "Reading Room Party," seeking to educate themselves politically; then later, with the assistance of the religious leaders, or *mullahs*, they conducted political meetings in the mosques. Gradually this political consciousness began to take firm roots, spreading from the intelligentsia to the people of the middle class, though not as yet to the peasants. Then the agitation was carried beyond the "reading rooms" and mosques to open meetings, until in 1931 the Maharaja gave his blessing to the foundation of three political parties in Kashmir. These were the Kashmiri Pandits Conference, the Hindu Sabha in Jammu, and the Sikhs' Shiromani Khalsa Darbar. This was obviously only a gesture on the part of the Maharaja because it included political representation only for the non-Muslim groups. As a consequence, the overwhelming majority of the population remained without any organized political party.

It was in 1931 that the growing dissatisfaction of the Kashmiri people burst into flame. It was led by a man of twenty-five, an unemployed teacher hitherto unknown but soon to play an important role in the political history of Kashmir—Sheikh Mohammad Abdullah.

Sheikh Abdullah was one of five children born at Sovrah, on the outskirts of Srinagar. His father, Sheikh Mohammad Ibrahim, was a dealer in shawls. The mother sent her son to the Islamic College in Lahore and to Aligarh University. Sheikh Abdullah was an imposing figure. His six feet four inches of height towered over his countrymen, and his intellect attracted the attention and respect of those who were associated with him in his revolutionary efforts.

The Maharaja reacted to the 1931 revolt with swift resolve. On September 24 he declared martial law and threw

Sheikh Abdullah into prison for several weeks. This first abortive attempt, however, was highly significant. For the first time in centuries the Kashmiri people responded to the leadership of one who sought to throw off the old yoke of oppression. They shed their docile and servile characters, and, as Sir Zafrulla Khan, the Pakistan Minister of Foreign Affairs, related before the United Nations on January 16, 1948, "they were mowed down by the bullets of the State Dogra troops in their uprising . . . but refused to turn back and received those bullets on their bared breasts."[12]

This first attempt was quelled, but the spirit of resistance continued to grow. Imprisonment brought to Sheikh Abdullah only further admiration from the Kashmiri people, and they rewarded him with the nickname *Sher-E-Kashmir*, the "Lion of Kashmir." After his release from prison, Sheikh Abdullah continued to work for the political rights of his people, and in October 1932 founded the All Jammu and Kashmir Muslim Conference, claiming to represent the state's Muslim population.

The British government, disturbed by the oppressive rule of the Maharaja and by the extent of the opposition, sent the Glancy Commission to Srinagar to investigate Muslim grievances. As a result of the inquiry the Maharaja was requested to introduce certain land reforms and to give the people the right to elect a legislative assembly. Whether the Maharaja ever intended to carry out the British recommendations cannot be known, but in 1933 revolt broke out once more, and once again on June 1 martial law was declared and the uprising crushed (Ordinance-Notification No. 19). A number of people were killed, and thousands were arrested without warrant. Property was confiscated and heavy fines imposed.

This revolt had been helped by Muslims from Punjab who in tens of thousands in organized groups (*jatha*) slipped through the open plains between Punjab and

[12] *Security Council Official Records*, Third Year, Nos. 1-15, p. 65.

Jammu. They were led by a Muslim political party, the Ahrar Party.[13] According to some sources their activity in this case was largely due to the fact that they felt they had compromised themselves in Punjab by attempting to collaborate with the Indian National Congress, and wished now to regain their popularity by such organized assistance to the Kashmir and Jammu Muslims.

After this second defeat a civil disobedience campaign was organized in the spring of 1934 by Sheikh Abdullah's closest political friend, Chaudhri Ghulam Abbas, but this met the same fate as the previous attempts to compel the Maharaja to liberalize his policy toward the Muslims.

But revolt continued to seethe in Kashmir, and finally, pressed by the British from above and by the Kashmiri people from below, the Maharaja on April 22, 1934, enacted the Constitutional Act, Regulation No. 1 of Samvat 1991 (A.D. 1934). In the first election ever held in Kashmir, in 1934, the Muslim Conference captured 14 out of 21 seats allotted to the Muslim voters in the State Assembly, *Praja Sabha.* It should be quickly pointed out, however, that this represented no great concession on the part of the Maharaja because the Assembly was composed of 75 members, 40 of whom were elected and 35 nominated. Also, the regulations which controlled the ballot (the voter had to be literate, have an income of $80 per year, and possess $1,500 worth of property) allowed only 8 per cent of the population to vote. Finally, the Assembly itself had only consultative powers. When this final fact became fully evident in 1936, all elected members of the Assembly walked out. Two years later new elections were held, and this time the Muslim Conference so controlled the Muslim voters of Kashmir that they elected 19 out of 21 seats allotted to the Muslims.

The year 1939 was a fateful one for the Muslims in Kash-

[13] Sir Geoffrey De Montmorency, *The Indian States and Indian Federation.* Cambridge University Press, 1942, pp. 73-74.

mir. As a matter of fact, the origins of the present tragic struggle can, in a sense, be traced back to those months. Up to that time the Muslims had been united through the Muslim Conference. In 1939 this unity was broken. Responsible for this tragic schism was none other than the popular Lion of Kashmir, Sheikh Mohammad Abdullah.

For some time Sheikh Mohammad Abdullah had been dissatisfied with the political program and practices of the Muslim movement on the Subcontinent, the Muslim Conference of Kashmir in particular. He objected to the fact that only Muslims were allowed to be its members. Then, too, its political leaders seemed to him to be preoccupied with the Muslim-Hindu struggle, unaware of the true significance of their own nationalist movement. They were, indeed, accused by the Indian National Congress leaders of reactionary tendencies and mediaeval theocratic thinking. Sheikh Abdullah's progressive, socially advanced mind did not find inspiration in this kind of political party. Instead, Nehru's secular and progressive concept of Indian society, including his dream of a united independent India, appealed to his way of thinking. In fact, the leadership of the Indian National Congress was permeated with ideas close to Abdullah's heart.

To advance these ideas, he and a Kashmiri Brahmin, Prem Nath Bazaz, founded in 1935 a weekly, *Hamdard*, printed in Urdu, in which he pleaded for admission of the Sikhs and Hindus to the membership of the Muslim Conference. At one time he became president of the All-India States' Peoples' Congress sponsored by the Indian National Congress. He also became a close friend of Pandit Nehru, to whom, it is said, he was introduced by Bazaz.

This development culminated in June 1939, when there emerged under Abdullah's guidance the All Jammu and Kashmir National Conference. Its first president was Ghulam Mohammad Sadiq, an old friend of Abdullah and, significantly enough, a man who was later to become the chief exponent of the Communist Party of India in Kashmir. Inevitably there soon developed between the Muslim leaders in Kashmir a split as definite and as pronounced as that between the Indian National Congress and the Muslim League.

In 1939 the Maharaja liberalized his rule somewhat, proclaiming the Jammu and Kashmir Constitution Act No. 14 of Samvat 1996 (A.D. 1939). This established an executive office, the Council of Ministers, and a juridical and legislative branch of public administration, but most of the decisive powers remained in the Maharaja's hands.

Two cities, Srinagar and Jammu, were administered by municipal councils, of which four-fifths of the members were elected; smaller towns were to be administered by town area committees, with one half of the members elected; and some 5,000 villages were administratively fused into 720 districts, *panchayats*. They all enjoyed only nominal authority, the most powerful persons being the district commissioner directly responsible to the government.

As in British India, however, where every political concession by the British government deepened the split between the Indian National Congress and the Muslim League, so in Kashmir, with every political concession made by the Maharaja, the abyss grew between the National Conference with its program of unity for all India and the pro-Pakistan Muslim Conference.

For some time, possibly because of the extreme popularity of Sheikh Abdullah, the All Jammu and Kashmir National Conference captured the attention of the Kashmiris. However, when in 1943 Mohammed Ali Jinnah visited Kashmir and presided over the annual congress of the Muslim Conference, he injected new life and authority into this organization.

In 1944 the popularity of the National Conference was still on the ascendancy, and one of its members, Mirza Afzal Beg, entered the Maharaja's government to become

Minister of Public Works. But events were soon to work against the National Conference. As Muslims in British India became more and more pronounced in their support of an independent Pakistan, the Muslims in Jammu and Kashmir began to return to the Muslim Conference led by Ghulam Abbas, abandoning the ranks of the National Conference of Sheikh Abdullah.

Then, in March 1946, Abdullah played a poor card. The British Cabinet Mission was to meet with Indian leaders to discuss the future of India, including the status of the Princely States. First, Mirza Afzal Beg resigned to free the National Conference of governmental responsibilities in these forthcoming negotiations. This was followed by a memorandum to the Mission from Sheikh Abdullah, declaring that "the fate of the Kashmir nation is in the balance and in that hour of decision we demand our basic democratic right to send our selected representatives to the constitution-making bodies that will construct the framework of Free India. We emphatically repudiate the right of the Princely Order to represent the people of the Indian States or their right to nominate personal representatives as our spokesmen."[14]

The memorandum was ignored, whereupon Sheikh Abdullah reacted by launching in May a "Quit Kashmir" campaign against the Maharaja. This sentiment would seem to be cause for rejoicing among the Kashmiris, but actually Sheikh Abdullah was accused of highly ulterior motives. It was charged that he opened this agitation solely in an attempt to regain the popularity which he had lost for his pro-India policy. Even his former close associate, Prem Nath Bazaz, accused him of opportunism and through his paper, *Hamdard,* denied him the right of claiming to represent both the Muslims and Hindus. He further asserted

[14] *Jammu and Kashmir Constituent Assembly,* opening address by the Honorable Sheikh Mohammad Abdullah, Srinagar, November 5, 1951. The Caxton Press, New Delhi, p. 14.

that the Muslims followed largely the Muslim Conference and the Hindus had their own parties.

Not only did this ill-fated gesture fail to strengthen Abdullah's position with the Muslims but also, because of his campaign against the Maharaja, he became unacceptable to many Hindus and Sikhs who looked upon the Maharaja as the main pillar of their privileged position in Muslim Kashmir.[15] Nor was his loss of political power his only reversal. Shortly thereafter he was arrested by the Maharaja, tried and sentenced to nine years in prison.

Then, in October 1946, Sheikh Abdullah and his political enemy, the leader of the Muslim Conference, Ghulam Abbas, were brought together by the Maharaja through a simple but not particularly happy expedient. Ghulam Abbas joined Sheikh Abdullah in jail for leading his Muslim Conference members in a "campaign of action" similar to Jinnah's in British India.

Sheikh Abdullah told me much later (in September 1948) about his many night-long conversations with Abbas in prison and how together they contemplated reconciliation and resumption of the common struggle. Ghulam Abbas had told me the same story one month before in Karachi. Both leaders recounted these conversations with feelings of sadness and nostalgia. They seemed to share the belief that the split in 1939 had been the beginning of all their troubles.

In January 1947 new elections were held in Kashmir. They were boycotted by the National Conference, and the Muslim Conference captured sixteen Muslim seats out of twenty-one. Both parties claimed victory in the elections. The National Conference pointed out that only 182,800 voters out of a possible 607,419 went to the polls. They drew from this the conclusion that their boycott had been highly successful and illustrated graphically their popularity.

[15] Prem Nath Bazaz, *Truth about Kashmir*. The Kashmir Democratic Union, 1950, pp. 4-5.

But the Muslim Conference, pointing to the impassable snow-clogged roads at the time of the elections, claimed that the polling of 30 per cent of the possible vote was a smashing victory and that the National Conference's appeal for a boycott had been largely ignored.

Meanwhile, the leaders of both parties lay in the Maharaja's prison, talking through the night about reconciliation. But it was a reconciliation that would never take place. For beyond the walls of the Maharaja's prison, indeed beyond the borders of his Princely State, historic forces were shaping their own pattern of events, which were soon to plunge Kashmir into another bloody chapter of its long and tragic history.

Over these forces neither Sheikh Abdullah nor Ghulam Abbas had any control.

2. The Real Issue

IF THE struggle for Kashmir were a struggle for territory, if it were a struggle for national resources, or for manpower, or for strategic position, or for any of the other prizes for which nations traditionally contest, it might well have been solved some years ago; it might no longer constitute for the entire Subcontinent the menace that today it remains.

But it is none of these. At least, not primarily. What makes the problem of Kashmir the nigh insoluble debacle that it is, what makes the leaders of both contending parties dispute in such bitterness and compromise with such grudging reticence, what makes the whole history of its attempted settlement such a record of frustration, annoyance, and exasperation is something more than these traditional causes for international dispute.

The real cause of all the bitterness and bloodshed, all the venomed speech, the recalcitrance and the suspicion that have characterized the Kashmir dispute is the uncompromising and perhaps uncompromisable struggle of two ways of life, two concepts of political organization, two scales of values, two spiritual attitudes, that find themselves locked in deadly conflict, a conflict in which Kashmir has become both symbol and battleground.

Simply, these two irrevocably opposed positions may be characterized thus: To India the Subcontinent is inescapably one nation. To Pakistan it is, just as inescapably, two. The examination of the intensity of these two beliefs, their nature, their origins, and the events that were and remain the expression of their conflict is essential to the full understanding of this conflict's present-day symbol, Kashmir.

Jawaharlal Nehru believed deeply and passionately in the national unity of all India. To him it was a natural consequence of the centuries of common history, of common achievements, common suffering, and the mutual influences of the varied cultures and customs of its diverse peoples.

He agreed with Vincent Smith that "India beyond all doubt possesses a deep underlying fundamental unity, far more profound than that produced either by geographical isolation or by political suzerainty. That unity transcends the innumerable diversities of blood, colour, language, dress, manners, and sect."[1] He explained the difficulties between Muslims and Hindus as a "dispute among upper-class people for a division of the spoils of office or of representation in a legislature."[2] He was convinced that the dispute was created and cultivated by the "third party," the British, who ruled over India by the method of *divide et impera*. This opinion was shared by Mahatma Gandhi.

Mohammed Ali Jinnah had no patience with Nehru's philosophy of the oneness of the Indian nation. For him, "It is extremely difficult to appreciate why our Hindu friends fail to understand the real nature of Islam and Hinduism. They are not religions in the strict sense of the word, but are, in fact, different and distinct social orders, and it is a dream that the Hindus and Muslims can ever evolve a common nationality, and this misconception of one Indian nation has gone far beyond the limits and is the cause of most of your troubles and will lead India to destruction if we fail to revise our notions in time. The Hindus and Muslims belong to two different religious philosophies, social customs, literatures. They neither intermarry nor interdine and, indeed, they belong to two different civilizations which are based mainly on conflicting ideas and conceptions."[3]

To Nehru, however, the conflict was not even one between two religions but "between those who stood for a nationalist-democratic-socially revolutionary policy and

[1] Smith, *The Oxford History of India, op.cit.*, p. x.
[2] Nehru, *The Unity of India, op.cit.*, p. 20.
[3] *Some Recent Speeches and Writings of Mr. Jinnah*, collected and edited by Jamil-ud-Dinahmad. Kashmiri Bazar, Lahore, 1942, p. 153.

26

those who were concerned with preserving the relics of a feudal regime."⁴ He was sure it would be settled after the "third party" withdrew and when the Muslims began to enjoy the blessings of living in a secular, united, and democratic India. To him, "The whole question of minorities and majorities in India is tied up with foreign and third-party rule. Eliminate that rule, and the basic aspect of this question changes."⁵ He saw in communalism, with its program of separatism, a reactionary force trying to throw India back to mediaeval feudalism. He recalled the humanitarian welcome which Hindus had extended to Christians, Jews, and Muslims alike, whatever might have been the motives for their appearance upon the soil of his ancient country. He was impressed by the endeavors of the great Muslim Emperor Akbar to lay foundations for a solid and consolidated country of one nation for all—Muslim, Hindu, and other religious communities. He bitterly opposed what he considered to be the aim of the Muslim League—to turn the clock back to the pre-Akbar days. "When the world is groping blindly towards a real Federation of Nations, it is suggested that India be split up into various parts,"⁶ he protested. He recognized the diversity of the nation's scores of patterns of life, but to him this diversity was only an ever-inspiring source of cultural and intellectual richness, giving real strength to the synthesis of one nation, one India. To Pandit Jawaharlal Nehru "one Indian nation in one united India" was the great ideal.

To Jinnah the Hindu-Muslim differences were of fundamental character, the cleavage too deep and sentiments too bitter for any lasting unity. What was to Nehru "unity in diversity" was to Jinnah "conflicting ideas"; and even more aggravating to him was the idea of political unity.

⁴ Jawaharlal Nehru, *The Discovery of India*. The John Day Co., Inc., New York, 1946, p. 399.
⁵ Nehru, *The Unity of India*, *op.cit.*, p. 233.
⁶ *Ibid.*, p. 388.

The Real Issue

One Nation—or Two

These two—Jinnah and Nehru—were the voices of the combatant schools of thought that had such diametrically opposed answers to the single question: Is the Subcontinent one nation or two? On both sides argument was piled upon argument, theory upon theory, promise upon promise. For centuries, argued the "one nation" school, the Hindus and Muslims in India had exerted profound influence upon each other. Actually, even before the Muslims invaded India (the first wave of penetration was traced to the eighth century, the last occurred in the eighteenth century) the Arab civilization came in contact with Hindu society through Hindu literature, merchants, and financiers. The Arabs were acquainted with Hindu science and writings. The courts of the Emperors of Iraq, Persia, and Syria received Indian merchandise. Basra was a busy meeting port of Hindus, Arabs, and Greeks.

True, Hindus were converted to Islam by Muslim rulers, Nehru maintaining that 95 per cent of today's Muslims were originally Hindus, Jinnah putting the figure at 75 per cent. But some enlightened Muslim Emperors recognized the greatness of the Hindu culture and supported its learnings, encouraging the study of Sanskrit and Hindu literature.

As these two religions came into contact, they developed ways of life in which each had deep and continuous impact upon the other. In the arts—for example, in music, architecture, and dancing—the two cultures created a synthesis of one artistic expression. The exception was painting and sculpture, where the laws of the Koran impressed upon the Muslims definite limitations, the Koran forbidding images.

Even as to dress, argued the "one nation" adherents, the differences were primarily those of wealth; the poor dressed simply, the rich subscribed to more elaborate and ornamented garments. There was, however, no difference in terms of Hindu or Muslim communities

The segregation of women—*purdah*—was an Islamic law. The intercourse of Muslims with Hindus introduced *purdah* among Hindu women as well.

Where villages and towns were composed of mixed population and the contacts became frequent and regular, inevitably various customs, rites, and ceremonies fused into one common way of social life. In villages especially, Hindus called upon Muslims skilled in some professions. The names of Hindus and Muslims were not always discernible, particularly among the lower strata of society. Even the name Jinnah, it was held, was a Hindu name.

Nor did language serve as an instrument of division along communal lines. Rather, the division developed according to geographical areas, Urdu and Hindi influencing each other. Such was the testimony of the "one nation" school.

The "two nations" school of thought had equally devoted disciples. Their arguments rarely contradicted the testimony of those who pleaded the "oneness" of the people of the Subcontinent. Rather, they dwelt on the differences, and argued that those differences were too great to be encompassed by one nation, no matter how many or how great the similarities. They pointed to the Hindu religion, which found its most characteristic expression in a caste system, the negation of the equality of men, and then to the Muslim religion, which was based upon this equality. They pointed to the Hindu philosophy of non-violence, strange to and incompatible with the militant and missionary zeal of Muslims. They enumerated the vast differences between their laws of succession, marriage, divorce, and adoption. These, they said, could never be compromised within one nation. Intermarriage was practically impossible. Members of the two groups would not share meals together. The caste system threw its heavy shadow over all social life. The capital of the nation, with the exception of landowning capital, was concentrated in Hindu hands, the Muslims being exposed to the exploiting practices of moneylenders. The Hindu concept of the sanctity of the cow was listed as an illustration of the extreme differences between the two cultures, a difference sharply apparent to thousands of Muslims who had been severely punished for inadvertent sacrilege to some bovine's "person."

The arguments for both points of view have here been both understated and oversimplified—nor is it possible to pass judgment too lightly on the relative merits of the two positions. But it must be emphasized that it is the emotional intensity of these contradictory Hindu and Muslim attitudes toward nationalism in India which has so decisively and gravely affected Indian and Pakistan policy toward each other and toward Kashmir.

This dilemma is one which has forever plagued students of political theory. Ever since nationalism became a factor in human relations, theories and practice have clashed with one another. Although nationalism has always proved to be an elusive concept, such prominent scholars as Arnold Toynbee, Ernest Renan, Frederick Hertz, Hans Kohn, to name only a few, have worked out at least one promising approach to the problem. They label it the subjectivist evaluation of the elements of nationalism. Its essence is that sentimental components must overweigh objective findings. According to them, such demonstrable unities as a common language, a common territory, or even a common culture are not the *sine qua non* of the community that is a nation. Instead, they insist, the essential quality of such a community is the knowledge, the feeling of a group of people, large or small, that they belong together; that there is a sense of solidarity, of mutual dependence, the desire to share in common the vicissitudes of life; that they feel themselves to be inextricably interwoven, for good or bad; that they wish to be or remain united forever; that there is among them a sufficient conformity of attitudes on the "fatal tests" of life.

Hans Kohn, whom D. W. Brogan called "the most learned historian of nationalism,"[7] wrote that "nationalism is first and foremost a state of mind, an act of consciousness. . . ."[8]

Would, then, the argument for the "oneness" of the Indian nation stand up against the requirement of a "state of mind, an act of consciousness"?

Hindus and Muslims on the Subcontinent have shared many things together: common rulers, common traditions, common history, common territory. The languages have not persisted along lines of religious affinities. Their cultures, customs, and habits have grown closer together under the pressures of physical intermingling.

Nevertheless, in the last seventy years all of these "objective" manifestations of "oneness" seem never to have achieved on the Subcontinent the spiritual synthesis that is perhaps the only enduring quality of national allegiance. And though such great minds as Nehru had no use for sentiment in politics and revealed somewhat scornfully that to "talk of a 'Muslim nation' . . . means, finally, just nothing at all except an emotional state of mind . . . ,"[9] contrariwise, the wise Rajendra Prasad, himself a one-nation advocate, conceded that "sentiment has its value and should not be lightly cast off. Nor can it be nonchalantly brushed aside."[10] It is quite possible that Nehru, with his more rational approach, misjudged the permanency of the cement that alone

[7] D. W. Brogan, *The Price of Revolution*. Harper & Brothers, New York, 1951, p. 127.

[8] Hans Kohn, *The Idea of Nationalism*. The Macmillan Co., New York, 1944, p. 10.

[9] Jawaharlal Nehru, *Autobiography*. The Bodley Head, London, 1949, p. 469.

[10] Rajendra Prasad, *India Divided*. 3rd Ed. Hind Kitabs, Bombay, 1947, p. 175.

had bonded Muslims and Hindus together—their struggle against their common overlords, the British.

The Burden of the Past

The pages of history are filled with stories of misery which have produced strange bedfellows. But the stories have a habit of ending in much the same way. As the misery lessens and the compulsions of unity subside, the animosities of such bedmates sharpen and their enforced union grows more and more repugnant. Then, when necessities of cooperation pass, one or the other or both want nothing so much as to be free of these bonds which once were ties between them but which now have the weight of chains.

The happenings on the Subcontinent have proved to be no exception. The struggle for freedom in India took concrete shape in the 1880's. It culminated in victory in 1947. But every event which brought the peoples of India closer to independence seems also to have been marked by growing differentiation and restlessness between the Hindus and the Muslims.

As far back, indeed, as 1857 when the famous mutiny was broken and the participants were severely punished, the treatment of Muslim mutineers, which was more severe than that meted out to their Hindu compatriots, produced resentment not only toward the British but toward the Hindus as well.

To produce among the masses stronger feelings of solidarity, the spiritual and political leaders of the nineteenth century dwelt in their writings on the illustrious past of the people of the Subcontinent, preaching a return to the spiritual and cultural values of ancient times. Raja Ram Mohan Roy in Bengal, in 1828, and Swami Dayanand Saraswati in Northern India, in 1875, tried to raise the spirit of resistance by spreading the gospel of "Back to the Vedas." Among the Muslims, Haji Shariat Allah, Dudhu Miyan, and Mirza Ghulam Quadiani harangued the masses with "Back to the

example of the Prophet," "Back to the early Khilafat."
Movements and institutions sprang up, calling for the puri-
fication of religion and of language. Old customs were
brought back from the shelves of forgotten history. As a
result, a national consciousness did indeed begin to take
roots, but from its fertile soil sprang also the first seeds of
separatism. "Hindus and Musulmans were going beyond
the last thousand years of *rapprochement* back to distant and
divergent traditions and heroes and, therefore, further away
from one another in some important spheres of life."[11]

In 1885, on the initiative of the Englishman Allan Oc-
tavian Hume, the Indian National Congress was founded
to foster the interest of the intellectual class in public affairs. Its founders and followers understood that the process
of national consciousness and self-reliance would develop
more quickly through education. Muslim society, on the
other hand, remained static, lagging behind the Hindu
cultural and educational activity, although intellectuals
among the Muslims found their way into the Congress.
But their number diminished when the suspicion spread,
well-founded or not, that the Congress, though professing
to be non-communal, was primarily defending and foster-
ing Hindu culture and interests.

Admittedly the Muslim leader, Sir Syed Ahmad Khan,
had recognized the weakness inherent in the backwardness
of his fellow countrymen and in 1875 he founded, as a
Muslim institution, the Anglo-Oriental College, later reorganized as Aligarh University. It was not until 1906, however, that the All-India Muslim League was founded, with
cultural and political aims similar to those of the Indian
National Congress. Originally, the two were not intended to
be rival organizations, though certainly they did at that time
bear testimony to a recognition of separate identities. It

[11] Beni Prasad, *India Hindu-Muslim Questions*. George Allen &
Unwin Ltd., London, 1946, p. 31.

33

was later that from within their ranks and around them separate national allegiances started to develop and grow.

Simultaneously with this cultural and intellectual growth came the expression of political aspirations. Among these— and one to which the British yielded—was the demand for separate Hindu and Muslim electorates for the local administration. Limited as these rights were, they nonetheless gave new impetus to the process of the separation of Hindu and Muslim interests. Sir Syed, the driving force behind the claim, argued that "The vigour of religious institutions has kept even neighbours apart; the system of caste is still dominant and powerful. . . . But, my Lord, in a country like India . . . where religious distinctions are still violent . . . the introduction of the election, pure and simple . . . would be attended with evils of greater significance than purely economic considerations. . . . The larger community would totally override the interests of the smaller community. . . ."[12]

In 1905, the Province of Bengal was actually partitioned largely along religious lines, and though this was abolished in 1911, the partition gave no small encouragement to the growing spirit of Muslim nationalism.

Then, in 1909, the Morley-Minto reforms, giving the people of India enlarged participation in local government, recognized the principle of separate representation. The Indian National Congress fought this tendency vehemently; among its opponents were also such Muslim leaders as the brothers Shaukat Ali and Maulana Mohamed Ali. But despite such opposition the process of growing divergence was not materially retarded.

World War I brought new hopes and opportunities to the Indian people in their struggle for freedom. Toward

[12] R. Coupland, *The India Problem*. Oxford University Press, London, 1944. Appendix II, Extracts from Proceedings of the Council of the Governor-General of India, 1883. Central Provinces Local Self-Government Bill, pp. 155-156.

the end of 1916 both the All-India National Congress and the All-India Muslim League met in Lucknow. Out of the conference came the historic document, the "Lucknow Pact," in which the two movements asked the British government for reforms, for a constitution, and for new elections for a central parliament and for the provinces. The most significant and important fact of this historic meeting was that the Congress concurred with the League upon the principle of separate electorates for the Muslim voters. This was a concession of great significance: it implied at least that both Hindus and Muslims anticipated the development of some political structure which would recognize separate Hindu and Muslim interests. It mattered little to the Muslims whether the concession was meant to be made to Muslims as a religious or an ethnical group; to them this was only another step which would eventually lead to their complete self-determination.

It may well be that the Congress leaders were not aware of the consequences of the Lucknow Pact. Indeed it was greeted by Hindus as well as Muslims as a great victory for their common cause. Victory it may have been for the Congress, a victory in their struggle for independence, but it also inevitably produced a strengthening of the very separatist inclinations which the Congress wished least to support.

If the Government of India Act of 1919 did not meet the Hindu-Muslim proposals as contained in the Lucknow Pact, and if it did not live up to the expectations aroused by the British promise to give to the Indian people "gradual development of self-governing institutions with a view to the progressive realization of responsible government of India" (August 20, 1917), the subsequent disappointment of the Indian people only intensified their struggle.

Once again, though now for individual reasons, the Muslims and the Hindus rallied their forces against the British rule. The Hindus, indignant over the tragedy at Amritsar

(April 13, 1919), where the British fired upon a gathering, launched their first non-violence movement. The Muslims, together with other Islamic brethren, joined the Caliphate movement in protest against the Allied policy towards defeated Turkey, the center of the Muslim world and the seat of the Caliph. The Congress supported the Muslims, and the Muslims in turn joined at least that portion of the non-violence Hindu policy which called for disobedience to British orders and the boycotting of British goods. Once again, in their mutual misery, facing the common enemy, these strange bedfellows found themselves united, albeit for different purposes and from different motives.

But the companionship did not last for long. The non-violence movement was called off in 1922, after Gandhi had condemned the killing of twenty-two policemen in the village of Chauri Chaura. To the Muslims the Hindu attitude toward a mild bloodletting was unnecessarily queasy. Nor were their bitterness and indignation in any way diminished when to their rage the Caliphate problem was solved by the Turks themselves, who denounced the Caliph, declared Turkey a republic, and signed the peace treaty in Lausanne in July 1923. This, be it recorded, was the last time that these two, the Congress and the League, found themselves in the same bed.

In the inter-war period the antagonism between the Muslims and Hindus grew until, by 1947, it reached unbridgeable proportions. Riots occurred, innocent people were killed, women were abducted. "The record of Hindu-Muslim rioting in India is long and tragic," wrote R. Coupland, who traced it back to 1809 and then listed recurrences in 1871, 1872, 1884, 1885, 1886, 1891, 1893, 1907-1914.[13] Dr. B. R. Ambedkar, the learned leader of the untouchables,

[13] *Ibid.*, p. 29.

described the riots as a "civil war between Hindus and Muslims, interrupted by brief intervals of armed peace."[14]

So the pages of history were repeating themselves. As British dominion decreased, as the prospect for freedom grew brighter, Hindus and Muslims (but more particularly Muslims) who had once united against a common enemy looked less and less at their common interests and fixed their attention more and more upon those characteristics of the other that irritated and annoyed them.

In 1928, when the Congress drafted a blueprint for a constitution of India with Dominion status, the Muslim leaders accused the Congress of having completely overlooked the special position of the Muslim population. As a reaction they met in Delhi and proclaimed, in 1929, their "Fourteen Points" asking for separate electorates, federal government, and qualitative rights in the parliament and the executive.

In 1930-1932 at the Round Table Conference in London, the British government was unable to reconcile both factions or to present them with reforms mutually acceptable to their separate political aspirations. The result was increased bitterness. Maulana Mohamed Ali, the prominent Muslim leader in the Congress, once its president and himself a protagonist of Hindu-Muslim unity, wrote from his deathbed to the Prime Minister of Great Britain, declaring his past attitudes mistaken and appealing for proper rights for the Muslims.

Mohammed Ali Jinnah, once also a member of the Congress (which he left in 1920 to remain aloof from politics for a number of years), declared that at the Round Table Conference he had received the shock of his life at the Hindu attitude.

Jinnah, whom the late Hindu woman leader, Sarojini Naidu, had once called "Ambassador of Hindu-Muslim

[14] Ambedkar, *Pakistan or Partition of India.* Thacker and Company, Bombay, 1945, p. 152.

unity," now became in the eyes of Congress leaders a traitor to the common cause of independence. Nehru accused him of having left the Congress, not because of any differences regarding the Hindu-Muslim question, but because he could not adjust himself to the progressive ideology of the Congress. He made no attempt to conceal his contempt for Jinnah and quoted openly a remark that Iqbal, the great poet of Islam of Kashmir origin, had made to him a few months before Iqbal's death in 1938: "What is there in common between Jinnah and you? He is a politician, you are a patriot."[15] The open recounting of such a remark was not calculated to repair any differences Nehru may have had with Jinnah.

Indeed, mutual suspicions continued to grow to the extent that even Mahatma Gandhi, whom Maulana Mohamed Ali called "the most Christ-like man," was now suspected of not wishing any sincere agreement with Muslims. Certainly, if there had been any hope of achieving the independence of a united India, the events of the 1930's shattered them.

The Muslim League, which since its beginnings in 1906 had been primarily a cultural organization, now grew into a full-fledged political party. For years its membership had been a few thousand intellectuals and landowners; but with the outbreak of World War II the membership rose to 590,919, and within two years, in 1941, it had mounted to 1,089,881 persons,[16] a not inconsiderable political force.

The last fifteen years prior to independence and partition were clearly marked by a growing animosity between the two political movements—the All-India National Congress and the All-India Muslim League.

The India Act of 1935 was meant by the British government as another step toward self-rule on the Subcontinent.

[15] Nehru, *The Discovery of India, op.cit.*, p. 355.
[16] T. A. Raman, *Report on India*. Oxford University Press, 1943, p. 175.

It envisaged almost full autonomy for the provinces and made provisions for a federal government with sovereign powers in internal affairs, external affairs, and defense remaining in the hands of the British. None of the parties concerned—the Congress, the League, nor the Princes—liked it. Nevertheless, they participated in the provincial elections of 1937, in which the Congress was victorious in seven provinces. It was in this period between 1937 and 1939 that the Muslim League complained bitterly about the behavior of the Congress Cabinets towards the Muslim population, and when, in 1939, all Congress Cabinets resigned as a protest against the British declaration of war without prior consultation with the Indian leadership, Jinnah called the occasion "the day of deliverance."

World War II offered a tremendous challenge to Hindu and Muslim leaders to press vigorously their right of independence. But at the same time, the cleavage between them continued to grow. While Congress leaders were arrested for undermining the war efforts by a campaign of non-violence, Jinnah, making clever use of the situation, moved toward conditional cooperation.

Then, in 1940, at the Lahore Conference of the League, Jinnah, feeling that freedom from British rule was upon them and that the issue must now be crystallized, openly, directly, and vigorously made the overt step. He demanded not only an independent but also a separate Pakistan.

In March 1942, the British Cabinet Mission of Sir Stafford Cripps tried to solve the deadlock. Sir Stafford invited the leaders to draft a constitution to give India a Dominion status which would be put in force immediately after the end of hostilities. It was to mean full independence, including external affairs and defense. It envisaged a Union of India but at the same time contained provisions for a separate homeland for Muslims should they wish to establish it. It also offered the Princely States their choice of joining the Union of India or maintaining their relationship to the British Crown. The proposal was rejected by the Indian leaders.

Another attempt to work out a suitable solution was made in June of 1945 at the Simla Conference. The Viceroy, Lord Wavell, proposed that a new executive council should be nominated, representative of all sections of the people and with authority over all affairs, the only exception being the functions of the Viceroy and the Commander-in-Chief, which were to remain in British hands. Jinnah agreed, but insisted upon the exclusive right of the Muslim League to nominate the Muslim representatives on the executive council. The Congress refused to accept any such proposal implying as it did a communal division. Jinnah's position, however, was considerably strengthened when in the elections of the winter of 1945-1946 the League received overwhelming majorities in the Muslim provinces.

The last attempt to give the Subcontinent freedom and at the same time maintain its unity was made in the spring of 1946. A cabinet mission visited Delhi and in May made public a plan which proposed a united, independent India but with safeguards guaranteeing rights and representation for minorities.[17] Most observers agree that this was the only occasion throughout ten long years that the Congress and the League seemed almost in agreement; for a moment there appeared some chance of saving the Subcontinent from dismemberment. But the plan collapsed. The cause of collapse had almost the shallowness of pretext. The parties could not agree on the composition of the government. Nothing could more graphically illustrate the depth of their mutual antagonism than this, for had any degree of will been present to establish a framework of one government for the Subcontinent, no technicality of the composition of the envisaged coalition government could have thwarted it.

From this point events plunged relentlessly onward toward inescapable separation, a separation that was to coin-

[17] Command Paper 6821.

cide with what should have been the Subcontinent's greatest day of rejoicing—its day of liberation.

The struggle had been long and hard fought. And who, even today, can pass final judgment upon the validity of one position or another?

Every student of international affairs who is aware of the havoc of excessive nationalism must be as inescapably attracted by the persuasiveness of Nehru's arguments as he must be repelled by those who argued separation. Without doubt reason was on his side. The undeniable facts of common history, customs, and mutual interests support him. And who, in these days, can look with dispassionate calm on the further splintering of an already too divided world?

But when the arguments of reason are opposed by deep-rooted, passionate, and somewhat justifiable emotions, then it would seem that reason must command itself to give way. It is, therefore, impossible to condemn Nehru and his colleagues for their stubborn insistence on Indian unity, but it is difficult to understand their inability to yield to the inevitable. Right as they may have been in their ideals of unity, they could not be unaware of the forces that would inevitably thwart them. Surely the Congress leaders sensed even among their own people the deep-seated, perhaps only semiconscious, resentment of the Muslims who in their well-remembered past had swarmed over the land, subjugating it to both a foreign dynasty and a strange religion. Surely they must have known that the Muslims, on the one hand personally and economically repelled by the caste system of the Hindus, on the other openly derisive of much of Hindu culture, could never (or at least not at the moment) shed both prejudice and contempt for the sake of an intellectual ideal.

Nehru often insisted that it was the British who were responsible for all the difficulties between these two peoples, playing one against the other throughout the history of their occupation. Even if this were true, the prejudices and animosities upon which the British played, however, were deeply rooted in the hearts of those who responded to the ruse. It appears that it was in their common hatred of this British rule that Hindus and Muslims found the principal reason for such mutuality of thought and action as did develop—a poor basis for the development of a unified national conscience.

That Nehru sensed the depth of this division may be found in his own admission that "the burden of the past, the burden of both good and ill, is overpowering and sometimes suffocating. . . ."[18] Another Hindu—himself an untouchable—Dr. B. R. Ambedkar, saw clearly that "the pity of it [the Hindu-Muslim problem] is that the two communities can never forget or obliterate their past. Their past is imbedded in their religion, and for each to give up its past is to give up its religion. To hope for this is to hope in vain. In the absence of common historical antecedents, the Hindu view that Hindus and Musulmans form one nation falls to the ground. To maintain it is to keep up an hallucination."[19]

How then, in this certain knowledge, we must ask ourselves, could the Congress have continued even to the day of separation not only to oppose the certainty of its occurrence but also to close their minds so completely to the humanity if not the wisdom of its inevitability?

But more important by far than this question is another one: For what reason does India continue this bitter fight for the ideal of "oneness" now that separation is an accomplished fact?

For the struggle for Kashmir is in every sense another battle in this continuing and by now irrational war of ideals. In the minds of Nehru and the Congress, Kashmir is, in miniature, another Pakistan, and if this Muslim nation can be successfully governed by India, then their philosophy of secularism is vindicated. Moreover, it would ease the ten-

[18] Nehru, *The Discovery of India, op.cit.*, p. 25.
[19] Ambedkar, *op.cit.*, p. 19.

sion among those forty million Muslims who still find themselves on Indian soil. But conversely, should the Muslim nation of Kashmir reject its present status and by plebiscite accede on the basis of its religion to Pakistan, then religious affinities and arguments of emotion have once more triumphed. This would be a damaging blow to Nehru's theory of secularism, and no one knows it better than Nehru. No one has expressed it more eloquently than he when he said, ". . . it is not Kashmir, therefore, but rather a much deeper conflict that comes in the way of friendly relations between India and Pakistan and the situation is a grave one. We cannot give up the basic ideal which we have held so long and on which the whole conception of our state is founded."[20] One must not overlook the fact that some prominent Muslim leaders as well have associated themselves with Nehru in his defense of this ideal of the oneness of the Indian nation. Nor must one overlook the fact that Nehru has combated courageously and consistently those Hindu nationalist extremists who have tried to compromise his philosophy of oneness.

This, then, is the setting for the tragic drama of modern Kashmir, a setting entirely essential to the full meaning of each scene. For only as Kashmir is viewed as one (though currently the most dramatic and foreboding) of many dramas in this tragic cycle of suspicion, fear, hate, and bloodletting that for so many years have wrecked the Indian Subcontinent, can its true significance be appreciated.

The prologue to this drama is identical to the epilogue of another. The place, the Subcontinent. The time, 1947. The argument, the final provisions for independence and the separation of Pakistan and India.

[20] Jawaharlal Nehru, *Report to the All-India Congress Committee,* July 6, 1951. The Hindustan Times Press, New Delhi, p. 17.

3. The Struggle Begins

By 1947 affairs on the Indian Subcontinent had reached the point that a declaration of independence could be delayed no longer. On February 20 the government of Great Britain announced its "definite intention to take necessary steps to effect the transference of power to responsible Indian hands by a date not later than June 1948."[1] Lord Mountbatten was appointed Viceroy and entrusted with the superhuman task of effecting a peaceful transfer of the administration from the British to the new authorities—either the government of a united India or the two governments of India and Pakistan.

This decision was not long in the making. Mountbatten came to Delhi on March 22, 1947, and almost immediately recognized the impossibility of bringing the Indian National Congress and the Muslim League together to create a common government. He declared he would proceed on the basis of two separate governments, and on June 3, acting upon his counsel, the British government published a plan for the partition of India. Six weeks later, on July 18, the Indian Independence Act was passed, stating that on August 15 India and Pakistan were to become independent countries.[2] The division was to take place according to communal allegiance; the predominantly Hindu provinces were to form the Union of India, and the predominantly Muslim provinces were to form Pakistan.

It is too early to judge every aspect of Lord Mountbatten's negotiations, and it would also exceed the nature of this study. Too few official documents have been published to throw sufficient light upon the deliberations among the parties concerned. No documents are needed, however, to establish that any mission designed to bring about the partition of a country which for so many years had developed

[1] Statement of H.M.G. of February 20, 1947.
[2] Command Paper 7136.

44

as an economic and military entity under one political authority must have encountered hundreds of complex and difficult problems.

Nor was Mountbatten's position made easier by the personal wrangling among the leaders of the political parties on the Subcontinent. It was a difficult collection of personalities with which he was to deal. There was Jawaharlal Nehru, the great and uncontested leader of the All-India National Congress, stubbornly unwilling to reconcile himself to the idea of an independent Pakistan. There was Vallabhbhai Patel, with the multiple function of Deputy Prime Minister and Minister of States, Home Affairs, Information and Broadcasting, calm, almost enigmatic, but with determined will. And there was Mahatma, with no official position but with overwhelming influence, exposing his views in daily articles, prayers, private conversations, and always ready to fast to rouse the conscience of millions.

There was Mohammed Ali Jinnah, *Quaid-i-Azam*, the "Great Leader," revered by Muslims as the chief protagonist of their independent country. He was described by the great Kashmiri poet Iqbal as "the only Muslim in India today to whom the community has a right to look for safe guidance. . . ."[3] Certainly he enjoyed unlimited authority among his followers. His opponents found him, however, a most difficult person with whom to negotiate. To them he was "a strangely negative person";[4] inaccessible, cold and yet passionate, stubborn and yet unpredictable, unwilling and perhaps unable to bring personal warmth into the delicate atmosphere of negotiations. He suspected the Congress leaders of bad faith and showed little belief in Lord Mountbatten's integrity. Few foreign observers or correspondents found it possible to establish cordial contacts with him. They all recognized, however, the power of his personality,

[3] *Letters of Iqbal to Jinnah.* Kashmir Bazaar, Lahore, p. 19.
[4] Nehru, *The Discovery of India, op.cit.*, p. 394.

his determined mind, and his perhaps unsurpassed ability in political strategy.

These were the principals with whom Mountbatten had to negotiate. But they were not the only ones. The Princes as well claimed the right to be heard and to take part in the historic decisions.

The Princely States

There were 584 of these Princely States scattered over the Subcontinent, covering 45.3 per cent of its surface and with a population of some 99 million people. Some Princes represented real power, such as the Nizam of Hyderabad, which had almost 17 million inhabitants and was about the size of Germany. Other Princely States were small in size and population. The overwhelming majority of them were Hindu; only a half dozen were Muslim.

The Princes were proud of their quasi-royal status and claimed unlimited obedience from their subjects and princely respect from abroad. They bore the elevated title of Maharaja (Hindu) or Nawab (Muslim), and they were addressed as "His Highness." The ruler of Hyderabad had the special title of Nizam and was addressed as "His Exalted Highness."

The relations between the British Crown and the Princely States were based upon treaties, "the paramount power" taking responsibility for their foreign affairs and defense, the Princes being guaranteed their rights of succession and autonomy in internal affairs. British India and the Princely States were linked by a sort of personal union: the Viceroy of British India acted also as the Crown's representative toward the Princes.

The Princes would have preferred to live in splendid isolation from the happenings in British India, but they were not able to quarantine their people against the infectious spirit of freedom which was sweeping the Subcontinent. In some states political parties appeared similar to the Indian

46

National Congress and the Muslim League. In 1921 the Princes constituted, in Delhi, a Chamber of Princes, composed of 108 rulers and 12 additional members representing 127 minor states. The Chamber was a consultative and debating body without any real authority. Its main political purpose was to bring the Princes closer to the political arena of Indian affairs and to make them aware of the impending realities of political life.

When the hour of decision struck in the spring of 1946 and the British government determined to grant independence to British India, the question of relinquishing its paramountcy over the Princely States was immediately posed.

In a "Memorandum on States' Treaties and Paramountcy," the Cabinet Mission informed His Highness the Chancellor of the Chamber of Princes that after the transfer of British powers to an independent government of India ". . . His Majesty's Government will cease to exercise the powers of paramountcy. This means that the rights of the States which flow from their relationship to the Crown will no longer exist and that all the rights surrendered by the States to the paramount power will return to the States."[5]

Four days later, on May 16, the Cabinet Mission reaffirmed its position on the Princely States, envisaging that, "There should be a Union of India embracing both British India and the States, which should deal with the following subjects: Foreign Affairs, Defence, and Communications . . ." and that "The States will retain all subjects and powers other than those ceded to the Union."[6]

Though the Cabinet Mission's proposal was rejected as a whole, its statements concerning the Princely States became the basis for future settlement of this particular problem. Nor was the principle of this declaration changed when in June of 1947 the decision for partition was announced.

[5] Command Paper 6855.
[6] Command Paper 6821.

On July 25, 1947, Lord Mountbatten appeared before the Chamber of Princes to offer them a more concrete interpretation of the Independence Act and to add to his previously private counsel a bit of public advice. "The States will have complete freedom," he told the Princes, ". . . technically and legally they become independent." But he reminded them that India had been operating as an economic entity, that this implied certain consequences and that "there are certain geographical compulsions which cannot be evaded."[7] The Independence Act made provisions for the temporary continuation of customs, transit and communications, posts and telegraphs (Section 7, sub-section 1, c), but Lord Mountbatten once again urged the Princes to enter into standstill agreements with the future authorities of India and Pakistan to make arrangement about such matters.

Lord Mountbatten stressed to the Princes that they would have to surrender to the central governments of India or Pakistan only defense, foreign affairs, and communications, without any financial liability, and that these governments would have no authority "to encroach on the internal autonomy or the sovereignty of the States."[8] He invited the Princes to make up their minds before long, as the day of transfer of power, August 15, was "very close at hand"; after that date they would have to take care of any arrangement by themselves as sovereigns of independent countries. The general assumption was that the Hindu States would join India and the Muslim States, Pakistan. Nearly all of the Princely States saw clearly the only possible and reasonable path open to them and acceded to one country or the other. Three Princes, however, those of Hyderabad, Junagadh, and Kashmir, chose to join neither dominion and on August 15 became technically independent states. Their subjects were to pay heavily for their rulers' policy. Junagadh, with a

[7] *Time Only to Look Forward*, Speeches of Rear Admiral the Earl Mountbatten of Burma. Nicholas Kaye, London, 1949, p. 52.

[8] *Ibid.*, p. 55.

Muslim ruler but with a Hindu population of about 700,000, acceded in September 1947 through the act of its Nawab to Pakistan, but the Indian army entered the country and assured the people of their right to express themselves about their future. They voted for India. In the case of Hyderabad, its Muslim Nizam tried to postpone indefinitely any decision concerning the fate of its predominantly Hindu population—but this too was solved by way of arms when the Indian army forced its way into the state in September 1948 and the country became part of India.

And Kashmir?

Flames of Civil War

It would be difficult to overestimate, then, the difficulties which Mountbatten faced when in March of 1947 he began his negotiations. Not only were there the perplexities of such problems as the Princely States and the deep-rooted antagonisms of the leaders of India and Pakistan, but there was also the knowledge that even as they worked, among the peoples of the Subcontinent the infernos of communal strife were already raging unchecked. Such bloodlettings were not new to the Subcontinent. But this time there was a difference. Now they were no longer outbursts of isolated political or religious feelings. Now they were part and instrument of a historical political struggle. Now the fate of a nation for centuries to come was at stake. Now the flames were fanned by winds of nationalism that threatened to engulf the entire Subcontinent.

The leaders of the Congress blamed the Muslim League for inciting outbursts of violence to prove that the Hindu-Muslim rift was irreconcilable. The leaders of the Muslim League accused the Congress of trying to decimate the Muslims.

A full and impartial story of the riots remains still to be written. The purpose of our study requires only the listing of some facts directly pertinent to the development in Kashmir.

Riots reached threatening proportions in several regions, particularly in Punjab, bordering on Kashmir. The reasons for this are readily understood when the conditions preceding the rioting are examined.

The population in Punjab was mixed. According to 1941 census, there were 16,217,000 Muslims living in the province, 7,551,000 Hindus, and (perhaps most important) 3,757,800 Sikhs.

Punjab was the motherland of the Sikhs, numbering altogether 5.7 millions. Originally they considered themselves as a religious group following the teaching of Guru Nanak (1467-1538), whose philosophy combined elements of both Hinduism and Islam: a belief in monotheism and a refusal to recognize the caste system. He wished to create something of a synthesis of both religions acceptable to all inhabitants of the Subcontinent, but his followers soon developed qualities distinctly antagonistic to both faiths. Eventually this included a vaunted militarism "to resist both Muslim aggression and Hindu intolerance."[9] In Punjab they established their own kingdom, but in 1846 they were crushed by the British, who had received, according to some sources, considerable Muslim assistance. Naturally enough this fact only served to intensify the Sikhs' hatred of the Muslims, a hatred which over the years found expression in much letting of blood. It was by no means rare for the otherwise quiet and stolid Sikh to pull out his sword, *kirpan*, the symbol of his virile, martial power, and burst into appalling murder.

Certainly, therefore, the presence of more than 3 million Sikhs in the primarily Muslim state of Punjab was a condition conducive to rioting and bloodshed. Another factor, however, was the presence in this unhappy territory of a

[9] *India, Pakistan, Ceylon.* Edited by W. Norman Brown. Cornell University Press, Ithaca, N.Y., 1951, p. 112.

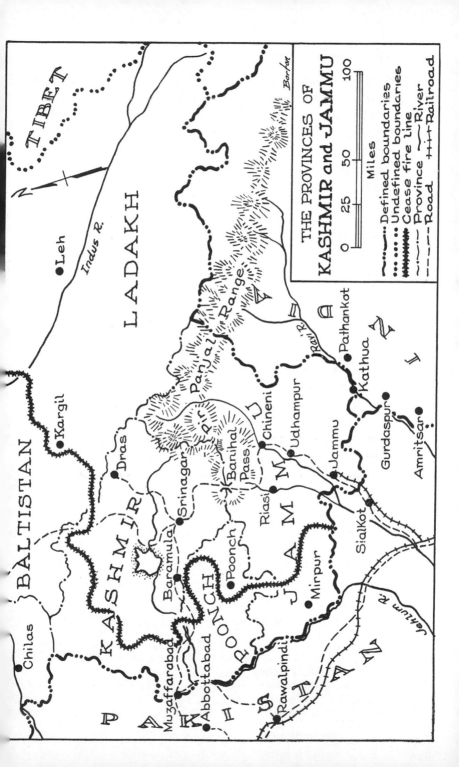

THE PROVINCES OF
KASHMIR and JAMMU

Miles
0   25   50   100

········· Defined boundaries
•••••••• Undefined boundaries
↜↜↜↜ Cease fire line
━━━ Province ━━ River
━━━ Road +++ Railroad

TIBET

LADAKH

•Leh

Indus R.

Pir Panjal Range

BALTISTAN

•Kargil

Dras

•Chilas

KASHMIR

•Srinagar

Baramula•

Banihal Pass

Chineni

Riasi•

Udhampur•

JAMMU

•Poonch

POONCH

•Mirpur

Jammu•

Sialkot

Kathua•

Pathankot•

Ravi R.

Gurdaspur•

Amritsar•

Muzaffarabad•

Abbottabad•

Rawalpindi•

PAKISTAN

Jhelum R.

Barbet

strong representation of the militant Hindu organization, *Rashtriya Swayamsevak Sangh* (RSS).

The RSS was founded in 1925, its leaders feeling that the traditional Hindu pacifist philosophy ill-equipped them to defend themselves against the bellicose Muslims. The RSS was organized as a secret group, and its founder, Dr. K. B. Hedgewar, and his successor, M. S. Golwarkar, were recognized and respected leaders—Fuehrers in the Nazi tradition.

In this same tradition, the members of the organization wore uniforms, were trained in terrorism, and were divided into military groups. It is thought that in 1935 they numbered only 25,000; by 1947 they had grown to 400,000, and these were supported by some 5,000,000 sympathizers.[10]

In Punjab there were, in 1947, some 30,000 of the RSS who were eager to lend their strength to the Sikhs' *kirpans*. Against both, the Muslim League assembled and armed the National Guard.

The Muslim leaders accused the Sikhs of having planned a wholesale massacre of the Muslims. Whatever the truth may be (and the findings of the Punjab Criminal Investigation Department, entrusted with the task of establishing responsibility for the riots, have never been brought to a conclusion), one officer of the Department reported to Mountbatten's mission that "These interrogations [of instigators of disturbances] and intelligence from other sources implicated the Sikh leaders in a number of sabotage plans, including a plot to assassinate Jinnah. . . ."[11]

As a matter of record also are such episodes as that which took place on February 23, 1947, when one of the Sikh leaders, Master Tara Singh, mounted the steps "of the Leg-

[10] For detailed study see J. A. Curran, Jr., *Militant Hinduism in Indian Politics, A Study of the R.S.S.*, International Secretariat, Institute of Pacific Relations, New York, 1951.

[11] Alan Campbell-Johnson, *Mission with Mountbatten*. E. P. Dutton & Co., New York, 1953, p. 149.

islative Assembly in Lahore. He unleashed his *kirpan,* waved it about and announced that the sword would now decide between the Sikhs and Muslims."[12] Other Sikh leaders followed his example.

Lord Mountbatten was gravely aware of the situation and the difficulty of negotiating with the Indian leaders in such an atmosphere. He induced Gandhi and Jinnah to appeal to the population to keep calm. "We deeply deplore the recent acts of lawlessness and violence that have brought the utmost disgrace on the fair name of India and the greatest misery to innocent people, irrespective of who were the aggressors and who were the victims," read their common declaration of April 15, 1947. "We denounce for all time the use of force to achieve political ends, and we call upon all the communities of India, to whatever persuasion they may belong, not only to refrain from all acts of violence and disorder, but also to avoid both in speech and writing any incitement of such acts."[13]

The appeal was not heeded for long. After the British government on June 3 announced its plan of partition, including the highly disputed partition of Punjab, rioting was resumed. The fighting spread to several Princely States. In Punjab it climaxed in August, even before the Radcliffe Award (made public on August 18) determined the boundaries between the western and the eastern parts of the province. Thousands of people were massacred, millions were expelled from their homes to seek refuge with their fellow countrymen and coreligionists; villages were burned, churches desecrated, trains carrying refugees dynamited; mass looting, abduction of women, and arson had no end.

Thus it was that the long-awaited day of independence, an event that should have produced general rejoicing, reverence, and conciliation, was instead for thousands of inno-

[12] From the speech of Sir Zafrulla Khan before the Security Council; *Security Council Official Records,* Third Year, Nos. 1-15, p. 42.
[13] *Time Only to Look Forward, op.cit.,* p. 272.

cent people a verdict of death. The British were evacuating their forces and offices; the newly established governments of the Union of India and Pakistan were unable to cope with the situation. Fighting went on in villages and towns, in provinces and Princely States. To a considerable extent this could not be stopped because the administration was similarly divided from top governmental posts down to the last local policeman. The central government became an unworkable team; the civil servants were grouped along the communal lines; the army broke into two hostile fronts bridged over only by a few British generals who tried to save the situation by wise and considerate advice. On local scenes of horror the constabulary sided with the community according to national and religious allegiances.

When the maelstrom of human tragedy had subsided, the Subcontinent was poorer by more than half a million people who had lost their lives in the mass killings. The misery of the displaced persons, fleeing from Muslim to Hindu territories or vice versa, staggers the imagination. Six million fled from Pakistan, 5,800,000 from India. But even such incredible migrations could not solve the problem of founding purely national states. After the large-scale flight of minorities was over, about 12 million Hindus remained in Pakistan and 40 million Muslims were left in India.

Nor did the religious frenzy which swept the Subcontinent stop at the boundaries of the Princely States, though some were spared because of their purely Hindu character. But Kashmir was not among these happy states.

Kashmir Involved

The Hindu Maharaja of these predominately Muslim people drew his army from Hindus, Sikhs, and Gurkhas. He knew that with the exception of the Kashmiris from the Vale of Kashmir the Muslims of Jammu and Kashmir were formidable fighters. In World War II, of the 71,667 citizens of the State of Jammu and Kashmir who served in the

British Indian forces, 60,402 were Muslims.[14] But the Maharaja also knew that as Muslims, they were not good risks as members of his army. When the Maharaja refused, after the war and demobilization, to accept these fighters in his military forces, most of them went back to farming in their home regions of Mirpur and Poonch. Meanwhile, the Maharaja strengthened his garrisons in these areas in the spring of 1947 by importing Sikhs and Hindus.

Political developments in Kashmir prior to 1948 paralleled happenings elsewhere. As in British India, the Muslim Conference in Kashmir had appealed on July 19, 1946, for "Direct Action." A few months later, its leaders were in jail.

Then, in the spring of 1947, the Maharaja brutally suppressed a Poonchis-instigated "No Tax Campaign," and as the fires of rebellion flickered, flared, and subsided, Muslims slipped in from Punjab to help their brothers in Jammu; Sikhs and Hindu extremists, on the other hand, crossed the border to aid the Maharaja forces.

Mountbatten Visits Srinagar

Lord Mountbatten could not have been unaware of the explosive character of the situation. There are no official documents published as to his negotiations with the Princes, and we are told that "Mountbatten . . . had no detailed directives from London to support him"[15] on how to handle the delicate problem of inducing the Princes to accede to one of the dominions before "the appointed day" of August 15. But it is now evident that although he apparently succeeded in convincing most of them to accede "in time," the Kashmir case proved to be beyond his persuasive powers.

Lord Mountbatten visited Kashmir on June 19 and remained four days. The immediate motives of this important visit appear to be unknown. The documentary diary of Allen

[14] *Jammu: A Muslim Province.* Kashmir Publications, Muzaffarabad, Azad Kashmir, p. 13.
[15] Campbell-Johnson, *Mission with Mountbatten, op.cit.,* p. 140.

Campbell-Johnson simply states that they were "visiting Kashmir on the 19th at the genuine invitation of the Maharaja."[16] It further reports, however (though only indirectly) certain interesting facts and background incidents related to him by Lord Mountbatten upon his return from Kashmir:

"Mountbatten has also seen for himself the paralysis of Princely uncertainty during his visit to Kashmir, from which he has only just returned today. Both Nehru and Gandhi have been very anxious that the Maharaja of Kashmir should make no declaration of independence. And Nehru, himself descended from Kashmiri Brahmins, has been pressing to visit the State himself to seek the release from prison of his friend, Sheikh Abdullah, now President of the States' Congress. Last year when Nehru visited the State he was himself placed under arrest by the Kashmir Government. Gandhi's view was that he himself ought to prepare the way for Nehru. The Maharaja has made it very clear that he does not welcome a visit from either. Mountbatten succeeded in deferring both visits by saying he himself had a long-standing invitation from the Maharaja and would like to see him first.

"When he got there he found the Maharaja politically very elusive and the only conversations that took place were during their various car drives together. Mountbatten on these occasions urged him and his Prime Minister, Pandit Kak, not to make any declaration of independence, but to find out in one way or another the will of the people of Kashmir as soon as possible, and to announce their intention by 14th of August, to send representatives accordingly to one Constituent Assembly or the other. He told them that the newly created States Department of India was prepared to give an assurance that if Kashmir went to Pakistan this would not be regarded as an unfriendly act by the Gov-

16 *Ibid.*, p. 117.

ernment of India. He went on to stress the dangerous situation in which Kashmir would find itself if it lacked the support of one of the two Dominions by the date of the transfer of power. His intention was to give this advice privately to the Maharaja alone and then to repeat it in the presence of his Prime Minister with George Abell [Private Secretary to the Viceroy] and the Resident, Colonel Webb, in attendance, at a small meeting where minutes could be kept.

"The Maharaja suggested that the meeting should take place on the last day of the visit, to which Mountbatten agreed, feeling that this would allow him the maximum chance to make up his mind, but when the time came the Maharaja sent a message that he was in bed with colic and would be unable to attend the meeting. It seems that this is his usual illness when he wishes to avoid difficult discussions.

"Needless to say, Mountbatten is very disappointed at this turn of events," concludes Campbell-Johnson in his diary.[17]

Though there is here no direct evidence concerning the conversation between Mountbatten and the Maharaja, there is reason to believe that the Pakistanis are mistaken in their conviction that Mountbatten from the beginning connived with the government of India to force the Maharaja and with him the State of Jammu and Kashmir into accession.

Lord Mountbatten was very anxious to dispel any doubt about his own position. Speaking before the East India Association in London shortly after his return from his historic mission in India, he repeated, "In the case of Kashmir I went up personally and saw the Maharaja. I spent four days with him in July [*sic*], on every one of those four days I persisted with the same advice: 'Ascertain the will of your people by any means and join whichever Dominion your people wish to join by August 14 this year.' He did not do that, and what happened can be seen. Had

[17] *Ibid.*, pp. 120-121.

he acceded to Pakistan before August 14, the future government of India had allowed me to give His Highness an
assurance that no objection whatever would be raised by
them. Had His Highness acceded to India by August 14,
Pakistan did not then exist, and therefore could not have
interfered. The only trouble that could have been raised
was by non-accession to either side, and this was unfortunately the very course followed by the Maharaja."[18]

It would seem, therefore, that up to this moment at least
Mountbatten applied the same formula for the future of
Kashmir after partition that he used so successfully with
the other Princely States. His failure to convince the Maharaja is surely no cause for Pakistani resentment. That this
was indeed the official position is only reinforced by the
knowledge that Lord Ismay, the experienced military adviser to Winston Churchill during the war, who served with
Mountbatten's mission in the capacity of Chief of Staff, also
tried his best while spending a few days in Srinagar at the
beginning of September 1947 to influence the Maharaja,
obviously with no success. Nothing official is known, however, about his conversations with the ruler.

Campbell-Johnson in his diary also returns several times
to the subject of Mountbatten's impartiality, apparently
deeply chagrined that suspicion should be thrown upon his
chief.[19] Lord Birdwood, a British expert on India, likewise
accepted "the truth of that position. After a certain amount
of inquiry and talk with those concerned, I certainly do
myself. If we accept it, then we must equally refuse the
Pakistan contention that there was some form of diabolical
plot between the Maharaja and the Government of India
to stage a situation which would precipitate accession to
India."[20]

[18] *Time Only to Look Forward, op.cit.*, pp. 268-269.
[19] Campbell-Johnson, *Mission with Mountbatten, op.cit.*, pp. 317,
358.
[20] Lord Birdwood, "Kashmir." *International Affairs*, Vol. XXVIII,

On the other hand one is forced to admit that Gandhi's and Nehru's ardent desire to visit Kashmir did nothing to allay Pakistan suspicion. The Subcontinent was in the throes of a deep communal and political crisis. The situation in Kashmir was tense. A Hindu Maharaja was in process of shedding the blood of Muslims whose prominent leaders, both of the National and Muslim Conference, were in prison. No Muslim leader visited such Princely States as Hyderabad or Junagadh in which Muslim rulers governed predominantly Hindu populations. Nor did they visit Kashmir.

Gandhi Visits Srinagar

In spite of Mountbatten's efforts to dissuade the Congress leaders from going to Srinagar, the Maharajas of Patiala, Kapurthala, and Faridkot and the president of the Indian National Congress, Acharya Kripalani, paid visits to the Maharaja. Then, early in August Mahatma Gandhi went himself.

Even the cautious *London Times* commented ". . . But the Union of India has been taking a lively interest in the subject and indications are that the Hindu Maharaja of Kashmir, Sir Hari Singh, has lately been much influenced by representations made by Mr. Gandhi who visited Kashmir three months ago and by other Congress leaders."[21]

Small wonder, then, that the Pakistanis are convinced that Gandhi succeeded in arriving at a definite commitment from the Maharaja, though no document supports their conviction. Such a possibility is, of course, in contradiction to the content of Mountbatten's June message to the Maharaja stating that the government of India had allowed him to "give to His Highness an assurance that no objection would be raised by them" if he acceded to Pakistan.

No. 3, July 1952, Royal Institute of International Affairs, London, pp. 301-312.
    [21] *The Times* (London), October 25, 1947.

On the other hand it is difficult to understand why the Congress leaders were anxious "that the Maharaja of Kashmir should make no declaration of independence." It is safe to assume that they would not have advised the Maharaja to accede to Pakistan, but then if they did not wish him to declare independence, for what purpose was their visit? It is perhaps understandable that Pandit Nehru might have wanted to visit Kashmir to intervene for his political friend, Sheikh Abdullah, who was in prison. But one wonders whether Nehru was interested in Abdullah's personal welfare—devoid of political implications—at a time when the Subcontinent boiled with insurrection and thousands of people were being killed.

The Pakistanis further support their conviction about the purpose of Mr. Gandhi's visit with the Maharaja by pointing to several political events which followed in the period between the visit and the act of accession. They point out, for example, that the Prime Minister of Kashmir, Pandit Kak, who had signed the standstill agreement with Pakistan, was replaced by Janak Singh and later by Mehr Chand Mahajan, who sided openly with India and was for the state's accession to India. They point to the dismissal of the British officers from the Kashmir police and army, including the Chief of the General Staff and the Inspector General of Police.

The Pakistanis have further maintained that as a result of Gandhi's negotiations it was decided to build a direct road between India and Jammu. It was reported that "orders have been issued by the Kashmir Government that a temporary boat bridge should be constructed over the Ravi near Pathankot [India] so that vehicular traffic could be maintained between Jammu and the Indian Union. The metalling of the road from Jammu [town] to Kathua [in Jammu Province] is also proceeding at top speed. The idea is to keep up some sort of communication between the State and the Indian Union, so that essential supplies and troops could be rushed to Kashmir without having to transport them through Pakistan territory. These orders were kept as top secret lest the Pakistan Government smell these shady moves. But somehow it leaked out and a local daily paper, belonging to the Kashmiri Pandit Sabha, published it. When other papers and news agencies tried to copy it, the censor stepped in and prohibited its publication in the State and circulation outside."

It was further reported three weeks later that, "The Kashmir Government has confirmed the news that it is linking the State, via Pathankot, with the East Punjab, and throwing a bridge over the River Ravi. The work is already proceeding at top speed. Temporary arrangements are also under way to make it possible for vehicles and other transport to cross the Ravi. In short, every effort is being made to render the State independent of the two existing arteries of communications that link Kashmir with the outside world. Both of these run through Pakistan.

"Once the communication lines between the State and Hindustan become actual, it is generally believed in the highest circles, that the Maharaja will burst forth with a declaration of accession to Hindustan. In the Muslim circles throughout the State, it is said that such a declaration would be tantamount to a declaration of war against 80% of the Muslim population of the State, as well as against Pakistan."[22]

The Pakistanis, then, assert that "with Indian assistance the State improved the road to Jammu, constructed a telegraph line along it, and started work on the road to link Bagh in Poonch with the main Jhelum Valley road to Kashmir near Chikar. This latter road was to give India through Jammu, Naushera and Kotli a road open throughout the

[22] *The Pakistan Times* (Lahore), September 27, October 17, 1947.

year to the Vale of Kashmir, which is normally inaccessible in winter by the Jammu-Banihal road."[23]

Now it cannot be assumed that a decision to link by highway two areas hitherto rather tenuously joined by inadequate transportation facilities is prima-facie evidence of either a secret agreement of eventual accession or military support in case of trouble. But the timing of such a decision, if it did come (as the Pakistanis claim) hard on the heels of Gandhi's visit, would be evidence enough for the Pakistanis. They were convinced that a plan to incorporate Kashmir within India had been prepared at the time of the negotiations concerning partition, when the Radcliffe Award assigned to India the district of Gurdaspur in spite of its slight Muslim majority. The district lies opposite Kathua and provides the only natural link between India and Jammu.

There is one piece of etymological fact that would seem to cast a different light on the question. This is the very name "Pakistan," with which the Muslims, ever since 1940, have associated the idea of national independence. It has a double meaning. One is Pak-i-Stan, meaning the "Land of Pure." The other is the fact that the name is composed of the initials of the regions from which Pakistan was to be created: P for Punjab, A for Afghan (North-West Frontier Province), K for Kashmir(!), S for Sind, and Tan for the ending of Baluchistan. Such a name would seem to imply that the Muslim leaders themselves had taken for granted that Kashmir would be an integral part of their future homeland. On the other hand, since the Indian National Congress failed to protest this highly political interpretation of the letter "K" in the name of Pakistan, it would seem to indicate at least its resignation to Kashmir's eventually becoming a part of Pakistan. If this is so, it would seem rather illogical to accuse the government of India of planning Kashmir's accession to India by force.

[23] *Jammu: A Muslim Province, op.cit.,* p. 17.

All these may seem to be trivial and bothersome details. Yet they are of material importance in view of the Pakistani suspicions which have cast heavy shadows upon the good faith and integrity of the Indian government. And such seemingly unimportant evidence, multiplied hundreds of times by the general distrust which clouded every detail of crucial negotiations in Delhi concerning the complex issues of the partition, added fuel to the flames of Hindu-Muslim hostility.

One fact, however, stands out amid the welter of claims and counterclaims. This is that of the other 584 Princely States not a single one with Hindu population became a part of Pakistan even though in two cases, Hyderabad and Junagadh, they were ruled by Muslim Princes. Nor did any state with a Muslim population (with the exception of the Sikh-ruled State of Kapurthala, in which almost all Muslims were killed or expelled) accede to India. Rather, they sought integration according to their religious affinity in every case save one—Kashmir.

Independence—and Bloodshed in Kashmir

Through all the mists of uncertainty that shroud the negotiations concerning the future of Kashmir, one fact alone is clear. This is the irresponsible behavior of the Maharaja. It was this that brought his nation uncommitted, his people's wishes unascertained, past the fatal day of partition, August 15, 1947. It was his stubbornness, his coy maneuvering, including his "attacks of colic," that brought upon his people unparalleled suffering and pain. In this respect at least, he was a worthy "Son of the Dogras."

When the fateful day of August 15 dawned, Muslims celebrated a "Pakistan Day" with flags enthusiastically displayed throughout the state. The Maharaja ordered them torn down and retaliated by closing all pro-Pakistani newspapers.

Still the pressure mounted, and the stories carried by

refugees pouring in from bloodsoaked Punjab by Sikhs, Hindus, and Muslims must have done little to allay the Maharaja's anxiety. Nor did the presence in Kashmir of these bitter and hysterical refugees do anything to reduce the tension within Kashmir.

The Maharaja's last-minute decision was, as history would indicate, no decision at all. It was only a final maneuver—a last vacillation. He apparently thought to temporize his position on August 12, three days before partition, by offering a standstill agreement with both India and Pakistan.[24] Under its terms, Pakistan would assume the responsibilities it now held as a part of British India and would continue to run the communications, postal and telegraph services. An agreement along these lines was signed with Pakistan on August 14. With India, however, such an agreement was never effected. There was no official explanation for this important omission until five years later when Sheikh Abdullah declared that India's decision to refrain from signing such an agreement was based upon the belief that "it could not consider any agreement entered into by the Government of the State valid until it had the approval of the people's representatives."[25] The fact that India accepted the all-important act of accession from the same Maharaja's government two months later, in October, casts some doubt upon Sheikh Abdullah's sincerity concerning India's motives. This abstention on the part of India has also been the basis for Pakistani accusations that the entire affair was a premeditated ruse on the part of both the Maharaja and India. They declare that the standstill agreement was designed to persuade Pakistan that no action was immediately anticipated; that India's failure to sign was based upon a fairly well-founded hope for a much closer political relationship.

[24] Campbell-Johnson, *Mission with Mountbatten, op.cit.*, p. 223.
[25] *Jammu and Kashmir Constituent Assembly, op.cit.*, pp. 15-16.

64

Who Coerced Whom?

The Indian government had an entirely different view about the development in Kashmir and the happenings connected with the question of accession. It admits that "Kashmir became crowded with a large number of refugees, both Sikhs and Muslims; the Muslim refugees passed through parts of the State on their way from East Punjab to West Punjab. This resulted in the State becoming a sort of channel through which they passed." Still, they insist that "Kashmir remained quiet . . . Kashmir had no disturbances at all when both East and West Punjab were in the flames of the communal passions and disturbances"; that ". . . there is no reason for any suggestion that anything has been done by the Dogra Raja or by the Dogras otherwise to molest the Muslims"; that they "have no facts which would show that any Muslims were killed in the Kashmir State by Sikhs or Hindus or even by the Maharaja or his Dogras before October 22, which is the date of the penetration and raid in Kashmir territory by the tribesmen."[26]

Indeed, says the Indian government, ever since the Maharaja failed to meet the time limit of accession the Pakistan government pursued a policy of coercing him into accession to Pakistan. It accused the Pakistani authorities of arousing feelings of communal hatred and giving support to acts of terrorism in Kashmir. Agents and religious leaders, it maintains, were sent from Pakistan to various parts of Kashmir to incite the Muslim population against Sikhs and Hindus. Raids were reportedly organized from Pakistan's West Punjab into Jammu Province, villages were burned, and non-Muslims murdered and robbed.

Furthermore, according to the Indian statements, Pakistan applied an economic blockade to Kashmir to coerce her into accession. She refused to honor her obligations towards

[26] From the speech of the representative of India, M. C. Setalvad, before the Security Council, *Security Council Official Records, op.cit.,* pp. 211, 212, 214.

Kashmir emanating from the standstill agreement and cut the country off from its supply of gasoline, wheat, salt, kerosene oil, and cloth. The postal system did not work, savings bank accounts were tied up, postal certificates were not cashed, and checks on West Punjab banks were not honored.[27]

The Pakistan government rejects emphatically these Indian accusations. It explains that the difficulties of supplying the state were caused by the dislocation of communications, by their being overloaded with the transport of refugees, by the failure of India to supply coal to Pakistan, by the fact that Muslim lorry drivers were afraid to carry supplies to Kashmir because the Sikhs and Hindus were attacking them. It further asserts that India violated the standstill agreement by having Kashmir included within her postal system, and as evidence it published a memorandum, dated September 1, 1947, almost eight weeks before the accession of the state to India, signed by the Director-General, Postal Telegraph, New Delhi, in which towns in the State of Jammu and Kashmir are listed as if they were part of India.[28]

Whatever the validity of the mutual accusations, there is little doubt that Kashmir was brewing with revolt against the Maharaja long before the tribesmen invaded the country. The political opposition launched in 1930 was carried into an open resistance in 1946. This was resumed in the spring of 1947, and it reached a critical climax in the summer when the news of the fratricidal struggle in Punjab echoed throughout Kashmir.

The Maharaja apparently was thoroughly aware of the situation. He strengthened the Sikh and Hindu garrisons in the Muslim areas. Then, towards the end of July, he

[27] See Government of India, *White Paper on Jammu and Kashmir*, pp. 2, 8, 9.
[28] See Sir Zafrulla Khan's statement before the Security Council, *Security Council Official Records, op.cit.*, pp. 101-103.

ordered the Muslims to deposit arms with the police. The Muslims answered by organizing themselves in guerrilla groups in the wild hills of West Poonch, where their movements remained unnoticed for some time. They were led by seasoned soldiers who previously had been demobilized from the British Indian army. They organized the smuggling of arms. Messengers were sent to the tribal areas of the North-West Frontier Province, where manufacturing of small arms and ammunitions had been practiced for years. The Muslim partisans in the hills were armed with these weapons. Many ex-servicemen from World War II, hearing about the Maharaja's expeditions against Muslim villages, evacuated their families to West Punjab, where their relatives lived, and returned to Jammu to fight the Dogra rule.

This movement was led by a young Kashmiri, Sardar Mohammed Ibrahim Khan, who since June had traveled throughout the country, arousing the spirit of his countrymen. In August he narrowly escaped arrest in Srinagar and fled to Pakistan. At Murree he laid the foundation for a political movement of liberation, out of which later grew the Azad (Free) Kashmir government.

The Maharaja admitted unrest when his government issued a statement on September 12, 1947, listing dates and places where agitation had been launched "by evilly disposed persons," and assured the population that the whole of Jammu was "now on the 10th of September pacified" and that "steps to restore control to civil administration of the area" were in progress.[29] But the revolt was not suppressed, and the fighting did not stop. From West Jammu it spread to the eastern part of the province, and massacres grew into mass proportions.

Richard Symonds, who served with a group of British Quakers in Punjab aiding innumerable victims of communal

[29] *Kashmir Before Accession.* Government Printing, Lahore, 1948; pp. 13-14.

strife, described the situation in Jammu and Poonch in the following terms:

"Poonch is a barren, rocky mountainous country, whose important export is military manpower. Sixty thousand Poonchis served in the Indian Army in World War II. They returned (they said) to find that during the war the Raja of Poonch, under whose mild, if unprogressive rule they had existed tolerably, had been dispossessed by a law suit and that the Maharaja of Kashmir's direct rule had imposed all the tyrannous taxes of Kashmir and Jammu. There was a tax on every hearth and every window. Every cow, buffalo and sheep was taxed and even every wife. Finally the Zaildari tax was introduced to pay for the cost of taxation, and Dogra troops were billeted on the Poonchis to enforce collection.

"As August 15 and the partition of India drew near, there were many meetings and demonstrations in Poonch in favour of Kashmir joining Pakistan. Martial law was introduced and meetings fired on. After one such incident on August 27 in Nila But, Abdul Qayyum, a young zamindar, started the revolt with a few friends. Substantial men told me that they would never have joined such a rash enterprise but for the folly of the Dogras who burnt whole villages where only a single family was involved in the revolt. Rapidly most of the Muslim ex-Servicemen joined Qayyum and in six weeks the whole district except for Poonch city itself was in rebel hands."[30]

About the middle of October, when the situation in Kashmir developed into mass killing, the governments of Pakistan and Kashmir exchanged a number of telegrams. Karachi accused Srinagar of organized expeditions against Muslims, and of the state troops' raids into West Punjab. The Maharaja government protested against the infiltration of Pakistani nationals and the smuggling of arms into

[30] *The Statesman* (Calcutta), February 4, 1948.

Kashmir. In one telegram, on October 15, it expressed readiness "to have an impartial inquiry made into the whole affair. . . ." But it warned at the same time, "If, unfortunately, this request is not heeded the Government much against its wishes will have no option but to ask for assistance to withstand the aggressive and unfriendly actions of the Pakistan people along our border. . . ."

The Pakistani government took a grave view of the threat of asking for an assistance which could not have implied anything other than help from India, but it accepted Srinagar's proposal to establish an inquiry committee. It expressed readiness to nominate its representative without delay.

A few days later, on October 18, the Prime Minister of Kashmir repeated the threat of asking "for friendly assistance," but, significantly, the previous offer of establishing an inquiry committee was omitted. The Governor General of Pakistan protested again, saying:

". . . the threat to enlist outside assistance shows clearly that the real aim of your Government's policy is to seek an opportunity to join the Indian Dominion, as a coup d'état, by securing the intervention and assistance of that Dominion.

"This policy is naturally creating deep resentment and grave apprehension among your subjects, 85 per cent of whom are Muslims. The proposal made by my Government for a meeting with your accredited representative is now an urgent necessity. I suggest that the way to smooth out the difficulties and adjust matters in a friendly way is for your Prime Minister to come to Karachi and discuss the developments that have taken place, instead of carrying on acrimonious and bitter controversy by telegrams and correspondence. I would also repeat that I endorse the suggestion made in your Prime Minister's telegram of 15 October, and accepted by my Government in their reply of 18 October, to have an impartial inquiry made into the whole affair."[31]

Several other telegrams were sent to Kashmir from Karachi, pointing to mounting oppression of Muslims and also to mountain tensions among the Pakistani nationals. But despite this insistent exchange of messages, nobody from the Maharaja's government came to Karachi, and no commission to carry out an "impartial inquiry" was ever established.

Abdullah Reenters the Scene

While this battle of telegrams between Karachi and Srinagar was going on, a highly curious event took place in Srinagar. Sheikh Abdullah was, without explanation, released from prison.

It will be remembered that Sheikh Abdullah, the leader of the National Conference, was sentenced in May 1946 to nine years in prison for having led the "Quit Kashmir" campaign, aimed against the Maharaja. Yet, on September 29, 1947, while the state was in the midst of a revolt, the Maharaja ordered his release.

There is no evidence of any official intervention with the Maharaja, but the only possible guess which suggests itself is that Abdullah was released on the intervention of the government of India, whose Prime Minister, Pandit Nehru, had been for years associated with him. That some such high-level intervention took place is supported by the fact that the leaders of the Muslim Conference, who had been far less pronounced in their hostility to the Maharaja than their political opponent, Sheikh Abdullah, remained behind bars. Abdullah's actions following his release are likewise significant and continue to imply that his freedom was no princely whim on the part of the Maharaja.

Immediately after his release, Abdullah set up a number of meetings and declared at a gathering of 100,000 people at Hazaribagh, in Kashmir, on October 5:

[31] The telegrams are quoted in the *Security Council Official Records; op.cit.*, pp. 75, 76, 77, 78, 79, 81-82.

". . . Our first demand is complete transfer of power to the people in Kashmir. Representatives of the people in a democratic Kashmir will then decide whether the State should join India or Pakistan. If the forty lakhs [4,000,000] of people living in Jammu and Kashmir are by-passed and the State declares its accession to India or Pakistan, I shall raise the banner of revolt and we face a struggle.

"Of course, we will naturally opt to go to that Dominion where our own demand for freedom receives recognition and support. . . . We cannot desire to joint those [in Pakistan] who say that the people must have no voice in the matter. We shall be cut to pieces before we allow alliance between this state and people of this type. . . .

"In this time of national crisis Kashmir must hold the beaconlight. All around us we see the tragedy of brother killing brother. At this time Kashmir must come forward and raise the banner of Hindu-Muslim unity.

"In Kashmir we want a people's Government. We want a government which will give equal rights and equal opportunities to all men—irrespective of caste and creed. The Kashmir Government will not be the government of any one community. It will be a joint government of the Hindus, the Sikhs and the Muslims. That is what I am fighting for."[32]

Such sentiments are of course eminently noble, but since, at the time he expressed them, the basic pattern for accession by the Princely States to India or Pakistan was being decided exclusively on a communal basis, there can be no doubt that the sense of Sheikh Abdullah's statement was decidedly pro-Indian—at least anti-Pakistani. The Sheikh's subsequent actions are likewise significant.

Soon after his release from prison and after a few days of campaigning in Kashmir, Sheikh Abdullah visited New Delhi. In two statements released through API (Associated

[32] *People's Age* (Bombay), October 26, 1947, as quoted in the *Security Council Official Record, op.cit.*, pp. 212-213.

Press of India) on October 10 and 21, he confirmed that the Poonchis were in open revolt against the Maharaja but he reaffirmed his policy against joining Pakistan. He sympathized with the Indian policy of Hindu-Muslim unity but insisted on "freedom before accession."

This, then, was the situation as darkness slid over the Subcontinent on the evening of the twenty-first of October, 1947. The independence of Hindus and Muslims from almost two centuries of British rule was only a little more than nine weeks old. But already, over vast areas of what should have been this happy land, an indigenous and complex tyranny was spreading—a tyranny of terror, product of a "fission" that was at once to the Indian leaders preposterous and to the Pakistanis, inescapable.

It was in Kashmir, peopled by Muslims, ruled by a Hindu, resting upon India, nestled against Pakistan, crossroad of refugees fleeing from the terrors of both Muslim and Hindu pillage and murder, that the most tragic explosion, product of this fission, was to take place.

In India, in Pakistan, in Kashmir on this evening of October 21, tension continued to mount. The press bayed accusation and counter-accusation. Hindus and Sikhs intensified the bitterness of their thrusts against Pakistan. The Muslims of Kashmir fell before the rifles and swords of the Dogras, and in Pakistan the tribesmen called for a *jehad*, a holy war of revenge against their brothers' killers.

The explosion had now become inevitable. It started at dawn of the twenty-second.

4. Invasion and Accession

"October 22nd. In the hour before dawn, Prithvinath Wanchoo, a young divisional engineer, staying in the dak bungalow at Domel near the Kashmir-North-West Frontier Province border, is rudely awakened by his servant hysterically shouting 'Dushman aagaya' (The enemy has come). Wanchoo runs barefooted into the verandah and sees the village of Nalochi, across the Kishenganga bridge, in flames. The Dogra garrison, caught unawares by the suddenness of the invasion, loses its hill-top positions and trenches and falls back to organize a new defensive position."[1]

THUS the curtain was raised on another scene of the drama of the Kashmiri people. It was the formidable Afridi and Mahsud tribesmen of Tirah and Waziristan who, aroused by stories of the slaughter of Muslims by the Dogra troops, crossed the Kashmir frontier at the strategic outpost of Domel and swept down, some 2,000 strong, along the Jhelum river valley, quickly overcoming the resistance of the state troops.

It had not required much effort to incite them into a "holy war." For years these tribes had been a thorn to the British in this all-important territory, where the British-Russian interests had often clashed in diplomatic squabbles. They were a restless people. Every man carried a rifle and recognized only one authority—his tribal chief. During the mild summers they were relatively quiet. But the winter snows covering their hilly motherland drove them to temporary quarters in milder valleys, and these seasonal migrations were by no means peaceable. On their treks they invaded villages, looted homes and shops, and abducted women. Then, their spirits satisfied and their greediness assuaged, they returned to their homes.

[1] D. F. Karaka, *Betrayal in India*. Victor Gollancz, London, 1950; pp. 173-174, quoting from the pamphlet by K. Ahmad Abbas, *Kashmir Fights for Freedom*; Kutub.

One British official document describing them as "among the hardest fighters in the world," says, ". . . only picked and highly trained troops can compete with them on anything like equal terms in their own hills. They are believed to number nearly three millions, of whom at least half are males and of the latter close on three quarters of a million are regarded as adults and fighting men. Their armament has vastly increased within the last few years, and as long ago as 1920 there were believed to be no less than 140,000 modern rifles in the territory."[2]

The British found one way to pacify them. They posted well-armed guards at all strategic locations and then paid subsidies to their chieftains. "It was also a fairly open secret, although exact figures cannot be obtained, that about thirty million rupees [approximately 10 million dollars] a year were spent in the shape of subsidies to various tribal chiefs in return for their goodwill. All this was done very quietly and details were known only to the very high ranking officials of the political department of the government of India."[3] (Some Pakistani sources put the figure at 70 million rupees, British sources at 17 million.)

When the British withdrew, however, the North-West Frontier Province outposts and subsidies were withdrawn also. Pakistan, which after the partition assumed responsibility over the area, found herself unable to pursue the British policy. In the first place the Pakistan army was too small (particularly in officer strength) to take over the garrisons held previously by the British in the area. Nor could the Pakistan treasury afford to maintain the subsidies. Instead it hoped to solve the problem by a program of public works which would keep the tribesmen busy in their own territory. But this would take years, and in the meantime

[2] J. Coatman, *India in 1927-28. A statement prepared for presentation to Parliament in accordance with the requirement of the 26th Section of the Government of India Act* (5 & 6 Geo. V., Chap. 61). Calcutta, Government of India, 1928, p. 280.

[3] Karaka, *op.cit.*, p. 171.

74

a resumption of the traditional raiding habits of these war-like tribesmen appeared to be inevitable. Under these circumstances it is understandable if the Pakistan government, without perhaps in any way inciting the invasion of Kashmir, felt some relief that the path of invasion turned toward that territory, particularly when such raids might well serve the national interests of Pakistan.

The invasion was easily incited by the stories brought into the North-West Frontier Province by Muslims, fleeing before the terror of Dogra troops in Kashmir. For centuries these tribesmen had believed that the Koran was the highest law and to defend it, nay, more, to spread it, was their sacred duty. Boundaries were no obstacle to them, certainly not in the sense of international law. "In Islam, every believer, wherever he may be, can serve any and all Muslim princes on the same terms and according to the same uniform law. In Islam, in consequence, the idea of frontiers has no juridical meaning. . . ."[4] Now Islam was in danger in Kashmir—and the tribesmen had swarmed across its border to defend the faith.

In quick succession, the tribesmen occupied Muzaffarabad and Uri, dispersing and liquidating the demoralized troops of the state army. In Jammu they were joined by the Azad revolutionaries and supported by Pakistani volunteers from West Punjab and the adjacent states of Swat and Dir. All of these groups were under the command of General Akbar Khan, who used the pseudonym of "General Tariq," the name of a Moorish hero who had defended Islam in Spain over a thousand years before. (It should be noted here that General Khan later became Chief of Staff of the Pakistan army—and still later was imprisoned for taking part in a plot against the government.)

The tribesmen pushed rapidly on, besieging the towns of Mirpur, Poonch, Kotli, Jhanger, Naoshera, and Bhimb-

[4] Robert Montagne, "Modern Nations and Islam." *Foreign Affairs*, July 1952, p. 581.

har. No one, especially the Hindus and Sikhs, was safe before their barbarous fury. The avalanche of looting, pillaging, burning, and abductions pushed irresistibly forward along the Jhelum river road.

On the fourth day of the invasion, October 26, the tribesmen swept into Baramula, the only major town on the open road to Srinagar, thirty-five miles farther southeast. Only 3,000 people out of 14,000 survived the raid. Even the Saint Joseph's Franciscan convent, church, and hospital were not spared. In the words of Father Shanks:

"The tribesmen—great, wild, black beasts they were— came shooting their way down from the hills on both sides of the town.

"A 20-year-old Indian nurse, Philomena, tried to protect a Muslim patient whose baby had just been born. She was shot dead first. The patient was next.

"Mother Superior Aldetrude rushed into the ward, knelt over Philomena and was at once attacked and robbed. The Assistant Mother, Teresalina, saw a tribesman point a rifle at Mother Aldetrude and jumped in front of her. A bullet went through Teresalina's heart.

"At that moment Colonel Dykes, who had assured us we would not be attacked, raced from his room a few yards along the terrace to get the Mother Superior out of danger, shouting at the tribesmen as he ran. But the Mother Superior fell shot, and Colonel Dykes collapsed beside her, with a bullet in the stomach.

"Mrs. Dykes ran from her husband's room to help him. She, too, was shot dead.

"While this went on Mr. Gee Boretto, an Anglo-Indian, was killed in the garden before nine nuns. Then the nuns were lined up before a firing squad.

"As the tribesmen raised their rifles a young Afridi officer, who once studied in a Convent school at Peshawar, rushed in and stopped them. He had been told his men were raiding a Convent, and had run all the way from the town. That saved all our lives by a few seconds.

"We did not find Mrs. Dykes until the following day. She had been thrown down a well."[5]

Srinagar trembled before the danger of the tribesmen's invasion. Sheikh Abdullah became a hero in his organization of the defense of the city, including the mobilization of a national militia. Some evidence, however, would seem to indicate that the chief activity of the state forces was the slaughter of Muslims in Srinagar. The Kashmir Muslim Association issued a statement describing the situation:

"Alarming reports are pouring in from Srinagar that during the last few days gangs of Dogra soldiers are combing out all those who are known to be supporters of Kashmir's accession to the Pakistan Dominion. Muslim personnel of the State military and police have either been disarmed or arrested; several important officials have been dismissed and hundreds of political workers have been lodged behind the iron bars of the dingy State cells. There have been innumerable instances of looting of the houses of political workers.

"In Baramula and Rampur, several people have been shot dead on the mere suspicion that they were welcoming the armies of liberation. A reign of terror has been unleashed against the peace-abiding population of the State. The life and honour of no self-respecting patriot, whether Hindu or Muslim, who wants the question of the State's accession to either of the Dominions settled in a democratic manner, is safe.

"The Hindu and Sikh refugees in the State are being armed by the Kashmir Government and are encouraged to kill Muslims and others whose loyalty Sheikh Abdullah's Conference considers to be dubious."[6]

The whole territory of Jammu and Kashmir burst into

[5] *White Paper on Jammu and Kashmir, op.cit.*, p. 25.
[6] *Security Council Official Records, op.cit.*, p. 70.

flame. Sikhs, Hindus, and state troops, supported by refugees and those who had infiltrated the territory for the specific purpose of communal slaughter, were killing Muslims. The Kashmir and Jammu Muslims, organized by Azad leaders and supported by Pakistan nationals, were killing Hindus and Sikhs. Over it all the tribesmen superimposed their own interests in looting, pillage, and abduction. Within a few days, 100,000 Muslim refugees fled to Pakistan, carrying their stories of the tragic happenings in their homeland.

Negotiation and Accession

The news about the invasion of the tribesmen reached Delhi on October 24. Events now moved swiftly. The following three days made history.

A meeting of the Defense Committee of the Indian government took place on October 25 under the chairmanship of Lord Mountbatten, now the Governor-General of the Indian Union. According to one authentic witness, the reaction of the Indian government was that "the Defence Committee considered the most immediate necessity was to rush in arms and ammunition already requested by the Kashmir Government, which would enable the local populace in Srinagar to put up some defence against the raiders. The problem of troop reinforcement was considered, and Mountbatten urged that it would be dangerous to send in any troops unless Kashmir had first offered to accede."[7] This witness made a further disclosure: "The Government were determined against the military advice both of their own Chiefs of Staff [who were British officers] and of himself [Mountbatten], to send in troops in response to a request from Kashmir for aid. . . . [Mountbatten] considered that it would be the height of folly to send troops into a neutral State, where we had no right to send them, since Pakistan could do exactly the same thing, which could only

[7] Campbell-Johnson, *op.cit.*, p. 224.

result in a clash of armed forces and in war. He therefore argued that if indeed they were determined to send in troops, the essential prerequisite was accession."[8] Furthermore, Mountbatten insisted that even such an act of accession should be considered as temporary and to be followed, upon the restoration of peace and order, by a plebiscite.

This testimony would indicate that the Maharaja had asked the Delhi government for military assistance as he had threatened to do in telegrams sent to Karachi. It further shows that the Indian leaders were resolved to send help to the Maharaja. But more important, it places upon Lord Mountbatten the responsibility for the idea that Kashmir accede, though conditionally, to India.

The importance of this decision to the subsequent history of the Kashmir dispute cannot be overestimated, for this decision and the events which it precipitated are responsible more than all else for the character of the crisis in Kashmir. It is a decision that is difficult to understand.

As impartial and as correct as was Mountbatten's attitude toward the problem of the accession of the Princely States during his viceroyalty, his attitude and advice in this case inevitably raise critical questions. Why, for example, did he advise that Indian military assistance to the Maharaja must be covered by the legal technicality of accession? How could he have reasoned that it would be illegal for Kashmir (which was at the time of invasion technically an independent country) to ask for military help from India without preceding the request by accession? He must have assumed that the Pakistan government would refuse in any case to recognize the legality of such accession brought about without prior determination of the will of the Kashmiri people. He must have known that if war over this issue were to develop between these two Dominions it would not be on the basis of the legality of such a method of accession, but rather over the fact itself. Why

[8] *Ibid.*, pp. 224-225.

was there at this point no appeal made to the United Nations from either the technically independent government of Kashmir or from Delhi? The record reveals no hint that such a possibility was even mentioned. But, finally, it is most difficult to understand why no one, particularly Mountbatten, advanced the most obvious idea—that of immediately getting into contact with the Karachi government for consultation.

Following the session of the Defense Committee, V. P. Menon, the right hand of Patel in the States Ministry, was dispatched to Srinagar to explain the situation to the Maharaja, including, without question, the suggestion that he sign an instrument of accession.

Nothing is known about the conversation between Mr. Menon and the Maharaja. Campbell-Johnson recorded only that "the information which V. P. [Menon] brought back to the Defence Committee the next day [October 26] was certainly disturbing. He reported that he had found the Maharaja unnerved by the rush of events and the sense of his lone helplessness. Impressed at last with the urgency of the situation, he had felt that unless India could help immediately, all would be lost. Later in the day, on the strong advice of V. P., the Maharaja left Srinagar with his wife and son. V. P. had impressed upon him that as the raiders had already reached Baramula it would be foolhardy for His Highness to stay on in the capital. The Maharaja also signed a letter of accession which V. P. was able to present to the Defence Committee."[9]

The letter of accession, dated October 26, 1947, read as follows:

"My dear Lord Mountbatten,

"I have to inform Your Excellency that a grave emergency has arisen in my State and request the immediate assistance of your Government. As Your Excellency is aware, the State of Jammu and Kashmir has not acceded to either the Dominion of India or Pakistan. Geographi-

[9] *Ibid.*, p. 224.

cally my State is contiguous with both of them. Besides, my State has a common boundary with the Union of Soviet Socialist Republics and with China. In their external relations the Dominions of India and Pakistan cannot ignore this fact. I wanted to take time to decide to which Dominion I should accede or whether it is not in the best interests of both the Dominions and of my State to stand independent, of course with friendly and cordial relations with both. I accordingly approached the Dominions of India and Pakistan to enter into a standstill agreement with my State. The Pakistan Government accepted this arrangement. The Dominion of India desired further discussion with representatives of my Government. I could not arrange this in view of the developments indicated below. In fact the Pakistan Government under the standstill agreement is operating the post and telegraph system inside the State. Though we have got a standstill agreement with the Pakistan Government, that Government permitted a steady and increasing strangulation of supplies like food, salt and petrol to my State.

"Afridis, soldiers in plain clothes, and desperadoes with modern weapons have been allowed to infiltrate into the State, at first in the Poonch area, then from Sialkot and finally in a mass in the area adjoining the Hazara District on the Ramkote side. The result has been that the limited number of troops at the disposal of the State had to be dispersed and thus had to face the enemy at several points simultaneously, so that it has become difficult to stop the wanton destruction of life and property and the looting of the Mahura power house, which supplies electric current to the whole of Srinagar and which has been burnt. The number of women who have been kidnapped and raped makes my heart bleed. The wild forces thus let loose on the State are marching on with the aim of capturing Srinagar, the summer capital of my Government, as a first step to overrunning the whole State. The mass infiltration of tribesmen drawn from distant areas of the

North-West Frontier Province, coming regularly in motor trucks, using the Mansehra-Muzaffarabad road and fully armed with up-to-date weapons, cannot possibly be done without the knowledge of the Provincial Government of the North-West Frontier Province and the Government of Pakistan. In spite of repeated appeals made by my Government no attempt has been made to check these raiders or to stop them from coming into my State. In fact, both the radio and the press of Pakistan have reported these occurrences. The Pakistan radio even put out the story that a provisional government has been set up in Kashmir. The people of my State, both Muslims and non-Muslims, generally have taken no part at all.

"With the conditions obtaining at present in my State and the great emergency of the situation as it exists, I have no option but to ask for help from the Indian Dominion. Naturally they cannot send the help asked for by me without my State acceding to the Dominion of India. I have accordingly decided to do so, and I attach the instrument of accession for acceptance by your Government. The other alternative is to leave my State and the people to freebooters. On this basis no civilized government can exist or be maintained. This alternative I will never allow to happen so long as I am the ruler of the State and I have life to defend my country.

"I may also inform Your Excellency's Government that it is my intention at once to set up an interim government and to ask Sheikh Abdullah to carry the responsibilities in this emergency with my Prime Minister.

"If my State is to be saved, immediate assistance must be available at Srinagar. Mr. V. P. Menon is fully aware of the gravity of the situation and will explain it to you, if further explanation is needed.

"In haste and with kindest regards,

Yours sincerely,

(Signed) Hari Singh."

As the Defense Committee discussed the letter of accession, once more Lord Mountbatten returned to his insistence that the accession of Kashmir "was not just an act of acquisition," and he urged the Defense Committee, "that in the reply his Government asked him to send on their behalf to the Maharaja accepting his accession offer he should be allowed to add that this was conditional on the will of the people being ascertained as soon as law and order were restored. This principle was at once freely accepted and unilaterally proposed by Nehru."[10]

On October 27, 1947, Lord Mountbatten replied to the Maharaja's letter as follows:

"My dear Maharaja Sahib,

"Your Highness's letter dated 26 October 1947 has been delivered to me by Mr. V. P. Menon. In the special circumstances mentioned by Your Highness, my Government have decided to accept the accession of Kashmir State to the Dominion of India. In consistence with their policy that in the case of any State where the issue of accession has been the subject of dispute, the question of accession should be decided in accordance with the wishes of the people of the State, it is my Government's wish that, as soon as law and order have been restored in Kashmir and its soil cleared of the invader, the question of the State's accession should be settled by a reference to the people.

"Meanwhile, in response to Your Highness's appeal for military aid, action has been taken today to send troops of the Indian Army to Kashmir, to help your own forces to defend your territory and to protect the lives, property and honour of your people. My Government and I note with satisfaction that Your Highness has decided to invite Sheikh Abdullah to form an interim Government to work with your Prime Minister.

(Signed) Mountbatten of Burma."[11]

[10] *Ibid.*, p. 225.
[11] *White Paper on Jammu and Kashmir*, *op.cit.*, pp. 46-48.

With this hastily arranged interchange of letters and the signing of the instrument, the accession of Kashmir to India became a *fait accompli*. Three days later, on October 30, the Maharaja appointed Sheikh Abdullah as the Head of Emergency Administration. But in a sense these are curious letters, and the points of view which they reveal and the appointment of Abdullah raise insistent questions.

Following as it did Menon's visit, it is not surprising that step by step the Maharaja's letter repeats the Mountbatten reasoning before the Indian Defense Committee only the previous day. But the language remains odd. "Naturally," says the Maharaja, "they cannot send . . . help . . . without my State acceding to the Dominion of India." But he had asked for help only a few days before—and apparently without the suggestion of accession. At least, the record would indicate that it was Mountbatten who first raised the danger of "aid without accession." It is quite probable, then, that the pressure of tribesmen only a few miles from Srinagar and the Maharaja's consequent desperation did much to make accession seem "natural" to him, particularly if it was revealed by Menon that such an act was prerequisite to military assistance.

On the other hand, Mountbatten's reply likewise raises questions. The proposal of a plebiscite "after the actual fact" is an odd one for a realist to make, and one must therefore ask whether Mountbatten was not at this point more interested in the principle of accession than in the final determination of the will of the Kashmir people by plebiscite. Though his letter to the Maharaja urged a plebiscite, Mountbatten certainly did not indicate that such was in itself a condition of aid.

But most curious of all was the sudden reappearance of Sheikh Abdullah. Almost as an afterthought in the Maharaja's letter is Abdullah mentioned as the one who would form the emergency government.

It was only in May of the preceding year that Abdullah

had been jailed under a nine-year sentence as a traitor by the Maharaja. Yet just a little more than a year later, less than thirty days before this date of October 26, he had been released. He had spent a few days in Kashmir making—if not pro-Indian—at least anti-Pakistan talks. Now, on October 26, he was asked by the Maharaja to form an interim government, and the appointment had been "noted with satisfaction" by Mountbatten. Could this have happened without pressure from Delhi? Could this, too, have been a condition of military assistance which the Maharaja could scarcely refuse? There is no documentary evidence. But the facts of accession and the appointment of Sheikh Abdullah are difficult to explain on the grounds of voluntary decision by the Maharaja.

In any case, military aid was dispatched the following morning, October 27, to Srinagar.

The Indian Army Intervenes

"Three hundred and thirty men of the First Sikh Battalion were flown in to block a major invasion by North-West Frontier tribesmen, who [were] moving rapidly on Srinagar, the summer capital."[12] The last-minute character of this intervention may be seen in the fact that on that very day the tribesmen were only four and one-half miles from the city, prepared to encircle the airport at which the Indian airborne troops were to land. But just before they moved, the troops were landed, the tribesmen repulsed, and Srinagar saved from destruction.

The Pakistanis insist that the dispatch with which aid was sent to Srinagar only further indicates that such aid had been planned for weeks. As a matter of record, General Sir Frank Messervy, who was the commander-in-chief of the Pakistan army from August 15, 1947, to February 15, 1948, asserted that there was "much evidence that this ac-

[12] Campbell-Johnson, *op.cit.*, p. 223.

cession had been deliberately planned for some weeks before the event."[13]

The Indian government insists, however, that the military aid sent to Srinagar was improvised upon receipt of word of the invasion of the tribesmen and their threat to the capital, and the testimony of General Messervy is contradicted by the three commanding officers in charge of the Indian armed forces, themselves all British: the commander-in-chief of the Indian army, General R. M. Lockhart; the Air Marshal commanding the Royal Indian Air Force, T. W. Elmhirst; and the Rear Admiral of the Royal Indian Navy, J. T. S. Hall. Jointly they issued the following statement:

"It has been alleged that plans were made for sending Indian forces to Kashmir at some date before 22 October, on which day the raid on that State from the direction of Abbottabad began.

"1. The following is a true time-table of events, as regards decisions taken, plans made, orders given, and movement started in this matter:

"2. On 24 October the Commander in Chief, Indian Army, received information that tribesmen had seized Muzaffarabad. This was the first indication of the raid.

"3. Prior to this date, no plans of any sort for sending Indian forces into Kashmir had been formulated or even considered. On the morning of 25 October, we were directed to examine and prepare plans for sending troops to Kashmir by air and road, in case this should be necessary to stop the tribal incursions. This was the first direction which we received on this subject. No steps had been taken, prior to the meeting, to examine or prepare such plans.

"4. On the afternoon of 25 October we sent one staff officer of the Indian Army and one of the Royal Indian Air

[13] General Sir Frank Messervy, "Kashmir." *Asiatic Review*, Vol. 45, January, 1949, p. 469.

Force by air to Srinagar. There they saw officers of the Kashmir State Forces. This was the first contact between officers of our Headquarters and officers of the Kashmir State Forces on the subject of sending Indian troops to Kashmir.

"5. On the afternoon of 25 October we also issued orders to an infantry battalion to prepare itself to be flown at short notice, to Srinagar, in the event of the Government of India deciding to accept the accession of Kashmir and to send help.

"6. On the morning of 26 October the staff officers mentioned in paragraph 4 above, returned from Srinagar and reported on their meetings with officers of the Kashmir State Forces.

"7. On the afternoon of 26 October we finalized our plans for the dispatch by air of troops to Kashmir.

"8. At first light on the morning of 27 October, with Kashmir's Instrument of Accession signed, the movement by air of Indian forces to Kashmir began. No plans were made for sending these forces, nor were such plans even considered before 25 October, three days after the tribal incursions began."[14]

The Pakistani government reacted swiftly to the Indian move. The Governor-General of Pakistan, Jinnah, at midnight October 27 (the Indian troops had arrived in Srinagar that morning) ordered the acting commander-in-chief, General Sir Douglas D. Gracey, to dispatch troops to Kashmir. The wise General, realizing the grave consequences of such an act, was not prepared to follow Jinnah's instruction without the approval of Marshal Sir Claude Auchincleck, who was the supreme commander in charge of administering partition of the Indian army. At Gracey's urgent request Auchincleck flew immediately to Lahore and urged upon Jinnah to withdraw his orders. Jinnah cancelled

[14] *Security Council Official Records, op.cit.,* pp. 222-223.

the order and invited Lord Mountbatten and Prime Minister Nehru to Lahore for the discussion of the situation.[15]

Negotiations Fail

This was probably the final opportunity to bring about a quick and peaceful solution of the Kashmir conflict. Perhaps, even at this point, Jinnah, Nehru, and Mountbatten could have solved at the council table what bullets, political maneuvering, and seven years of subsequent diplomatic effort have not yet solved. It was not to be. Prime Minister Nehru was exhausted and sick. Lord Mountbatten's press attaché "was shocked to see how haggard and ill Nehru looked."[16] In addition, the Indian Cabinet, Patel most of all, was against anyone going to Lahore. Later, Mountbatten's view prevailed, and the Cabinet decided on October 30 that both the Governor-General and the Prime Minister would go to Lahore, where a meeting of the Joint Defense Council was to take place. Finally, however, Mountbatten went alone, as the doctor had forbidden Nehru to leave.

Meanwhile the government of Pakistan branded Kashmir's accession as an act based on "fraud and violence" and refused to recognize it.

The two Governors-General met in Lahore the next day, November 1, and had a three-and-half hour talk. The conversation revealed little more than the powerful position of Jinnah in the Pakistan government and the constitutionally limited powers of Mountbatten in the Indian government.

Jinnah formally presented a three-point proposal embodying a cease fire, a mutual withdrawal of all "alien" troops, and a plebiscite. Herewith is the text:

"1. To put an immediate stop to fighting, the two Governors-General should be authorized and vested with full

[15] Campbell-Johnson, *op.cit.*, pp. 226, 241.
[16] *Ibid.*, p. 225.

powers by both Dominion Governments to issue a proclamation forthwith giving forty-eight hours' notice to the
two opposing forces to cease fire. We have no control over
the forces of the Provisional [Azad] Government of Kashmir or the tribesmen engaged in the fighting, but we will
warn them in the clearest terms that if they do not obey
the order to cease fire immediately the forces of both Dominions will make war on them;

"2. Both the forces of Indian Dominion and the tribesmen to withdraw simultaneously and with the utmost expedition from Jammu and Kashmir State territory;

"3. With the sanction of the two Dominion Governments, the two Governors-General to be given full powers
to restore peace, undertake the administration of Jammu
and Kashmir State, and arrange for a plebiscite without
delay under their joint control and supervision."[17]

Mountbatten rejected Jinnah's proposal, pointing out his
constitutional inability to act without his government's advice. He, in turn, suggested a plebiscite under United Nations auspices, but this Jinnah would not agree to, insisting
that the two Governors-General should organize it.

Lord Mountbatten's caution not to exceed his constitutional rights is understandable, but it is difficult to understand why the government of India, under the grave circumstances that occasioned his visit to Lahore, could not
have bestowed upon him the special right to co-act as an
authority supervising a plebiscite, especially since under the
act of accession the territory of Kashmir was considered a
part of the Indian Union and the holding of such a plebiscite was one condition of that accession. It may have been
that the Indian government felt that the participation of
the Pakistan Governor-General in the supervision of the
plebiscite would imply doubt as to the validity of the accession.

The tragedy, of course, is that no matter what condi-

[17] *White Paper on Jammu and Kashmir, op.cit.,* p. 60.

tions limited or seemed to limit Mountbatten's ability to accept Jinnah's proposals, had he been able to accept them there is much reason to believe that the fighting could have been stopped, the raiders withdrawn, and the plebiscite carried through quickly and without too many complications. Kashmir would have been spared months of further cruel fighting and years of partition, and, more important, the two Dominions could have smoothed out their present bitter estrangement, so dangerous to the peace of the world.

The day following the meeting in Lahore, on November 2, Pandit Nehru made a broadcast in which he failed to mention the Lahore meeting and Jinnah's proposal. Instead he repeated the suggestion made by Mountbatten to Jinnah of a plebiscite held under the United Nations auspices.

Then for about ten days, negotiations (if this term can be used) were carried on by telegrams between the Prime Ministers of the two Dominions—each elaborating and restating their case against the other.

On November 16, the Prime Minister of Pakistan, Liaquat Ali Khan, issued a press statement. It was something of a surprise move, accepting (at least in principle) and elaborating Nehru's suggestion of reference of the dispute to the United Nations. Said Liaquat Ali Khan,

"The fundamental principle of the Charter of the United Nations is to prevent might prevailing over right. The whole dispute should, therefore, be brought before the bar of international opinion. We are ready to request the United Nations Organization immediately to appoint its representative in the Jammu and Kashmir State in order to put a stop to fighting and to the repression of Muslims in the State, to arrange the programme of withdrawal of outside forces, set up an impartial administration of the State until a plebiscite is held, and undertake the plebiscite under its direction and control for the purpose of ascertaining the free and unfettered will of the people of the State on the question of accession. . . ."

To this proposal Pandit Nehru replied five days later, on November 21, and his answer, given here in part, revealed the measure of disagreement:

"Since the United Nations have no (repeat no) forces at their disposal, we do not see how they can put a stop to the fighting or to the alleged repression of Muslims. This can only be done by an organized military force, and is being done by our troops. The fighting would also stop as soon as raiders were made to withdraw, and I have repeatedly asked your cooperation in stopping transit [of] and supplies to raiders through Pakistan territory.

"It is not clear to me what the United Nations Organization can do in the present circumstances in Kashmir until peace and order have been established. We are convinced that Sheikh Abdullah's administration is based on the will of the people and is impartial. Only he who goes to Kashmir and sees things for himself can appreciate this. Moreover, we have pledged that, so long as our forces are in Kashmir, protection of all sections of the community will be their first and sacred duty. This duty will be discharged without fear or favour.

"I have repeatedly stated that as soon as the raiders have been driven out of Kashmir or have withdrawn, and peace and order have been established, the people of Kashmir should decide the question of accession by plebiscite or referendum under international auspices such as those of the United Nations. It is very clear that no such reference to the people can be made when large bodies of raiders are despoiling the country and military operations against them are being carried on. By this declaration I stand. . . ."[18]

[18] For full texts and details see *White Paper on Jammu and Kashmir, op.cit.,* pp. 61-67. Also, *Security Council Official Records, op.cit.,* pp. 90, 92, 94-96, 97; Campbell-Johnson, *op.cit.,* pp. 229-230, 245, 251.

Then, on December 12, Nehru dispatched still another telegram to Karachi, this one saying, "We have given thought . . . to the question of inviting the United Nations to advise us in this matter. While we are prepared to invite United Nations observers to come here and advise us as to the proposed plebiscite, it is not clear in what other capacity United Nations help can be sought. . . . I confess, however, that I find myself unable to suggest anything beyond what I have offered already; namely, to ask the United Nations to send impartial observers to advise us regarding the plebiscite."

With this statement it became apparent that the Kashmir dispute was to be placed by Indian decision before the United Nations—not on the basis of a direct intervention in the dispute but rather as a request for advice limited to the conducting of an eventual plebiscite. The breach between the two nations, even on the issue of the nature of a United Nations intervention, was only widening.

Meanwhile in Kashmir the fighting had slowed, partly because the Indian troops had blunted the tribesmen's offensive, partly because winter had set in, which necessarily all but immobilized the two contending forces. The slaughter of civilians continued, however, and by the end of the year some 200,000 Muslims had fled Kashmir to Pakistan. Only one region—Gilgit—was not affected by the violent struggle. Here the people seized the Maharaja's agent and through a bloodless revolution established their own local government, which immediately acceded to Pakistan. The Karachi government, however, cautiously refrained from accepting the act of accession, possibly because it feared that such acceptance might imply their approval of a division of the state.

The year 1947 finally drew to a close. Few concerned with the awesome problems of the vast Subcontinent were loath to see it go. But the coming year offered no prospect of relief from the violence of its predecessor.

Clearly, Kashmir was now not an issue of territory; it was an issue of principle between the second and sixth largest nations in the world, India and Pakistan.

And who could judge the real issue—the rights or the wrongs, the wisdom or the foolishness, the logic or the illogic of the issue that created Kashmir, the issue of partition? All that could now be judged was the symbol and the product of partition—the problem of Kashmir. And in the judgment of this issue the world wanted to know a few facts. Principally, it wanted to know the extent to which Pakistan was, if not the instigator, at least the silent partner, in the invasion of Kashmir by the tribesmen.

Who Was Responsible?

Many highly competent and politically neutral correspondents descended on Kashmir and Punjab and the North-West Frontier Province. But even these failed to agree.

Margaret Parton reported to the *New York Herald Tribune*:

"If Pakistan is giving direct assistance to 'Azad' ('Free') fighting forces in Kashmir, evidence is not on the surface to be seen by prying foreigners. Below the surface is a mass of rumours, contradictions and paradoxes which, during a just completed week along the border of Pakistan and Kashmir, have alternately baffled and amused groups of press correspondents who followed Liaquat Ali Khan, Prime Minister of Pakistan, on his tour of the frontier.

"During the entire 600 miles trip we saw no raiders' bases, no training centers, no stocks of arms and ammunition and no Pakistan soldiers slipping off to the Kashmir front. Even those reliable 'neutral observers'—British officers and civilians—denied the existence of any of those material aids which India charges Pakistan is giving the fighters in Kashmir. . . ."[19]

[19] *New York Herald Tribune*, January 24, 1948.

The *London Times* on the other hand reported:

"That Pakistan is unofficially involved in aiding the raiders is certain. Your correspondent has first hand evidence that arms, ammunition and supplies are being made available to the Azad Kashmir forces. A few Pakistani officers are also helping to direct their operations. . . . And however much the Pakistan Government may disavow intervention, moral and material support is certainly forthcoming. . . ."[20]

The *New York Times* published an interview which its correspondent in India, Robert Trumbull, had with a former sergeant of the U.S. Air Force, Mr. Haight. He had once served with the Azad forces with the rank of brigadier general but now denounced them to Mr. Trumbull:

"I interviewed Mr. Haight clandestinely in Lahore, Pakistan, twelve days ago," Mr. Trumbull wrote, "but I agreed to hold his story until he let me know by code telegram that he was leaving the country. This was because there had already been three attempts on his life, and when I met him he felt that his safety in Pakistan was none too secure. He was in fact very decidedly 'on the lam'—whatever that may mean. . . . Mr. Haight said gasoline—a scarce and strictly rationed commodity—was supplied plentifully to the raiders by the Pakistan authorities. . . . Mr. Haight also found Pakistan Army personnel running the Azad Kashmir radio station, relaying messages through their own Pakistan Army receivers, organizing and managing Azad encampments in Pakistan, and supplying uniforms, food, arms and ammunition which, he understood, came from Pakistan Army stores through such subterfuges as the 'loss' of ammunition shipments.

"Although he insisted that the Kashmir fighting broke out in rebellion against atrocities committed upon Muslims by the Hindu Maharaja's Dogra troops, Mr. Haight characterized the Azad Kashmir Provisional Government,

[20] *The Times* (London), January 13, 1948.

94

headed by Sardar Mohammed Ibrahim Khan (who is now in New York), as 'Pakistan puppets.' He also deeply implicated high Pakistan Government officials, notably the Premier of the North-West Frontier Province."[21]

The Indian army's general staff also displayed as evidence collections of captured weapons which they were convinced were delivered to Kashmir straight from Pakistani army stores. They also presented a number of soldiers' record books as evidence that regular Pakistani troops were taking part in the fighting.

There is also the known fact that five years later, in the summer of 1952, the Khan of Mamdot claimed from the Pakistan government the sum of 68,000 rupees which, he asserted, as Chief Minister of Punjab at that time, he spent out of his own pocket to facilitate the tribesmen's invasion.

In all the inundation of contradictory reports, mutual accusations, and denials, the true picture is difficult to ascertain. It would appear that the Pakistani central authorities did not initiate the tribal invasion. On the other hand it would also appear that the Prime Minister of the North-West Frontier Province, himself a Kashmiri, and his officers did give the tribesmen help. Certainly all Pakistanis viewed with open sympathies the struggle of the Kashmiri Muslims against the Maharaja and were ready to give them all political and moral support. When, however, the Indian army was sent to intervene in what up to that time was considered to be primarily a civil war, an unknown number of Pakistani nationals joined the Azad forces for whom the Pakistan government was undoubtedly responsible. Then, when the Indian forces succeeded not only in stopping the tribesmen at the gates of Srinagar but began to push them back toward the borders of Pakistan, the Pakistan government became thoroughly concerned about the outcome of the struggle and undoubtedly helped with officers and equipment. Pakistan became alarmed that the intervention of

[21] *The New York Times*, January 29, 1948.

the Indian army was not to be limited to Kashmir. She suspected that this was the beginning of an Indian onslaught against Pakistan herself. And it was this fear which perhaps was largely responsible for the extent of Pakistan's participation in the struggle, a fear which Liaquat Ali Khan expressed in a telegram which he addressed to Nehru:

"It is a matter for deep regret that even today responsible members of the Government of India, including yourself, openly declare their intention or hope of bringing Pakistan back into the Indian Union well knowing that this could be done only through conquest of arms. . . . In other words Pakistan's very existence is the chief 'casus belli' so far as India is concerned. . . . India never wholeheartedly accepted the partition scheme but her leaders paid lip service to it merely in order to get the British troops out of the country. . . . India is out to destroy the State of Pakistan. . . . The fraudulent procurement of the accession of Jammu and Kashmir State [is an act] of hostility against Pakistan whose destruction is India's immediate objective."[22]

Jawaharlal Nehru not only emphatically rejected Ali Khan's accusations but also hurled the counter-accusation that Pakistan complicity in the Kashmir fighting was "an act of aggression."

Once again the real issue had broken through. It was the old issue of partition.

[22] *White Paper on Jammu and Kashmir, op.cit.*, pp. 83, 85.

5. The United Nations Intervenes

ON JANUARY 1, 1948, the Security Council of the United Nations was called upon by the government of India to intervene in the Kashmir conflict. Since that date, for almost seven years, it has devoted countless meetings to the issue; it has sent a commission and two representatives to the Subcontinent, all dedicated to the task of seeking a peaceful settlement to the dispute. But the conflict has not been solved. The danger of war between India and Pakistan over Kashmir cannot be excluded and in addition somber Soviet-Communist activities behind the scene point to the possibility that Kashmir might eventually become a hub of Communist activities in Southern Asia.

No full analysis of the deliberations of the Security Council and its commission and representatives will be undertaken in this review; instead only the main stream of their deliberations and actions will be described. A few of the principal documents are presented in the Appendix.[1]

In its letter of January 1, 1948, addressed to the president of the Security Council, the government of India recalled Articles 34 and 35 of the Charter of the United Nations, according to which, it stated, "any Member may bring any situation, whose continuance is likely to endanger the maintenance of international peace and security, to the attention of the Security Council." The letter continued: "Such a situation now exists between India and Pakistan owing to the aid which invaders, consisting of nationals of Pakistan and of tribesmen . . . are drawing from Pakistan for operations against Jammu and Kashmir, a State which has acceded to the Dominion of India and is part of India. The Government of India request the Security Council to call

---

[1] For convenience, the United Nations documents are referred to in an abbreviated form as used by the UN Secretariat: S refers to the Security Council's documents; S.C.O.R. refers to the Security Council Official Records.

upon Pakistan to put an end immediately to the giving of such assistance which is an act of aggression against India. If Pakistan does not do so, the Government of India may be compelled, in self defence, to enter Pakistan territory, in order to take military action against the invaders. The matter is therefore one of extreme urgency and calls for immediate action. . . ."[2]

The Indian complaint described the situation in Kashmir, how the fighting had started, how India had accepted the accession of the state and sent in troops. It considered India's steps fully justified and labeled Pakistan an aggressor. It reiterated the pledge, "that once the soil of the State had been cleared of the invader and normal conditions restored, its people would be free to decide their future by the democratic method of a plebiscite or referendum which, in order to ensure complete impartiality, might be held under international auspices." It requested the Security Council: "(1) To prevent Pakistan Government personnel, military and civil, from participating or assisting in the invasion of the Jammu and Kashmir State; (2) To call upon other Pakistani nationals to desist from taking any part in the fighting in the Jammu and Kashmir State; (3) To deny to the invaders: (a) access to and use of its territory for operations against Kashmir, (b) military and other supplies, (c) all other kinds of aid that might tend to prolong the present struggle."

The President of the Security Council, Mr. F. Van Langenhove, the Belgian delegate, appealed immediately, in a telegram, to both governments "to refrain from any step incompatible with the Charter and liable to result in an aggravation of the situation. . . ."[3] He received assurances in that sense from both parties in dispute.[4] But the fighting in Kashmir went on.

[2] S/628 of January 2, 1948.
[3] S/636 of January 4, 1948.
[4] S/639 and S/640 of January 9, 1948.

The Security Council met on January 15. The representative of India was Mr. N. Copalaswami Ayyangar, one of the leading statesmen of India and former Prime Minister of the State of Jammu and Kashmir under the Maharaja rule. He was assisted by Mr. M. C. Setalvad and Sheikh Abdullah, who, it will be remembered, had been asked by the Maharaja at the moment of accession to form an interim government. Mr. Ayyangar stressed at the beginning of his address "the threat to international peace and security with which it [the situation in Kashmir] is pregnant if it is not solved immediately."[5] He reminded the members of the Security Council of the statement made by the Governor-General, Lord Mountbatten, upon the accession of Kashmir to India, pledging that "the question of the State's accession should be settled by a reference to the people," and described this statement and policy as "high-principled statesmanship." He insisted upon the issue being not one of "a dispute about territory" (the implication being that Kashmir belonged undisputably to India), but one of requiring Pakistan to refrain from giving aid to the invading tribesmen and to forbid her nationals to take part in the fighting in Kashmir. As to the future status of Kashmir, Mr. Ayyangar reiterated, ". . . whether she should withdraw from her accession to India, and either accede to Pakistan or remain independent, with a right to claim admission as a Member of the United Nations—all this we have recognized to be a matter for unfettered decision by the people of Kashmir after normal life is restored to them."[6]

The Pakistan representative requested that deliberations be postponed to allow him time to prepare the answer, but the Indian representative declared emphatically, ". . . the situation does not brook delay."[7]

This declaration, read as it is today after a period of almost seven years of little but delays, postponements, and

5 S.C.O.R. Third Year, Nos. 1-15, p. 10.
6 *Ibid.*, p. 29.   7 *Ibid.*, p. 31.

debate, is not so impressive as it must have been in January of 1948.

The Pakistan government first replied in writing to the Indian complaint and presented its own counter-complaint.[8] It was a lengthy paper consisting of three documents. In Document I, replying to India's complaint, Pakistan denied giving aid to tribesmen and thereby committing an act of aggression. On the contrary, the Pakistan government "continued to do all in their power to discourage the tribal movement by all means short of war." It admitted though that "a certain number of independent tribesmen and persons from Pakistan are helping the Azad Kashmir Government in their struggle for liberty as volunteers. . . ."

In Document II, the Pakistan government raised numerous counter-complaints of its own:

1. It charged India with widespread genocide against the Muslim population, pursued by responsible officials of the Princely States and the Union of India in the period preceding and following partition.

2. It accused India of having forced by way of arms and occupation Junagadh, a predominantly Hindu state with a Muslim ruler, into accession to India, though the ruler had acceded to Pakistan. "This action on the part of the Government of India amounted to a direct attack upon and aggression against Pakistan which Pakistan was entitled to repel by force," maintained the Pakistan document in an obvious attempt to make the Indian accusation boomerang.

3. It gave the genesis of the Kashmir case and denied the validity of Kashmir's accession to India. It protested against Indian forces being sent to Kashmir "without consultation with, or even any notice to, the Government of Pakistan with which the State had concluded a standstill agreement." As to the Indian promise about a plebiscite in Kashmir, Pakistan expressed through this document the strong conviction that a plebiscite would be but a farce if it were con-

[8] S/646 and Corr. 1 of January 15, 1948.

ducted in the presence of the Indian armed forces and if proper conditions were not established to guarantee to the people of Kashmir complete freedom to express their will.

(4) It protested that India had failed to fulfill various agreements reached in connection with the partition, such as division of military stores, cash balances, and other matters.

After summing up its complaints, the government of Pakistan in this section of its reply requested the Security Council: (1) to call upon the government of India to desist from acts of aggression against Pakistan and implement all agreements she had signed with Pakistan; (2) to appoint a commission charged with the task of investigating all the accusations against India, arranging cessation of hostilities in Kashmir, enforcing the withdrawal of all outsiders whether they came from India or Pakistan, facilitating the return and rehabilitation of Kashmiri refugees, establishing an impartial administration in Kashmir, and, finally, conducting an impartial plebiscite.

In Document III, the Pakistan government gave detailed information on the preceding matters, stressing that "even the Kashmir episode in all aspects is but one link in the chain of events which has been unfolding itself ever since it became obvious that there was no solution of the Hindu-Muslim problem except the partition of India," with which, the Pakistanis suspected, India had never been reconciled and, as a consequence, harbored hostile intentions towards Pakistan. As to Kashmir, the document concluded, "The Pakistan Government have not accepted and cannot accept the accession of Jammu and Kashmir State to India. In their view the accession is based on violence and fraud."

As both parties presented the issue to the Security Council, the sharply different views of the two nations not only on the cause and nature of the conflict but also on the ways of solving it became immediately apparent. To India, the cause of the conflict was the tribal invasion and Pakistan's participation in it. She therefore limited her presentation and defense of the case before the Security Council to these two acts. To Pakistan, however, the hostilities in Kashmir were only a part of the whole picture of unhappy Indo-Pakistani relations, and her presentation was therefore an exhaustive account of all problems dividing the two countries.

After the Indian delegate had placed his government's complaint before the Security Council, the Pakistan delegate, the Minister of Foreign Affairs, Sir Zafrulla Khan, presented the Pakistan picture. In a speech which for length made a record in the annals of the United Nations (it lasted five hours) Sir Zafrulla went into the details of the "story of Kashmir." He linked it with the generally unsettled situation on the Subcontinent, with the communal strife, with the political struggle of Kashmiris for freedom. He agreed with the Indian delegate in one thing only: "that the situation is grave and urgent and needs to be dealt with on the basis of immediacy."[9]

The Pakistan attitude was summed up by Sir Zafrulla Khan when he concluded, "What is to be done? . . . All that we want to ensure is this: Everyone who has gone into Kashmir should go out: Sikh bands, Rashtriya Sewak Sangh volunteers, other people who have gone in, tribesmen, and any other people who may have gone in from the Muslim side, and men from Pakistan, Muslims who are Indian nationals and who were refugees in Pakistan—everybody. They must get out, including Indian troops. . . .

"Therefore, by whatever means may be necessary, the condition to be brought about is this: whether by joint administration under the two Governors-General, by joint occupation of predominantly Muslim areas by Muslim troops from Pakistan and predominantly non-Muslim areas in Kashmir by Indian troops, by joint occupation in each place, by inviting Commonwealth forces, non-Indian forces altogether; or whether through the United Nations—Kash-

[9] S.C.O.R. Third Year, Nos. 1-15, p. 36.

mir must be cleared. Fighting must stop. Kashmir must be cleared of everybody. Normal administration must be restored. There should be no kind of pressure, either from the Muslim Conference being in power and holding the administration or the National Conference being in power and holding the reins of administration. No kind of pressure should be brought upon the people. The people should then be invited to express the way in which they want to go, and whatever they decide, they should be welcome to do it. . . ."[10]

The Security Council passed a resolution recognizing the urgency of the case and called upon both governments to do everything in their power to improve the situation and to do nothing that might aggravate it. It agreed to bring the representatives of India and Pakistan together to try, with the help of the President of the Security Council, "to find, as from now, some common ground on which the structure of a settlement may be built."[11]

A Difficult Start

Thus the negotiations entered that type of informal conversations which were meant, in the spirit of Chapter VI of the United Nations Charter, to seek settlement by direct attempts of the parties in dispute, before the Security Council would have to intervene and make decisions.

Indeed, as a result of these conversations, at least one agreement was reached and on January 20, 1948, the President was able to present "also on behalf of both parties" a proposal which was embodied in a Security Council resolution establishing a three-member commission with the task to "proceed to the spot as quickly as possible" in order to investigate the facts relevant to the complaints of the two governments and exercise "mediatory influence likely to smooth away difficulties."[12]

It was a highly modest resolution. It made no mention of

10 *Ibid.*, pp. 119-120. 11 *Ibid.*, p. 125.
12 S/654 of January 20, 1948.

the withdrawal of either the tribesmen or the Indian army, or of the plebiscite which supposedly would be dealt with at a later stage. But both parties agreed to the resolution, and it was adopted by nine votes, with the Soviet Union and the Ukraine abstaining.

It is tragic, in retrospect, that such a commission as was agreed to was not constituted and dispatched to the Subcontinent without delay. Even if it had not been able to stop the fighting, in all probability the commission could have prevented, through its mere presence in Kashmir, the spring offensive and the continuance of large-scale operations. But this was not done—and the United Nations documents do not offer explanation for the omission—and inevitably the bitter wrangling broke out again in an intensified form. The representatives of both countries returned to mutually bitter accusations as to what had happened between the Hindus and Muslims before, during, and after the partition, what had been taking place in Kashmir before and after her accession to India, and as to the actual fighting and the horrors of persecution which were going on in the state. Both representatives tried to prove their points by extensive quotations from the world press. The conciliatory and sober spirit of the resolution of January 20 was buried under piles of speeches and an avalanche of poisoned invective. In this debate and in the informal consultations which followed, the great gap between the two delegations as to the proper means of reaching a solution became clearer and clearer. Finally, India presented to the Security Council a proposal which indicated some concessions concerning at least the eventual plebiscite.

The Indian delegation proposed that: (1) the fighting in Kashmir must stop and the tribesmen and Pakistan nationals must withdraw; (2) after restoration of peace, refugees were to return, law and order must be maintained, and the security of the state assured. It declared that India was responsible for the defense of the state but would progressively reduce its forces to a strength compatible with the external security of, and internal order in, Kashmir; (3) Sheikh Abdullah would be Prime Minister; and (4) the United Nations Commission should proceed to India at once to mediate and supervise the cessation of fighting and the termination of military operations.

As to the plebiscite, the Indian delegation proposed: (1) to have a National Assembly elected (apparently under Sheikh Abdullah's administration); (2) to constitute, then, a National Government; (3) this government to arrange for the plebiscite to be taken under the advice and observation of the United Nations; (4) to have, then, the National Assembly frame a new constitution.[13]

The Pakistan request was in many ways diametrically opposed to the Indian proposal. It wished to vest in the Commission of the United Nations the authority to arrange for: (1) the establishment of an impartial interim administration in the state; (2) the withdrawal of all troops from Kashmir; (3) the return of refugees; (4) the holding of a free, fair, and unfettered plebiscite.[14]

It is important to keep in mind these major points of difference in order to judge the subsequent developments. It is equally important to keep in mind, however, that both parties from the beginning were agreed on one thing—the principle that Kashmir's future would finally be settled by a plebiscite. The principal cleavage was this: India wished the fighting to stop first and before anything else; Pakistan insisted upon first reaching an agreement on the plebiscite, asserting that the people would stop fighting only if they had guarantees that a fair plebiscite was forthcoming.

Thus, the first stage of the Security Council deliberations revealed Pakistan's fears that once the fighting had stopped and the military situation had become stabilized, a *de facto* political stabilization would evolve which would mean at

[13] S.C.O.R., Third Year, Nos. 1-15, pp. 266-267.
[14] *Ibid.*, pp. 267-268.

best a partition of the country with India in possession of the more important sections, particularly the Vale of Kashmir.

A long debate before the Security Council ensued. Nine members of the Security Council eventually endorsed the Pakistan position, the Soviet Union and the Ukraine abstaining from both the debate and voting. All others agreed that the problem had to be considered as a whole, that the cessation of hostilities could not be treated apart from the prospect of the final settlement of the dispute.

The Indian delegate made a strong plea. "We seem here to be fiddling while Kashmir burns," declared Mr. Ayyangar. He reminded the delegates of their condemnation of Yugoslavia, Albania, and Bulgaria for giving assistance to the rebels fighting the government forces in Greece. Now, argued Mr. Ayyangar, the tribesmen, who are Pakistani citizens, were similarly taking part with Pakistan assistance in fighting against the lawful government of Kashmir. He saw the situation as similar to that in Greece and was convinced that it was the duty of the Security Council to stop fighting first and to compel Pakistan to make the tribesmen withdraw.

The Indian delegate maintained that if peaceful measures could not prevent the tribesmen from infiltration into Kashmir, it was "the obligation of the Government of Pakistan to resort to measures of war against these tribesmen."[15] This, of course, was exactly what the Pakistan Governor-General, Jinnah, had proposed to Lord Mountbatten when they had met in Lahore in November 1947 in the early days of the conflict, providing there was a concurrent withdrawal of Indian troops. But the Indian government had refused this offer at that time.

A temporary armistice in the struggle in the Security Council took place when, on January 30, 1948, it met under the grave impact of the tragedy which had occurred in

[15] *Ibid.*, p. 301.

Delhi two days before. Mahatma Gandhi, the great apostle of Hindu-Muslim amity and unity, was assassinated by a Hindu fanatic. All present at the Security Council table, including Sir Zafrulla Khan, paid moving tributes to his greatness. The meeting was then adjourned.

But the struggle was renewed with vigor at the following session. The Indian delegate, feeling that the trend of thinking of the Security Council was developing against his concept of a solution, stressed the internal nature of the problem of administering Kashmir. He advanced an argument that neither India nor Pakistan nor the Security Council had any jurisdiction about the form and composition of the Kashmir government, and he suggested that the Security Council had no right even to conduct the plebiscite, only "that the plebiscite should be conducted under the advice and observation" of the United Nations, but "the actual plebiscite, the actual taking of it . . . is a matter for the Government and people of the State of Jammu and Kashmir."[16]

When it was the Pakistan delegate's turn to speak, he stuck consistently to Pakistan's original demand for a "foolproof" plebiscite under an impartial administration and with no troops on the territory of the state.

Again, the members of the Security Council supported the Pakistan point of view. They attached great importance to having the plebiscite conducted by the United Nations and under an impartial government. They rejected the Indian contention that the administration and actual conduct of a plebiscite was an internal affair for Kashmir. The American delegate particularly, Mr. Warren Austin, subjected the Indian argument to a critical, juridical analysis. He pointed to the Kashmir sovereignty being now exercised by India as a result of accession, India having pledged herself to a plebiscite under United Nations auspices.

The question as to whether or not a plebiscite on such an

[16] *Ibid.*, pp. 329-330.

issue and its conduct are actually an internal or international affair was more than once declared by various international bodies or conferences to be of an international nature. The plebiscites over Schleswig, Marienwerder and Allenstein, Upper Silesia, Klagenfurt, and Sopron were supervised by inter-Allied plebiscite commissions in 1920 and 1921. The plebiscite over the Saar territory, in 1935, was organized and supervised by the League of Nations Plebiscite Commission. The Conference at Yalta in February 1945 made provisions for the composition of the Polish and Yugoslav governments and for the conduct of free elections in the two countries. It agreed also upon "The Declaration on Liberated Europe," which embraced all European countries, to assist them in establishing democratic governments through the process of free elections. The elections in South Korea in May 1948 were held under the observation of the United Nations Temporary Commission. The elections in Greece in March 1946 and the plebiscite in September 1946 took place in the presence of observers representing the United States, Great Britain, and France. In the case of Germany, the Western powers proposed several times that a United Nations commission or other impartial body investigate whether conditions existed there which would warrant free elections. All these instances point to a legitimate international interest and intervention in such a technically "internal affair" as a plebiscite or election or even the composition of a government.

The debate before the Security Council continued for weeks, however, and proposal after proposal was advanced. The Canadian, Belgian, and Colombian delegations presented draft resolutions or memoranda. They accepted, more or less, the Pakistani point of view. Only the Chinese representative gave support to the Indian position. He pointed to the difficulty of changing Kashmir's administration and proposed a progressive withdrawal of the Indian army from Kashmir. He further advised the Security Coun-

cil to concentrate its work on the machinery of the plebiscite.

Still the debate went on. On one occasion, on February 5,
Sheikh Abdullah spoke. His speech was blunt, direct, and
devoid of diplomatic language. In that respect it differed
conspicuously from the polished, subtle, and cultured presentation of the Indian and Pakistan chief delegates. Sheikh
Abdullah contested with particular bitterness the proposals
to change the Kashmir administration in the interests of
the impartiality of the plebiscite. "There is no power on
earth which can displace me from the position which I
have there. As long as the people are behind me I will remain there," he declared, not bothering to offer any explanation as to how he had discovered that the Kashmiris were
behind him. "The dispute arises when it is suggested that,
in order to have the free vote, the administration must be
changed," he continued. "To that suggestion we say 'No.' "[17]

A few days later, on February 8, the Indian delegation
asked the Security Council for adjournment, as it had been
ordered by its government to return immediately to Delhi
for consultation. The explanation for this unexpected move
was to be found in the Indian press, which was increasingly
critical of the Security Council's policy. The Indian government felt that its representatives had not done too well in
putting the case before the United Nations and that the
Pakistani Foreign Minister, "an experienced and popular
practitioner in United Nations dialectic, who was as suave
and smooth as the Indian delegates were awkward and an-
gular," had scored considerable success. Feelings in India
were aroused, and, according to governmental sources, the
belief was also spreading "that India has most to hope,
whether in terms of mediation or even of the veto, from
Soviet Russia and her satellites."[18]

Most delegates expressed concern at the request for ad-

[17] S.C.O.R. Third Year, Nos. 16-35, pp. 23, 25.
[18] Campbell-Johnson, *op.cit.*, p. 287.

journment, reminding the Indian delegate that they had been told that the gravity of the situation in Kashmir did not allow any delay in decision. The Chinese delegate, however, again supported the Indian position and moved a resolution for adjournment.

Meanwhile the Security Council discussed the complaint of Pakistan concerning the State of Junagadh. It should be stated, without describing in any way the nature of this conflict, that both sides used it to strengthen their position on Kashmir. The Pakistan representative pointed to the inconsistent attitude of India, which refused to respect the validity of the Junagadh ruler's accession to Pakistan, and yet insisted upon the legality of the Kashmir Maharaja's accession to India. India protested, by the same token, against Pakistan's contradictory approach of defending the steps taken by the ruler of Junagadh as legally correct, but rejecting the validity of the steps taken by the Kashmir ruler.[19]

On March 8, after the Indian delegation had returned from Delhi to Lake Success, the discussion on Kashmir was resumed. Mr. Ayyangar's speech indicated that the consultations in Delhi confirmed his previous attitude. At this juncture the President, who was the Chinese delegate, Mr. T. F. Tsiang, volunteered to follow the example of his predecessors and as chairman have informal conversations with the contending parties. He then submitted a draft resolution to the Security Council,[20] the main feature of which was to leave in the hands of the Indian government the reconstruction of the Jammu and Kashmir administration and to assign the United Nations Commission a modest and vaguely defined task of mediation.

In the light of recent developments, particularly the insistent Indian policy in the United Nations since 1950

[19] For the discussion of the Junagadh case see S.C.O.R. Third Year, Nos. 16-35, pp. 189-209, 322-343; Nos. 36-51, pp. 44-65.
[20] S/699 of March 18, 1948.

aimed at unseating the Chinese Nationalist delegation from the Security Council, the friendly attitude of Mr. Tsiang towards India in the case of Kashmir makes rather pathetic reading.

But if the Indian delegation was willing to accept the Chinese proposal in regard to Kashmir, the Pakistani delegate opposed it and found support for his opposition among other members of the Security Council. Sir Zafrulla Khan did not find it difficult to prove the partiality of Sheikh Abdullah's administration and of any plebiscite conducted under such circumstances. He needed only to quote the latter's statement made only a few days before: "We shall prefer death rather than join Pakistan. We shall have nothing to do with such a country."[21]

Another precious month elapsed before the Security Council met again to continue its efforts to bring the Kashmir issue closer to a peaceful settlement. Six delegations, including those of the United States and Great Britain, presented a draft resolution which was a combination of various proposals made before. Individual sponsors of the draft characterized it as "our most considered views on the best approach we could propose to this problem," "the best advice which completely objective and fairminded thought could bring to the difficult problem," "fair, just and necessary," "the considered judgement of six delegations," "the only possible proposal," and "the best that our judgement affords."

The Indian delegate subjected the draft resolution to severe criticism. He objected that he found in it no condemnation of Pakistan's aggressive policy. He protested against the idea of establishing a coalition government in Kashmir which would include "enemies of State or [those] in sympathy with the raiders." Who these enemies of the state were had been explained rather fully by Sheikh Abdullah, who had declared that his cabinet "would be chosen

[21] S.C.O.R. Third Year, Nos. 36-51, p. 122.

according to only one criterion, their loyalty to the National Conference and their country."[22]

The Indian delegate also revealed that "When the whole of the State thus comes under one administration . . . India's garrisons will need to be planted at her outer frontiers on the West of the Jammu and Kashmir State."[23] This, of course, would actually mean stationing Indian armed forces over the territory which was now under the actual control of the Azad government.

The UN Resolution

Despite Mr. Ayyangar's objections, however, on April 21, 1948, six months after the fighting in Kashmir had started and almost four months after the Security Council had undertaken to settle the dispute, the resolution was carried by nine votes against none, with the Soviet and Ukranian delegations again abstaining.[24]

The Indian press was highly critical of the Security Council resolution for not having condemned Pakistan as aggressor, insisting that reports were still coming in of her complicity in building the military strength of the Azad revolutionaries. Pandit Nehru described the resolution as "unreasonable," and declared, "We can neither execute nor accept many points."[25] The government of India sent a letter of protest to the United Nations and refused cooperation in any implementation of the resolution.

One month later, however, the Indian representative was somehow more conciliatory, "If . . . the Commission is still sent out to India . . . the Government of India have already stated that they would be glad to confer with it."[26]

The Pakistani delegate was not wholly satisfied with the

[22] *The Hindustan Times* (Delhi), March 7, 1948.
[23] S.C.O.R. Third Year, No. 60, p. 14.
[24] For the text of the resolution, see Appendix I.
[25] *New York Herald Tribune*, April 25, 1948.
[26] S.C.O.R. Third Year, No. 74, pp. 6-7.

proposal, but his criticism did not imply outright rejection.

Nevertheless, the governmental circles in Karachi made no secret of their feeling that the original trend of the debate before the Security Council, which had been favorable to Pakistan, was importantly modified by the United States and Britain out of a strong desire to mollify India. Great Britain was subjected to particular criticism for endeavoring to "strike a balance" between two members of the Commonwealth. Some Pakistani papers indicated that the government ought to seek help from the Soviet Union, and the opening of diplomatic relations with Moscow was regarded as a happy omen for such policy.

The resolution of April 21 was of cardinal importance. It outlined the Security Council's stand on the Kashmir conflict, recommended the method of its solution, and became the principal term of reference for various United Nations representatives who ever since have been trying to bring about a peaceful and final settlement of the problem.

The resolution did a number of things. It increased the membership of the Commission to five and instructed it to proceed to the Indian Subcontinent at once to place its good offices and mediation at the disposal of the governments of India and Pakistan. It recommended to the government of Pakistan that it secure the withdrawal of tribesmen and Pakistani nationals from Kashmir; and to the government of India, a subsequent and progressive withdrawal of the Indian forces to the minimum strength required for maintenance of law and order. It suggested formation of a coalition cabinet of the State of Jammu and Kashmir which would be representative of all major political groups. To insure freedom and impartiality in an eventual plebiscite, the resolution envisaged that a plebiscite administrator be nominated with powers adequate to prepare and conduct the plebiscite and that measures be taken for the return of refugees, for the release of political prisoners, and for political freedom. The Commission was to be allowed to establish observers and it was finally to report to the Security Council as to whether the plebiscite was free and impartial.

The main purpose of the resolution was to stop fighting and to establish conditions in the state which would allow the population to express freely, without threat of physical or psychological coercion, their desire to accede to either India or Pakistan. Acting under Chapter VI of the United Nations Charter, the Security Council did not direct the parties in dispute what to do but only passed a recommendation. This bound the parties only morally—not juridically. The Commission's role, therefore, was one of mediation without any right to impose its will. It was thus limited in its activities, allowed to make contact with the Indian and Pakistan authorities and make recommendations carrying the weight only of the persuasiveness of its arguments and its political prestige. The final issue remained with the government of India and Pakistan and depended on their good will.

Furthermore, the Security Council avoided taking sides in the dispute. It did not, as India requested, condemn Pakistan as aggressor, nor on the other hand did it touch upon the legal aspect of Kashmir's accession to India.

As a matter of fact, the Security Council avoided any consideration of the juridical aspect of the accession, a perfectly plausible procedure under Article 96 of the Charter, according to which the Security Council "may request the International Court of Justice to give an advisory opinion on any legal question." It would seem to be obvious that the handling of the dispute would have been easier had the International Court been asked to declare itself on the subject. One of the parties would then have been in the wrong, and the Security Council would in turn have had a stronger moral and political position for the recommendation of appropriate measures. The fact that neither India nor Pakistan asked for such a juridical finding would also indicate their mutual uncertainty about the validity of the accession. If the question was studied informally by the members of the Security Council, their policy not to ask the court for such a decision could be interpreted only as a failure on the part of some members to understand the complexity and seriousness of the Kashmir problem. They probably felt that a fair, impartial, and rather mild resolution recommending to India and Pakistan certain measures and carrying the political and moral prestige of the United Nations would be sufficient to bring about a quick and peaceful solution of the dispute.

There is, perhaps, one other explanation. The Security Council is a political body. It may have felt that diplomacy and mediation might provide adequate means for settling the conflict, whereas a juridical verdict would have put one of the parties in dispute in the light of being wrong, with the quite possible result that that party would turn politically against the United Nations or the sponsors of such a procedure. There was, of course, no guarantee that the parties would accept and respect the pronouncement of the International Court, but at least the rest of the world would clearly know which stand to take in the dispute.

Another question also poses itself in regard to the Security Council's actions. Why did it not act according to Chapter VII of the Charter, which deals with threats of war? Both India and Pakistan had repeatedly pointed out before the Security Council the gravity of the situation, accusing each other of acts of aggression. They urged the Council for an immediate solution and stressed its urgency. They even claimed the right of resorting to war if their interests in Kashmir (and Junagadh) were not honored. The Indian delegate emphasized the imminence of war between the two Dominions, and indeed, fighting in Kashmir was going on while the Security Council was deliberating upon the issue.

Whereas provisions of Chapter VI of the Charter limit

the Security Council to acts of negotiation, mediation, conciliation, and arbitration, Chapter VII entrusts the Security Council with the right to enforce its decisions and imposes on all members of the United Nations the obligation to abide by these decisions.

Once again it would seem that the Security Council avoided consideration of the Kashmir problem under the provisions of Chapter VII because the parties themselves invoked Chapter VI in their requests and the Security Council itself failed to recognize the full gravity of the situation. It is true that in the history of the United Nations, the Security Council has always been reluctant to apply the provisions of Chapter VII because it has wished to avoid an unnecessary sharpening of the issues. Furthermore, there is always the greater risk of a Soviet veto under Chapter VII. But one may speculate that the Soviet representative on the Security Council would not have vetoed a resolution under Chapter VII on Kashmir because Russia did not wish to estrange either India or Pakistan. The fact that she abstained in all debate and voting on the Kashmir dispute at least indicates the possibility that she might not have exercised her veto power in this case. On the other hand it could be argued that her failure to participate in the discussions and the voting on the Kashmir problem stemmed from a desire to see the dispute continue. Certainly such a rift between two such great nations could only be in her interests. It could, then, further be argued that her failure to use her veto power on the resolution of April 21, 1948, was due precisely to its obvious lack of resoluteness and to the fact that she could foresee with hope that the fighting in Kashmir would continue. Had the conflict been approached by the Security Council according to Chapter VII with the probability of more resolute action offering better hope for an early settlement, Russia might have vetoed such a resolution.

Another reason for the Council's overcautious treatment

of the Kashmir conflict might have been its preoccupation with other explosive situations—in Palestine, Indonesia, and Czechoslovakia.

Nevertheless, one must be somewhat critical of the Security Council's procedure. It is true that it handled the Kashmir problem impartially, that its recommendations were just and fair to both parties, that it approached it with the skill of experienced diplomacy. But it did not handle the situation adequately. Its approach was timid. Its evaluation of the situation in Kashmir was far from realistic, as was shown only a few weeks later. The prolongation of the debate, the endless wrangling of the parties, the adjournment of the deliberations, the one-month intervals in the debates were unnecessary. With every day that passed, the tensions and the political cleavages in Kashmir grew, and as they grew the plebiscite which was finally to decide the fate of the country became increasingly difficult.

It is also impossible to understand the delay in sending the Security Council Commission to the Subcontinent. The Commission was established by the original resolution, passed on January 20, and accepted by India and Pakistan. True, its described powers were vague, but its mere presence in the area might have reduced the intensity of the fighting, already slowed to local skirmishes by the high snows of the Kashmir mountains. But with the melting of the snow in May and before the long-delayed Commission had arrived, fighting had been resumed with full fury.

When at last the Commission was dispatched to India and Pakistan, it found the situation politically and militarily quite different from what the Security Council had thought it to be when it had passed its mild and necessarily noncommittal resolution in April.

6. The UN Commission at Work

ELEVEN weeks dragged by after the Security Council resolution of April 21, before the Commission got to work. Meanwhile affairs in Kashmir moved toward all-out war. According to a newspaper report based on a most reliable and authoritative source, it was only the British government's threat that it would withdraw all British officers in their service should Pakistan engage her air force in Kashmir that restrained that alleged impulse.[1] Nor did the attitude of the contending nationals toward the Commission make its task easier.

India objected to its being entrusted with the investigation of the other complaints which Pakistan had brought before the Security Council, namely the accusations of genocide, the case of Junagadh, and other matters. Robert Trumbull reported, "The Indian press has begun to lay the groundwork for the rejection of any recommendations that the Commission may make unless they favor India. Dispatches from Kashmir make it plain that the pro-India government of Sheikh Abdullah is now unwilling to accept even an impartial plebiscite."[2] The Pakistan press warned that the Commission would be received in Pakistan by a display of black flags.

On June 15, 1948, however, the Commission did convene in Geneva. As finally composed, it consisted of five members: Argentina, nominated by Pakistan; Czechoslovakia, nominated by India; Colombia and Belgium, selected by the Security Council; and the United States, named by the Council's president. It had been my pleasure to be assigned as the Czechoslovak member of this group on February 5, 1948, and the record of the Commission's activities, ob-

[1] *The Hindustan Times* (Delhi), August 7, 1948.
[2] *The New York Times*, June 16, 1948.

servations, and conversations herewith presented are largely a product of that memorable experience.[3]

The Commission's first act was to prepare its rules of procedure, and this was followed by an exchange of letters with the governments of India and Pakistan. The early days of its deliberations did not seem promising.

Most of the members were only vaguely informed about the dispute, and only the American delegation, led by Ambassador J. Klahr Huddle, was properly equipped with an expert political, military, and secretarial staff. Each member, therefore, faced the unhappy prospect of fighting his way through piles of documents and lengthy speeches, separating, where possible, facts from propaganda and finding points directly relevant to the issue from masses of informative background.

Everyone, however, appeared anxious to get down to work. There seemed to be a strong feeling that the long struggle of the ancient people of the Indian Subcontinent for that greatest of all treasures, freedom, should not, at the last, be negated by a senseless war. Each member of the Commission seemed to feel a personal responsibility to restore freedom and peace to Kashmir. The American delegate, a seasoned diplomat, spoke with tears in his eyes when, opening a session, he pledged all his efforts to the noble and honorable task with which he had been entrusted.

The first few days were given over to such formalities as the selection of an official title—itself a precarious task, lest in the name some unintentional offense be given to India or Pakistan. The name finally chosen was the United Nations Commission for India and Pakistan. And concur-

[3] Other members of the Commission were: for Argentina, Ricardo J. Siri and his alternate Carlos A. Leguizamon; for Belgium, Egbert Graeffe and his alternate Harry Graeffe; for Colombia, Alfredo Lozano and his alternate Hernando Samper; for the United States, J. Klahr Huddle and his alternate C. Hawley Oakes. Erik Colban served as personal representative of the United Nations Secretary-General.

rent with such preliminaries were others still less pleasant—
the inoculations against typhus, cholera, smallpox, diph-
theria, plague, and yellow fever. Finally, however, on July
5, the Commission left by chartered plane for Karachi,
the capital of Pakistan. The plane, a DC-3, carried on both
wings huge letters: U.N.[4]

First Contact

The Commission stopped in Karachi for a short formal
visit to pay its respects to Governor-General Mohammed
Ali Jinnah and the Pakistani government. Mr. Jinnah,
however, was seriously ill, secluded at Ziarat, a hill station
in Baluchistan. Although every major decision affecting
the Commission's work was made by him, it was never our
pleasure to meet him. He died three months later.

At first glance, the city of Karachi with its modern
harbor gave the impression of great industry. But as the
paralyzing heat of noon descended, we saw that almost all
movement ceased and a vast calm covered the capital, a
calm of exhaustion and uneasiness. And on every hand
were the refugees, thousands of them—eloquent testimony
to the upheaval which had swept the Subcontinent.

The Pakistani government offered us Jinnah's residence
for our accommodation, and the Commission accepted
the invitation with thanks. For the three days of our visit
we were well taken care of by an array of servants and
served excellent food by the maître d'hôtel, a Russian
refugee, Mr. Beck. Faithful to his Russian patriotism he
called his meals beefsteak à la Tolbouhine, melba à la
Stalingrad!

The visit with Prime Minister Liaquat Ali Khan was

[4] For details about the Commission activities in the period from
June 15 to September 22, 1948, see *Interim Report of the United
Nations Commission for India and Pakistan*; S/1100 of November 9,
1948. S.C.O.R. Third Year, Supplement for November, 1948, pp.
17-144.

limited strictly to an official exchange of greetings; the word "Kashmir" was not mentioned. Then followed a visit with the Minister of Foreign Affairs and Commonwealth Relations, Sir Zafrulla Khan. He received the Commission in a small, modestly furnished house—whether his residence or office or both, we never discovered.

At this meeting Sir Zafrulla gave the Commission a three-hour discourse on his concept of the background of the Kashmir conflict. His tone was calm, his language precise, and, following the best traditions of his English schooling, his narration was broken by good stories.

Then came the first bombshell. Sir Zafrulla Khan informed the Commission that three Pakistani brigades had been on Kashmir territory since May. He explained the measure as an act of self-defense. The Indian army had opened a large-scale offensive in the spring. Local Azad forces and tribesmen had been pushed back close to the Pakistan border. The Indian army was indeed in sight of the canal waters flowing to Punjab. Pakistan could not, Sir Zafrulla asserted, sit passively back, unmindful of the danger that the Indian army might invade her own territory. For these reasons, Pakistan had felt militarily and politically justified in reinforcing the defense-line held by the Azad forces and the tribesmen.

The Commission preferred not to express its opinion openly about this new and most important element in the picture, but to one another the members admitted that the presence of the Pakistani troops in Kashmir made of the situation something far graver and far more disturbing than what it had appeared to be to the members of the Security Council at faraway Lake Success. When asked whether the government of Pakistan had informed the Security Council about the action of its army, the Foreign Minister answered in the negative, offering as explanation that by the time of Pakistan's active intervention in Kashmir the United Nations Commission was nominated and was daily expected on the scene. He had now seized the first opportunity to acquaint the Commission with this development.

That evening, the government arranged a dinner to honor the Commission, but the members soon discovered that the "honor" was in name only. No seating arrangements had been made, and as no one suggested to any of the United Nations delegates that he share a table, they found themselves sitting at the same table, isolated from the more than two hundred guests. Coincidence brought them together with the Prime Minister, but no mention was made of Kashmir. It soon became quite evident that the Pakistan government felt most uncertain about the Commission's policy and intent and preferred to wait and watch. The press, less diplomatic than members of the government, did not disguise its mistrust.

Three days later we flew to Delhi. The first impression was not more promising. The heat struck with merciless brutality. The Commission found accommodations in the Cecil Hotel and established its office in Faridkot House, some ten miles away. Distances in Delhi are enormous, and the Commission went by car twice a day to and from the office, winding slowly past the hundreds of sacred cows calmly lying in the middle of the streets. In Delhi as in Karachi thousands of refugees were lying along the streets, hungry and exhausted, more dead than alive, their only comfort the monsoon rains which often flooded over the city, sending streams of water over their aching bodies.

The Commission was received by the Right Honorable Pandit Jawaharlal Nehru: a thin man, small of figure, with a beautiful face, deep, dark eyes, small, refined hands. He spoke with us about the economic problems of India, about the movement of people away from cities to villages—a movement quite the reverse of that in Europe—making industrialization difficult. He spoke, too, about the eight cultures of Delhi. And as he spoke he seldom raised his head to look into our eyes. Nor did he utter a word about Kashmir.

The Indian papers received the Commission in calmer tones than was the case in Karachi, but they offered it only "a conditional cooperation."

An audience with Governor-General Chakravarti Raja-gopalachari was a solemn, official event following precise rules of diplomatic protocol. Delegates were assembled in a semicircle with some fifty guests behind them. The old gentleman slowly entered the room, quiet, gentle, almost ethereal, his thin figure covered by a white garment like that worn by the Mahatma. He welcomed us with his palms together as in prayer.

Then tea was served, and this time we were seated at various tables with our Indian hosts. It was a pleasant time, and as we sat there we sensed a certain satisfaction in seeing these national leaders play the host in this spacious governor's palace which for so long had been the seat of foreign viceroys. Pandit Nehru came later and exchanged a few words with each delegate. But still not a word about Kashmir.

Indignation in Delhi

The formalities finally came to an end and the real work began. On July 13 Sir Girja Shankar Bajpai, Secretary-General of the Ministry for External Affairs, was invited to present the Kashmir case before the Commission. Sir Girja, a small man with a shy smile, perfect manners, and ivory-cut hands, with the English of Shakespeare and himself the quintessence of ancient Indian culture and Oxford schooling, was a great diplomat of the English school. He had served in the British India government and during the war had represented India in Washington.

He reminded the Commission of the dissatisfaction of the Indian government with the Security Council proceedings where "in the four months' debate that had followed, the issue . . . had got lost in a miasma of dialectics." He then passed on to the crucial point, one which, since our visit in Karachi, was very much in our minds. "Since the Council had passed its resolution," he said, "a great change had occurred in the situation. . . . Our troops were fighting the regular armed forces of Pakistan on all fronts in and around Jammu and Kashmir State. We had abundant evidence of this. . . . What was in progress today was an undeclared war between India and Pakistan." He reproached the Security Council for having ignored the moral aspect of the Kashmir issue and insisted that the Indian government attached "the highest importance to the declaration of Pakistan's guilt and, if this guilt were proved, to Pakistan being directed to do what, seven months ago, we had asked the Council that Pakistan should be asked to do. Until this matter was settled, there could be no question of discussing the details of a plebiscite. . . . If the future of Jammu and Kashmir was to be determined by the arbitrament of the sword, then, without in any way wishing to utter a threat, or use the language of menace, I should like the Commission, as realists, to recognize that the offer of plebiscite could not remain open. If Pakistan wanted a decision by force and that decision went against Pakistan, it could not invoke the machinery of the United Nations to obtain what it had failed to secure by its chosen weapon of force. . . ."[5] Sir Girja Bajpai added to this alarming conclusion, ". . . the sands of time are running short; if the problem is not resolved by reason, the sword will find the solution."

The Commission was now face to face with the already-well-known aspect of the Kashmir problem: India's insistence that Pakistan be branded as aggressor. But now, with the Pakistan army actually taking part in the fighting,

[5] S.C.O.R. Third Year, Supplement for November, 1948, pp. 126-127.

the insistence came with increased resoluteness and indignation.

Individual members of the Commission then held informal conferences with Mr. Nehru, Ayyangar, and Sir Girja Bajpai. Their attitudes were identical: condemn Pakistan of aggression; then—and only then—would they be willing to consider the implementation of the Security Council resolution. The Commission knew that such a policy would immediately close the door to any further negotiations with Pakistan. Moreover, the Commission was bound to follow the Security Council directives embodied in its resolution of April 21, which deliberately proscribed any pronouncement of judgment concerning guilt or the juridical validity of accession.

The Commission had several meetings with high officers of the general staff to hear their description of the military operations and to examine the material the Indian army had captured from the enemy. These men dated Pakistan's active participation in the fighting back to March. In moments of informal conversations these officers did not conceal their distaste for fighting officers who once had been their comrades in the British Indian army, many of whom had received common training at Sandhurst. If it were left to them, they said, they would stop the fighting immediately. But the politicians would not.

The fact that there were some 300 British officers of high rank serving in the Indian army and 700 in the Pakistani army (though none of them in an operational command in Kashmir) was highly embarrassing to the British government. After all, India and Pakistan were members of the Commonwealth. Actually, a withdrawal of British officers was often contemplated, but this was offset by the knowledge that their presence in India and Pakistan might exert at least a calming influence on both belligerents.

Meanwhile, fighting in Kashmir went on unabated, and scores of letters reached the Commission from individuals and organizations reciting stories of atrocities perpetrated by both sides against the civilian population. Increasingly it seemed unreal to debate about procedural matters and details of a plebiscite, hundreds of miles away from the area of fighting. The Commission, therefore, explored unofficially with the government of India the idea of flying to the Kashmir capital, Srinagar. It felt that it might be better able to grasp the complexity of the problem if it were closer to the country in dispute and that its mere presence in Kashmir might diminish the intensity of the struggle. However, though Sheikh Abdullah conveyed to the members of the Commission through private channels his hope of welcoming us very soon in Kashmir, we were told politely that the Kashmir issue would be decided, not in Srinagar but in Delhi and Karachi.

Disturbed by the reports of fighting, the Commission determined to attempt a first step which seemed to be most urgent. It investigated, again informally, the possibility of an unconditional cessation of hostilities. It further felt that a cease-fire would inevitably open an avenue to further negotiations in a more friendly atmosphere. It addressed a resolution to both governments, urging them "to take immediately those measures within their power which can improve the situation and to refrain from making or causing to be made any statements which might aggravate the situation."[6] Both governments answered in reassuring terms; but the fighting and furious newspaper comments continued.

One evening the Commission was honored at a dinner given by Pandit Nehru in the governor-general's palace. Some one hundred people were present: members of the government dressed in white, grey, or black long coats; their wives in richly ornamented saris and wearing precious jewels; diplomats, and officers in decorative uniforms.

The dinner was served according to precise court proto-

[6] *Ibid.*, pp. 127-128.

cal and in a typically English social tradition. The British
emblem with the writing "Dieu et Mon Droit" still adorned
the silver dishes. The Soviet Ambassador K. V. Novikov
looked at his plate with unconcealed curiosity, turning it
around in his hands.

In the background an orchestra discretely played nostalgic Indian airs. On the walls of the long dining room
hung portraits of the former British Viceroys, many of
them great figures in British history. As they looked down
from their elevated position at the strange gathering which
was a mixture of the new life of Indian national sovereignty
and of old imported British customs, one felt that they
followed the development with wise understanding and
approval—that for once a national revolution had not destroyed the old values, had not indeed torn this very gal-
lery to pieces.

Following dinner, we went into the palatial gardens,
with their spacious soft meadows and glittering fountains.
The night was mild and humid, and the icy atmosphere of
official contacts seemed to thaw somewhat in the balmy
air. It seemed a propitious time to put out feelers on Kashmir, and Pandit Nehru indicated to us that he would like
to talk the matter over with each delegate, separately, at
informal lunches or dinners. We eagerly agreed and prepared ourselves for our separate meetings by a thorough
re-examination of the situation.

When I lunched with Mr. Nehru, he talked freely and
fully about the problem. "It does not correspond with our
mentality to wage wars," he said. "We had the British
here for 150 years and fought for our independence by
peaceful means and not by arms. Now that we have
achieved our goal, we find we must fight against people
who for so many years have lived here with us. We have
always been for a united India, but when we saw no other
solution than partition we accepted it. It should be so
natural to have with Pakistan the closest possible coopera-

tion. We want to cooperate and work towards cooperation, and one day integration will inevitably come. If it
will be in four, five, ten years—I do not know.

"The background of the partition is economic," Nehru
continued. "We Indians have always advocated political
freedom and social progress. First, we had to get rid of
British domination and now we must try to achieve economic prosperity and social progress. Some people have
been against this policy. But as nobody can possibly stand
up publicly against the independence of a nation and
against the prosperity of the broad masses, these people
had to find other arguments to preserve their privileged
position. So they used religion.

"In reality, it is not at all a dispute between religions.
We give to all people full religious freedom. Besides, it is
impossible to divide the country according to a religion.
Even now there are still some forty-two million Muslims
in India. It is, then, a struggle between freedom and progress and a group of wealthy men. Jinnah abandoned us
[the National Congress] thirty years ago and founded the
League—not to defend Islam, as he asserts, but to defend
privileged materialistic rights. It has nothing to do with
religion; he himself is not a religious man. But there was
no other solution to this problem in our struggle for independence, so we agreed to the establishment of Pakistan.

"Pakistan, however, is developing today as an Islamic,
feudal state. It is backward, reactionary, economically weak,
administratively disrupted. The army is led by British
officers. If they left there would be no Pakistani army. We
have some few British officers, too, but step by step all
functions are being taken over by our own people.

"This, then, is the background of our differences with
Pakistan, and it applies also to Kashmir. It would never
have occurred to us to send an army to Kashmir had she
not been invaded by tribesmen, supported by Pakistan,
and exposed to the danger of wholesale pillage and murder.

And other parts of our country were in danger too; the tribesmen advanced, shouting that they were on their way to Delhi.

"Now the question is to find a solution. We have been greatly disturbed by the policy of the Security Council which accepted the allegations of the Pakistan delegation, though we proved the complicity of Pakistan in the invasion of Kashmir. You talk about a cease-fire. But Pakistan does not admit having her own army in Kashmir. It means that a cease-fire would apply only to us. We must insist upon the withdrawal of the Pakistani army and then we would be willing to negotiate. It must be publicly declared that her army has withdrawn from Kashmir, with the condemnation of Pakistan thus implied. As things now stand, the presence of her army in Kashmir is not publicly known, and we instead of Pakistan are thought of as the aggressors.

"We do not insist upon the right of our army to advance and occupy the territory which would be evacuated by Pakistan. On the other hand there must not be a vacuum there and we shall be satisfied with the recognition of the authority of the State over all its territories and with the occupation of advanced positions important to us strategically and economically."

Upon my remark that the Prime Minister's original intent would be carried out only if the Indian army also withdrew from Kashmir, Mr. Nehru continued, "We would withdraw as the situation permitted; the campaign costs us money and people. But we must insist on having our army stationed at strategically important posts.

"And Pakistan must be condemned. I do not require any solemn, formal verdict, but a clear declaration about the Pakistani army's presence in Kashmir and its withdrawal."

I tried to suggest that a peaceful solution of the problem depended very much upon the good will of both parties, and I said, "The Commission's possibilities are limited. We do not overestimate our powers. The success of our mission is in your hands; we depend upon your good will. If we find a solution it will be to the benefit of the whole world, of the United Nations, and above all, of India and Pakistan. You have just stressed the distaste with which you have taken up arms and your desire to end the conflict. Could you not use the presence of the Commission to seek, together with us, a solution? Can you indicate what final solution you would have in mind if we succeed in arranging a cease-fire?"

"I have already indicated the solution," Mr. Nehru answered, "and I am going to add: We ourselves asked for a plebiscite. We wish the nation of Kashmir to decide for itself. We did it spontaneously and not because of Pakistan. But now for almost ten months there has been a war going on in Kashmir. The country is devastated, the administration disrupted, the situation different from what it was. The preparation for a plebiscite would of course require the withdrawal of the Pakistani forces and then a prolonged period of adjustment preceding the elections, including such necessities as the return of refugees, their settlement and the like. It means that the plebiscite could not take place before one year after the cessation of hostilities."

I attempted to appeal to his inspiring leadership and suggested that India might be in a position to make a gesture of concession to Pakistan. Pandit Nehru reacted vehemently. In a flash of bitterness he leaped onto a chair, shouting, "You seem not to understand our position and our rights. We are a secular state which is not based on religion. We give to everyone freedom of conscience. Pakistan is a mediaeval state with an impossible theocratic concept. It should never have been created, and it would never have happened had the British not stood behind this foolish idea of Jinnah."

My meeting with Nehru was not a profound success. Other delegates had a similar experience as they talked privately with him. He felt strongly about the righteousness of India's case, was indignant about Pakistan, insisted she should be condemned by the United Nations, was ready to stop the fighting if Pakistan units withdrew but in addition wished the Indian forces to advance to the strategic places now under Pakistan control. For the first time he revealed skepticism about a plebiscite and expressed the thought that he would not be opposed to the idea of dividing the country between India and Pakistan. To one delegate he displayed a map on which the Indian border stretched far west towards Pakistan, including the crucial Valley of Kashmir and even part of West Jammu.

Meanwhile, two delegates were in consultation with the Pakistan Foreign Minister, Sir Zafrulla Khan, exploring the possibilities of an unconditional cease-fire.[7] Sir Zafrulla was not impressed by the Indian indignation. Indeed, he felt that a better case could be made for Pakistan's assistance to Azad Kashmir forces, which at least were the product of a Muslim population, than could India for the armies which she sent to Kashmir at the request of the hated Maharaja. He refused the suggestion of an unconditional cease-fire and was ready to consider it only if the Indian troops also withdrew, if the Muslim population was given adequate protection, and if the views of the "Azad Kashmir Government" were taken into consideration. "Under no circumstances would his government consider the partition of Kashmir," declared Sir Zafrulla, as this would "considerably extend the Kashmir-India frontier and would constitute a constant threat to Pakistan."[8] As he had once placed his confidence in the Security Council when it handled the dispute at Lake Success, so also he

[7] For details see S.C.O.R., Third Year, Supplement for November, 1948, pp. 87-94.
[8] *Ibid.*, p. 93.

expected the Commission to assume more authority and to take a strong action by phrasing its decisions in terms of directions rather than recommendations.

Certain valuable lessons were learned by the Commission from its first, though unsuccessful, attempt at a "meeting of minds." It now could know for certain that the two governments would agree on one matter only, namely, that neither wished to stop the fighting without certain conditions which were respectively inacceptable to the other. What was even more important, it now knew that in the background of the dispute lay deep mutual suspicions as to the motives of each party's policy. In Delhi this suspicion was evidenced by a pronounced and unconcealed contempt towards Pakistan, the very existence of which Nehru found it difficult to accept. In Karachi it grew from a deep-seated mistrust of any move coming from India. On both sides there was an absence of that which is the paramount prerequisite for negotiation among any group of countries: a semblance of good will.

It soon became apparent that if the Commission wished to achieve any results, it must exercise its utmost skill in diplomacy. It must demonstrate to the governments of India and Pakistan its complete integrity and impartiality, and it must present to them only such proposals as were balanced to the point of perfection in all political and military aspects, every word of which could be defended by unshakable arguments.

Any student of the case will find from the United Nations documents that the Commission held a number of meetings and a number of official and informal conversations with both governments. He would not be able to detect in their official language, however, the spirit of the Commission's work. Step by step an atmosphere of complete mutual confidence developed among its members. Unhampered by the burden of power politics, refusing to apply in the Kashmir dispute the East-West rift which had so often poisoned the work of the United Nations in other cases, it proceeded as one body. The delegates lived mostly in the same hotels, and if the official proceedings indicated meetings of three or four hours' length, the fact is that the Kashmir dispute was on the agenda from morning till late at night: at breakfast, lunch, and dinner. The delegates became emotionally attached to the cause of Kashmir as if it were their own cause. I had attended many international conferences, but I had never witnessed anything like this.

Perhaps the press in Karachi and Delhi sensed the Commission's devotion; at any rate it soon became more friendly toward its endeavors. Also, individual members of both governments uttered here and there commendable comments upon its cautious and impartial attitude. But despite this, little or nothing was achieved in terms of any *rapprochement* of the diametrically opposed views of both parties. Instead, the fighting went on, and the misery of innocent people increased. In fact, the situation deteriorated materially from what it had been in the spring when the Security Council had passed its resolution. It might have been possible ten months before to bring the leaders of the Muslim Conference and the National Conference together, when the struggle had just begun and the leaders on both sides still remembered the days of their common fight for liberation from the oppressive rule of the Maharaja. But now their hatred was an abyss between them, and their political aims were irreparably divergent; now the National Conference linked its fate with India, the Muslim Conference with Pakistan. Sheikh Abdullah secretly indicated his willingness to meet the leader of the Azad Kashmir, but the Commission was unable to move in this direction, knowing that it would be accused by the government of India of intrigue.

Under such circumstances it seemed out of the question to contemplate the original directive from the Security

Council: the creation of a coalition administration in Kashmir. A new approach would have to be found if the Commission was to accomplish its final aim of establishing conditions in Kashmir which would guarantee freedom of plebiscite. But in the meantime if it was at all possible and if any hope of eventual solution was to be retained, it seemed imperative to try for a cease-fire arrangement.

In spite of the Pakistan refusal to stop fighting without certain preceding conditions, the delegates now had a feeling that Pakistan might be persuaded to accept their proposal. Indeed, in a letter sent later to the Commission, the Pakistan Foreign Minister expressed regret that the Commission had not actually made a proposal.[9]

Certainly, now that the Indian army was on the offensive, advancing closer and closer to her border, Pakistan might find it very much in her interest to stop fighting, particularly if by the establishment of a cease-fire line this advance could be terminated. We also knew that when the case was before the Security Council, India had insisted upon cessation of hostilities as a first step. Now that Pakistani troops had entered the conflict, she had acquired, however, a considerably different point of view.

I had once asked Mr. Nehru if he would consider again the idea of an unconditional cease-fire order, and he had replied, "How can you ask for something like that? It means that you are putting us on the same platform with the other side—the intruder and the aggressor. It is your duty, as a Commission, to condemn Pakistan for having an army on our soil. You should compel them to withdraw. Otherwise, it would be as though a thief had broken into my house, and you would then tell him to stay and not to move out until some further measure had been taken. You treat the thief and the owner of the house as equals. First, the thief must get out, and then we can discuss further steps."

[9] *Ibid.*, p. 130.

The prospect for any immediate cease-fire arrangement had to be abandoned. Nevertheless, all members of the Commission felt they must proceed in their mediatory efforts.

Suspicion in Karachi

The Commission moved to Karachi to get a firsthand picture of the situation there and to try to detect the mood in Pakistan's governmental circles. As in Delhi, the Commission held a number of official and informal meetings with the Prime Minister, Liaquat Ali Khan; the Foreign Minister, Sir Zafrulla Khan; the Minister of Finance, Ghulam Mohammed; the government's Secretary-General, Mohammed Ali; and other prominent members of the government. All these conversations were discouraging, adding as they did only additional proof of the profound abyss which lay between the governments of India and Pakistan.

One Sunday afternoon I was the guest of Ghulam Mohammed, now Governor-General of Pakistan. He spoke at length about Kashmir and Indo-Pakistan relations. With the fire of a fanatic believer he concluded, "For thirty years I have been a friend of Nehru, fighting alongside him against the British. Now we are free and have our own independent countries. But Nehru hates the mere existence of Pakistan and wants to destroy us. Well, he can do so. He has an army and weapons; we have none. He can march to Karachi, come to this house and thrust a dagger into my heart. I may die, but I will never surrender, and the great idea for which I have lived will live forever. We shall never give up our Kashmir."

After a few such conversations, the Commission reluctantly not only abandoned the prospect of any immediate cease-fire arrangement but alas, and even more discouraging, began to doubt the possibility of ever being able to arrange an impartial plebiscite.

It was quite obvious to us that the people of Kashmir

were not politically educated to vote and that, under any feeling of pressure, they would not express their wish freely. Only an almost completely demilitarized country would enable them to express themselves honestly at the polls. But there appeared no hope that India would agree to such a substantial demilitarization. Besides, the country was so vast and so rugged, villages were spread over such enormous distances, that the mere technicality of carrying out the plebiscite seemed beyond the scope of reality.

It was at this point that the idea of partitioning Kashmir began slowly to emerge as at least one line of action. Such a partition would be based largely on ethnical principles though giving due consideration to economic, geographical, and strategic needs. The Commission had no mandate from the Security Council even to explore such a possibility, but we felt by this time that any solution acceptable to India and Pakistan would be welcomed.

I spoke at length with Sir Zafrulla Khan about the idea of a partition. I told him about the discouraging experiences we had had in Europe with plebiscites which had turned into mere instruments of propaganda, pressure, and falsification, and I cited those conducted by Hitler and by the Communists. He realized all this but insisted that it was up to the United Nations to secure conditions conducive to a free plebiscite in Kashmir.

When on another occasion I proposed to Ghulam Mohammed that he consider the idea of partitioning Kashmir, telling him that India was inclined to such a solution, he told me that no partition which would give India more than East Jammu would be acceptable; all the rest of the country, being predominantly Muslim, would have to go to Pakistan.

Once again the Commission was thwarted. There seemed to be no line of exploratory investigation that did not run into the stubborn resistance of either Delhi or Karachi. So, perhaps out of sheer desperation, the Commission returned once more to its original mission as determined by the Security Council.

We determined to draw up a resolution—no matter how mild—that would be acceptable to both Delhi and Karachi and that would, if nothing more, initiate the habit of mutual agreement. But from the first we realized one thing: that no resolution of any type would be at all acceptable to Delhi unless it expressed disapproval of the presence of the Pakistan army in Kashmir.

We also thought that at this point Pakistan was most vulnerable, that perhaps we could impress her with that vulnerability to the place that she would, though reluctantly, accept in our resolution some statement of disapproval of the presence of her troops in Kashmir. For this reason, we launched an investigation into this phase of the problem.

Sir Ambrose Dundas, the governor of the North-West Frontier Province, gave the Commission a three-hour discourse on the tribesmen among whom he had lived for twenty-five years. He spoke about their history, their political and economic problems, their political organization and military passions, their religious zeal and their crusading spirit. He described the British policy of keeping them calm with financial subsidies and military vigilance, and the policy of the present government of Pakistan to pacify them with a spirit of friendliness. He explained their invasion of Kashmir as a response to the communal strife in Punjab and to the oppression of Muslims in Kashmir by the Maharaja. Once it started rolling, this onslaught could not be stopped, and any attempt to do so would have been met with fury, inviting war with Pakistan.

He claimed the further necessity of channeling the invasion by giving the tribesmen gasoline and letting them board trains. Pakistan herself was in a stage of administrative chaos, militarily weak, inundated by millions of refugees, absolutely unable to resist the fanatical onslaught.

General Sir Douglas Gracey, the commander-in-chief of the Pakistan army, presented to the Commission a lengthy exploration of the military situation and elaborated the reasons which had led the government, upon his recommendation, to the decision to send its army to Kashmir. It will be remembered that this was the same General Gracey who, in October 1947, had refused to follow the order of Governor-General Jinnah to send the Pakistani army to Kashmir, after the Indian army had come to rescue Srinagar from the tribesmen. But when, in May 1948, the Indian army began to approach the borders of Pakistan, he felt she could no longer remain passive.

The Pakistani army's intelligence service, he reported, was in possession of reports indicating that the Indian army had been preparing itself for a general offensive with the aim of finishing off the Kashmir campaign. The plan was to reach strategic places in the northwest and southwest areas of the state very close to the Pakistan boundaries. These were overpopulated regions, almost 100 per cent Muslim.

Had the plan been accomplished, the Pakistani authorities maintained, it would have meant disaster for Pakistan herself. First, the Indian government would have put before the whole world the possession of Kashmir as a *fait accompli*. Second, it would have inundated Pakistan with an additional several hundreds of thousands of refugees who would have further disrupted her chaotic economy. Third, it would have placed the Indian army on the long Pakistan border and within thirty miles of the strategic railway leading from Peshawar through West Punjab to Lahore. Pakistan would then have been at the mercy of India, which, as people in Karachi were convinced, desired nothing less than to remove Pakistan from the map. Fourth, to weaken Pakistan from within, the Indian push toward the north would allow the Indian army to reach the boundaries of the Pakistani states, Chitral and Swat, and further establish a physical link with the leaders of the anti-Pakistani movement for independent Pathanistan, with whom the Indian government was suspected to be in contact. It would have opened the opportunity also for a pincers movement against Pakistan by India and Afghanistan, the latter having shown a suspicious interest in the Pathan movement. Fifth, the occupation of the lower waters of three Kashmir rivers flowing to Pakistan would have placed India in a position to strangle Pakistan economically.

This latter economic threat was highly important in the minds of the Pakistani leaders. The waters of six rivers—the Indus, Jhelum, Chenab, Ravi, Beas, and Sutlej—with their elaborate systems of irrigation canals had been indispensable to the agriculture of the Subcontinent. The partition brought the river Beas under the complete control of India. The Ravi and Sutlej flow through both India and Pakistan, but their headwaters are in India. The Indus begins in Tibet and flows through Kashmir; the Jhelum and Chenab headwaters are in Kashmir. A land of 35 million acres had been irrigated by 16 canals before the partition. Now the boundary lines cut through both rivers and canals, but their waters would still irrigate 19 million acres of land in Pakistan. The occupation of these rivers and their dams by the Indian army and the eventual diversion of their waters through canals would have meant Pakistan's quick economic death.

The Indian government rejected with indignation the accusation of having ever planned such a project, pointing first to the physical impossibility of diverting these waters and to the financial burden of such an idea, and, second, to the enormous quantity of these waters, which are more than sufficient to satisfy the needs of both countries.

But the Pakistani government, despite India's denials, lived in intense fear that the approach of the Indian army to the Pakistan border would spell the end of her independence. To avoid this danger, said her leaders, the Pakistan army was ordered to move to Kashmir and stop the advance of the Indian troops.

The Commission listened sympathetically to this detailed explanation. Nevertheless, it explained to the Pakistanis, the movement of these troops into foreign territory without the invitation of that territory's government was a violation of international law; it had seriously aggravated the problem and had given India certain rights to complain. These complaints, it then further explained, must be reflected in any Commission findings and, moreover, the Commission would necessarily, on the same grounds, have to give some expression to the complaint. Having thus prepared Pakistan for what was coming, the Commission prepared a resolution and adopted it on Friday, August 13. The resolution was carried unanimously.

The Resolution—The First Pillar

Lack of space does not allow a complete analysis of every paragraph of the most important terms of the resolution. It will suffice to say that its main purpose was to arrange for a cessation of hostilities, to define in broad outlines the conditions of a truce, and to restate the principle that the final fate of the State of Jammu and Kashmir would be decided by a plebiscite. Accordingly, the resolution was divided into three parts.[10]

In Part I the governments of India and Pakistan were to agree upon the issuing of a cease-fire order within four days after their acceptance of the resolution. The Commission would appoint military observers to supervise the observance of the cease-fire.

In Part II both governments were to accept the following principles of a truce agreement: (1) Pakistan would withdraw her troops from Kashmir, "as the presence of troops of Pakistan in the territory of the State of Jammu and

[10] For the text of the resolution, see Appendix II.

Kashmir constitutes a material change in the situation since it was represented by the government of Pakistan before the Security Council. . . ." (This was the slap on the wrist the Commission delivered to Pakistan. It could hardly be labeled a denunciation, but though Nehru later described it as at best "feeble" he accepted it as at least an admission of the illegal presence of the Pakistani army in Kashmir.) (2) The tribesmen and Pakistani nationals would withdraw. (3) The territory evacuated by the Pakistani troops would be administered by the local authorities under the surveillance of the Commission. (4) The government of India would begin to withdraw the bulk of its forces from Kashmir after the Commission had notified them that the tribesmen and Pakistani nationals had withdrawn and that the Pakistani forces were being withdrawn. (5) Pending the acceptance of the conditions for a final settlement of the dispute, India would maintain within the lines existing at the moment of cease-fire a minimum force to assist local authorities in the observance of law and order.

According to Part III, both governments were asked to reaffirm their agreement that the future of Kashmir would be determined in accordance with the will of the people.

The Commission split into two sections to present its proposal simultaneously in Delhi and Karachi and to put its services at the disposal of both governments if any explanations were required. They were required. Every word was carefully weighed in both capitals.

In Delhi the Commission was received by the Prime Minister, who put to its members scores of such questions as: Will the Indian forces be permitted to occupy strategic points? Would not the acceptance of the cease-fire give certain legality to the presence of Pakistani troops in Kashmir? Did the wording of the resolution imply any legal change in the status of the Kashmir government? Did the term "law and order" imply security from external aggression? And the cardinal question: May the government of India suggest any change in these proposals? The answer to this final question was "no."

The Prime Minister also expressed concern about the danger of Pakistan's violating the truce. I answered, on behalf of the Commission, "Should the eventuality . . . occur, the whole weight of the United Nations would be turned against Pakistan."[11] The Prime Minister merely raised his eyes and smiled with gentle but obvious skepticism. The look told us with convincing clarity of the delicate and difficult position of a Commission representing the United Nations, whose prestige had suffered so much from its previous failures to solve international disputes.

However, one week later, on August 20, the government of India signified to the Commission its acceptance of the resolution, accompanying it with a number of points of interpretation previously agreed upon. Mr. Ayyangar had expressed the view privately that "the resolution was a remarkable piece of work."

Meanwhile, another diplomatic struggle went on in Karachi between the government of Pakistan and the other section of the Commission. It was a more difficult, a harder, and a fiercer struggle than in Delhi. Sir Zafrulla Khan harassed the Commission with a number of questions which plainly revealed his suspicion of the Commission's impartiality and his resentment at what he felt to be the inadequacy of its proposal. He formulated his inquiries in writing, and it took several days to prepare an answer.[12]

The Commission then spent more than ten days in Karachi, giving oral and written "explanations, elucidations, and interpretations" of its resolution. Conversations with Sir Zafrulla lasted hours on end and touched upon almost every word and its exact meaning. Every eventuality was scrutinized by him. What would happen . . . ? What would the Commission do if . . . ? Did you bear in mind the

[11] S.C.O.R. Third Year, Supplement for November, 1948, p. 103.
[12] *Ibid.*, pp. 129-138.

possibility of . . . ? What is meant by "local authorities"? "evacuated territory"? "surveillance"? Could you specify the role of military observers? What do you mean by "the future status of the State of Jammu and Kashmir"? and hundreds of other questions. They were aimed in part at removing all doubt or possible misinterpretation, but they revealed as well a deep-seated mistrust of India.

Sir Zafrulla proved to be a master of brilliant juridical analysis, and as I was chairman of the Commission at the time, he hurled interrogations at me until I was exhausted. He assured the Commission of his complete trust in its integrity, but suspected India. The Commission could only reply that good faith in the intentions of the other party is the only possible basis for negotiation and that the Commission had no power to impose anything, only to mediate.

A remark that India would be exposed to the moral condemnation of the United Nations, and possibly to even graver consequences if she violated the resolution, evoked from Sir Zafrulla a reaction similar to that given me by Pandit Nehru. It was disturbing to say the least to see so clearly this lack of belief in the prestige and power of the United Nations. But the discussions continued, with oral explanations supplemented by lengthy letters.[13]

Then the Commission met informally (at a tea party in order not to cause resentment in India) the leaders of the Azad Kashmir government, Chaudhri Ghulam Abbas and Sardar Mohammed Ibrahim Khan, to hear their reactions to the resolution and to attempt to convince them of its fairness.

Meanwhile the government of India, which had accepted the resolution more than two weeks before, began to urge the Commission to publish the resolution and the accompanying documentation because of an impending session of the Indian Parliament. But nothing could be done until we

---

[13] *Ibid.*, pp. 39-47.

had heard from Pakistan, and for that answer we waited with trepidation.

The answer came on September 6, 1948.[14] The government of Pakistan accepted the resolution—but it attached so many reservations, qualifications, and assumptions that the Commission had to consider its answer as "tantamount to rejection." Again a number of letters were exchanged, but they did little to bring Pakistan closer to actual acceptance. Among many objections, Pakistan's main preoccupation was the absence of detailed guarantees for a free plebiscite in Kashmir. Basically the Commission was in full agreement with this Pakistani position, but its resolution was designed first to stop hostilities and later to negotiate about the details of the plebiscite. Pakistan obviously was of the opinion that once the fighting had stopped, India would be satisfied with a *de facto* division of Kashmir (the better part of which was in her possession), the situation would subsequently become stabilized, and India would then obstruct a free plebiscite.

The Commission was bitterly disappointed. Its efforts seemed frustrated by Pakistan's suspicions of India (suspicions which in the light of present-day developments may have been justified), but at that time the profound hope of reaching some agreement made Pakistan's position seem unnecessarily recalcitrant. The Commission decided to leave the Subcontinent and prepare a report for the Security Council.

In retrospect, two questions emerge as to the wisdom of the Commission's procedure in regard to the resolution. The first of these is, Was it wise to have presented the resolution to the two parties on such a (as a member of the Indian government phrased it) "take it or leave it" basis? Would it have been better to have presented it as a tentative proposal, subject to negotiation and modification? Many worthy arguments might be presented for either

[14] *Ibid.*, pp. 41-45.

course of action, but in the minds of the Commission members the time had come when concrete proposals, carefully prepared and based on our best understanding of the problem, should be rather unequivocably presented. Any other approach we felt would only produce additional wrangling, consultations, and postponements—but no action.

The second question was the product of Pakistan's reaction, which was tantamount to a rejection of the resolution. Under these circumstances, was it wise to leave the Subcontinent? Should we not remain and try again? Once more it could be readily argued either way, but the subsequent developments in Paris would seem to indicate that the decision was a correct one.

But before we left for Paris one further step seemed imperative—a visit to Kashmir, the area in dispute.

To Srinagar at Last

Part of the Commission left immediately for Srinagar, to be joined later by the rest, who, headed by the American member, Ambassador Klahr Huddle, had been investigating the situation on the Azad Kashmir side.

Our UN marked plane flew over the snow-covered Pir Panjal mountains. Unlike the rocky, barren hills of Jammu lying south of Pir Panjal, on the north an impressive panorama of fresh meadows, forests, lakes, rivers, and streams presented itself. It was the fabulous Kashmir Valley. We landed at the Srinagar airport, which only ten months before had almost fallen to tribesmen. We were accommodated in one of the Maharaja's guest houses, enjoying, after two months of oppressive heat in Delhi and Karachi, the refreshing air of Srinagar.

We went for walks and tried to mingle with the local people, but they returned our overtures with anxiety, as if afraid to talk to us. The streets of Srinagar were busy, but the shops were empty, and one could immediately observe that with the war the main source of income, the tourists, had gone. The first evening we took a pleasure trip on Dal Lake. Along its shores and on the river were hundreds of houseboats, mostly abandoned. Only a few families of former British officers and civil servants continued to spend their quiet days on the placid waters of the lake, undisturbed by the fury which had so recently surrounded them.

The time spent in Kashmir was most revealing. The Commission used it to good advantage, exchanging views with the members of Sheikh Abdullah's government and visiting the scene of several battles.

The contacts with Sheikh Abdullah and his colleagues developed slowly. At first they were reluctant to speak up. On one point, however, they expressed themselves fully: they disliked the fact that negotiations about the fate of Kashmir had taken place outside Kashmir and without their participation. They resented the fact that the Commission had come to Srinagar only after it had passed its resolution. Apparently they did not know that their own central government had discouraged an earlier visit. But after the ice was broken, the Kashmiri leaders began to speak with frankness.

One evening Sheikh Abdullah gave a reception for the Commission in the famous Shalimar gardens. They were even more beautiful than legend would lead one to believe. The sun bathed the snows of the Himalayas in gold and threw a fantastic display of colors over the calm waters of Dal Lake. Between the heavy green lawns of the gardens, built in a sequence of terraces, elaborate streams of water slipped softly from one terrace to another, and throughout the garden massed banks of tulips flared in riotous colors. The orchestra of bagpipers reminded us of the British past.

After the party I went for a walk with Sheikh Abdullah. He spoke at length about the origin of his movement, his fight against the Maharaja, and the problem of accession. Here was a Muslim leader who believed, as did India, in a noncommunal, secular state but who was aware of the fanatical devotion of his followers to Islam. What, then, should he do? Pakistan was a reactionary country, he said, and he was convinced that a union of Kashmir with Pakistan would finally work against the interests of his people. They would be better off with India—but what could he do if the sentiments of his people pushed them in a direction against his better judgment?

Sheikh Abdullah did not conceal his helplessness. "I have meditated about four possible solutions to our problem," he said. "First or second—accession to India or Pakistan through a plebiscite. This could not take place in less than three years because of the destruction of the country and the dislocation of its population. Even then it would be difficult to ascertain impartially the wishes of the people scattered over large areas and possibly subjected to intimidation. Would such a plebiscite be democratic and would India or Pakistan accept the verdict?

"Third, there is a possibility of independence under the joint guarantee of India, Pakistan, Afghanistan, China, and the Soviet Union. I would be willing to meet the leader of Azad Kashmir, Ghulam Abbas, with whom I was once tied by bonds of friendship and a common struggle. We had been together in prison and often had discussed the future of our country. But even should Kashmir's powerful neighbors agree to give us a guarantee of independence, I doubt that it could last for long.

"There is in my opinion, therefore, only one solution open," Sheikh Abdullah concluded. "That is the division of the country. If it is not achieved, the fighting will continue; India and Pakistan will prolong the quarrel indefinitely and our people's suffering will go on."

I asked whether the conflict could not be settled by way of arbitration. He replied that he personally would be agreeable to an attempt, but was convinced that neither India nor Pakistan would agree, and most certainly not on the composition of an arbitration committee.

147

It was difficult to judge from his rather melancholic reasoning whether Abdullah fully followed the attitude of Pandit Nehru. The Indian government had indicated previously its willingness to divide Kashmir between India and Pakistan. But there seemed to be this important difference —that while India seemed ready to divide the country as a realistic solution, Sheikh Abdullah saw in it an act of desperation and last resort.

We knew, however, that Pakistan would refuse to consider any division of the country which would give the Valley of Kashmir with its overwhelming majority of Muslims to India. She felt she could not abandon the fate of the Kashmiris who preferred (the Pakistanis were sure) to join Pakistan. And indeed the Commission's experience in Kashmir supported this opinion.

Time and again the individual members of the Commission and its secretariat were secretly approached, and the people—simple, modest, and humble Kashmiris—would tell them with tears in their eyes how anxiously everyone awaited the arrival of the United Nations Commission. In shops, in streets, and through letters written by various women, youth organizations, and anonymous individuals, the Commission was beseeched to undo the wrongs, to stop the political terror and corruption, and to make it possible for them to choose freely.

One morning the government at Srinagar arranged an excursion for the Commission to Baramula, a town thirty-five miles from the capital. On the way one could see the evidences of the tribesmen's savage attack: houses were destroyed, small villages burned to the ground. Baramula itself was a place of destruction and misery. The Commission went from one place to another encircled by the police and accompanied by thousands of wretched people. At one place a meeting was arranged and someone spoke. Groups of people among the crowd responded with "India, Kashmir, Sheikh Abdullah, Zindabad! Long live the union between India and Kashmir!" Anyone who had lived in a totalitarian country immediately recognized that the methods of organizing a "spontaneous" expression of the masses were the same the totalitarian world over.

At one moment a young man broke the police cordon, threw a paper in front of the Commission, and shouted in English, "I want to tell you that these people oppress us." The police took him away immediately, but one could still hear him shouting from among the crowd, "Long live Pakistan!"

This was a disturbing scene for the Commission, which had been assured that the people enjoyed political freedom in Kashmir. It asked its host, the district commissioner, to send for the man and to bring him before the Commission. A few minutes later a man appeared, but it was quite obviously not the young man who had spoken to us. When this fact was brought to the commissioner's attention, he insisted that it was the same person, but the substitute himself disrupted the attempted deception. "Yes," he said, "I am somebody else. My friend is in prison, but it does not matter; I can also tell you that we want to join Pakistan."

On the other hand, back in Srinagar that afternoon we received quite a different impression. We attended a service at an old mosque where Sheikh Abdullah was preaching to several thousand believers. While small groups of Muslims prayed, completely submerged in religious devotion, Sheikh Abdullah spoke before a microphone from a window to some 4,000 people who sat quietly in an open space listening with rapt attention, their faith and loyalty quite obvious in their faces. Nor could we notice any police, so often used to induce such loyalty.

At Srinagar and elsewhere we spoke with Indian officers. They had no stomach for the war, nor did they conceal their loathing of the Kashmir government. Some of them, whose darker skins indicated that they came from South India, showed complete disinterest in the Kashmir conflict, saying they never had any sentimental attachment to the country or any political understanding of why Kashmir should be part of India.

The Commission was getting well acquainted with the situation in the country. A military subcommission prepared a detailed study of the military aspect of the Commission's work, while another committee of alternates inquired thoroughly into its political and economic phases. The picture they acquired was in no way encouraging.

To blacken it even more, the death of Mohammed Ali Jinnah threw a dark shadow of uncertainty over the entire scene. The Indian army marched into Hyderabad, and in Palestine the United Nations representative, Count Bernadotte, was assassinated. None of these events contributed to the position of the Commission.

On September 21, 1948, the Commission left Srinagar for Geneva to prepare its report to the Security Council, which was in session at that time in Paris. It left Kashmir, deeply disappointed that it had been unable to stop the fighting and thereby bring some degree of peace to the suffering Kashmiris.

Pakistan's refusal of the Commission's resolution had been discouraging, but even more so was the general attitude of both governments towards its efforts. The Prime Ministers of both countries would say, "We want to assist the Commission," or, "We wish to facilitate your task," speaking as though the struggle in Kashmir were exclusively a United Nations affair in which India and Pakistan were only interested observers. Even more disheartening were such opinions as those expressed by the Indian Deputy Prime Minister, Sardar Patel, who, after the Commission had left the Subcontinent, openly criticized the United Nations, declaring that the Kashmir conflict could be solved if India could be released from the embarrassment of the United Nations investigation, adding to his criticism the shocking comment that the Security Council had become an "insecurity council and a disturber of peace."[15]

The Commission, however, did not give up hope. It continued its work in Paris in the optimistic expectation that the international atmosphere of Paris, where the General Assembly of the United Nations and prominent statesmen from all over the world were assembled, would be conducive to further negotiations. Developments did not fall short of these expectations.

The Commission held a number of meetings and reentered formal and informal consultations with the Indian and Pakistan representatives in Paris. Its work was for a while disrupted by news, submitted by Sir Zafrulla Khan, about increased military activities. The Indian government denied this report and rejected the Pakistani complaint, but the Commission made use of the opportunity to secure from both governments their approval for the dispatch to the Subcontinent of a military adviser to the Commission.

The Commission then drafted a proposal, the main purpose of which was to supplement its resolution of August 13 by enunciating principles which would govern the envisaged plebiscite. It hoped thus to satisfy Pakistan's request for more assurance of an eventual plebiscite.

Another Resolution—The Second Pillar

The new proposal, therefore, stated unequivocally, "The question of the accession of·the State of Jammu and Kashmir to India or Pakistan will be decided through the democratic method of a free and impartial plebiscite." It also made provisions for the nomination of a plebiscite administrator who would be "a personality of high international standing and commanding general confidence." Though he was to be formally appointed by the government of Jammu and Kashmir—for the technical reason of not interfering with the sovereign rights of that country—it was provided

[15] *The Times* (London), October 2, 1948.

that he would possess such powers as he would consider "necessary for organizing and conducting the plebiscite and for ensuring the freedom and impartiality of the plebiscite."

After the fighting had ceased and the truce agreement as envisaged in Part II of the resolution was implemented, the Commission and plebiscite administrator, in consultation with the government of India and the Azad authorities, would determine the final disposal of the Indian and Azad forces respectively. The purpose of this formulation was to bring about a further withdrawal and disarmament of the military units in Kashmir to the absolute minimum required for the security of the state and below a point that could expose the population to the possibility of threat or intimidation.

The proposal then went on to elaborate the principles of securing the return of refugees and the freedom of political activities during the period of plebiscite preparations and actual voting.

The Commission sent its member for Colombia, Mr. Alfredo Lozano, and his alternate, Mr. Hernando Samper, to the Subcontinent to be at the disposal of both governments for any explanation of the proposal. Pandit Nehru expressed concern as to whether the proposal did not exclude the possibility of seeking other methods for ascertaining the wish of the Kashmir people if the holding of a plebiscite should prove to be impossible, though he insisted that the government of India still adhered to this method. He was opposed to the idea of appointing the plebiscite administrator before the truce would be fully implemented; he did not wish the plebiscite administrator to have powers which would imply any right of interference in the administration of the state; he insisted upon large-scale disbandment and disarming of the Azad forces; he regarded appeals to religious fanaticism as going beyond the scope of legitimate political activities; he emphasized the supreme importance of the maintenance of the security of Kashmir and hinted that adequate Indian forces should remain in the country during the plebiscite period.

Sir Zafrulla Khan wished, on the other side, that the plebiscite administrator be selected "as soon as possible" and that the organizing and conducting of the plebiscite fall within his exclusive responsibility.

Despite these reservations, questions, and dissents, however, both governments finally accepted the proposal and, as the first step, ordered a cease-fire in Kashmir effective one minute before midnight, January 1, 1949.

For the first time in fourteen bitter months the Kashmiris found relief from the nightmare of killing and were given some hope for a peaceful future. Hundreds of homes had been destroyed. An unknown number of people had been killed, and hatred plagued those who survived. The number of refugees had reached overwhelming proportions: 525,000 in Pakistan and the Azad territory (375,000 and 150,000 respectively), and 226,000 in India and on Sheikh Abdullah's territory (45,000 and 181,000 respectively), among them 20,000 widows.

It would be difficult to describe the feeling of the members of the Commission. The long months of labor, for which so frequently the reward had been disappointment and frustration, had finally produced at least this one important result—had at least brought some peace and promise to the suffering Kashmiris. Perhaps, too, this first step would open the gates to friendlier collaboration between Pakistan and India. Certainly also in their minds was the profound hope that this success would strengthen the prestige of the United Nations.

On January 5, 1949, the Commission met at Lake Success to embody its proposal in a formal resolution.[16] I was honored as the chairman of the Commission to report to the Security Council the happy conclusion of the first part

[16] For the text, see Appendix III.

of its mission.[17] The Commission had held all together 113 meetings, and one of its most remarkable achievements was that all its decisions had been unanimously supported.

But this unanimous approach to further problems which arose in implementing the Commission's resolutions of August 13, 1947, and January 5, 1949, was not to last. I left the Commission for political reasons, and the Communist government of Czechoslovakia nominated a delegate who almost immediately embarked upon the Soviet-Communist tactic of disrupting the structure of peace.

Implementation of the Resolutions

The Commission returned to the Subcontinent on February 4, 1949, to implement the terms of the cease-fire, put into effect the truce agreement, and prepare the plebiscite. Its activities were as strenuous as those of its first mission. It held another 126 meetings in Delhi, Karachi, Srinagar, and Rawalpindi. It negotiated with the Indian and Pakistan representatives officially and conversed with them informally. It travelled extensively in Kashmir and constituted subcommissions to study specific problems. But it ran into enormous difficulties, which were partly due to its own lack of cohesion. The Czechoslovak delegate sabotaged the Commission's efforts, encouraged intrigue among individual delegates, and reported regularly to Sheikh Abdullah on its confidential meetings.

If the Commission's activities are dealt with somewhat briefly it is because their detailed description and analysis would prolong this account beyond reasonable limits.

Before the Commission arrived, the commanders-in-chief of the Pakistan and Indian armies had already met on January 15 and arranged, in the presence of the Commission's military adviser, the details of the cease-fire order. India already had withdrawn one squadron of her air force, and

[17] For details and the Second Interim Report of the UN Commission see S/1196, of January 10, 1949.

Pakistan had also begun to withdraw. Local adjustments of the cease-fire line were agreed upon, and proposals were prepared to effect the truce. Agreement also was reached on exchange of prisoners of war.[18]

When the Commission met the Pakistan Foreign Minister, he was in a position to inform them "that considerable progress had already been made in the withdrawal from the State of Jammu and Kashmir of tribesmen and Pakistan nationals not formally resident therein, who had entered the State for the purpose of fighting," and "he believed that by the middle of that month [February], the obligation of the Pakistan Government in this respect would have been fulfilled."[19] He pointed to the necessity of defining the terms "evacuated territory," "local authorities," and "surveillance," as they appeared in the Commission's resolution.

A few days later, the representative of India, Sir Girja S. Bajpai, suggested that "the scope and the meaning of the resolutions of August 13 and January 5 should be clearly understood," as well as the terms "local authorities," and "surveillance." Then came the jolt. He named "the disbanding and disarming on a large scale of the Azad forces as an essential condition to be fulfilled before any plebiscite could be held."[20]

This statement heralded new difficulties. The terms of the Commission's proposals, accepted by both governments as the basis for the truce, had contained no suggestion of disbanding or disarming the Azad forces during the truce period. Now India had thrust this new element into the picture. Pakistan, disturbed by the proposal, once again questioned India's good will.

Meanwhile, at Lake Success, a man was hard at work on preparatory studies for the conducting of a plebiscite in

[18] For details see S.C.O.R. Fourth Year, Special Supplement, No. 7, Annex 47, pp. 169-172.
[19] *Ibid.*, p. 29.　　　　　[20] *Ibid.*

Kashmir. He had been nominated in March, 1949 by the United Nations' Secretary-General, Trygve Lie, after consultation with the governments of India and Pakistan and at the recommendation of the Commission.

This man was Fleet Admiral Chester W. Nimitz, the former commander-in-chief of the Pacific Fleet and Pacific Ocean Areas in World War II. There could have been no better choice. A man of unquestioned integrity, of recognized international prestige, with a knowledge of and experience in administrative and organizational tasks, a person of charming and modest manners, though with an air of authority, Admiral Nimitz accepted the task of plebiscite administrator with devotion and thoroughness. He spent several months reading the literature on India, Pakistan, and Kashmir; he studied the geography of Kashmir; acquainted himself with the political, cultural, religious, health, and economic conditions of the country; he became acquainted with the voting rolls and analyzed the technical aspects of the envisaged election which was to be the first universal and democratic plebiscite in Kashmir. He outlined in full detail the work of the staff which was to assist him in his task. Had the governments of India and Pakistan reached agreement on measures to be taken preceding the actual carrying out of the plebiscite, Admiral Nimitz could have moved to Srinagar to undertake his task without delay.

But, first, Kashmir had to be demilitarized—and this was going badly. The two governments were asked by the Commission to present a plan of their own for the withdrawal of their forces. The proposals differed materially. The Commission then submitted its own proposal, which had been elaborated in the spirit of its resolutions. Neither India nor Pakistan accepted it. The Commission, trying again to reconcile the views of both governments, prepared another proposal for the demilitarization of Kashmir as envisaged in the truce agreement and asked for its "unreserved acceptance." The answers were again in the negative. The Commission made another attempt by sending its representatives to Delhi and Karachi to discover "on what conditions they would accept the truce terms." Again it was evident that India was principally preoccupied with the control of the sparsely populated areas north and northwest of Kashmir proper, a control which clearly went beyond the stipulations of the accepted resolutions. She also continued to insist upon the disbanding and disarming of the Azad forces, an act never envisaged at that stage by the Commission. Pakistan's final answer elaborated on a number of points of the Commission's truce terms, but principally she based her rejection upon the fact that India refused to reveal the scope and schedule of the withdrawal of her troops from Kashmir.

The Commission tried hard to overcome these differences by suggesting a common meeting with the representatives of both governments; but they could not even agree upon the nature of the agenda, and the idea of a common meeting had to be abandoned.

After all mediation efforts were exhausted, the Commission suggested an arbitration of all differences which had arisen about the implementation of the truce agreement. Fleet Admiral Chester W. Nimitz was proposed as arbitrator. This move was supported by President Truman and Prime Minister Attlee, who sent messages to the Prime Ministers of India and Pakistan, urging them to accept the Commission's proposal. Pakistan accepted, but India rejected the proposition of international arbitration. Her concrete objection was that the scope of the arbitration was not known in advance and the government of India considered that "this procedure [was] novel and without precedent and could hardly be justified"; she could "only express surprise and disappointment at the attitude of the Commission,"[21] as it was forgetting the past, namely, the moral aspect of the Kashmir conflict.

This opinion was openly voiced by Pandit Nehru, who further declared his surprise "at the intervention of President Truman and Prime Minister Attlee in the Kashmir dispute." He reminded the world of Pakistan's "unwarranted aggression against international law," and felt that ". . . it is not right to sidetrack the basic cause of the conflict."[22] He considered that "Pakistan's perfidy and her part in despoiling Kashmir which, in spite of her vigorous denial, the Commission itself found true, are sought to be forgotten."[23]

And so, once more, all the months of labor and frustration were in vain. The resolutions of the Commission of August 13, 1948, and January 5, 1949, surely provided a solid basis for the final settlement. But their implementation had been defeated once more by the lack of mutual trust on the part of the two nations, by their totally different evaluation of the causes of the Kashmir conflict, and especially (for so it must appear after all the Commission's efforts) by a lack of good will on the part of India.

Once again it was the old story. India, clinging to the legality of the accession, considered it her right and duty to defend Kashmir against the danger of renewed external aggression. She persistently refused to disclose to the Pakistan representatives the strength of her army in Kashmir, the bulk of which she had agreed to withdraw, this despite the fact that in negotiations between the two countries she had repeatedly asserted her wish to establish friendly relations. Such a procedure could only strengthen Pakistan's suspicions as to India's real intentions.

On the other hand, the problem of disbanding and disarming the Azad forces proved equally difficult. The Com-

[21] *Ibid.*, p. 143.
[22] From Nehru's speech in Allahabad, September 4, 1949.
[23] From Nehru's speech at Ferozepore, September 18, 1949.

mission's resolution of January 5 spoke clearly about this phase of demilitarization. It was to be effected as the last measure preceding the actual act of plebiscite. But now, in the summer of 1949, the situation was much different from what it had been at the beginning of the year. The Azad forces were reorganized, rearmed, and well-trained. Before, they had been loosely knit guerrilla groups; now they were a seasoned and well-equipped army of thirty-two battalions.

India had valid reason to be worried about these Azad forces. They were composed of soldiers who once had been considered among the best in the British Indian army. India could by no means be sure of the ability of the Kashmiris who lived in the Indian part of the country to resist the Azad people either politically or militarily, though they were in a numerical majority at a rate of 2 to 1. Moreover, once the Indian army had withdrawn, it would be difficult to get them back over high mountains and long distances. On the other hand, should the Azad forces suddenly erupt into a holy war, Pakistani supplies, weapons, and perhaps once again troops could be easily and immediately available.

So the problem of demilitarization was a real one, but it should not have presented any great difficulties if there had been good will and some mutual confidence. The government of India did not accept the Commission's proposal, and its own counterproposal "was, in the opinion of the Commission, far from a fulfillment of India's undertaking under the terms of the 13 August resolution."[24] The government of Pakistan also had a number of objections to the Commission's plan of demilitarizing the country; nevertheless it agreed to accept the final judgment of an arbitrator.

Having exhausted all possibilities of mediation and facing the Indian refusal of arbitration, the Commission returned from the Subcontinent to present another report to the Se-

[24] S.C.O.R. Fourth Year, Special Supplement, No. 7, p. 50.

curity Council and to make a recommendation as to further procedure. It concluded in solemn and correct terms, "The roots of the Kashmir dispute are deep; strong undercurrents —political, economic, religious—in both Dominions have acted, and do act, against an easy and prompt solution of this outstanding dispute between India and Pakistan. These currents, which at this early stage of national formation are often antagonistic, account to a considerable degree for the misgivings, reluctance, and hesitancy which the Commission felt were often present in the negotiations and which restricted both governments in the concessions which they might otherwise have been prepared to make to facilitate agreement."[25]

The Commission considered that in view of the developments in the military situation its resolutions were now inadequate and outmoded. It recommended that the entire problem be turned over to one person as a mediator, instead of to a commission. It further recommended the use of arbitration should further attempts of mediation again fail.

On the whole, the Commission's report was markedly critical of the Indian attitude. This was quite different from its first report, which had been slightly critical of the Pakistan attitude. But in all fairness it was balanced and impartial. It was no longer, however, a unanimous report. As could be expected, the four members of the Commission were burdened with the Soviet-controlled intervention of the Communist delegate of Czechoslovakia. He presented a minority (one member) report, critical of the whole work of the Commission, of the Secretariat of the United Nations, and, faithful to the Communist pattern, full of abusive attacks on the American and British governments.[26] This disruptive activity of the Communist delegate was enough to justify dissolution of the Commission and the transfer of its functions to a single mediator.

[25] *Ibid.*, p. 60.   [26] *Ibid.*, pp. 195-204.

Commenting on the Commission's work, a British expert, Sir Godfrey Davis, wrote, "Good will and devotion . . . could do no more. It is true that the Commission failed in its final objective, but the devoted labours of the members must still be an asset to the cause of peace."[27]

Soldiers Guard the Peace

Of no small importance, at least to the Kashmir people, were the cessation of hostilities and maintenance of armistice. While political negotiations about further procedures were being held in Delhi, Karachi, Srinagar, Rawalpindi, Geneva, Paris, and New York, quiet but strenuous, unostentatious but important activities were being carried on along the cease-fire line.

A group of United Nations military observers was dispatched to Kashmir to assist the Pakistan and Indian military authorities in demarcating the line and to oversee the armistice. The first group arrived in January 1949; since then, the number has varied from 40 to 60 members.

In response to the Secretary-General's request, twelve members of the United Nations assigned officers from their armed forces for service as military observers. Australia, Belgium, Canada, Chile, Denmark, Ecuador, Mexico, New Zealand, Norway, Sweden, Uruguay, and the United States were represented by one or more officers in an international United Nations team headed by a chief military observer with the rank of brigadier to lieutenant-general appointed by the Secretary-General. The team established headquarters in Srinagar and Rawalpindi and sent out groups of two to strategically important posts on both sides of the cease-fire line. The posts were linked together and with headquarters by a radio communications network operated by United Nations personnel. The task of the observers was to be of assistance in the local adjustment of the line

[27] Sir Godfrey Davis, "Kashmir—A Sovereign State." *The Asiatic Review*, January, 1951, XLVII, p. 35.

and its final demarcation, and particularly in investigating any violations of the truce. Supervising the armistice along a line of more than five hundred miles in primitive mountainous country required enormous efforts. The two hostile armies facing each other could resume open war at the slightest provocation. But the presence of the United Nations observers, identified by their arm bands carrying the letters UN, contributed considerably to the calming of hostile spirits.

There were several hundred reports of violations of the armistice, but with very few exceptions they proved to be unfounded or of a civilian, non-military nature. When any such report reached the headquarters of the military observers, it was passed to the headquarters on the other side. Both sides would then send a team of observers to the spot to investigate the accusation and if possible settle the problem locally. The observers travelled by planes, jeeps, horses, and mules; they crossed rivers on "flying boxes," and often had to walk, sometimes several days and in high snow, to reach the area of trouble.

As a rule, the investigations revealed that the alleged violation had been caused by local people: by cattle thieves who respected no cease-fire line, by peasants who crossed it for harvesting, by girls involved with lonely soldiers.

Illustrative not only of the necessity of the observers' work but also of its vexations is the case of the soldier seen bayoneting and burying a civilian. News of the incident spread rapidly. When it came to the ears of the UN observers, teams from both sides set out for the spot. For seven days they struggled over exhausting terrain to reach the place of the incident. Upon their arrival they quickly established the facts. What the soldier had bayoneted and buried had been, not a civilian, but a wild dog!

The case proved rather trivial, but it serves as a vivid illustration of the effectiveness of the day-to-day work of the United Nations observers. One can easily imagine that, had it not been for the prompt deflation of the word-of-mouth report, the rumor might have spread and grown: the lone civilian might easily have become a group of defenseless women and children and the simple soldier might have grown to a platoon.

If the results of most investigations are anything but sensational, the process of investigation itself is not devoid of drama. It often involves danger and the risk of death. The Chief of the Military Observer Group, Brigadier Harry Angle of Canada, was killed in an airplane crash in the treacherous mountain passes of the Subcontinent. Two United States officers and a member of the United Nations Secretariat lost their lives in the same accident. One observer was killed in a jeep accident. Other observers have suffered injuries in carrying out their duties.

There were moments when the truce was in real danger. Whenever relations between India and Pakistan deteriorated or the endeavors of the United Nations resulted in another failure, tensions increased in faraway Kashmir. But they subsided again, thanks partly to the calming presence and the tireless work of these observers.

This kind of United Nations activity does not lend itself to publicity. Newspapers have little to say of such a peace mission. But, undramatic as it is, it remains one of the most commendable and admirable activities carried on by the United Nations. And it continues. For the Kashmir dispute has not yet been solved, and the military observers continue their seven-year-old task of unselfish, unheralded, and unsung devotion to the quiet ways of peace.

Their peaceful mission has not been always fully appreciated, nor have they pursued it in an altogether friendly atmosphere. The government of Kashmir accused them of several cases of interference in its internal affairs. After Pakistan was promised military assistance from the United States, in February 1954, Nehru declared concerning the eighteen Americans serving on the United Nations group of military observers that they "can no longer be treated by us as neutrals in this dispute and hence their presence appears to us improper."[27] The State Department regarded this informal request for their withdrawal as a matter between the Government of India and the United Nations, by whom these observers had been appointed. The Secretary-General, Dag Hammarskjold, anxious as he was to avoid friction, was equally concerned with the principle involved. It was his feeling that persons serving the United Nations were "denationalized" and apart from their national allegiances. In April, the issue was reported as settled by an informal consent of all parties involved that American officers on the team of observers would not be replaced after the normal term of service of those presently in Kashmir had expired. The incident itself is probably of no serious significance, but it does illustrate the high tensions that evolve from the Kashmir dispute and it reflects more broadly Nehru's irritation over the American policy of military help to Pakistan.

[27] *Indiagram* (The Embassy of India, Washington, D.C.), No. 403, March 3, 1954.

7. The United Nations
Representatives

On December 29, 1949, the Security Council met to consider what further steps could be taken in the Kashmir dispute. For two years the Council had wrestled with the problem, but solution seemed far away. True, a cease-fire had been achieved, and United Nations military observers were now stationed along the line of action to guard the armistice. But it was an uneasy peace between two restless armies, and behind them loomed India and Pakistan—still suspicious, bitter, and resentful, their original convictions about Kashmir only better muscled by two years of vigorous exercise. The ultimate destiny of four million people was as uncertain as during those fateful days of invasion and accession in 1947.

The deliberations continued against the background of renewed tensions between India and Pakistan. For, beginning in September 1949, the two countries further aggravated the already precarious situation by engaging in a bitter economic war. As a consequence of the devaluation of the currency by India, and Pakistan's refusal to devaluate her own, the governments refused to trade in coal and jute, the two most important materials for their respective industries. Old controversies and unsettled problems were revived—the disputes over the canal waters, over Junagadh, evacuee property, and liquidation of other mutual claims raised by the two governments. The problem of the canal waters, which flow from India and Kashmir and irrigate vast fields in Pakistan, was a nightmare to the Karachi government. It raised vigorous complaints against the government of India that it had several times deliberately shut off these waters and exposed the Pakistanis to the danger of starvation.

The Deputy Prime Minister of India, Sardar Patel,

termed the Indo-Pakistan relations as being "capable of provoking war," and he wanted "the nation to be prepared for the worst."[1] Pandit Nehru apparently sensed the powder-keg character of the situation and therefore proposed a joint declaration of the two governments "that they condemn resort to war for the settlement of any existing or future disputes between them." To this proposal, the Pakistan Prime Minister answered, ". . . there should be tangible action to match the spirit of the declaration, since peoples and governments are judged by their actions rather than by their words."[2] A number of letters were exchanged between them but with no result.

Then a particularly pressing and painful issue brought the two Prime Ministers together. In February 1950 riots broke out in East and West Bengal. Hundreds of people were killed and thousands sought refuge in India or Pakistan. Finally, on April 8, an agreement on minorities was signed. This was followed a few days later by a partial agreement on the reopening of trade. But other serious problems remained unsolved, and Kashmir was among them.

The Security Council, burdened with many other and more burning issues, seemed satisfied with the cessation of hostilities and was reluctant to risk by more resolute action any possible protest or overt defiance from either of the two principal contenders. Instead it based all further deliberations upon the two resolutions of the Commission already approved by the governments of India and Pakistan, the core of which was the conducting of a plebiscite in Kashmir.

The Negotiations Continue

The great Canadian statesman, General A. G. L. Mc-

[1] *The New York Times,* January 5, 1950.
[2] Government of Pakistan, *No War Declaration and Canal Waters Dispute.* Correspondence between the Prime Ministers of Pakistan and India, pp. 1, 4.

Naughton, was entrusted, as President of the Security Council, to negotiate informally with the Indian and Pakistan representatives. Following these talks, he presented to the Council a plan whereby both sides would simultaneously and progressively demilitarize to the point where the remaining forces would "not cause fear at any point of time to the people on either side of the cease-fire line." The northern, sparsely populated areas of Baltistan and Gilgit would be administered by local authorities, subject to the United Nations supervision, and a United Nations representative with wide powers would be appointed to carry out the Council's decision.[3]

Pakistan was ready to accept General McNaughton's plan with some provisions of minor importance. India, however, insisted upon the complete disbanding and disarming of the Azad forces and the occupation of the northern areas by the Indian army.

The Security Council listened once more to lengthy speeches by the representatives of India and Pakistan. Recriminations were repeated, reminiscent of the original diatribes; new accusations were exchanged, and the atmosphere was heavy with bitterness and hostility. Sir Benegal N. Rau, the Indian delegate, objected to the McNaughton proposals, saying, "They completely ignore the legal and moral aspects of the question; . . . in effect, therefore, in crucial respects the new proposals are the old proposals minus some of the small concessions previously made to India plus certain new concessions made to Pakistan. Is it a matter of surprise that India has been unable to accept them as they stand?"[4]

Three more meetings were devoted to the discussion of the McNaughton proposals, which were meanwhile embodied in the draft resolution sponsored by Cuba, Norway, the United Kingdom, and the United States. Eight dele-

[3] S/1453 of February 6, 1950.
[4] S.C.O.R. Fifth Year, No. 5, pp. 10, 17.

gates out of eleven supported the draft; the Soviet Union's Jakob Malik kept quiet, and Yugoslavia expressed doubts. India, at that time a member of the Security Council, expressed views as a party in dispute but abstained from voting.

The resolution was carried on March 14, 1950, by eight votes with two abstentions (India and Yugoslavia) and in the absence of the Soviet Union, which at that time was boycotting the Security Council. It called upon India and Pakistan "to prepare and execute within a period of five months from the date of this resolution a programme of demilitarization on the basis of the principles of paragraph 2 of General McNaughton's proposal."[5] It further decided to replace the United Nations Commission by a representative entrusted with arbitrary powers "to interpret the agreements reached by the parties for demilitarization," in case they should agree in this most important matter. It also requested this representative to make any suggestions which would in his opinion expedite and offer an enduring solution to the Kashmir dispute.

Pakistan accepted the resolution; India reiterated her strongly critical position, but also accepted it. One could read in India's reluctant acceptance of the Council's draft resolution that she recognized the authority of the United Nations, and that, faced with the pressure of the world organization and world opinion, she was willing to make what she considered to be concessions—a position which should have indicated to the Security Council its future method of procedure.

One is also bound to state, at this juncture, that throughout the endless deliberations of the Security Council on the Kashmir issue, the majority of the Council was closer to the Pakistan point of view than to that of India. Not only were its permanent members—the United States, Great Britain, France, and China, with the Soviet Union largely

[5] S/1469 of March 14, 1950. For the text of the resolution see Appendix IV.

neutral—inclined to support a procedure acceptable to Pakistan rather than to India, but the elected members also, as they served their term, associated themselves with this same general position. Included in the roster of these elected nations during the 28 months since 1948 were Argentine, Belgium, Canada, Colombia, Syria, Egypt, Cuba, Ecuador, Brazil, Holland, Turkey, and at a later period Lebanon, Greece, Chile, and Norway. Was it because all these members, permanent or elected, had some special reason to support Pakistan? It would be hard to argue along these lines. As a matter of obvious fact, all were well aware of the paramount importance of the great Indian democracy to the cause of peace and freedom, and out of this awareness must have arisen basic desires to support India's position. But the Council members could not follow the arguments and proposals presented by the Indian delegates, ably as they were stated by such prominent Indian leaders as Mr. Ayyangar and Sir Benegal Rau. Despite the serious charge that Pakistan had at least aided and abetted the tribesmen and that she had sent troops to Kashmir, the basic position taken by all these representatives largely coincided with Pakistan's insistence that the population of Kashmir be given full guarantees of an unfettered opportunity to express its desire to be a part of India or Pakistan.

The world press had up to now reported the Kashmir story without taking sides. It usually noted only the Muslim majority of the Kashmir population and voiced its expectation of an eventual plebiscite. Now, with the problem back before the Security Council, world opinion began to be critical of India's attitude. Representative of this point of view was the London *Economist*, which remarked, ". . . But the whole world can see that India, which claims the support of this majority [of the Kashmir people] . . . has been obstructing the holding of an internationally supervised plebiscite. From this the world opinion can only conclude that . . . India really has no confidence that the vote would go in its favour."[6] Pandit Nehru, usually sensitive to world opinion, asserted at a press conference that these critical comments were only "blatant and lying propaganda in the foreign Press."[7]

Sir Owen Dixon Mediates

The Security Council nominated the prominent Australian jurist and member of the High Court of Justice, Sir Owen Dixon, as the United Nations Representative. The reaction in India and Kashmir was not calculated to inspire him with self-confidence. The Indian press warned that the replacement of the Commission by a representative would not change one iota India's basic stand. Sheikh Abdullah, referring to the new mediator, declared, "If he tries to base his proposals on the McNaughton formula, failure is certain."[8] A special convention of the Kashmir National Conference was called on April 18 and passed a strongly worded resolution warning the United Nations not to bypass the crucial aspect of the dispute, namely that Pakistan was the aggressor.

Sir Owen Dixon arrived on the Subcontinent on May 27, 1950, accompanied by a member of the United Nations Secretariat, Arthur Campbell, who had been associated with the Kashmir case from its beginning. He visited the capitals of both countries, travelled extensively in Kashmir, and on July 20 opened a four-day conference in New Delhi with the Prime Minister of India, Jawaharlal Nehru, and the Prime Minister of Pakistan, Liaquat Ali Kahn. He did not leave for the record any document about the day-to-day activities, but every scrap of information available and his subsequent report[9] to the Security Council mark him as a great man, a keen observer with a penetrating analytical mind and a sense of justice.

[6] *The Economist* (London), February 18, 1950.
[7] *The Times* (London), February 7, 1950.
[8] *The Statesman* (Calcutta), March 21, 1950.
[9] S/1791 of September 15, 1950.

Though Sir Owen's report makes no mention of the fact, there is no doubt that his work was made intensely difficult by the further deterioration of the situation in the Far East. The Korean War broke out in June 1950, and the Indian government, which had recognized the government of Communist China, was more than cautious in its policy on the Korean affair. More than this, it made elaborate comparisons between the attitude of the United Nations toward Korea and toward Kashmir. If the North Korean Communists had invaded South Korea, they argued, so had the Pakistanis invaded Kashmir. Why, then, were they not condemned as were the North Koreans? Why had the United Nations failed to take action against Pakistan?

Upon his arrival in Delhi from Lake Success, ten weeks after the resolution of the Security Council had called on both parties to prepare and execute the demilitarization of Kashmir within five months, Sir Owen found that nothing had been done. "The situation as I found it presented strange features," he wrote. "The parties had agreed that the fate of the State as a whole should be settled by a general plebiscite but over a considerable period of time they had failed to agree on any of the preliminary measures which it was clearly necessary to take before it was possible to set up an organization to take 'plebiscite.' "[10] Not too dismayed, however, he set to work on his own proposal. Partially because of Indian insistence that Pakistan be declared an aggressor and partially because he himself saw in the tribesmen's incursion and the advance of Pakistan troops onto Kashmir territory an act contrary to international law, he asked that the Pakistan troops be withdrawn. This was followed by a request to both sides to demilitarize the territory to a minimum of forces (Azad, state troops, Indian army, and local militia) consistent with law and order.

The Prime Minister of Pakistan agreed to take the first

[10] *Ibid.*, p. 3.

step to withdraw the Pakistan army. But Sir Owen's grati-
fication was short-lived. The plan for demilitarization was
rejected by India.

Then Sir Owen attempted to deal with the problem of
the administration of the Azad territory, suggesting (as had
his predecessor, the Commission) that the task be assigned
to the local authorities, namely, district magistrates, whose
powers would be supervised by United Nations officers.
India objected. He then turned his attention to the territory under Sheikh Abdullah's government, making proposals to ensure for the Kashmiri population complete freedom of choice in a plebiscite. By now he must have anticipated the answer. India said "No." She based her opposition upon a number of things—the need of assuring the
defense of Kashmir and of maintaining law and order. But
she objected most vehemently to any proposal which either
treated Pakistan as an equal or failed to take into account
the violation of Kashmir territory by the Pakistanis.

Patiently Sir Owen Dixon then suggested an alternative
procedure. He suggested that for the period of the plebiscite a single government for the whole state—a coalition
government composed of the two hitherto hostile parties,
or a neutral administration by trusted persons outside politics, or an executive constituted of United Nations representatives—be organized. Sir Owen's report did not record
Pakistan's acceptance of his proposals, but the fact was
implicit. India's reply was in the negative. "None of these
suggestions commended themselves to the Prime Minister
of India," Sir Owen almost plaintively reported to the
Security Council. And then he added, "In the end, I became convinced that India's agreement would never be
obtained to demilitarization in any such form, or to provisions governing the period of the plebiscite of any such
character, as would in my opinion permit the plebiscite being conducted in conditions sufficiently guarding against
intimidation, and other forms of influence and abuse by

which the freedom and fairness of the plebiscite might be imperiled."[11]

Then Sir Owen came up with another plan, and no one reading his report could doubt either his persistence or his ingenuity. He tried to ascertain the views of both governments on taking a plebiscite region by region, allocating each to Pakistan or India according to the result of voting; or allotting to either of the two countries areas which unquestionably would vote for Pakistan or for India, limiting the plebiscite to the Valley of Kashmir. Here, however, he encountered sturdy opposition from the Prime Minister of Pakistan. India, Pakistan insisted, was committed to a plebiscite in the State of Jammu and Kashmir as a whole. On the other hand, India indicated her willingness to consider such a plebiscite, limited to the Kashmir Valley and some adjacent areas. But her suggestions as to which territories should be allotted to Pakistan or India, stated Sir Owen, "appeared to me to go much beyond what according to my conception of the situation was reasonable. . . ."[12] Pakistan refused to budge from her position, though she indicated her willingness to straight partition if the Valley were allocated to her. This was unacceptable to India.

As a last resort, Sir Owen Dixon presented both governments with another proposal. In broad lines, he called for a partition of the country and a plebiscite for the Valley, itself completely demilitarized, conducted by an administrative body of United Nations officers. This proposal Pakistan rejected but reluctantly accepted Sir Owen's further suggestion that the two Prime Ministers meet with him to discuss the issue. However, wrote the now thoroughly frustrated Sir Owen, "The Prime Minister of India answered by telegram expressing an emphatic refusal to agree to any such provision."[13]

All avenues of mediation exhausted, Sir Owen Dixon

[11] *Ibid.*, p. 16.   [12] *Ibid.*, p. 19.   [13] *Ibid.*, p. 23.

left the Subcontinent on August 23, 1950. In the concluding part of his report he wrote, patient and thoroughly moderate man that he was, "There is I believe on the side of India a conception of what ought to be done to ascertain the real will of the people which is not that tacitly assumed by me. Doubtless it is a conception which Pakistan does not share."[14]

Sir Owen Dixon's failure was certainly through no fault of his own. His approach had been thoughtful, his alternative proposals many and varied, his authority unquestionable. But the method of mediation in this dispute had revealed its own aridity. The concluding part of his report indicates something of the despair which this hard-working and conscientious man must have felt. There was no hope, it indicated, of solving the problem of Kashmir by agreement. So perhaps all that could now be done was the division of the country along the cease-fire line. This would bring about stabilization and peace, albeit forced and uneasy, a peace born of appeasement, a peace which neglected entirely the justice of determining from the people involved their will for their nation.

One cannot criticize Sir Owen's motives in his concluding recommendation. He appeared skeptical of the ability of the United Nations to force upon India any just solution. On the other hand, he felt strongly that the United Nations could not be a party to any compromise which would cast any doubt on its integrity. Any solution short of a completely free plebiscite would, in his opinion, be such a compromise. Unable to achieve agreement on a plebiscite, he wearily concluded that the only course open was for the United Nations to toss the responsibility for any further development in Kashmir back to the parties concerned, India and Pakistan. And perhaps, at least for the Kashmiris themselves, there was some value in the temporary armistice.

[14] *Ibid.*, p. 26.

But one may criticize his conclusions, for the assumptions upon which they are based are dangerous. The nationalist elements in Pakistan were increasingly impatient with the United Nations efforts, and from time to time cries of settling the problem by means of the sword were heard from the Azad people and from Pakistani extremists. There was no assurance that these cries would quiet, should the Security Council resign itself to failure. On the contrary, people well acquainted with the situation were afraid that the Council's failure would tend to guarantee a renewal of war. Besides, had the Security Council adopted Sir Owen Dixon's recommendation, it would have been a humiliating admission of its own impotence, another grave blow to the prestige and authority of the world organization.

As a matter of fact, even the immediate deadlock in the Kashmir negotiations had a serious effect on Indo-Pakistan relations. The press of both countries resumed their sharp attacks, each blaming the other for Sir Owen's failure. Articles appeared asking for the withdrawal of the Kashmir case from the Security Council, and some extremists called for the withdrawal of India and Pakistan from the United Nations.

The world press, as a whole, spoke critically of India's reaction to Sir Owen Dixon's proposals. The *London Times*, always cautious in comments on international affairs, and more particularly on Commonwealth relations, wrote, "Like most great men, Nehru has his blind spot. In his case it is Kashmir, the land of his forebears which he loves 'like a woman.' Because he is not amenable to reason on this subject, but allows emotion to get the better of common sense, Kashmir remains a stumbling block in the path of Indo-Pakistan friendship. So long as it is so India's moral standing is impaired, her will to peace is in doubt, and her right to speak for Asia is questioned by her next-door neighbour. Critics may well ask, if self-determination under United Nations auspices is valid for Korea [as India advocates], why is it not valid for Kashmir?"[15]

And so, with India and Pakistan still at each other's throats, with the world press increasingly critical, and with the very authority of the United Nations at stake the Security Council did not follow Sir Owen Dixon's advice of "hands off" and wearily decided to resume its study of the Kashmir dispute.

The Commonwealth Mediates

But five long months were to elapse before active consideration took place. One of the reasons for the delay may have been the meeting of the British Commonwealth Prime Ministers in London in January 1951, and the hope that perhaps this group might handle what was obviously an intra-Commonwealth quarrel. But the British government was extremely cautious about showing any initiative in that direction. A number of communications had been exchanged between Delhi and Karachi and London on the subject, but the British were aware of a deep-seated suspicion on the part of India towards anything coming from His Majesty's government, and were apparently anxious to avoid taking sides in the conflict. Even so, the Indian government accused the British of giving unjustified support to Pakistan.

At the January 1951 meeting the Prime Ministers did discuss informally the conflict for seven hours, but only because Liaquat Ali Khan had warned that he would not attend the meeting if it by-passed the Kashmir problem. Nothing was achieved, however, the main issue continuing to be how to demilitarize Kashmir in the period preceding a plebiscite without exposing her to the danger of "external aggression."

Three proposals were suggested by the Australian Prime Minister, Robert Gordon Menzies: (1) to station Com-

[15] *The Times* (London), September 6, 1950.

monwealth troops in Kashmir; (2) to have a joint Indo-Pakistan force there; (3) to entitle the plebiscite administrator to raise local troops. Pakistan accepted any of the three propositions. India refused them all.[16] Pandit Nehru explained later to the Indian Parliament, on February 12, 1951, that he could not agree to the presence of the Commonwealth forces because of suspicions arising out of the recent past and those growing out of current international tensions; that the second solution would place Pakistan, the aggressor, on an equal footing with India; and that although the third proposal could be considered, India must still be responsible for the security of the state and would continue to station troops in Kashmir.

Frank P. Graham Mediates

So on February 21, 1951, the Security Council once again faced the diplomatic battle of Kashmir. The representative of Great Britain, Sir Gladwyn Jebb, reminded the Council that "developments in Asia the ten months since this question was last debated by the Council have clearly demonstrated the urgent need for removing the obstacle to cooperation and mutual assistance between the governments of India and Pakistan. Never was it more necessary, indeed, than it now is for the two great peace-loving states to give practical evidence that these issues which divide them, great and troubling though they are, are still capable of adjustment in accordance with the purposes and principles of the organization to which both belong."[17]

The delegations of Great Britain and the United States submitted a draft resolution on February 21 and another slightly modifying draft a month later.[18] This proposal reaffirmed the two original resolutions of the Commission of

[16] *The Times* (London), January 17, 1951.
[17] S/PV. 532, p. 3.
[18] S/2017/Rev. 1 of March 21, 1951. For the text of the resolution see Annex V.

August 13, 1948 and January 5, 1949 accepted by India and Pakistan, and in fact stressed their mutual acceptance of a plebiscite. Once more it appointed a United Nations representative to effect, after consultation with the governments of India and Pakistan, the demilitarization of Kashmir within three months and in case of failure to report to the Security Council points of difference between the parties in regard to the interpretation and execution of the Commission's resolutions. It called upon the parties to accept, in case of failure, arbitration by an arbitrator or a panel of arbitrators appointed by the President of the International Court of Justice after consultation with the parties.

The preamble of the resolution expressed concern with the internal development in Kashmir, where Sheikh Abdullah was preparing elections for a Constituent Assembly allegedly entitled to decide the question of the final accession of the state. (This and other internal developments in Kashmir during the period of this long diplomatic struggle are described and analyzed in another chapter.)

The Anglo-American proposal was followed by eight long meetings. In addition to the sponsor-delegations, the representatives of Brazil, the Netherlands, Turkey, Ecuador, France, and China supported it warmly and convincingly, and the resolution was carried on March 30 by eight votes, with the Soviet Union, Yugoslavia, and India abstaining, the latter on the basis of Article 27, paragraph 3 of the Charter, of "being a party in dispute." One month later, Dr. Frank P. Graham was appointed the United Nations Representative.

Pakistan accepted the resolution. India rejected it, principally because of the new proposal for arbitration. Pandit Nehru and his followers in Kashmir declared that they would not permit the fate of four million people to be decided by a third person.

But this was overclouding the issue. It had never been

recommended, nor can one seriously believe that Nehru actually thought it had been, that the final fate of Kashmir should be decided by a tribunal. The resolution continued to insist, and both parties to the dispute had agreed, that the final fate of Kashmir would be settled in one way— by plebiscite. The Security Council, its Commission, and Sir Owen Dixon had repeatedly on every occasion confirmed this agreement. It was only the extent and procedure of the state's demilitarization which was to be submitted to arbitration, should the parties again fail to agree.

At this point India cannot escape criticism. It is true that seldom in the history of international relations do countries readily submit their quarrels to a tribunal, although such a procedure is by no means unique. The United States, for example, up to 1914 had submitted 86 cases to international arbitration. Furthermore, the United Nations Charter, which binds India as well as all other signatories, states in paragraph 1, Article 33, "The parties to any dispute . . . shall, first of all, seek a solution by negotiation, enquiry, mediation, conciliation, arbitration, judicial settlement. . . ."

One could therefore expect that a country of such undisputed greatness, led by a man of Nehru's stature and integrity, would have reacted more favorably to such a valid and, under the Charter of the United Nations, recommended technique of international cooperation.

On one occasion Nehru had thoroughly endorsed a policy proposed by the National Congress when it had still hoped for a united India, to have all disputes concerning minorities, i.e., Hindu-Muslim relationship, "referred to arbitration to the League of Nations or the International Court at The Hague or any other impartial body mutually agreed upon."[19] Certainly such a policy as this goes far beyond the technicality of the mere interpretation of an international agreement. Indeed, it goes far beyond the compass of na-

[19] Nehru, *The Unity of India, op.cit.,* pp. 366-367.

tional sovereignty; it constitutes, in fact, a material infringement upon the sovereign rights of a country in internal jurisdiction. But it would seem that it is one thing to be a great leader of a national movement in opposition to foreign rule, meditating theoretically on principles and policies, and another to be a statesman operating under the compulsions of internal political pressures.

Even so, the leaders of the Republic of India cherished the high ideals of solving international disputes by means of arbitration. Article 51 of the Constitution states, "The State should endeavour to . . . (c) Foster respect for international law and treaty obligations in the dealings of organized peoples of one nation; (d) Encourage settlement of international disputes by arbitration."

Pandit Nehru himself, at the beginning of 1950, suggested a "No War Declaration" with Pakistan, in which specific mention was made of settling all disputes "through recognized peaceful methods such as negotiation, or by resort to mediation or arbitration. . . ." When, however, Liaquat Ali Khan made the more concrete proposal that the Kashmir dispute be arbitrated as well as other Indo-Pakistan issues, Nehru replied that the Kashmir dispute was "a non-justiciable and political issue and cannot be disposed of by reference to a judicial tribunal."[20]

India again based her whole stand on Kashmir upon the conviction that Kashmir was already a part of India, against which Pakistan had been an aggressor. She expressed thorough indignation that this important fact had been ignored by the Security Council, by the Commission, and by Sir Owen Dixon.

This was not quite the fact, of course; both the resolution of the Commission and the recommendation of Sir Owen had given concrete expression to its disapproval of the Pakistani army's presence in Kashmir. On the other

[20] Government of Pakistan, *No War Declaration, op.cit.*, pp. 1, 20.

hand, if India felt so strongly that the aggressiveness of Pakistan in Kashmir was the heart of the dispute, why had she not asked the Security Council to deal with it according to Chapter VII of the Charter, which is concerned with "Acts of Aggression"? Why had she invoked only Chapter VI concerning "Pacific Settlements of Disputes"? This may, of course, have been a serious error in political judgment on her part which she was now attempting to correct. But it is highly questionable whether, having decided to follow one procedure, India could now legitimately insist that the Security Council could proceed only on the basis of the assumption of Pakistan's "act of aggression." But finally, and it would appear decisively, India had already accepted as the basis for the solution of the Kashmir dispute the Commission's resolutions which contained no direct condemnation of Pakistan, and by so doing had forfeited the right to fall back on such arguments as Pakistani "aggression."

One would be more readily inclined also to understand the moral motives which underlie the Indian attitude toward the Kashmir conflict if they emanated from principled policy applicable to any international situation. But if India seriously considered Pakistan to be an aggressor in Kashmir, how could she decline to see an act of clear-cut aggression in the participation of Chinese troops in the war against the United Nations in Korea? In the case of Kashmir, the basic premise of India's charge against Pakistan—that Kashmir was a part of India—has never been ruled upon by the United Nations. But in the case of Korea, the United Nations had openly condemned the aggression of the North Korean Communists; it had called upon its members to assist the victim of aggression; and when the Chinese forces joined in the invasion, it passed a resolution branding China as aggressor. Nevertheless, India refused to vote for the resolution, and Pandit Nehru called the move unwise, declaring, "It was clear it wouldn't help to call a country an aggressor when you intended having dealings with it in order to reach settlement by negotiation and the two approaches are directly opposed to each other."[21] There is apparently some inconsistency between this attitude and his continued insistence that Pakistan be named as an aggressor in Kashmir, a dispute which he has always declared should be settled by negotiation.

Under these circumstances, the failure of the Security Council's resolution of March 30 was almost certain. Nehru condemned the resolution as "highly objectionable," "a challenge to India's self-respect." At a press conference, he stated that the United States and Great Britain "have completely lost the capacity to think and judge anything. . . . No organization and no country has any business to interfere with what is done in Kashmir by India or the Kashmir people. . . . So far as we are concerned, we will tolerate no nonsense about Kashmir come what may. . . . The whole thing is a fantastic nonsense."[22]

In Kashmir, demonstrations were arranged against the United Nations, and placards like "Graham, don't come and confound confusion" were displayed. Sheikh Abdullah went ahead with his plan to have his Constituent Assembly confirm "the final accession of Kashmir to India." Nehru advanced a legal theory that would confound most students of international law. "The Republic of India," declared Nehru, "inherited the position left behind by the British Government. Apart from accession, it has to be remembered that India today is a continuing entity, taking over all the rights and liabilities of the old India. . . . These rights and responsibilities included the protection of not only the Indian States that have acceded to us, but also other states that had not acceded to Pakistan. Thus, irrespective of accession, we would have had the obligation to protect the people of Kashmir against aggression. Kashmir has at no

[21] From Pandit Nehru's speech in Parliament, February 12, 1951.
[22] *The Hindu* (Madras), June 12, 1951.

time been recognized as a state under international law, but has been an integral part of India. Partition made no difference to our responsibilities in regard to Kashmir as long as it did not deliberately accede to Pakistan."[23]

Regardless of Nehru's juridical arguments, his attitude continued to display how deeply he felt his policy on Kashmir to be right and just and to explain his intransigeance and indignation on the last resolution of the Security Council.

The atmosphere awaiting Dr. Graham on the Subcontinent could scarcely have been worse. The two countries were again in the grip of tensions which culminated in the concentration of troops in West and East Punjab. The Pakistani press hurled new insults against India. New resolutions called for *jehad*, holy war. The World Muslim Conference met in Karachi in February 1951 and among many decisions adopted a resolution urging all Muslim governments to support at the United Nations the cause of the people of Kashmir, "whose ties with the people of Pakistan no power on earth can break."[24] The Grand Mufti of Jerusalem, known for his doubtful role during World War II, visited Azad Kashmir in March 1951 and called for *jehad*.

Three religious leaders of Iran, Iraq, and Maghreb, visiting Pakistan on a later occasion, declared in an interview, ". . . the Muslim masses the world over are solidly behind the Government and people of Pakistan in the latter's demand for a just and speedy solution of the Kashmir issue."[25]

Many journalists from Arab countries visited Pakistan and the Azad government towns, spoke at meetings, and expressed in their newspapers the complete solidarity of the Middle-East Muslims with the struggle of Pakistan for Kashmir.

From time to time the Pakistani press grew bitter at

[23] From Nehru's speech in the Parliament, March 28, 1951.
[24] *The Times* (London), February 15, 1951.
[25] *Dawn* (Karachi), March 12, 1952.

what they described as the noncommittal attitude of the British and Americans toward the Kashmir dispute and their pampering of India, and advocated a shift in foreign policy towards the Soviet Union. "If Pakistan's foreign policy should take the direction that increasingly is being advocated here, the United States will have lost one sure friend in South Asia," reported Robert Trumbull from Karachi.[26]

Oddly enough, in India the seeming detachment of the Soviet Union in the Kashmir dispute received the approval of the Indian press. "To the Soviet's credit it may be said that it has so far taken little interest in the strategic and political possibilities of Kashmir—further proof that it is undue Anglo-American interest which provokes Soviet intervention anywhere," wrote *National Herald*.[27]

During the summer of 1951 India and Pakistan reached the very brink of an all-out war. Pakistani cities staged blackouts. Pandit Nehru accused Pakistan of concentration of troops in West Punjab, with aggressive intentions, and of gross violation of the truce in Kashmir.

Liaquat Ali Khan protested against the concentration of Indian troops in Kashmir and East Punjab along the Pakistan border. The two Prime Ministers exchanged a number of telegrams accusing each other in barbed language of hostile intentions.[28] The U.S. Secretary of State, Dean Acheson, conferred with the Ambassadors of India and Pakistan and expressed to them "his country's concern over the danger and tension developed in the situation. . . ."[29]

Still later, in his 1952 New Year's message, Jawaharlal Nehru warned Pakistan, ". . . if Pakistan by mistake invades Kashmir, we will not only meet them in Kashmir,

[26] *The New York Times*, September 15, 1951.
[27] *National Herald* (Lucknow), March 31, 1951.
[28] Government of Pakistan, *India's Threat to Pakistan*. Correspondence between the Prime Ministers of Pakistan and India. White Paper.
[29] *The New York Times*, August 9, 1951.

but it will be a full-scale war between India and Pakistan."[30]

It was in this atmosphere that Dr. Frank Graham was to attempt to effect the demilitarization of Kashmir. His mission was limited to this particular task, which was the essential prerequisite to a free plebiscite. The Security Council requested him to report in three months the result of his work. Three years have now passed, and Dr. Graham has not been able to report success.

Dr. Frank P. Graham has been United States senator from North Carolina, president of the University of North Carolina, defense manpower administrator in the Department of Labor, and member of the United Nations Committee of Good Offices for Indonesia. Above all, Dr. Graham is a man of deep humanitarian understanding, courageous optimism, rare patience, perseverance, and a belief in the good faith and good will of men. Only a man of these qualities could have continued in his task through such weeks and months of frustration without losing hope.

Dr. Graham, accompanied by Miguel A. Marin and Elmore Jackson of the United Nations Secretariat and by the experienced military expert, General Jacob L. Devers, carried on extensive activities in an attempt to bring the parties in dispute to an agreement on the demilitarization of Kashmir. Dr. Graham travelled to and negotiated in Delhi, Karachi, Srinagar, Geneva, Paris, New York; he studied in detail all aspects of the demilitarization; he sent questionnaires and submitted numerous proposals to the two governments; he drafted and redrafted his own plans of demilitarization. Five reports have been submitted to the Security Council,[31] and still, at the Council's request, his efforts continue.

His work has revealed a painstaking, relentless effort to

[30] *The Hindu* (Madras), January 2, 1952.
[31] S/2375 of October 15, 1951; S/2448 of December 19, 1951; S/2611 of April 22, 1952; S/2783 of September 19, 1952 S/2967 of March 27, 1953.

narrow, step by step, the differences between the governments of India and Pakistan. After a thorough investigation of their attitude he defined his own plan in twelve proposals. Most of them were of a general nature and did not present serious obstacles to acceptance. Finally, however, he reached the point where inevitably the governments of India and Pakistan had to take a stand on his two most crucial proposals: the time for the induction into office of the plebiscite administrator, Fleet Admiral Chester Nimitz, and the scope of the demilitarization of Kashmir.

On the first point, Pakistan insisted on Admiral Nimitz's taking the office as soon as possible; India considered this premature, asserting that the demilitarization must first be carried out. On the second point, Dr. Graham had to face insurmountable, though now thoroughly familiar, obstacles.

The United Nations representative first proposed, as a basis for discussion, that 12,000 to 18,000 soldiers be retained on the Indian side, plus the local state militia of 6,000 men; and 3,000 to 6,000 Azad soldiers on the Pakistani side, plus 3,500 scouts in the northern area. Then, he modified this proposal, suggesting 18,000 and 6,000 men respectively.

Neither of his proposals was acceptable to India. She insisted that 21,000 soldiers was an absolute minimum and refused to include in this figure the state militia. In addition, she insisted on the complete demilitarization of the Azad Kashmir and the substitution of the present armed forces there by a civil force of 4,000 men (one-half armed and one-half unarmed), this force to be composed of 2,000 followers of the Azad government and 2,000 men normally resident in the Azad territory who were not followers of the Azad government.

This of course was an entirely new element, never before considered. It would have meant in essence that the proposed plebiscite would be carried out in Sheikh Abdullah's territory in the presence of 27,000 soldiers friendly to India and Abdullah; and on Azad territory, in the presence of 4,000 men of a civil force, only partially armed, and one half of whom would be recruited presumably from refugees living under Sheikh Abdullah's administration.

Pakistan considered the number of soldiers left in Kashmir still too high but indicated she was ready to accept Dr. Graham's proposal. When the Security Council, on December 23, 1952, passed a resolution[32] urging the governments of India and Pakistan to agree within thirty days on the demilitarization of Kashmir on the basis of Dr. Graham's proposal, India once more refused and once more Pakistan accepted the resolution.

Nevertheless, the negotiations between the representatives of India and Pakistan were resumed, first in New York and then, in February 1953, in Geneva. Dr. Graham's zeal, which by now could be termed nothing less than missionary, led him to present another six suggestions on both the manner of demilitarization and the time of the induction of the plebiscite administrator into office. Among these he reiterated his previous proposal that the Azad troops be limited to 6,000 men. On the other hand, he met India's request and increased the number of Indian soldiers to 21,000. He attached added importance to the induction of the plebiscite administrator into office, as he assumed that in the last analysis it would be for him and for the United Nations representative to determine later, in accordance with the procedure envisaged in the resolution of January 5, 1949, after the implementation of the truce agreement, the final disposal of the rest of the armed forces on both sides.

This proposal broke against the insurmountable opposition of both governments, and the conference finally dissipated in a mood of resignation. Dr. Graham found himself precisely where Sir Owen Dixon had been in September 1951. In the conclusion of his fifth report to the Se-

[32] S/2883 of December 24, 1952.

curity Council, he expressed the hope, ". . . may the leadership of over 400,000,000 people, with the good will and assistance of the United Nations, join in negotiating and reporting an agreement on Kashmir and thereby light a torch along the difficult path of the people's pilgrimage toward peace."[33]

Once more a thoroughly frustrated negotiator had arrived at the same conclusion as Sir Owen: that the inability of the two parties to agree under United Nations mediation left no solution except that they agree between themselves! It is difficult to envisage that any torches lighted under these circumstances would be for the purpose of illuminating the path to peace.

Dr. Graham's methods differed somewhat from Sir Owen Dixon's approach. Sir Owen, having presented proposals which led directly to the crux of the problem, moved swiftly and when they were not accepted put the blame where he believed it belonged. After three short months of negotiations, he assumed the role of the realist, and gave the whole thing up. Dr. Graham, on the other hand, chose the method of the patient mediator, who listened, ascertained the points of disagreement, and, until his fourth report, abstained from recommendations of a concrete nature. He worked first on questions of minor importance in the hope that agreement on these might induce a habit of agreement conducive to the settlement of the more crucial problem of demilitarization. When he had arrived in Delhi on his first mission in the summer of 1951, "he did not even once refer to the Security Council's resolution," in the words of Mr. Nehru. "It was as if the resolution was not there."[34] Undoubtedly it was there, but also in Dr. Graham's mind was the knowledge that this resolution had already been rejected by the government of India. When he succeeded,

[33] S/2967 of March 27, 1953, p. 21.
[34] Pandit Nehru's speech in the House of the People, February 12, 1952.

one and one half years later, in bringing the parties together again in Geneva to discuss the problem of demilitarization, he did not even then refer to the Security Council's last resolution urging India and Pakistan to come to an agreement in thirty days. Once again he was aware that the government of India had already rejected this resolution.

Dr. Graham's methods can be evaluated properly only against the background of his knowledge of the attitude of responsible Indian and Pakistani officers and, above all, the happenings in Kashmir. He knew that Mr. Gopalaswami Ayyangar, the Minister of Defense and one of the most influential leaders in India, had declared on the eve of Dr. Graham's arrival in the Subcontinent, "Kashmir is in India and is going to remain in India."[35]

He knew that the Kashmir Deputy Prime Minister, Bakshi Ghulam Mohammed, had declared that the Kashmir people had already made up their mind to join India and "no power on earth could swerve them from their chosen path."[36]

All of these pressures Frank Graham knew and understood as he proceeded with his mission, and, peaceful spirit that he was, he studiously avoided any possible statements or proposals that would increase these antagonisms or destroy his mission. But even so, his every step was prejudged —his mission hopeless.

The Indian press treated his mission in a conciliatory way only so long as he remained on the level of inquiry concerning the problems of demilitarization; as soon as he presented concrete proposals they became reserved and mistrustful to the point of stating that "the failure of his negotiations was a foregone conclusion" and ". . . the failure . . . will cause small surprise," and "it is not entirely his, Graham's, fault."[37]

---

[35] *The Hindu* (Madras), June 26, 1951.
[36] P.T.I. (Press Trust of India), August 11, 1951.
[37] *Hindustan Standard* (Delhi), September 26, 1952; *The Times of India* (Delhi), September 26, 1952; *Delhi Express*, September 26, 1952.

If the Indian press, of which only a few examples are quoted here, was exerting public pressure upon its government, the Pakistani governmental representatives and the press were increasingly indignant and restless about the prolonged negotiations, which they viewed only as unnecessary procrastination. They felt, perhaps with some justice, that although they had accepted almost all the proposals of Dr. Graham, the United Nations had let them down. Their statements grew increasingly bellicose.

Sardar Ibrahim, then Prime Minister of the Azad government, threatened in the summer of 1951 that the Kashmir issue would not be settled at Lake Success, "but will be decided only on the battlefield."[38] In September 1952 he criticized the United Nations inactivity, accused the Pakistan government of "dilly-dallying," and called for resumption of "liberation" fighting. Thus the Pakistan government faced serious internal difficulties in keeping the Azad forces patient and quiet during this continually prolonged period. The president of the Sind Provincial Muslim League, Mohammad Ayub Khurro, declared in the Parliament, ". . . if no immediate action is taken in the Kashmir issue there might be an upheaval of revolution in Pakistan which might be difficult for the Government to control."[39] The Azad government warned that, "Azad Kashmiris themselves . . . would be responsible for the liberation of their brethren across the cease-fire line and the war would be this time fought to the bitter end, irrespective of circumstance."[40] The Prime Minister of Pakistan, Khwaja Nazimuddin, declared, ". . . there is a limit to our patience," and he promised, ". . . God willing we shall never rest until we have liberated the people of Kashmir."[41] At the annual conference of the Muslim League, the most powerful political party in Pakistan, a resolution under the chairmanship of

[38] *The Hindu* (Madras), June 26, 1951.
[39] *The New York Times*, March 28, 1952.
[40] *Ibid.*, September 10, 1952.   [41] *Ibid.*, August 15, 1952.

the Prime Minister appealed to the government to liberate the Kashmiri people "by all possible means" and to Pakistan to be "prepared for an all-out struggle."[42]

On October 24, 1952, a "Kashmir Day" was observed throughout Pakistan, and scores of meetings were held and resolutions passed urging action, condemning the "dilatory policy" of the United Nations, asking for Pakistan's withdrawal from the United Nations, and warning that "the Muslim World may be forced to revise its attitude towards the United Nations."

Whatever may have been the purpose of the avalanche of these threatening statements—whether to put pressure on the Pakistani government, or on the Indian government, or on the Security Council, or on Dr. Graham—they were certainly a clear and convincing expression of the indignation and resentment of the Pakistani people over the failure to bring the Kashmir issue closer to the final solution. That there has yet been no outbreak of armed hostilities offers some hope for peace, but all informed observers believe that the situation continues to be grim; that the powder keg of the Kashmir issue, which threatens so dangerously the welfare of Pakistan and India as well as the peace of the world, might yet explode without warning.

Perhaps it is this deadly possibility, plus his own optimism, that has kept Dr. Graham from succumbing to what would be an easily understandable exasperation over the frustrations of his prolonged efforts to mediate. Dr. Graham's patience and persistence arouse admiration. But there is another side of the coin. This is that the endless negotiations have allowed for profound political changes in Kashmir which not only are dimming the hope that an impartial plebiscite will ever take place but also are implying serious dangers to the cause of peace and democracy.

[42] *Ibid.*, October 15, 1952.

Bilateral Negotiations

Now, of course, another event has taken place which vitally affects the United Nations role in the Kashmir dispute. Whether from lack of good will, or out of the weariness of the people directly involved in the Kashmir procrastination, or more probably because of the dissatisfaction of both parties in dispute with the United Nations policy, the governments of India and Pakistan in 1953 decided to excuse the United Nations from active participation in the issue, and to try again, as they did in 1947, to prepare the solution in bilateral negotiations. In the spring of 1953 Mohammed Ali, the Ambassador of Pakistan to the United States, was appointed Pakistan's Prime Minister. He made several optimistic statements on the Kashmir problem and stressed the necessity of establishing close and friendly relations between India and Pakistan. The latter statements were reciprocated by New Delhi.

In June 1953 Mohammed Ali and Jawaharlal Nehru discussed the Kashmir issue informally in London, where they met on the occasion of the coronation of Queen Elizabeth. Then, on July 25, Nehru paid a visit to Karachi, where the problem was discussed, among other questions, in general terms. Further negotiations were envisaged. The press of both countries was friendly as it had never been before.

On August 9, however, Sheikh Abdullah was abruptly dismissed from office and Ghulam Mohammed Bakshi was nominated Prime Minister of Kashmir (the event is described in detail in the following chapter). Once again Muslims were killed in the Vale of Kashmir. It was as though a stroke of lightning had shattered the promising atmosphere of Indo-Pakistani relations.

Mohammed Ali rushed to Delhi, partly because he wished to avert the danger of a violent outburst of indignation on the part of the Pakistanis, partly because he probably wanted to use the events in Srinagar to convince Nehru of the necessity of an early settlement of the Kashmir dispute.

After four days of consultations, the two Prime Ministers issued a joint press communiqué on several matters concerning the Indo-Pakistani unsettled problems. The part on Kashmir read:

"The Kashmir dispute was specially discussed at some length. It was their firm opinion that this should be settled in accordance with the wishes of the people of that State with a view to promoting their well-being and causing the least disturbance to the life of the people of the State.

"The most feasible method of ascertaining the wishes of the people was by fair and impartial plebiscite. Such a plebiscite had been proposed and agreed to some years ago. Progress, however, could not be made because of lack of agreement in regard to certain preliminary issues.

"The Prime Ministers agreed that these preliminary issues should be considered by them directly in order to arrive at agreements in regard to this. These agreements would have to be given effect to and the next step would be the appointment of a plebiscite administrator.

"In order to fix some kind of a provisional time-table, it was decided that the plebiscite administrator should be appointed by the end of April 1954. Previous to that date the preliminary issues referred to above should be decided and action in implementation thereof should be taken. With this purpose in view Committees of Military and other experts should be appointed to advise the Prime Ministers.

"On the plebiscite administrator's formal appointment and induction into office by the Jammu and Kashmir Government he will examine the situation and report on it. He will then make such proposals as he thinks proper for preparations to be made for the holding of a fair and impartial plebiscite in the entire State and take such other steps as may be considered necessary therefor."[43]

[43] *APP* (Associated Press of Pakistan), August 20, 1953.

The communiqué marked a new phase in the long attempt to solve the Kashmir problem; in a way it marked too its new treatment. It confirmed the old agreement to let the people of the entire State of Jammu and Kashmir decide their future by a free and impartial plebiscite, but it also meant that the problem of demilitarization ("certain preliminary issues") would be considered by the governments of India and Pakistan directly upon the advice of their experts and without direct assistance from the United Nations. It further envisaged their implementation prior to the appointment of a new plebiscite administrator to succeed Fleet Admiral Nimitz, this to take place by the end of April 1954.

Strangely enough, the communiqué did not mention the United Nations, though certainly the Kashmir dispute remains on its agenda. Unfortunately, however, the proverbial ink of the communiqué had hardly dried when its wording, instead of strengthening Indo-Pakistani friendship, freshly established and still fragile, provoked critical reaction among the rightist parties in India and among almost all papers in Pakistan. The Azad leaders even declared at a press conference in Karachi that "It has been natural for Bharat [India] to devise some means to blanket her stark misdeeds and to camouflage the real situation in the Valley. It is our considered opinion, which we express with considerable pain, that the Delhi Agreement has been used to serve exactly this end, and no other. . . . It has not brought the plebiscite a bit nearer than it was in 1949."[44]

Fleet Admiral Nimitz was improperly involved in the sharp exchange of views on the Delhi agreement of August 20. Nehru expressed preference for a national from a smaller European or Asian country, to avoid involving both India and Pakistan in power politics. "In any case," he declared somewhat undiplomatically, "the fact of the Nimitz nomination as administrator by the United Nations is now

---

[44] *Dawn* (Karachi), August 29, 1953.

an historical memory and I have almost forgotten about it."
The Pakistanis, however, insisted on Nimitz' retention and
branded Nehru's attitude as "deliberate shock tactics designed to drive a wedge between Pakistan and the United
States."[45] As the newspaper war continued, Jawaharlal
Nehru and Mohammed Ali exchanged several letters, which
have not as yet been published, on the "preliminary issues,"
as envisaged in the Delhi agreement.

Four months passed before expert representatives of India and Pakistan met to advise their Prime Ministers on the
most important preliminary issue, the demilitarization of
Kashmir. The meeting could not have taken place under
less favorable circumstances. On the initiative of Nehru, a
campaign was in progress against the negotiations concerning American military assistance to Pakistan. Nehru declared in the House of the People that these negotiations
might affect the solution of the Kashmir problem. Indeed,
the experts' conference in Delhi towards the end of December 1953 ended without having made any tangible
progress. They have not met since. The Prime Minister of
Pakistan requested in a number of letters a meeting with
the Prime Minister of India, but with no success. Nehru
declared on various occasions that the Delhi agreement had
been reached in the context of a situation which now was
altered by Pakistan's acceptance of American military help.

The two Prime Ministers did see each other at the Colombo Conference of India, Pakistan, Ceylon, Burma, and
Indonesia toward the end of April, and Mohammed Ali
tried to have the Kashmir issue put on the agenda, but failed
against Nehru's opposition. The latter declared that the
problem could not be solved in a few hours if it had escaped
solution for seven years. So the awaited month of April
passed and no "preliminary issue" was solved, no plebiscite
administrator was appointed. People who believed and
hoped that the solution of the problem might be facilitated

[45] *The New York Times*, August 29, 1953.

by keeping the United Nations out of the picture could not be encouraged by the outcome of one year of bilateral negotiations.

No supporter of the United Nations could be pleased by Delhi's and Karachi's decision to by-pass, though perhaps only temporarily, the world organization. But the United Nations, unlike national governments, is not concerned with prestige in matters of procedure, and it would wholeheartedly welcome any solution which would come out of the bilateral negotiations between India and Pakistan. However, the United Nations cannot give up in its major responsibility in maintaining peace among the nations, and it must be ready to reassume without delay its role of mediation should the bilateral approach fail.

In any therapy, when the disease persists, there comes a time for a change of treatment.

What Next?

Why, for example, should not the Kashmir conflict be taken off the agenda of the Security Council and passed on to the General Assembly, whose recommendations carry the authority and moral support of the majority of its sixty members? The General Assembly could appeal to India and Pakistan to demilitarize Kashmir according to those proposals already endorsed by the Security Council resolution of December 23, 1952, and to proceed with the plebiscite as it had been agreed upon under the resolution of the United Nations Commission.

Is it not perfectly proper and plausible that the General Assembly could simultaneously, or in case of the failure of such a recommendation, ask the International Court of Justice for an advisory opinion on the legal validity of Kashmir's accession to India?

Certainly the General Assembly could appeal to Pakistan and India to accept arbitration on at least the process and scope of the demilitarization of Kashmir and on the interpretation of other clauses of the United Nations Commission's resolutions, in case of further disagreement between the parties in dispute.

Or, the General Assembly could propose to the disputing parties to station United Nations troops along the Kashmir-Pakistan border on Pakistan's territory, thus allowing the State of Jammu and Kashmir to be completely demilitarized. The United Nations units could be composed of nationals of the countries which are neither politically nor geographically directly concerned with the issue. This could exclude also nationals of the five permanent members of the Security Council.

It might be very difficult for Pakistan to accept this proposal, but while it would relieve India of any concern over the defense of Kashmir against the danger of an external aggression, it would also meet Pakistan's aim of complete demilitarization of the country and the assurance of real freedom for a plebiscite.

It is, of course, entirely possible (perhaps probable) that such suggestions would likewise encounter opposition—perhaps rejection. But behind these proposals would be the moral weight of both the individual and collective nations of the world, one portion of which, at any rate, can hope for nothing good from any further prolonging of this struggle. It is reasonable to expect that a fair resolution would be carried by an overwhelming majority of the General Assembly, perhaps only with the exception of the Soviet bloc and one of the parties in dispute. At least the world would know where each member of the United Nations stands.

There are, of course, other peaceful ways of solving the Kashmir dispute as long as the wishes of the Kashmir people are respected and their freedom of expression fully assured. But all of these are predicated upon the presence of good will. Without it, even the most ingenious proposal is condemned to failure.

8. The Kashmir Scene Changes

SEVEN YEARS have passed since India and Pakistan began their struggle for the State of Jammu and Kashmir. The world press, which once headlined the dispute, now reports it only sporadically. Only the press of India and Pakistan retell the whole story on every possible occasion. But though few correspondents now cover the scene as once they did, life in Kashmir goes on under its burden of strife. The parties in the divided areas continue to entrench themselves until today Kashmir is in effect two countries, led by two governments, their policies and aims irreconcilable.

Should a plebiscite take place now, the pent-up bitterness of seven years would drive the members and followers of the losing side from the country. All are aware of this, and with little question it is this fact that makes the prospect of a plebiscite remote. For the party which has the more serious reason to be fearful of the result of a plebiscite—the government in Srinagar—has been doing everything in its power to delay this day of reckoning. It has been working hard to change the conditions of life under the Maharaja and to bring some relief to the poverty-stricken masses. Indeed, it has introduced some healthy economic reforms. But as the process goes on, it becomes simultaneously apparent that Kashmir is on the road to a radical left-wing totalitarian dictatorship.

Before we examine this pattern further—it is a familiar one in the twentieth century—let us review the situation briefly. Since those October days of 1947, the State of Jammu and Kashmir has been split into two parts. The western and northern part adjacent to Pakistan, to Afghanistan, to Sinkiang, and, for a short strip of territory, to the Soviet Union, consists of the Azad region, Gilgit, northern Ladakh, and Baltistan. The other part consists of the Vale of Kashmir, a part of Jammu, and a part of Ladakh.

The Azad Government

The Azad territory has an area of 5,000 square miles and a population of 700,000 plus some 200,000 refugees. It is overwhelmingly Muslim, since the pre-war non-Muslim 12.5 per cent minority has been reduced to 2 per cent. The temporary capital is Muzaffarabad.

The country is governed by the Azad Kashmir government, which is in charge of all affairs of a local nature. The postal and telegraph systems and defense are in the hands of the Pakistan government, which exercises these functions through a Ministry of Kashmir Affairs, established at the beginning of 1949. Foreign affairs are also the concern of the government of Pakistan. The armed forces are under the command of the Pakistani general staff; they are composed of units of the Pakistani army and local Azad troops. The tribesmen withdrew in 1949.

The government is composed of five members headed by the Supreme Head of the Azad Kashmir government. In March 1948 this title was conferred upon Ghulam Abbas, the old warrior of freedom for the Kashmir people. He held this position as well as that of the presidency of the All Jammu and Kashmir Muslim Conference until December 1951, when he resigned for reasons never publicly explained. It would seem, however, that he and his younger colleague, Sardar Mohammed Ibrahim, the talented and radical leader who had raised the banner of revolt in Jammu in the spring of 1947 when Ghulam Abbas was in prison, felt considerable dissatisfaction with what they considered the timid policy of the Pakistani government on Kashmir. On several occasions both Abbas and his young Prime Minister had pressed for a vigorous military action, and when it was not forthcoming they apparently resigned in protest. Both continue to be very active in the Muslim Conference, however, taking part in its meetings and criticizing both the Azad government for its lack of democracy and the Pakistan government for its lack of resoluteness. The Azad government is now headed by Colonel Sher Ahmed Khan.

Both the driving and the controlling force behind the Azad government is the All Jammu and Kashmir Muslim Conference. It determines the policy of the government and nominates its members, who, in turn, are responsible to the Conference for their actions. In 1949 it claimed a membership of 300,000 people. It holds annual general congresses, and in March 1952 one thousand delegates participated at its gathering. Its leading body is the Working Committee of 19 members.

The Muslim Conference is the only party in Azad Kashmir and in that sense is in fact no more democratic than its opposite number, the National Conference. There have been no elections in the country. But all observers who visited the Azad territory or who have studied the conditions there are agreed on its vast and popular following. Its main aim is to unify Kashmir and to unite with Pakistan. Unlike the National Conference, the Muslim Conference has never indicated that it would be willing to consider the alternative of establishing an independent Kashmir.

Under the Azad government administration the old system of feudalism was abolished, though no radical land reform was introduced. In April 1949 land revenues were cut by 50 per cent and some others were discontinued. In October 1951 the land tax was 4 annas (about 7.5 cents) to 1 rupee (about 30 cents) per *kanal* (8 kanals equals one acre). The country raises few agricultural products. Its chief export is timber, the forests being owned by the government. Industry is very small, employing only some 20,000 workers. About 400 cooperatives functioned in the country at the end of May 1953.

With the financial help of the Pakistani government the Azad government has devoted considerable effort to the construction of roads and public buildings and to the improvement of education and social and medical services. It maintains the Oriental College at Muzaffarabad, 12 high schools, 37 middle schools, and 492 elementary schools. It also supports 8 hospitals, 22 village dispensaries, and 6 mobile medical units, but it is in dire need of doctors and nurses. It runs several refugee camps. The Pakistan Red Cross operates 6 hospitals in Azad Kashmir. Health centers and dental clinics are established in the more important towns, and new ones are being planned. Some 700,000 dollars are spent a year for medical services. All this indicates a very low standard of living, and much remains to be done. Only recently, in May 1954, at a press conference in Karachi, critics of the Azad Kashmir government, Sardar Mohammed Ibrahim among them, raised vigorous protest against bribery, corruption, and embezzlement in the governmental circles. They also accused the Ministry of Kashmir Affairs of pursuing a policy of colonialism in the Azad territory. They urged the government to conduct democratic elections in the country. Perhaps as a concession to these popular pressures, the Azad Kashmir government in June promised (without specifying any date however), general elections based on adult franchise.

The northern areas consist of a vast expanse of 54,000 square miles with a scattered population living in remote villages, hidden in valleys or lying at the gateways to various mountain passes. They are politically controlled in only the vaguest way by the Pakistani government through a political agent. The actual political power is exercised by local chieftains, and police functions are fulfilled by some 3,500 scouts. The area is essentially, though mildly, agricultural in nature. Life is primitive, and such political aspirations as exist have been satisfied by the allegiance of the population to Pakistan. According to some sources, there has been some infiltration of Communist agents in Gilgit from the Soviet Union and from Communist Sinkiang. In April of 1953 Sir Zafrulla Khan protested to the Chinese government against violations of Sinkiang-Gilgit borders.

In Gilgit there are only 8 schools—one of them a middle school—one civilian and one veterinary hospital, and 14 dispensaries. In Baltistan and northern Ladakh there are only 33 schools and 3 hospitals. The Pakistan government endeavors to maintain regular air communication with these faraway mountainous regions and for that purpose has constructed an air strip at Gilgit proper, at Skardu, and at Chilas. Gilgit could be reached before only on foot in a 12-day journey from Peshawar, in the North-West Frontier Province. Now the 250 miles may be traveled daily by air transport. The old caravan route has also been widened for jeeps, which can make the trip in four days.[1]

In general, one would say that the western and north-western areas of the State of Jammu and Kashmir form part of Pakistan, tied with her by the strong links of Islam, though this has not as yet found expression in any formal act. Legally they continue to be part of the State of Jammu and Kashmir. Their individual regions enjoy rights of wide autonomy, but they are far from being democratic. This can be partly explained as a consequence of the old feudal traditions of their primitive society and partly by the necessities of the war. But the internal organization of the Azad territory is not the problem. Rather, it is that as the years go by, the people continue to seethe with anger over their enforced separation from their fellow countrymen on the other side of the cease-fire line. It is in this respect that the policy of their leaders, if it is not extraordinarily wise and prudent, may have far-reaching and disastrous consequences for the free world.

It is in the other half of this divided State of Jammu and Kashmir, which is under the Srinagar administration, that the internal political development gives reason for real international concern.

[1] The foregoing paragraphs are based on information from Pakistani governmental sources.

New Kashmir

In 1944, four years before Sheikh Abdullah came to power, the National Conference prepared its political program, embodied in a document called *New Kashmir*. First published as a booklet, its cover was decorated with the red flag and white plough[2] which has since become the national flag of Kashmir. The declaration is often referred to as the Magna Charta of the Kashmiri people and it has become the bible of Kashmir's economic life.

In the Introduction, Sheikh Abdullah declares that the National Conference fights "for the poor, against those who exploit them; for the toiling people of our beautiful homeland against the heartless ranks of the socially privileged. . . . The history of freedom movements . . . had only one lesson to teach—that freedom from all forms of economic exploitation is the only true guarantee of political democracy. . . ."

Then Abdullah continues, "In our times, Soviet Russia has demonstrated before our eyes, not merely theoretically but in her actual day-to-day life and development that real freedom takes birth only from economic emancipation."

New Kashmir contains a proposal for a constitution, a national economic plan, and a women's charter. The constitution lists and guarantees the basic human and political rights: equality of all citizens; freedom of conscience and worship, of speech, press, assembly, street processions; inviolability of the person; and a universal, equal, direct suffrage by secret ballot. In that respect it does not differ from the best constitution of any democratic country. But for that matter, neither does it vary from the constitutions of those Communist countries which, having inscribed these human and political rights in their basic constitutional law, have violated them daily.

The constitution proposed by *New Kashmir* also guarantees to all citizens the right to work, to rest, and to have

[2] *New Kashmir*, Kashmir Bureau of Information, New Delhi.

material security in old age, sickness, and in case of loss of capacity to work. It guarantees the right to education and equal opportunity for all children. It guarantees the right of personal property, within the limits of an economy planned by the state.

The country's highest organ, according to *New Kashmir*, is the National Assembly with usual legislative powers but also with the jurisdiction to represent the state in external relations; to organize the defense of the state; to prepare the national economic plan; and to develop executive activities which are as a rule pursued by governments. The Council of Ministers is responsible to the National Assembly, and the ruler is the constitutional head of state. Judges are independent of the government in fulfilling their duties.

"The economic life of the State shall be determined and directed by the National Economic Plan . . . ," continues the *New Kashmir* program. "Cooperative enterprise should be stressed as opposed to destructive competition. Marketing and trade must not be spontaneous but controlled and organized." This means, in agriculture, the abolition of landlordism, assignment of land to the tiller, cooperative association of peasants, people's control of forests, organized cultivation according to a plan, better utilization of land; development of culturable waste, of animal husbandry; organization of fruit cultivation; development of bee-keeping, of fish cultivation; utilization of timber, fuel and grazing wealth of the forests. A national agricultural council is envisaged to execute and supervise the national agricultural plan.

Then follows the peasant's charter, assuring him of the right to work on the land, freeing him from debts, and guaranteeing to him numerous material, social, and health facilities.

A chapter on industry stresses the principle that industrial advancement is the key to a progressive standard of living.

All key industries are to be in the hands of the people's government, and therefore the large private capitalist is to be abolished, private monopoly forbidden, and forests, important industries, and mineral deposits to be worked only by the state. "Private small-scale enterprise will be allowed only in strict conformity with the need of the National Plan, and will be subject to supervision by the National Industrial Council."

The chapter on industry then includes the worker's charter, according to which every citizen has the right to demand work from the state, consistent with his honor and self-respect, the right to a higher standard of living than the mere subsistence level, the right to associate in trade unions, freedom to change occupation, an annual fortnight's leave with full pay, insurance, free medical facilities and education.

The problem of transport and distribution is another part of the *New Kashmir* program. The government is to take care of both. To safeguard the health of its citizens *New Kashmir* includes a national health charter; to foster education it plans the activities and the tasks of the national educational council; to develop housing it proposes to establish a national housing council. Banking, currency, and finance matters are nationalized under the control of the national economic council.

New Kashmir concludes with the women's charter, which assures the Kashmir woman "her just and rightful place in society" in the political, social, economic, legal, educational, and cultural life of the country.

New Kashmir offered, obviously, a detailed program in all spheres of life. The historic events of 1947 gave Sheikh Abdullah the opportunity to implement it.

The Lion of Kashmir

It has already been related how Sheikh Abdullah had been released from prison a few weeks before the struggle for Kashmir began and how, in October 1947, he had been named Head of the Emergency Administration by the Maharaja, once his fiercest enemy. In March 1948 the Maharaja was "advised" to end the emergency administration and nominate Sheikh Abdullah Prime Minister of Kashmir. The State Assembly was dissolved because its Muslim members represented exclusively the "enemy" party, the Muslim Conference. The Maharaja, living in an enforced exile in Bombay, lost all authority over internal affairs. As a result, Abdullah and his associates became the real and only rulers of the country.

The Kashmir people had every right to expect that their popular leader would live up to his promises. To them he was "the Lion of Kashmir"; to detached observers, a democrat and socialist. However, as years went by, his policy cast increasing shadows over the enlightened scene of his theory.

In 1947, before Kashmir was invaded, Sheikh Abdullah had called for the freedom of his country, before its accession to either India or Pakistan. In 1948, when he became Prime Minister, he declared that he would accept the will of his people. In May 1949, addressing himself in Srinagar to Pandit Nehru, he said, "I want you to believe that Kashmir is yours. No power in the world can separate us. Every Kashmiri feels that he is an Indian and that India is his homeland."[3] From time to time he clamored for complete independence for Kashmir, and on other occasions he declared that independence was not a practicable idea.

In March 1952 he stated, ". . . neither the Indian Parliament nor any other Parliament outside the State has any jurisdiction over our State. . . . No country—neither India nor Pakistan—can put spokes in the wheel of our progress."[4]

A few days later he envisioned Kashmir as a bridge between Pakistan and India which "can again be reunited and

[3] *The Statesman* (Calcutta), May 31, 1949.
[4] *Delhi Radio*, Indian Information Service, March 31, 1952.

become one country."[5] But two days later he considered relations between India and Kashmir "irrevocable and no force on earth can render us asunder."[6] Back to warn the Indian government, he declared "that the existence of Kashmir did not depend on Indian money, trade, or defence forces, and he did not expect any strings to be attached to Indian aid. Threats and taunts would not intimidate him into servile submission."[7]

In actual fact, he led Kashmir step by step farther away from India. One of his political rivals has characterized him as a "communalist in Kashmir, a Communist in Jammu, and a nationalist in India."[8]

The story of Sheikh Abdullah is a sad and sorry one. It is the story of a patriot, once passionately devoted to his people's welfare, but one whose patriotism was too shallow to reject the temptations of power. Once a fighter, he turned into an opportunist and, worse, a dictator who at the end found himself entangled in the web of his own methods and policy.

One-Party System

There are several political parties in the State of Jammu and Kashmir. Most of them, however, exist only on paper or function as a small group of intelligentsia. These are the Kisan Mazdoor Conference (in Kashmir), the Kashmir Socialist Party, the Democratic Socialist Party (in Jammu), the Kashmir Democratic Union (a small exiled group in New Delhi around Prem Nath Bazaz), and the Sikh Akali Party. One party of importance is the Praja Parishad (in Jammu), the only one which is in any real sense the opposition party to the one in power—the All Jammu and Kashmir National Conference.

[5] *The Hindu* (Madras), April 12, 1952.
[6] *Ibid.*, April 14, 1952.
[7] *The Times* (London), April 26, 1952.
[8] Pandit Premnath Dogra, from his statement in Madras. *The Hindu* (Madras), October 15, 1952.

In truth the National Conference is the only effective political party in Kashmir, with local organizations in almost every village. Although on the surface considerable progress has been achieved in local self-government, in reality it is the local National Conference organization which decides everything: who is going to be elected to what office, who will get a job, who will receive the supplies which it alone distributes.

The Statesman, a prominent Indian newspaper which consistently supported Sheikh Abdullah's policy, observed in March 1949, "There are signs of establishment of a police State—futile notices in restaurants forbidding political conversations when everybody talks politics; more 'Public Safety' prisoners than are healthy. . . ."[9] Some eighteen months later, Sir Owen Dixon observed during his mission that "the State government was exercising wide powers of arbitrary arrest."[10]

Such strict police measures would be justified in a period of war, and one would also understand that no freedom of action could be permitted for the members of a party which advocated accession to Pakistan even before the actual plebiscite campaign took place. But all observers who have had the opportunity to visit Kashmir recently agree that the rule of political persecution still continues and that the police terror perpetuates itself, though fighting has been stopped for six years.

There are two government-owned radio stations in the country, but with the exception of a few wealthier families and high state officials there are no privately owned sets. Instead, the government has established a community broadcasting system by installing 218 listening posts in Kashmir and 150 posts in Jammu. For lack of electric current the sets are on batteries which are regularly serviced from Srinagar and Jammu town. The sets are under the control of the

[9] *The Statesman* (Calcutta), March 1, 1949.
[10] S/1791 of September 15, 1950, p. 24.

local organization of the National Conference, all "tuned to radio Kashmir, fixed and sealed," as a governmental publication quite candidly and perhaps naïvely announced.[11]

A governmental Field Publicity Organization carries on a program of audio-visual education, the chief features of which are five vans, rigged with public address equipment, that travel from one village to another voicing for the most part political propaganda. There were in 1949 four daily newspapers in Srinagar, two English-written weeklies, and about twenty-five weeklies printed in the vernacular language. The total circulation of the dailies is reported to be about 100,000 copies; they are also reported to be essentially government-controlled or under strict censorship.

The government attaches great importance to education, and much has been done in this field. New schools have been opened, some 60 of them for children from three to five. In addition to the older The Prince of Wales College at Jammu, now called Gandhi Memorial College, a university was established in 1948 at Srinagar.

The government has set up a Textbook Advisory Board to prepare new textbooks for all kinds of schools, to be written in the spirit of *New Kashmir*. The government sources claim that up to 1950, 2,790,500 volumes of these textbooks have been published. Refresher courses have been organized to indoctrinate "New Teachers" in the spirit of *New Kashmir*. "A network of social education centers has been spread over the entire area of the State to educate public opinion in the ideology of New Kashmir," wrote Sheikh Abdullah.[12]

The Land Reform

The government introduced the most radical and far-reaching reforms in agriculture following its declared pol-

[11] *Jammu and Kashmir, 1947-1950*. Printed at the Ranbir Government Press, 1951, p. 32.

[12] Sheikh Mohammad Abdullah, *Jammu and Kashmir*. Printed at the Ranbir Government Press, p. 5.

icy of the "land to the tiller." The total cultivated area in the state was about 2,200,000 acres, most of which belonged to the Maharaja or his feudal vassals. The landlords rented the land to peasants under medieval conditions of exploitation. There were, generally speaking, three classes of such economically privileged persons: *jagirdars, muafidars,* and *mukarraries.*

The jagirdars owned vast areas of land, *jagirs,* and were paid by the tenants partly in crops, partly in cash. The muafidars, who were individuals such as pandits and faqirs, or institutions such as mosques and temples, received part of the land revenue. There were 396 jagirdars and muafidars in the state collecting 556,313 rupees annually.

The mukarraries received cash payments from the state treasury under various religious and nonreligious titles. There were 2,347 mukarraries in the state drawing 177,921 rupees a year. All these privileges were abolished by Sheikh Abdullah's government with the exception of some grants allotted to the religious leaders for church purposes.

The government also enacted laws for the protection of tenants. They could no longer be ejected from the land; a moratorium was declared on their debts; and they could have reinstated their rights in mortgaged property.[18] Previously the tenants had had to provide seed and agricultural implements and give the landlord 50 per cent of the crop. Now he was allowed to retain three-fourths of the production of rice, wheat, and oil-seeds, and two-thirds of the production of cotton and pulses and other agricultural products.

In April 1949 a committee was set up to prepare a plan for the transfer of land to the peasants. Eighteen months later, the Big Landed Estates Abolition Act superseded most of the preceding temporary measures and legalized a

[18] The Tenants (Stay of Ejectment) Ordinance, S. 2004 (1947). –The Tenancy (Amendment) Act, S. 2005 (1948).–The Realization of Debts (Temporary Stay) Ordinance, S. 2006 (1949).–The Distressed Debtors' Relief Act, S. 2006 (1949).–The Restitution of Mortgaged Properties Act, S. 2006 (1940).

sweeping land reform. The landlord was allowed to keep not more than 160 *kanals* (20 acres) of agricultural land, 8 kanals (1 acre) of land for residential use or vegetable gardening, 4 kanals (½ acre) as residential site, and 10 kanals (1.25 acres) of orchards—altogether 182 kanals (22.75 acres). Also, it was stipulated that the landlord must work on his land; otherwise it would be expropriated. Extremely interesting was the provision for the confiscation of the property of "enemy agents," these agents being largely defined as persons who had expressed a desire for Kashmir to join Pakistan.

This expropriated land was to be transferred in full ownership to the maximum of 160 kanals (20 acres) to the tenant, who was to pay the government a regular land tax and a temporary special tax, known as the "land development cess." All lands which were not under cultivation or not rented and in excess of 182 kanals were transferred to the government for redistribution or for collective farming. For the expropriated land the government was to pay to the former owner for the first year after expropriation an amount equal to 3/4 of the land revenue of the expropriated land, for the second year 2/3, and for the third year and subsequent years 1/2 of such land revenue, these sums never to exceed 3,000 rupees a year. The tiller is not allowed to transfer the newly acquired property without governmental permission. No one other than a Kashmir citizen is entitled to acquire land. If a proprietor or tiller dies without heir, or transfers the land or any interest therein in contravention of the law, or sublets it continuously for two harvests, he loses the right of ownership, which lapses to the government.

In most cases the government failed to receive the land tax from the peasants for the simple reason that they had no cash with which to pay. As a logical consequence, former owners rarely had any indemnity paid to them—for precisely the same reason. On March 26, 1952, the Constituent Assembly relieved itself of this embarrassment by deciding to confiscate all landed estates without any compensation.

The land reform laws changed drastically the agricultural and social structure of Kashmir. The feudal system was abolished, landlordism disappeared, and thousands of peasants living before in virtual slavery became landholders. According to Kashmir government sources, by the end of March 1953, 188,775 acres of land were transferred to 153,-399 tillers. This would indicate that each peasant therefore received an average of 1.23 acres of land under this program. In fact, however, many landless peasants received considerably less than the average, because many local officials were given more and better land, sometimes even above the maximum of 20 acres.

The government also established collective farms on lands which were not distributed among the peasants. Collective farms have been established at such places as Gopalpora, Shalteng, and Harwan, and by April 1953, 87,500 acres of land were government-owned.

The government endeavored to increase the production of land by repairing old irrigation canals and constructing new ones. The Awantipura Canal was built at the cost of 8 million rupees to irrigate more than 4,000 acres, as well as to increase electrification.

All these measures seem impressive, freeing as they do the Kashmiri peasant from the unbearable burden of complete economic dependence on the landlord. They signaled a new era of peasant emancipation. However, on second thought one finds that in practice there is a striking similarity between these measures and the agricultural policy of Communist countries. The former proprietors are not guaranteed any indemnity, even in principle, though lack of funds may have justified a moratorium on paying the indemnity for some years. The peasant is not allowed to sell his land. He is given such a small strip to cultivate that as soon as his first enthusiasm has paled, he comes face to face with the hard fact that he simply cannot live on its production. Meanwhile, in the vicinity of his one-acre "field" a collective farm is established and is given various privileges, technical and financial, which he does not enjoy. Under the circumstances, then, he is led to realize that it is often better to join the collective farm than to toil on his own property. Exactly the same method was applied in Communist Poland, Hungary, Bulgaria, and Yugoslavia. It is unlikely that this could be coincidental, nor does it seem unfounded to assume that the member of the Land Reform Committee, Ghulam Sadiq, got his inspiration for this policy from his fellow comrades.

The practice of collecting taxes in kind and of obligatory redemption of agricultural products has been widely criticized. "Government officials are harassing cultivators and petty landholders to procure mujawaza [taxes in kind] and surplus food grains," wrote a newspaper in Srinagar. ". . . From the complaints which are being received from the kisans [peasants] of various areas, it is evident that in procurement of mujawaza . . . and surplus paddy, the poor kisans are being subjected to inhuman treatment. Sometimes they are forced to sell all of their belongings in order to pay government taxes. A number of complaints depict very horrible conditions. It appears that human feelings and gentlemanliness are being sacrificed at the altar of barbarity as if law is helpless before these corrupt and barbaric officers. Money is being illegally extorted from poor people in every town and village. The local officers were resorting to all sorts of irregularities in order to deprive petty landowners of their produce. Mujawaza has been realized from kisans of Badgam tehsil [district] twice or thrice. The Revenue officials have made the life of the cultivators extremely miserable. . . . The Police have even surpassed the Revenue authorities in barbarities. In one case a tehsildar [district official] had issued warrants of arrests for a person and when on payment of mujawaza his warrants were cancelled, the police refused to let him off without receiving [a] bribe which the poor fellow could not pay and had to remain in prison. In Kulgam tehsil one old woman had to sell her cow in order to pay mujawaza. . . . The government is not paying any attention to redress the grievances of the people whose demands have failed to evoke any interest in government quarters."[14]

Another report evaluating practical aspects of the land reform stated, "Ironically enough, the beneficiaries [of the land reform] themselves have yet to reap the full advantage out of their ownership which is currently operating more as a liability than as asset; for the cancellation of agricultural indebtedness, with the stroke of a pen, has left a serious void in the rural credit system which the regime has been unable to fill, with the result that more often than not, the new owner has no money to buy a bullock or agricultural implements with."[15]

Thousands of people heavily indebted to moneylenders profited from the government policy of investigation of the nature of debts. Debt Conciliation Boards disposed in less than three years of 48,000 applications; debts were scaled down by about 80 per cent, from 11.1 million to 2.43 million rupees.[16]

Kashmir economy was dealt a heavy blow when its chief source of income, forestry, was disrupted by the division of the country. Timber which once was economically floated down the rivers to Pakistan now had to be transported by trucks on the road to Pathankot in India. The government claims, however, to have restored the timber trade to the

[14] *Al-Haque* (Srinagar), as quoted in *Kashmir Affairs* (Rawalpindi), Vol. v, No. 12, March 21, 1953 (5 months later, on August 14, further publication of *Al-Haque* was banned).

[15] *The Hindustan Times* (Delhi), May 23, 1953.

[16] *Indiagram*, No. 218, May 21, 1953 (Washington, D.C.: Embassy of India).

extent that in 1949 it yielded 5.5 million rupees to the state treasury in comparison with 2.9 million in 1947.

The Policy of Nationalization

Considerable governmental support was given to the silk industry through the importation of silkworm eggs which were distributed among rearers and through three government-owned silk-weaving factories. Other industries include manufacture of wool, sports goods, drugs, matches, and carpets. The available sources of information do not indicate which of these factories are government-owned, but they all depend on governmentally distributed supplies and marketing.

Special attention is given to cottage industries, such as hand-loom weaving, hosiery, furniture, ceramics, paper manufacturing, embroidery, and papier-mâché. Artisans of these industries are organized into industrial societies, Inducos. The government owns two printing houses, Ranbir and Partab Government Press.

In the program of reconstruction old public buildings, bridges, and roads were repaired, new buildings and telephone lines were erected. Several projects are in the stage of planning.

Great emphasis is put on the cooperative movement, "with the object mainly of bringing the entire village life within its fold."[17] The purpose of cooperatives is to scale down the debts of the members, spread the reduced debt over a number of years, lease the expropriated land to the members, finance crops, supply daily commodities, and facilitate the marketing. In 1948 there were 222 multipurpose cooperative societies in the country with 25,673 members; in 1949 the figures rose to 347 and 56,499 respectively. Statistics for 1950 give the figures of 1,731 agricultural cooperatives, 386 purchase and sale cooperatives, and 378 non-agri-

[17] *Jammu and Kashmir, 1947-50, op.cit.*, p. ix.

cultural credit cooperatives. Basically, this policy would be sound and of great help to poor peasants whose association in cooperatives would substitute for their financial misery. But in practice it turned into an instrument of the National Conference party politics. Moreover, as the government itself had to admit in the summer of 1953, the cooperatives completely collapsed because of "corruption and maladministration" of governmental officials.

All foreign trade is done through the governmental Kashmir Peoples' Cooperative Society, K.P.C.S. It is handled by Emporia, with depots in New Delhi, Bombay, Simla, Lucknow, Madras, and Calcutta. Nationalized bazaars are organized for trade within the country.

The transport is managed by the government's Transport Department, which owns some 500 vehicles, most of which operate on the mountainous road connecting Srinagar and Jammu town with India. All commodities and other supplies are distributed by the Supplies and Control Department. Food is rationed, and its distribution is under governmental control.

The Kashmir Chamber of Commerce (still mostly of Hindu membership) submitted in the spring of 1953 a memorandum to the government in which it asked for immediate abolition of state trading; effective decontrol of all commodities; introduction of free and healthy competition in purchase, distribution, and sale; removal of restrictions on private transport; and cancellation of existing monopolistic licenses in favor of a few individuals and firms. It asserted that the "absence of free competition in transport has enabled the government to charge arbitrarily, thereby increasing the price level by about 50 per cent more so far as freight is concerned and throwing scores of people depending on private transport to penury and starvation." The president of the Chamber described the "miserable plight of the people of Kashmir as a result of the 'dreadful' controls and State trading run by certain departments of the government."[18]

One of the important sources of income used to be the tourist trade. It gave a living to boatmen, cooks, artisans, owners of ponies. In the old days some 30,000 tourists visited Kashmir every year, providing an income for some 200,000 people. This source of revenue has dropped considerably. In 1949, 3,700 visitors came to Kashmir, of whom only 426 were non-Indians; in 1950 the figure rose to 5,355. In July 1954 Indian sources reported, however, that, up to that date, 21,000 tourists had already visited Kashmir.

The state's finances had been necessarily unbalanced, the budget for 1952-1953, for example, being in deficit by 700,000 rupees. The financial year 1954-1955, however, claimed a budget surplus of 48 million rupees. This probably could not be achieved without material help from India, from which, according to a statement of Bakshi Ghulam Mohammed, Kashmir has received since the signing of the instrument of accession, in October 1947, 86.15 million rupees.[19] Also, the government, paralleling the Indian Five Year Plan, prepared a plan of its own for the period 1951-1952 to 1955-1956. It provides for 100 million rupees expenditure, of which the Kashmir government is to provide 30 million and the rest is expected to be met by the government of India. The main undertaking is to construct a tunnel through the Banihal Pass at an elevation of 7,000 feet. One and a half miles in length, it will be the longest tunnel in Asia and will cost 30 million rupees. Fifty-six million rupees are also earmarked for the construction of roads and canals as well as for flood control and hydroelectric plants.

Undoubtedly, many of these projects will remain on paper for a long time, their principal importance having been

[18] *Hindustan Times* (Delhi), May 2, 1953.
[19] *The Hindu Weekly Review* (Madras) and *The Statesman* (Calcutta), April 5, 1954.

their propaganda value. Even so, the changes, especially in agriculture, have been remarkable. It would be wrong to judge them according to Western standards and principles of economic liberalism. It may well be that the task of raising the standard of living of a primitive society must be based upon active intervention by the state in economic and social affairs and the assumption of responsibility for planning and implementing production. Such a society often has no spontaneous incentive to improve living conditions; usually it lacks capital and frequently will not admit foreign investment. But if the government completely ignores those guarantees of political rights which it solemnly gives to its citizens, if it introduces a one-party system, and if it monopolizes all means of education and cultural enlightenment, it inevitably becomes a totalitarian dictatorship with all power concentrated in the hands of a few leaders.

If one compares the program and policy of the Communist satellites in Europe with *New Kashmir* and the practices of the Kashmiri government, one cannot escape the conclusion that Kashmir has already reached the first step toward communization.

Drifting from India

Simultaneously with these political and economic trends, Kashmir has also undergone radical development in her constitutional position. Principally through the shrewd maneuvering of Sheikh Abdullah and his associates, she has succeeded in securing privileged rights within the Republic of India which no other Indian state enjoys.

It will be remembered that according to the promise given by Lord Mountbatten as Viceroy of India and by Nehru's government, the Princely States were assured of retaining all powers and asked to hand over to the central government only foreign affairs, defense, and communications. These provisions were stipulated in detail in the instruments of accession signed by the Maharajas. But almost inevitably the Princely States soon found themselves stripped of all powers and their states amalgamated within individual provinces of the Indian Union.

Kashmir, however, did not fuse with the Indian Union, but retained rights of autonomy. The Maharaja of Kashmir in one sense followed the fate of his princely colleagues, but he was deprived of his powers, not by the government of India, but rather by his own Prime Minister, Sheikh Abdullah. The Maharaja, partly because he was unable to exercise his prerogatives from exile and partly as a protest against Sheikh Abdullah's policy, issued on June 20, 1949 a proclamation through which he turned over to his son, the Yuvaraj Shri Karansinghji Bahadur, all his princely rights. From that time until the summer of 1953 it was Sheikh Abdullah's systematic policy, using this son as a figurehead, to keep and maintain Kashmir autonomy against any infringement by the Indian government.

In September 1949 the National Conference met in Srinagar. Celebrations were held, meetings organized, and resolutions passed. The Prime Minister of India, Jawaharlal Nehru, was present. "During the entire celebration when Srinagar wore a festive appearance with flags . . . the Indian National Flag was conspicuous by its absence. The State Flag of the ruling dynasty has practically disappeared. . . . The flag of the National Conference which has been adopted as the State flag is perhaps rightly flown all over the place," wrote an Indian newspaper.[20] The meeting passed a resolution reaffirming the National Conference decision not to accept any limitation on Kashmir autonomy. It expressed faith in the *New Kashmir* program and appealed "to the freedom-loving peoples of the whole world, to the indivisible fraternity of all true democrats in all lands to lend their moral and material support to our cause." Significantly enough, it also stated that "nobody will . . .

[20] *The Hindu* (Madras), September 29, 1949.

deny that ugly communal elements keep raising heads in India. . . ."[21]

Many politicians in New Delhi expressed dissatisfaction with these manifestations of Sheikh Abdullah's independent-mindedness and pointed to the fact that it was Indian money which was footing the bills for this Kashmir government, which now, with the assistance of these same grants, was drifting away from its Indian protector. The Indian government attempted several times, but with no success, to convince Sheikh Abdullah to fall in line with other Princely States and merge with India.

On October 17, 1949, the Constituent Assembly in Delhi passed a new article of the Constitution, according to which constitutional provisions concerning the Princely States do not apply to the State of Jammu and Kashmir and stating further that certain specified matters can be legislated by the Indian Parliament only in concurrence with the state's government.[22] The spokesman of the Indian government, G. Ayyangar, who defended the amendment in the face of opposition from several quarters, expressed the hope "that in due course Jammu and Kashmir will become ripe for the same sort of integration as has taken place in the case of other States."[23] If Mr. Ayyangar had expected to woo the Kashmiris with such generosity of spirit, he was sadly disappointed. Sheikh Abdullah, now even more firmly entrenched in power, only reaffirmed his position and his policy of autonomy from India.

The young Maharaja-Regent on occasion attempted to slow down the policy of radical reforms. But Sheikh Abdullah always moved with vigor. On one occasion particularly he warned the Maharaja that not only would he never be allowed to return to Kashmir but also that if his son persisted "in seeking the advice of reactionaries and com-

---

[21] *Ibid.*, September 24, 1949.
[22] Art. 238,370 of the Constitution of India.
[23] From G. Ayyangar speech in the Parliament, October 17, 1949.

munalists, I can only tell him . . . that his future will not be far different from that of his father."[24]

By eliminating the Maharaja from any voice in Kashmir affairs, Sheikh Abdullah's government followed the policy of giving to its own position an appearance of legality and democratic procedure. In October 1950 the General Council of the National Conference passed a resolution asking for elections for a Constituent Assembly which would determine "the future shape and affiliations of the State of Jammu and Kashmir." As could have been expected, Pakistan's Foreign Minister, Sir Zafrulla Khan, raised a protest with the Security Council against this policy, which in his view prejudiced the final determination of whether Kashmir would join India or Pakistan.[25] The Security Council affirmed in its resolution of March 30, 1951 that the convening of a Constituent Assembly and any action concerning the future of the state would not be in accordance with the previous agreement on plebiscite.[26] The Indian government, though insisting that the Constituent Assembly could not be physically prevented from expressing its opinion about the future of Kashmir, declared that it would not be bound by this opinion.

The government of Sheikh Abdullah was not discouraged by the Security Council resolution. In May 1951 the Yuvaraj issued a proclamation convoking a Constituent Assembly on the basis of free elections by all citizens of the state over 21 years of age by means of a direct and secret ballot. The elections were prepared in the summer of 1951 and were held in September and October on three consecutive dates. People were to elect 75 deputies, 45 of whom were to represent Kashmir and Ladakh, and 30 Jammu. In Kashmir and Ladakh the elections, if they can be so called, were fairly simple. Forty-three candidates were elected unop-

[24] *The Hindu* (Madras), April 8, 1951.
[25] S/1942 of December 14, 1950.
[26] S/2017/Rev. 1 of March 30, 1951.

posed one week before the election date, and two independent candidates withdrew under pressure later. There
was actually no balloting. In Jammu the authorities rejected
the nomination papers of the Praja Parishad, the opposition
party, in 13 constituencies on the pretext that they were
not properly presented or, as the leaders of the party put
it, "on the flimsiest grounds and under pressure from the
government."[27] Thus, before the election date Sheikh Abdullah was assured of 58 friendly members in the Constituent Assembly. Three days before the elections in Jammu, on
October 12, the Praja Parishad announced a boycott of the
elections and accused the government of "illegal practices
and official interference, wholesale rejections of Parishad
nomination papers."[28] This gave to the National Conference
another 15 seats. The last two contestants dropped out at
the last moment. Before the polling began, therefore,
Sheikh Abdullah's followers were sure of the full 75 seats.
No dictator could do better. Nehru stated that he was "sure
that the way people had voted showed clearly that they
were with the National Conference and with India."[29]

The Constituent Assembly met on October 31, 1951.
Its chairman declared, ". . . Kashmir was not interested in
the United Nations, which was the victim of international
intrigues. The path of Kashmir and U.N. lay in different
directions. . . . It is well known that the National Conference had gone to the people of the State with a programme
of accession to India and this programme of accession had
been ratified by every single adult voter of the State."[30]
Nehru sent to the opening session of the Assembly greetings
and best wishes.

A few days later, on November 20, the Constituent Assembly passed "The Jammu and Kashmir Constitution Act,

[27] *The Times of India* (Bombay), September 27, 1951.
[28] *The Times* (London), October 13, 1951.
[29] *The Hindu* (Madras), October 19, 1951.
[30] *Ibid.*, November 1, 1951.

1951," which stripped the Maharaja of virtually all powers, allowing him to act only on advice of the government, which, in turn, was made responsible to the Assembly. The law reaffirmed the principle of Kashmir's autonomy in all affairs with the exception of defense, foreign affairs, and communications. Sheikh Abdullah, now assured "constitutionally" of a supreme position in the state, opened a political offensive.

In March 1952 he appealed to the Azad people to make "positive efforts" to liberate themselves "from the present Pakistani rulers whose attempt always is to mislead you and keep you away from knowing the true facts about us." He promised them to "continue our efforts to liberate you."[31]

Sheikh Abdullah also opened his guns against India. To put his position on autonomy beyond doubt he made a speech on April 10 at Ranbirsinghpura in Jammu in which he criticized India for communalism and warned against applying the Indian Constitution to Kashmir in all respects. He qualified these attempts as "unrealistic, childish, and savouring of lunacy," and added, "No one can deny that communal spirit still exists in India. Many Kashmiris are apprehensive as to what will happen to them and their position if, for instance, something happens to Pandit Nehru."[32]

The speech caused an uproar in India, and Nehru, who otherwise had been giving public and continuous support to the policy of his long-time friend, declared he didn't like it either, especially its tone. Although Sheikh Abdullah tried to appease Nehru with another speech, this one more carefully worded, he nevertheless refused to come to Delhi for several months. He did send his emissaries to prepare the ground for an agreement which would stipulate the privileged autonomous position of Kashmir in the Indian Union.

[31] *The National Standard* (Bombay), March 12, 1952.
[32] *The Hindu* (Madras), April 12, 1952.

The Kashmir Scene Changes

On July 24, 1952, Jawaharlal Nehru announced in the House of the People the terms of an agreement which he had signed with Sheikh Abdullah after a week of negotiations. The agreement gave to Kashmir special rights which no other constituent unit of India enjoys.

It was agreed that the hereditary ruler would be replaced by a Head of the State who would be elected for a term of five years by the Constituent Assembly and "recognized" by the President of India. In all other states of India, this function is held by governors who are nominated by the President. Fundamental rights that are guaranteed by the Indian Constitution apply to Kashmir, subject to the provision that they will not encroach upon the program of land reform, including the expropriation of land without compensation, nor must they hamper the state's measures concerning its security. The government of India further agreed that the Kashmir legislature "shall have the power to define and regulate the rights and privileges of the permanent residents of the State, more especially in regard to the acquisition of immovable property, appointments to services and like matters." This means that although Kashmiris enjoy the same rights as Indian citizens all over India, Indian citizens have no right to acquire land in Kashmir.

The jurisdiction of the Indian Supreme Court was to be limited, as regards Kashmir, to inter-state disputes, to the fundamental rights which were applied in the state, and to matters of defense, foreign affairs, and communications. The government of India also wished the Supreme Court to be the final court of appeal in all civil and criminal cases, but Sheikh Abdullah wanted to leave the question open.

The national flag of India was to be recognized by the State of Jammu and Kashmir as supreme, but the Kashmir state flag was to be maintained. In financial matters, the government of India would have preferred an integration, but Sheikh Abdullah wished again to reconsider the matter.

The most important provision of the agreement between

Sheikh Abdullah and Jawaharlal Nehru concerned the emergency powers of the President of India. According to Article 352 of the Constitution, the President has the right to declare a state of emergency in case of invasion, external danger, or internal disturbances. The agreement provided that in the latter case the President's power can be applied in Kashmir only "at the request or with the concurrence of the government of the State." This would mean that in case of a violent uprising in Kashmir, the President of India would have no right to declare a state of emergency and to intervene unless the Srinagar government asked him to do so.

The Nehru-Sheikh agreement met with severe criticism in some Indian newspapers and parliamentarian circles. They were concerned both with the fate of the Hindus in Jammu and with the privileged position Sheikh Abdullah had managed to carve out for himself. They wished to see the state integrated with India as were all other constituent units of the Republic. Pandit Nehru, however, defended the agreement against the critics, pointing to the necessity of having confidence in Abdullah's friendship towards India and of acting in good faith. In this he was to be within one year gravely disappointed.

Sheikh Abdullah now set to work to put the agreement he had signed with Nehru into force. First, he wished to solve the problem of the headship of the state. The function was offered to the Regent-Maharaja, Yuvaraj Karan Singh, apparently in an attempt to ease the transfer of a hereditary rule to an elected Head of State and to alleviate the misgivings of the Hindu minority in the state. The opposite was achieved. Many Hindu leaders visited the Yuvaraj and advised him not to accept the new function. They expressed to him the fear that he would serve only as a puppet for the Sheikh's policy. Their statements were published in the Jammu and Indian papers and once more stirred up the spirit of opposition. Nehru had to visit Srinagar in September to counterbalance this opinion, advising the Yuvaraj to accept the office.

On November 12, 1952, the Constituent Assembly in Srinagar formally adopted an amendment to the Constitution replacing the Maharaja rulership by the function of an elected Head of State, Sadar-i-Riyasat. Two days later the twenty-one-year-old Yuvaraj, Prince-Regent, was elected to the office. "His Highness" became Mr. Karan Singh. His election was then formally recognized by the President of India. This act brought to fulfillment the abolition of the hereditary rule of the hated Dogras, a tyranny which had cursed the State of Jammu and Kashmir since 1846.

Separatism in Jammu

No one could realize that the fanfares of Abdullah's victory over the medieval rule of the Maharaja and over the control of the central government in Delhi carried the first undertones of his political doom. Lack of coherence between individual regions of the state now found a serious outlet in Kashmiri politics.

The opposition party in Jammu, the Praja Parishad, appeared only to be waiting for an opportune moment. Its field was limited to eastern Jammu, where the majority of the population, after the expulsion and escape of many Muslims, is Hindu and Sikh. Economically it represented that group of wealthy people who, as the Maharaja's active supporters, once enjoyed the privileged position of landlords but who have been dispossessed by the land reform, and of government officials and businessmen. Politically, however, it found its principal support in the great majority of the non-Muslims who were becoming increasingly worried about Abdullah's tendency to draw the State of Jammu and Kashmir away from India. In the Jammu district alone, the Praja Parishad had 16,000 members while the National Conference had 6,000.[33]

[33] *The Times of India* (Bombay), September 12, 1952.

The platform of the Praja Parishad dates back to the beginning of 1949. Soon after the fighting stopped, the Hindus began to worry about their fate under the Abdullah government. In March 1949 Mihir Lal Chattopadhaja, a member of the Indian Constituent Assembly, addressed a report to the government of India based on his visit to Jammu. He stated that all Hindus were convinced that in a plebiscite 90 per cent of the Muslims would vote for Pakistan and that the Hindus, who once had been supported in their position by the Maharaja, were concerned about his gradual elimination from power.[34]

The Praja Parishad led several demonstrations against Sheikh Abdullah's government; and the more apparent his policy of estrangement from India became, the more virulent grew the Hindu opposition. The demonstrations were always suppressed and many people arrested. In February 1952, after a particularly violent outburst, a curfew was imposed on Jammu town for 72 hours, the army was called in to break up the demonstration, and a government communiqué described the situation as "extremely critical." The chairman of the Praja Parishad, Premnath Dogra, was among the hundreds who were arrested.[35]

The movement was not halted, however, and when the Nehru-Abdullah agreement was signed in the summer of 1952, it reached a climax. Its leaders demanded full merger of the state with India, and they threatened that, should this not be achieved, they would detach Jammu from Kashmir and make it an integral part of India. They found some support among a few members of the Indian Parliament but were openly and severely rebuffed by Jawaharlal Nehru. Sheikh Abdullah pointed to the seriousness of the situation in a broadcast on September 1, 1952. According to him, the whole noncommunal structure of the state was in danger.

[34] *Dawn* (Karachi), March 30, 1949, reprinting the report published in Calcutta's *Nation*, March 19, 1949.
[35] *The Hindu* (Madras), February 12, 1952.

The Kashmir Scene Changes

In December 1952, according to the government's admission, another wave of demonstrations precipitated the arrest of nearly 500 persons, and 213 rioters were sent to prison.

At the beginning of 1953 Robert Trumbull reported, ". . . dissatisfaction . . . is erupting into almost daily violence with mob demonstrations against authorities. Five hundred demonstrators—unofficial sources put the figure higher—have been arrested within recent weeks, and several persons have been killed in clashes with the police."[36] Among those arrested was Premnath Dogra, who was sentenced to 18 months at hard labor.

Separatism in Ladakh

These feelings were not limited to Jammu. They found similar expression in Ladakh, though not in such a violent and organized form since there the Buddhist population is widely scattered and of a rather passive, peaceful temper. On the other hand, such unrest is particularly dangerous because of Ladakh's proximity to Communist Tibet and Sinkiang.

Ladakh, as noted before, is divided into two parts, the northern being Pakistan-held and the districts (*tehsils*) of Leh and Kargil, Indian-held. The people of Ladakh live in appalling poverty. For centuries it has been isolated from the outside world, dependent entirely on the will of its Buddhist leaders, the lamas. Land was the property of the church and was rented to the peasants under most exploitative conditions. Ninety per cent of the Ladakhis were in heavy debt, paying 25 per cent interest. Porters, cooks, owners of ponies and mules, and local merchants used to draw some income from caravans passing through the capital, Leh, on their way along the rugged trails from India to Yarkand in Sinkiang and Lhasa in Tibet. With the communization of China and Tibet, however, and as a conse-

[36] *The New York Times*, February 2, 1953.

quence of the Indo-Pakistan dispute over Kashmir, this trade has been brought to a standstill. Were it not for the Indian army, which garrisons at Leh, the Ladakhis would find a rupee a rare sight indeed.

The government of Sheikh Abdullah, which technically was responsible for Ladakh, was trying to bring some measure of improvement to the almost hopeless condition of its people. A high school was opened at Leh and a few elementary schools were founded; telephone communications were established (mainly for military purposes), forests taken away from the church, and some other development undertaken. Plans have been prepared for the construction of roads and for irrigation and basic medical services, but they remain on paper for lack of funds. There is no electricity in the country, and the price of kerosene oil is beyond the means of the would-be customer.[37]

Land reform has made little progress in Ladakh. Figures differ on the scope of the land distribution, but probably no more than 10,000 acres have been affected. The major part remains in the hands of monasteries, since the government in Srinagar does not dare to move against this stronghold of political and economic power.

The Buddhist leaders showed resentment against the Srinagar policy. They objected to the centralizing tendencies of the Abdullah government and complained that Ladakh was left without economic help. The Buddhist Ladakhis would not wish to join Pakistan, but at the same time they resented being "governed" from Srinagar. As do the Jammu Hindus, they prefer to be autonomous within India. The problem of the Kashmir Muslims is to them both remote and of small concern.

The lamas in Leh play their own political game on the chessboard of competing interests in this crucially exposed area. Spiritually, they owe allegiance to the Dalai Lama at

[37] For details see Sheikh Mohammad Abdullah, *Ladakh Today*, Kashmir Bureau of Information, New Delhi, 1952.

Lhasa, but at the same time they are aware of the fate of their superior, who yielded to Chinese Communist control. So to keep their precarious position in balance they flirt with the government in Srinagar, opposing at the same time such policies as land reform. Attempts at pressure from Srinagar are answered with coy hints that "across the border lies Tibet—perhaps here lies their destiny."

The Head Lama of Ladakh, Kushuk-Bakola, is a member of the Constituent Assembly in Srinagar, but from time to time he likes to assert his independent position and to promote the slogan "Ladakh for Ladakhis." Towards the end of 1949, however, he saw the Communist shadow sliding over Tibet. He then declared that "the people of Ladakh were growing anxious about the security of their land and their culture and religion. This menace from outside is threatening not only Ladakh but the whole of Jammu and Kashmir State,"[38] and pleaded with Srinagar for appropriate defense measures. When, however, he began to realize his position between the "devil" of land reform and the "deep blue sea" of a Communist rule in Tibet that might engulf him, he began to put increased emphasis on the claim of autonomy within India. But should this fail, he warned in June of 1952, Ladakh may seek political union with Tibet "as a last course left to us."[39]

The Communists have been watching the situation in Ladakh with keen interest. As early as 1947 Robert Trumbull reported that according to an American visitor to Ladakh there had been some pro-Russian activity developed at Leh and a few agents from Sinkiang were arrested there.[40] Other reports have also appeared in other newspapers from time to time about Chinese Communists infiltrating in these areas.

Justice William O. Douglas recorded in his admirable

[38] *The Hindu* (Madras), November 11, 1949.
[39] *The Christian Science Monitor*, June 27, 1952.
[40] *The New York Times*, October 29, 1947.

book the conversation he held with the Head Lama of Ladakh on the subject of Communist activities. There was no Communist activity in Ladakh, the Lama told him, and the Soviet Union showed little interest in the happenings in the country, and yet he expressed concern over events in the making. "The Communist strategy in the Buddhist world is first to get control of the church. That requires not propaganda but control of the ecclesiastical hierarchy," he said. "The Communists will use every means to get control of the wealth of the monasteries. My fear is that they will succeed. . . . The monasteries will then become so poor that they cannot carry on their work, or they will become dependent on the Communist government for their financial support. . . . The Dalai Lama is the spiritual head of the Mahayan school of Buddhism, which embraces China, Japan, Mongolia, Nepal, Tibet, Ladakh, Bhutan, Lahul, Sikkim, and Spiti. Buddhists in these countries look to him as Catholics look to the Pope in Rome. If the Communists control the Dalai Lama, they are in a fair way of controlling that part of the world."[41]

People who have observed the methods of the Communist governments which brought the Orthodox Churches to subservience in Russia, Yugoslavia, Rumania, and Bulgaria would not be prone to underestimate the seriousness of the predictions made by the Head Lama of Ladakh. When considered in conjunction with other factors, they appear all the more alarming. To the poverty-stricken people of Ladakh, for whom there is small hope for immediate improvement, the apparent economic activity in near-by Communist Sinkiang must be attractive. On top of this, the border between China and Ladakh is not internationally defined—an open invitation to plot and intrigue. And if help were needed, all Ladakhis know that the Indian military bases are hundreds of miles away.

[41] William O. Douglas, *Beyond the High Himalayas*. Doubleday and Company, New York, 1952, pp. 213-214.

The Kashmir Scene Changes

At the very moment, therefore, that Sheikh Abdullah was reviewing with satisfaction the autonomous status he had wrested from the central government in Delhi for his country, his hands were full with the separatist tendencies in Jammu and the centrifugal trend of thinking in Ladakh. His own policy appeared to have heaped upon him a series of incongruities and contradictions.

Here was a Hindu as Head of State in a predominantly Muslim country, with even the Hindu minority opposed to the policy which had produced him. Here was his government, claiming to represent the entire nation, but with two segments of it, the Jammu Hindus and the Ladakh Buddhists, clamoring for separation from Kashmir and for integration with India. Here was the Sheikh himself, claiming to be the uncontested leader of the Kashmir Muslims, while in spite of the benefits he had brought to the people, the all-pervading force remained the spirit of Islam, a spirit which continued to demand unification with their Muslim brothers.

All these contradictions and incongruities soon found an explosive outburst which buried their symbol and product, Sheikh Abdullah himself. The agreement which he had brought triumphantly to Srinagar proved to be a year later his political grave.

The Misery of Victory

Soon after he had begun to implement his summer agreement with Nehru, Sheikh Abdullah was accused of ignoring those sections which confirmed Kashmir's ties with India. The opposition elements in Jammu and Ladakh gathered new strength, and in the spring of 1953 there burst out, more particularly in Jammu, an open and well-organized action.

The Praja Parishad led demonstrations in various towns in Jammu, and its leaders organized sabotage in factories and the blowing up of bridges and governmental buildings.

Police detachments from Indian Punjab had to be called upon to assist the local police in maintaining law and order. Demonstrators were arrested in the hundreds. Nehru termed the movement "most pernicious and malignant" in its "narrow, bigoted, reactionary and revivalist approach,"[42] and pointed to its dangerous repercussions. In this evaluation he was probably correct, but in spite of this, the movement, as a foreign observer put it, ". . . has gone deep into the rural areas where the masses take part in Parishad processions and demonstrations and stubbornly endure police baton charges and tear-gas attacks."[43]

Similarly in Ladakh, the Head Lama revived his tactic of looking toward Ladakh's autonomy within India and of flirting with Tibet. In an interview he stressed, "It should be clear . . . that there shall be no place for us in a virtually independent Kashmir. The only bond that linked Ladakh with Kashmir in the past was the Maharaja. With the abolition of hereditary rulership, that bond has, however, broken." He complained against the Kashmir police for perpetrating atrocities on Ladakhi peoples, "many of whom have begun to look towards changes in Tibet as a solution of their ills." In the spring of 1953 he pleaded "for complete integration with India," but at the same time did not fail to mention that the "Ladakhis were distinct people from Kashmiris—racially, linguistically, and culturally."[44]

Sheikh Abdullah chose to face these growing threats of disintegration by a policy of blowing both hot and cold. He was prepared to make some concessions to the separatists, but simultaneously he tightened the police regime and even threatened to break away from India.

[42] From Jawaharlal Nehru's speech in the House of the People; *The Hindu* (Madras), April 26, 1953.

[43] *The Times* (London), January 24, 1953.

[44] Quotations are in sequence from U.P.I. as quoted in *Kashmir Affairs* (Rawalpindi), No. 49, December 6, 1952; *The Times* (London), December 24, 1952; *Times of India* (Bombay), April 30, 1953.

The Kashmir Scene Changes

The Basic Principles Committee of the Constituent Assembly was instructed to study the idea of extending autonomy to each province of the state. A plan was prepared to establish five autonomous regions: the Vale, Jammu, Gilgit, Ladakh, and a region consisting of the districts of Mirpur, Rajaouri, Poonch, and Muzaffarabad (though it must be remembered that Gilgit, part of Ladakh and of the last composite region, are under the pro-Pakistani administration). The Vale and Jammu would each have a separate legislature and a council of ministers for local affairs. Ladakh would be ruled centrally with an elected advisory district council. The state's name would be "Autonomous Federated Unit of the Republic of India."[45] Subsequent events prevented Abdullah from materializing this atomization of Kashmir.

The proposed reform failed to reconcile the opposition forces. Rather, they were encouraged by the happenings in India. Three communalist parties, Hindu Mahasabha, Jan Sangh, and Ram Rajya Parishad solidarized themselves with the Praja Parishad movement and opened a nationwide campaign of *satyagraha* for full incorporation of Kashmir within India. Their strength should not be overestimated, as they have been more vocal than popular among the Indian people; and yet even Jawaharlal Nehru, who has been courageously combating the ugly communalist elements in Indian politics, could not ignore their voice altogether, the more so since his own party, the National Congress, has not remained entirely deaf to their cries.

The leaders of Jan Sangh went so far as to appeal to their followers to organize militant groups, *jathas,* and to "march to Jammu." Abdullah answered by repressive measures in Jammu and by deliberately relaxing his vigilance in the Vale of Kashmir. In May of 1953 he issued an ordinance forbidding, under imprisonment, any person to enter the state without special permit. He issued a ban on public meetings. Two papers were suppressed and others were put under

[45] *The Hindu* (Madras), April 27, 1953.

strict censorship. Meanwhile, in the Vale of Kashmir an opposition group, Kashmir Awami Conference, was allowed to come into existence within the ranks of the National Conference. Workers, stricken by unemployment and hunger, organized protest meetings, and pro-Pakistani elements, encouraged by the happenings in Jammu and by Abdullah's wavering attitude in Srinagar, managed for a short while to demonstrate in larger numbers.

The news of a forthcoming meeting between the Prime Ministers of India and Pakistan gave a new impulse to every group engaged in the struggle for power in Kashmir. Each pressed its position in the hope that it might influence the outcome of the meeting.

The President of the communalist party Jan Sangh, Dr. S. P. Mookerjee, demonstratively traveled in May to Jammu and was arrested. The following month he died in prison in Srinagar of a heart attack. Rumors about the circumstances of his death added new fuel to political passions, which were already running high.

Sheikh Abdullah, in a speech made in June, reminded the public that back in the fateful fall months of 1947 he had pleaded for "freedom before accession." Exposed to increasing pressure from several quarters in his own country and compelled to witness passively the negotiations between Delhi and Karachi, he protested that "a decision about Kashmir cannot be taken behind closed doors without approval of the people of Kashmir."[46] As he had done before on various occasions, he again hinted at the idea of independence. In the Indian papers appeared the draft of a new Kashmir constitution which called for independent Kashmiri armed forces and left to India responsibility only for Kashmir's foreign affairs.

In this policy of ascertaining his independent position, Sheikh Abdullah presumably relied on the undivided support of his political party, the National Conference. He was

[46] *The Hindu* (Madras), June 16, 1953.

profoundly convinced of the incontestability of his leadership. In this estimation he proved to be fatefully wrong. There were in the Srinagar government and in the National Conference some leaders who showed more pro-Indian inclinations than Abdullah and who were against his policy of drifting away from India. They were led by Abdullah's right-hand man, Bakshi Ghulam Mohammed.

Bakshi was the chief organizer of the National Conference, and in the government he was Deputy Prime Minister and Home Minister. In this latter capacity he was the chief of police in Kashmir. Bakshi had embraced Christianity in his school years but later returned to Islam, and since the nationalist riots in 1931 he was closely associated with Sheikh Abdullah. His brother is a wealthy military contractor, and other relatives occupy important positions in the economic life of Kashmir. Bakshi found it profitable to be in charge of state supplies, public works, and transport. A popular wit has given to his wide interests and associations a name—the Bakshi Brothers Corporation. Paradoxically, he prided himself on having once whipped a black marketeer on the streets of Srinagar. His ambition has been power—if possible with comfort. The increasing rift between India and his superior, Sheikh Abdullah, offered Bakshi the opportunity to realize more of both than he had previously enjoyed.

Nehru flew to Srinagar in May and attempted to patch up the differences in the government, but apparently with no success. "I invited Sheikh Abdullah to come to Delhi," Nehru explained at a later occasion. "In fact, even when I was in Europe I had sent word that he should be invited. On returning, I invited him. He did not come; then he said he would come a little later. Later again, this invitation was repeated by telephone, by letter. Ultimately he did not come. Meanwhile—in fact, before I had come back—Sheikh

Abdullah and some others began speaking in a way which seemed strange to me and distressed us greatly."[47]

If Abdullah declined to visit New Delhi, his deputy, Bakshi, went. So did the Head of State, Mr. Karan Singh. In the same period, at the beginning of July, the three Hindu communalist parties heeded Nehru's repeated appeals and called off the *satyagraha* agitation for complete integration of Kashmir with India, with the explanation that the "movement has achieved the purpose of impressing on the government and on the country the urgent necessity of tackling the problem in an objective manner."[48] There is no proof of any connection between the behind-the-scene happenings and this sudden change in their policy, but the coincidence is conspicuous.

When a country is thrown into a turmoil of political uncertainties and confusion, suspicions and intrigues, then fantastic combinations mushroom. Kashmir was not spared from such an experience. Rumors soon had it that Sheikh Abdullah was now ready to save of his policy what he thought to be available and what was dearest to his heart: the Vale of Kashmir. He was suspected of planning a session of the Constituent Assembly, which, instead of ratifying the accession of the State of Jammu and Kashmir to India, would declare the Vale of Kashmir independent. On top of these reports came the highly inflammatory rumors that the United States was backing the idea of Kashmir independence and that Sheikh Abdullah had been encouraged in it when Adlai Stevenson had visited Srinagar in May. Indeed, Robert Trumbull reported (as did Reuters) that even the governments of India and Pakistan were believed to have come to an agreement on the solution of the Kashmir dispute. Accordingly, the Kashmir Valley would gain independence, possibly guaranteed by both

[47] From Jawaharlal Nehru's speech in the House of the People, September 17, 1953.
[48] *The Hindustan Times* (Delhi), July 8, 1953.

countries, and the rest of the state would be partitioned between them roughly along the present cease-fire line. It was rumored, without official verification, that John Foster Dulles supported a solution of this nature.[49]

The Pakistani Prime Minister denied the reports as "mischievous and false." The government of India denied them too. The American Ambassador to India, George V. Allen, and Adlai Stevenson himself denied any interference in the Kashmir situation. Jawaharlal Nehru declared later, somewhat vaguely, "Now, a great deal has been said, much has been said about foreign interference in Kashmir. These kinds of charges are often made, and if there is a modicum of truth in them that is greatly exaggerated as expressed it becomes a little difficult to deal with them. In a matter of this kind it is not easy for me to state every fact that may come in our knowledge, before the House, but, broadly speaking, I would say in the course of the last few weeks, in the course of the last few months and sometime more, hard cases of this type of interference have come before us—individual interference. It would not be correct to call it governmental interference, but individuals have not behaved properly, because again you must remember the basic fact that Kashmir is a highly strategic area."[50]

In the other camp of the struggle for Kashmir, on the Azad side, it was re-emphasized that "no solution other than the holding of an impartial plebiscite in Kashmir and Jammu State would be acceptable to the people."[51]

The scene was now complicated enough to climax the tragic drama of Kashmir. The two factions of the National Conference split openly and supported their differences in public meetings. Vehemently the independence-minded Sheikh Abdullah warned that "the communal happenings

[49] *The New York Times*, July 5, 1953.
[50] From Jawaharlal Nehru's speech in the House of the People, September 17, 1953.
[51] *Dawn* (Karachi), July 16, 1953.

of last year have shaken the foundation of this [Indo-Kash-miri] relationship," and at the beginning of August he made "the astounding statement that Kashmir's initial accession to India was forced on her because of India's refusal to give any help without the State's accession." With equal vehemence the more pro-Indian Bakshi declared that "Kashmiris would defend at the cost of their lives the State's accession to India and a special position granted to Jammu and Kashmir in the Indian Constitution."[52]

The cup of suspicion over Abdullah's intentions must have overflowed when he, according to a disclosure made later by a Pakistani newspaper, prepared a speech in Urdu and sent it to New Delhi for translation. In the prepared text he expressed his views on the definiteness of accession, "Though the accession of Kashmir to India is complete in all aspects it is conditional and temporary in the sense that the people of the State have to ratify it. Therefore, it is not final." He also questioned the Delhi agreement stating that it was "transitory and temporary." But more than that, he was now suddenly ready to admit that Kashmir was geographically so situated that her prosperity depended on trade with both India and Pakistan, that her people had cultural relations with both the West (Pakistani) and the East (Indian) Punjab and the North-West Frontier Province, and that "the rivers and roads of Kashmir lead to Pakistan. The nearest railway station to Kashmir is Rawalpindi. Kashmir traders use Karachi as their port." He criticized the Praja Parishad agitation, which was supported "monetarily and morally in India," and declared that the Kashmir Muslims were forced to ponder whether they could rely on Indian promises. He admitted that the National Conference had lost to some extent its hold on the Muslims. "The Muslims and not non-Muslims of the State have to take a

[52] The quotations are in sequence from *The Hindustan Times* (Delhi), July 24; *The Hindu Weekly Review* (Madras), August 10; *The Hindustan Times*, July 27, 1953.

decision in regard to the accession of the State to India," stated Abdullah. "Because non-Muslims could not even think of any alternative, I do not have to assure Hindus and Sikhs that their future will be safe in India because to say that is unnecessary. In this respect I have been misunderstood. Whenever I have tried to secure their just rights for the Muslims or voiced their views about their future in India my friends labelled me as a 'communalist.' . . . But, unfortunately, the Praja Parishad agitation, on the one hand, has created doubts in the minds of Muslims and, on the other the Muslim middle class is finding out that whereas accession to India has opened to Hindus and Sikhs various doors of progress, Muslims have become a frog in the well. In departments which are under the direct control of the Government of India there has been not only no progress towards better representation of Muslims but there has been actually decline in this representation."

Sheikh Abdullah intended to conclude his speech with these questions: "1. Is there no possibility of any change in Kashmir's relationship with India in view of the international situation? 2. Will all of the people of the State irrespective of religious and cultural differences enjoy the same rights and opportunities under this relationship? 3. Is it possible to overcome the natural and geographical obstacles facing the State and obstructing its progress and prosperity even while maintaining this relationship?"[53]

This was another Abdullah from the one of five years or even one year ago. He never gave the prepared speech. It was confiscated and counteraction followed immediately.

Events then moved swiftly toward a cloak-and-dagger denouement. On August 7, three members of the government, led by Bakshi, accused Abdullah in a memorandum of making arbitrary decisions, of being responsible for deterioration in the administration, despotism, inefficiency, and wanton wastage of public resources. "You have tended

[53] *Civil and Military Gazette* (Lahore), February 3, 1954.

to act in a manner that has generated uncertainty, suspense, and doubt in the minds of the people of the State in general and of those in Jammu and Ladakh in particular," stated the memorandum. "All these factors have combined to strengthen the disruptionist forces seeking the disintegration of the State. . . . You have arbitrarily sought to precipitate a rupture in the relationship of the State with India. . . . Under these circumstances, what seems inevitable is that interested foreign powers may well take advantage of and exploit the situation for their own selfish purpose. . . . You have connived in all these unfortunate happenings and thus strengthened and encouraged the forces of disruption." The memorandum informed Sheikh Abdullah, in conclusion, that the cabinet had lost the confidence of the people.[54]

The memorandum was submitted to the Head of the State, who suggested an emergency meeting of the government. Abdullah refused the request and, probably sure of his unshakable leadership, went to Gulmarg, a beautiful summer spot, to spend the weekend there.

In the early hours of the morning of August 9 a Shakespearean-styled drama developed in the legendary Maharaja's palace. The Head of the State, the son of the Maharaja who had been exiled by Sheikh Abdullah in 1947, now avenged his father. He dismissed Abdullah and nominated Bakshi as Prime Minister. Abdullah, resting at Gulmarg, was arrested and taken to prison. Thus ended, at least temporarily, the meteoric political career of the man who began as a national revolutionary, "the Lion of Kashmir," who thought as a socialist, acted as a dictator, maneuvered as a petty Machiavellist, and finally succumbed at the hands of his lifelong associates by arms which he had often used himself.

The new Prime Minister, immediately upon taking the oath of office, went before the microphone to make a policy statement. He stated that Abdullah's independence policy

[54] *The Times of India* (Bombay), August 10, 1953.

had "naturally the connivance and support of interested foreign powers who have all along been resisting the exercise of the right of the people of the State to freedom and self-determination. . . . An 'independent' Kashmir under the influence of imperialist power will be a great threat to the freedom and independence of Indian and Pakistani people. In view of the geographical position of the State, such independence is bound to involve us in a bitter and violent international controversy and another Korea may be staged here, as a result of the armed conflict between interested powers." He then had words of praise for India with which Kashmir had established "indissoluble links." He indicated, however, that the key to the governmental crisis was "the deep economic discontent of the masses of the State." He disclosed shortcomings which in a totalitarian country often remain concealed from the public, to be brought to light only in time of a violent change of government as something of a scapegoat. He, of all people, the principal of "Bakshi Brothers Corporation," blamed the corruption of Abdullah's administration for the failure of its agricultural policy. He admitted that the local authorities behaved arbitrarily, that cooperatives became a symbol of tyranny, that the bureaucracy in education caused great hardships.[55]

The abrupt change in the Kashmir government and the detention of Sheikh Abdullah was received in some quarters with shock and amazement, in others with satisfaction. Jawaharlal Nehru, on August 10, made a statement in the House of the People in which he explained that the government of India had been informed about the crisis in Srinagar, "but our advice was neither sought nor given." He understood that Abdullah, his political friend of twenty years, had been detained "in the interest of the peace of the State, which was threatened in various ways." Nehru's words disclosed the dilemma of choosing between personal friend-

[55] *Ibid.*, August 11, 1953.

ship and political interests. He solved the painful difficulty in favor of what he considered to be in the interests of his country and of Kashmir.

If the public in India was in general bewildered by the disappearance of Sheikh Abdullah, the three communalist parties were enthusiastic and saw in the change the first step towards the complete integration of Kashmir with India. However, the Kashmiri people, supposedly the beneficiaries of the change, were enraged. Thousands of them demonstrated against the new government and for Abdullah. Hundreds were arrested and many were killed (figures given by various sources vary from 30 to 800).

In Pakistan the happenings in Srinagar prompted a wave of indignation. Large meetings were organized and extremists called again for *jehad*, holy war. In Karachi Fatima Jinnah, the sister of the late founder of Pakistan, led a procession of demonstrators who in a resolution appealed to "the Pakistanis to volunteer their services and join their Kashmiri brethren in their righteous cause and fight for freedom."[56] The newspapers accused India of having overthrown Sheikh Abdullah, until then a Quisling in the opinion of the Pakistanis but now, through a twist of history which did not lack its somewhat comical aspects, almost a martyr in the struggle of the Kashmiri Muslims.

As could have been expected, Indo-Pakistani relations underwent a profound shock. They had greatly improved in the spring of 1953 after the new Pakistani Prime Minister, the youthful Mohammed Ali, had made several gestures of friendship to India and personally to Nehru. Now, however, they once again reached a dangerously low ebb.

It was in and because of this atmosphere of tension and new outbursts of newspaper attacks that Mohammed Ali rushed to Delhi. On August 20 the two Prime Ministers signed a joint communiqué (referred to and analyzed in the

---

[56] *Dawn* (Karachi), August 17, 1953.

preceding chapter) in which they reaffirmed the previous agreement to have a plebiscite in Kashmir.

Thus the danger of open hostilities was averted, but the confirmation of the plebiscite agreement quickly revived the old disruptive voices in Kashmir and India. Bakshi in Srinagar paid lip service to the Delhi agreement of August 20, but almost immediately thereafter stated that Kashmir was an integral part of India and "no power on earth can separate the two countries." The Head Lama of Ladakh concurred: "Plebiscite or no plebiscite, Ladakh has made its choice, and its decision to accede to India is irrevocable." The communalist parties in India thundered in almost identical language that "the accession of the State to India was final and irrevocable and there was no question of holding a plebiscite to determine its future status." They called the Delhi agreement "a colossal blunder" which "is bound to end in disaster and loss of both Jammu and Kashmir to India." They provoked new incidents in Jammu. Even the leader of the Praja Socialist Party of India, Dr. R. Lohia, declared that "the Kashmir problem would not be solved by plebiscite."[57]

In Kashmir the new Prime Minister lost no time in strengthening his hold on the government. Without any apparent difficulties he sent to prison Abdullah's political friends who remained faithful to their old leader in the days of crisis. He reshuffled various committees of the National Conference. To gain some respite from the enraged Kashmiris he dealt quickly, as every shrewd politician would do, with the most pressing grievances. He partially restored free trade, eased food rations, abolished import duties on salt, raised governmental wages, and promised investigation of corruption and nepotism and reforms in education. He expected the government of India to foot the bill. Indeed, in

[57] The quotations in sequence from *The Times of India* (Bombay), August 24, 27, 24, 1953; *The Hindustan Times* (Delhi), September 8; *The Times of India*, September 2, 1953.

December 1953 it advanced a loan to Kashmir of 14.49 million dollars.

In the redistribution of portfolios in the now five-member government, Bakshi reserved for himself a wide range of responsibilities embracing political, police, trade, judiciary, economic, tourist, militia, and labor fields.[58]

A National Conference meeting convened in September and, attended by several hundred delegates, passed a resolution which condemned the policy of Sheikh Abdullah, but confirmed the policy of New Kashmir and of accession to India, while preserving Kashmir's autonomous status. It opposed any association with "the ruling clique in Pakistan" and her "reactionary and feudal policy." It attacked foreign powers which were using Pakistan "to bring pressure on India to yield to their persuasion." At the beginning of October Bakshi won a unanimous vote of confidence from the Constituent Assembly.

As the year 1953 drew to a close, Bakshi appeared to be well established in power in Srinagar. In large part he followed the path of his predecessor. He continued Abdullah's dictatorial methods and apparently was far from eager to have the Kashmiri people decide their fate freely. He enjoyed the confidence of Jawaharlal Nehru, who strangely enough shut his eyes to the totalitarian methods applied in Kashmiri politics—methods which he would not use or tolerate in India herself.

Assured of Nehru's support and of the subservience of the purged Constituent Assembly, Bakshi now moved toward what he considers the final step of Kashmir's integration with India. This was to be materialized by ratification of Kashmir's accession to India and by clarification and implementation of the Delhi agreement of July 1952, which Abdullah had been accused of sabotaging.

[58] For the text of the governmental order published in the Jammu and Kashmir Gazette see *The Statesman* (Calcutta), September 10, 1953.

On February 6, 1954, after Bakshi's return from consultations in Delhi, the Constituent Assembly ratified the accession. Of the seventy-five member Assembly, sixty-four were present and voted unanimously; of the eleven absent members, six were under detention.[59] Bakshi accompanied the act with a triumphant speech in which he expressed confidence, without bothering to support it by facts, that the Azad Kashmiris would accept the decision of the Constituent Assembly, if they did not live "the lives of prisoners" and were not "victims of tyranny." He further repeated the conviction that Kashmir had "irrevocably acceded to India more than six years ago and today we are only fulfilling the formalities of our unbreakable bonds with India."[60]

At the same session which ratified Kashmir's accession to India, the Basic Principles Committee reported on the regulations concerning the relations between the government in Delhi and Srinagar. The report stated that "in order to enable the Centre [the government of India] to discharge its responsibilities, which devolve upon it under the Constitution, those provisions of the Constitution of India which may be necessary for this purpose should be made applicable to the State in an appropriate manner. While preserving the internal autonomy of the State, all obligations which flow from the fact of accession and also its elaborations as contained in the Delhi agreement should find appropriate place in the Constitution."[61]

As a practical consequence of the report, in which the government of India apparently acquiesced, the customs barrier was removed on April 13, and thereby Kashmir became economically an integral part of India. The government of India agreed to pay to Srinagar 2 million rupees a year for the loss of customs revenue. To demonstrate the

---

[59] *The Statesman* (Calcutta), February 17, 1954.

[60] *Indiagram* (The Embassy of India, Washington, D.C.), No. 388, February 9, 1954.

[61] *The Hindu Weekly Review* (Madras), February 8, 1954.

solidity of Kashmiri-Indian relations, Dr. Rajendra Prasad, the President of India, visited the country in April. In a statement in Jammu he declared that "history and mutual understanding had cemented the ancient ties between Kashmir and India to such an extent that any break in the relationship was inconceivable."[62] One month later, on May 14, 1954, the President, under Article 370 of the Indian Constitution, issued an order endorsing the relationship between the Republic of India and Kashmir as it had been formulated in the Delhi agreement and adopted by the Constituent Assembly in Srinagar. Most of the provisions of the Indian Constitution now apply also to the State of Jammu and Kashmir. Exception is made in regard to the position and function of the Head of the State and the rights to acquire immovable property in the state and to employment and settlement therein. These rights are left to the authority of Kashmir's legislature to safeguard the interests of the state's permanent residents. Also, the state legislature, for reasons of security, is empowered for a period of five years to impose restrictions on basic political rights otherwise guaranteed by the Indian Constitution. The Kashmir land reform has been confirmed and special status has been given to the Kashmir High Court, from which the right of appeal to the Supreme Court of India is limited to certain cases in civil and criminal proceedings. The Presidential order implies both further strengthening of India's hold on Kashmir and recognition of a privileged position of Kashmir within the Indian Republic.

None of these moves was calculated to alleviate the anxieties and indignation in Karachi and on the Azad side. The act of ratification was obviously against the spirit and letter of the Security Council resolution of March 30, 1951 (S/1469) and against the spirit of the Nehru-Mohammed Ali agreement of August 20, 1953. Indeed, Mohammed Ali

[62] *Indiagram* (Embassy of India, Washington, D.C.), No. 431, April 13, 1954.

condemned it as "an insult to the United Nations" and appealed to Nehru to repudiate it. The Indian Prime Minister considered such a request as "manifestly absurd"; in his view the Constituent Assembly's decision "represented the wishes of the elected people in Kashmir." He, however, confirmed that it "did not come—it cannot come—in the way of our observing our international commitments in regard to a plebiscite."[63]

Few people in Pakistan found consolation in Nehru's commitment to plebiscite—a commitment which he had put on record so often in the past. On the contrary, many again urged an early settlement of the dispute. The Azad leader, Ghulam Abbas, declared at a public meeting that the people should depend solely on their own efforts and not look to the United Nations or any other international power for the liberation of Kashmir. "We are now convinced beyond doubt," he stated, "that India is not for a plebiscite. She is afraid of the result." One of the leading chiefs of the tribesmen warned, "Thirty-two lakhs of tribesmen [are] ready to stake their all for Pakistan and their Muslim brethren in Kashmir," and at a meeting at Peshawar a resolution was passed appealing to the government of Pakistan to remove all restrictions on the tribesmen from opening a front in Kashmir.[64] Bellicose speeches were again pronounced in the Pakistani parliament.

Perhaps these threats and outbursts are only outlets for an uncontrolled anger; perhaps they are instruments of political pressure. No one can predict with assurance what they mean. Undoubtedly, however, they do illustrate the potential gravity of the Kashmiri nightmare, which may one day burst into reality, into a horror of killing and bloodshed, over which governmental authority may have no control.

[63] *Ibid.*, No. 399, February 25, 1954.
[64] *Kashmir Affairs* (Rawalpindi), Vol. VI, No. 11 (no date); *Dawn* (Karachi), February 22, 1954; *Kashmir Affairs*, Vol. VI, No. 14, April 3, 1954.

9. Communist Harvest

DURING the long seven-year struggle for Kashmir, one dangerous fact seems to have escaped the notice not only of the rest of the free world but of the two major participants themselves: the serious danger that, to quote the old proverb, "while the lion and the tiger fight each other, the jackal may run off with the prize."

The political dangers arising from the dispute, the continuing threat of open warfare between India and Pakistan, the heavy economic burden of maintaining armies in the disputed area—all these are apparent and are sufficient cause for a grave and continuing concern.

But apparently unseen, unrecognized, is the equally dangerous fact that in this atmosphere of instability, of economic and political uncertainty, Kashmir is being subjected to a systematic process of communization. With all of its economic misery, its internal corrosion, its religious feuds, and its geographic proximity to Communist Sinkiang and Tibet, Kashmir offers an ideal ground for subversive designs. The evidence of the last few years points to the fact that neither the Soviet representative at the United Nations nor the Communist Party of India has overlooked its potentialities.

Indeed, the first Kashmiri revolt of centuries, which occurred in the early 1930's (see page 17), has been ascribed by some writers to "Bolshevik influence."[1] But the Soviet writer I. Mazdur disclaims "the honor" and asserts that the upheavals were organized by bourgeois elements and were of a bourgeois-religious character. "There is no evidence from the material at [our] disposal of any participation of the revolutionary Indian organizations in the Kashmir insurrection," writes Mazdur. "Only the Communist Party of India leading the struggle of peasantry can bring them

[1] Sir William Barton, *The Princes of India*, Nisbet & Co., London, 1934, p. 127.

249

to the possession of land and liberation from feudal and imperialistic oppression," he concludes.[2]

Whatever may be the truth of the political background of these initial acts of discontent, they undoubtedly did serve notice that there was a revolutionary potential in Kashmir. In any case, when in May 1946 Sheikh Abdullah launched a "Quit Kashmir" campaign aimed against the Maharaja (see page 22), the Communists this time were full of praise for such revolutionary fervor. "After the Second World War," wrote the foremost Soviet specialist on India, A. M. Diakov, "a national movement in Kashmir developed the program of doing away with the Maharaja, of turning Kashmir into a democratic republic, of giving to the people of Kashmir the right of self-determination." Sheikh Abdullah was to him "a man of progressive, democratic opinions."[3] Still later, in 1951, Diakov evaluated the endeavors of the National Conference in more concrete terms. "Till 1946," he wrote, "the National Conference was under the leadership of bourgeois elements which stood close to the 'leftist' wing of the All India National Congress. In 1946, however, the Kashmiri peasants accepted a plan according to which workers joined actively in. Under the influence of the masses the National Conference accepted a democratic program."[4] The Azad leaders assert that the "Quit Kashmir" program was Communist in origin and led by agents from Russia.

When Abdullah opened his campaign of "freedom before accession" upon his release from prison in September of 1947, the Bombay monthly, *Communist*, supported his declarations with a significant comment: "It is imperialism's

[2] *Revoliutsionyi Pod'em v Indii.* Sbornik, Moskva: Partiinoe izdatel'stvo, 1933. I. Mazdur's study on the revolt in Kashmir, pp. 167-182; quotations, p. 182.

[3] A. M. Diakov, *Natsional'nyi Vopros i Angliiskii Imperialism v Indii*, Ogiz, 1948, pp. 107, 195.

[4] A. M. Diakov, *Indien und Pakistan*, Kultur und Fortschritt, Berlin, 1951, p. 22.

game to disrupt the great democratic movement led by the National Conference. . . . There is no doubt that the National Conference would defeat these disruptive efforts by placing in the forefront the issue of ending the present autocratic regime and establishing a fully democratic government in accordance with its programme."[5]

After Sheikh Abdullah had been installed in power as the Prime Minister of the State of Jammu and Kashmir, the Soviet journalist O. Orestov, who had witnessed these events, wrote about them, "This [National] Conference, headed by Sheikh Abdullah, had always been in the lead in the people's struggle against the British colonizers . . . and it had the ready following of the population." After the tribesmen had been repelled from Srinagar, the city, according to Orestov's description, was flooded with red flags, a red rosette on every breast, and the central square was renamed Red Square. Though "Sheikh Abdullah's government, brought to power on the rising tide of a truly popular movement, had proved impotent in the face of the Indian reactionaries . . . nevertheless, in Kashmir, this friendship [for the Soviet Union] and the people's interest in the life of the Soviet Union are particularly great."[6]

Infiltration

The events of the next few years clearly indicate that this burgeoning of Communist interest in Kashmir was well founded. For the policy of the National Conference which came to power with Sheikh Abdullah was almost tailor-made for Communist infiltration.

As early as the end of 1948, it was reported by *The Statesman* that "Communist activity . . . has been on the increase

[5] *Communist,* October 1947, as quoted in Rajbans Krishen, *Kashmir and the Conspiracy against Peace,* People's Publishing House, Bombay, 1951, pp. 3-4.

[6] O. Orestov, "The War in Kashmir." *New Times* (Moscow), No. 40, September 29, 1948, pp. 24-30.

in Kashmir for some time and a marked change in their attitude towards the National Conference and the present administration is noticeable. Though small in number Communists have already gained a toe-hold in the State. A number of them are working with the National Conference Committees here and there. The Communists are, however, stated to be very critical of this organization and the State Government which is run by the National Conference, although criticism has been subdued and indirect. It is also understood that Communists have got into local labour unions and similar organizations. It is commonly believed here that two prominent Communist leaders of India managed to enter Kashmir."[7]

Another newspaper reported, "Having lost their face in Hyderabad, the Communists it appears have now concentrated their attention on Kashmir which according to them is yet the weakest link in the Indian Union. I have reasons to state that for some weeks past, Communists have been organizing themselves in the State at top speed to fish in troubled waters. A few days back, prominent leader Sardar Kulvir Singh, is said to have been in Kashmir on a 'secret mission.' According to reports current here even Comrade Ranadive, General Secretary of the Communist Party of India, was in Kashmir recently."[8]

The process of infiltration quickly placed Communist sympathizers in high governmental positions and within the circle of leadership of the National Conference. Chief among these was and is Ghulam Muhammad Sadiq. Until 1951 he was Minister of Development, then the President of the Kashmir Constituent Assembly, and more recently also the Minister of Education.

Sadiq, 45 years old, comes from a rich family. He studied at the Aligarh University and practiced law at Srinagar. In 1934 he entered the Muslim Conference, but three years

[7] *The Statesman* (Delhi edition), December 31, 1948.
[8] *Amrita Bazar Patrika* (Calcutta), December 31, 1948.

later contacted the Communist leaders in Punjab, Abdullah Safdar and Fazal Elahi Qurban, and took part in anti-governmental activities. He then followed Sheikh Abdullah and participated at the foundation of the National Conference in 1939.

He played a prominent role in Abdullah's "Quit Kashmir" movement and as a consequence was jailed. When the country was invaded by the tribesmen, he displayed both his energy and his administrative ability. He quickly organized the National Militia, the Women's Defense Corps, and the National Cultural Front. He has become undisputed leader of the labor institutions. In the summer of 1950 he organized demonstrations in Srinagar in support of the Stockholm Peace Congress. In the fall of 1952 he organized a People's Peace Congress in Jammu, and more recently joined the Communist chorus in accusing the United States of waging germ warfare in Korea. He has been most active in disseminating, through governmental channels and through the National Conference, Communist propaganda materials. He maintains close contact with the Communist leaders in India. In the Kashmir issue he has frequently used the most violent language about "the Anglo-American imperialists" and has had highly gratifying words to say about the Soviet Union.

The other members of the government with Communist leanings were Durga Parshad Dhar, Deputy Home Minister, and Girdari Lal Dogra, Finance Minister, both former lawyers and long associates of the Prime Minister.

The Revenue Minister, Mirza Mohammad Afzal Beg, a man of peasant origin, was the leading spirit behind the land reform in Kashmir. Though not a Communist, he fell undoubtedly under their influence. In his book *On the Way to Golden Harvests*, in which he analyzed the class interests of the working masses and the irreconcilability of the capitalist and socialist systems, he wrote, "Insofar as the State of Jammu and Kashmir is concerned, we have decided to

own that system which gives no quarter to production for
private profit, where no private manipulation can bring
about economic crisis, endangering the life of millions. This
decision of ours is only an implementation of the promises
which the standard bearer of freedom's forces [Sheikh Ab-
dullah] had held out to the people from time to time.
Building a socialist order is our objective. . . . The capitalist
system is the biggest barrier to human progress."[9] He maintained, however, that the Kashmir government believed "in
changing the social system by a process of evolution. We
wish to bring it about peacefully."[10] Events have indicated,
however, that they have failed to practice what they preach.

The Communist party's chief agent in Kashmir is Niran-
jan Nath Raina, who owns the New Kashmir Book Shop in
Srinagar and publishes a weekly, *Azad*. In Jammu the chief
agent was Dhanwantry, under whose guidance was published
a daily, *Shamshere*. Still another Communist, B. P. L. Bedi,
is considered to be the author of the National Conference
program, *New Kashmir*, and was the *éminence grise* behind
the Abdullah government. His European wife, Freda, sat on
the governmental committee for the preparation of school
textbooks.

Sadiq and other Communist members or fellow-travelers
do not speak of themselves as Communist party adherents.
Instead, they are all prominent leaders of the National Conference. But whether members or sympathizers, they have
exerted decisive influence upon the policy of the government and the National Conference without committing
themselves to public and official responsibility for government measures. This ambiguous arrangement gives them
the advantage of claiming the credit if the government introduces, for instance, the land reform, and of free criticism
if it fails.

[9] Mirza Mohammad Afzal Beg, *On the Way to Golden Harvests*.
Government of Jammu and Kashmir, pp. 4, 5.
[10] *Ibid.*, p. 58.

The Communists use the government propaganda channels for their own ideological purposes and at the same time
exploit the dissatisfaction of the masses. Their techniques
of dissension are familiar. Most of them support Kashmir's
union with India; a few of them preach accession to Pakistan; and still others cried till recently for the independence
of Kashmir. In Jammu they abuse the separatist tendencies
of the Hindus, incite the people against the Indian army,
and feed the general dissatisfaction of the population.

The Communist position in the labor movement is reported to be strong. Ghulam Sadiq organized a Central
Labor Union (Mazdoor Sabha) with which are affiliated
the Government Transport Association, the Government
Sericultural and Silk Labor Union, the Jammu Turpentine
Labor Union, and the Rent Payers Association. The Telegraph Employees Union is also under Communist influence.
In Kashmir alone there are 100,000 members of these labor
organizations, including not only workers but peasants.

Communists have infiltrated the Students Federation,
the Democratic Youth League, the Cultural Front, and are
in control of the Progressive Writers' League, which publishes a monthly, *Kung Posh.*

Sanctuary of Isolation

The National Conference and its Communist associates
did not at all like the United Nations intervention in the
Kashmir conflict. Not only might its mediation lead to the
plebiscite, the result of which could deprive them of all
their labors, but also they preferred to pursue their policy
in a sanctuary of isolation from any international attention.
The Soviet Union in the Security Council and the Communist Party of India developed, therefore, a well-concerted policy of undermining the mediatory efforts of the
United Nations with the aim of eliminating them altogether. The National Conference joined in the campaign

on the local Kashmiri scene while continuing its policy of communization.

In Security Council discussions of the Kashmir conflict, the Soviet representative for a long time remained aloof. He showed no interest in bringing the fighting in Kashmir to an early end. He let the British and American representatives pursue the thankless efforts toward reconciliation. When the resolution came to a vote on April 21, 1948, Mr. Gromyko and his Ukrainian colleague, Mr. Tarasenko, abstained. Nor did the Soviet Union declare its own views on the subject, apparently to preserve freedom of future action. One might easily speculate also that it was not in the interests of Soviet policy to bring about an early settlement of the Kashmir conflict; the Soviets preferred its continuation in the hope that the two young countries, Pakistan and India, already so preoccupied with other grave problems, would be exhausted.

But the attitude of the National Conference, influenced as it was by Communist members, was quite outspoken. It declared openly on April 22, 1948 that the Security Council resolution was "yet another feature of power politics on which the Security Council has embarked ever since its inception." The General Secretary of the National Conference, Maulana Syed Masoodi, declared, "In regard to the Kashmir issue the imperialist powers like America and Britain had made out Pakistan as the innocent party. This was being done to further their own ends with a view to establish bases here for the coming war." Sheikh Abdullah, too, spoke about "imperialist powers" which "saw Kashmir only as a neighbour of Russia and therefore an essential base in the encirclement of Russia for future aggression."[11]

The pro-Communist Bombay weekly, *Blitz*, published on June 9, 1948 a special issue, "Great Conspiracy," in which G. K. Reddy, the author, "proved" that the invasion of

[11] Rajbans Krishen, *op.cit.*, pp. 19, 20.

Kashmir was planned and supported by the British and American governments. He had somewhat mysteriously served as the Azad Kashmir government director of public relations, but he escaped and brought the information on the "great conspiracy" to the paper.

The Communist *People's Age* evaluated the United Nations Commission report to the Security Council as "the culmination of the nefarious intrigues of the British and American imperialists against the democratic mass movement of Kashmir and Jammu. The policy that was being pursued by them till now through the instigation of war and intervention in Kashmir and Jammu with the help of Pakistan reactionaries, mainly the annihilation of the democratic mass movement and the enslavement of their people, and the setting up on this soil of Anglo-American warbases directed against the Socialist Soviet Union and the democratic forces in China, would now be attempted to be carried forward to completion through 'peaceful' means and under cover of the 'free and impartial' plebiscite that will now be held under the direction of the military and political agents of American imperialism, masked as the UNO Commission officers."[12]

The Communist writer Rajbans Krishen devoted a book to the task of "proving" that the United Nations, its Commission, and its representative, Sir Owen Dixon, acted on order of the Anglo-American warmongers and wished to liquidate Sheikh Abdullah's progressive movement and to establish in Kashmir, with the help of Indian and Pakistani capitalists, a military springboard for an attack on the Soviet Union.[13] Only the Czechoslovak Communist member of the Commission, O. Chýle, deserved the author's praise for having uncovered the big plot against Kashmir's democracy.

[12] *Ibid.*, p. 38.
[13] Rajbans Krishen, *op.cit.* (The book was extensively quoted and highly praised in *Izvestia* (Moscow), on February 6, 1953, in an article, "Anglo-Amerikanskie proiski v Kashmire.")

In the fall of 1949 the annual session of the National Conference passed four resolutions. Their language was revealing. One resolution referred to the world tensions as "the direct consequence of the basic tussle between the forces of progress and reaction on the global scale." It recalled the adoption, in 1944, of the *New Kashmir* program, which was the "National Charter of the People's Demand." It quoted the resolution of the National Conference session in Srinagar, in 1948: "After mature consideration of the issue it [the National Conference] is definitely of the opinion that Kashmir with its unflinching faith in New Kashmir and with the very advanced outlook of the fundamental issue cannot find its proper place in Pakistan, which today has become the main citadel of reaction and decaying feudalism. . . ." Another resolution contained this self-explanatory statement, "The history of the creation of Pakistan as an imperialist maneuver for weakening the freedom movement surging in the Indian Subcontinent and for undermining the anti-imperialist forces in Asia through the division of India lends further strength to our misgivings and doubts." The resolution referred to "the machinations of warring imperialism" and it confirmed the National Conference leaders' "total refusal to be made the springboard of power politics or to be reduced to pawns in international racketeering." Another resolution expressed belief in "the principle that the concept of freedom all the world over is indivisible and that the fighters for true democracy are linked together with a bond of fellowship which recognizes no boundaries." Another resolution reiterated the National Conference's "worthy participation in the historic resurgence of the people of the East and working masses of the world."

Scores of speeches made by the Kashmiri and Communist leaders revealed the same pattern which has become such a familiar trademark. The American and British policies were always inseparably linked with the devilish forces of imperialism, conspiracy, capitalism, intervention, oppression, exploitation. The Sheikh's government was called Awami Raj—People's Government; there were Peace Brigades, People's Guards, People's *New Kashmir*. The right of self-determination was put forward as an ideal to which the United Nations, controlled as it is by the Anglo-American imperialists, was opposed. Only the true democrats and the working masses could understand and help the true democracy in Kashmir.

It has become one of the major tragedies of our age that Communists have stolen the terms "democracy," "peace," "self-determination," and "freedom," which for centuries have been the powerful sources of inspiration to mankind in its struggle for a better world and better life, and have twisted their meaning and used them as mere instruments of policy. This method of grand deceit has reached the point that one begins to reach for his gun whenever these voices speak of peace; that one is never so worried about another violently expansionist move as when its proponents speak about self-determination; that when they speak of democracy, one is prepared to witness the extremes of totalitarian dictatorship. Kashmir has unhappily become an admirable training ground for these ominous exercises in Communist semantics.

This travesty of freedom, democracy, peace, and self-determination as understood by the government in Srinagar found an experienced and well-coached actor in the representative of the Soviet Union on the Security Council. Following attentively the development in Kashmir, the Soviet Union eventually abandoned the tactic of abstaining from the debates on the issue. Time had finally worked to the advantage of Soviet policy. Four years had passed, the conflict was unsettled, and the internal situation in Kashmir pleased the Soviets. The Constituent Assembly was elected, "truly democratic," all its members belonging to Sheikh Abdullah's party. Now Moscow considered it opportune to intervene actively in the Security Council's deliberations on the Kashmir dispute.

"The United States and the United Kingdom have been . . . particularly active in the discussion of this matter . . . ," declared Jacob Malik in January 1952, and continued, with cynicism characteristic of Soviet policy: "The United States and the United Kingdom are continuing as before to interfere in the settlement of the Kashmir question, putting forward one plan after another. All these plans are failing [as they] . . . are of an annexionist, imperialist nature, because they are not based on an effort to achieve real settlement of the Kashmir question. . . . The purpose of these plans is interference by the United States and the United Kingdom in the internal affairs of Kashmir, the prolongation of the dispute between India and Pakistan on the question of Kashmir, and the conversion of Kashmir into a protectorate of the United States and the United Kingdom. . . . Finally, the purpose of these plans . . . is to secure the introduction of Anglo-American troops into the territory of Kashmir and convert Kashmir into an Anglo-American colony and a military and strategic base." He accused the American and British governments of taking "all steps to ensure that no opportunity should be given to the people of Kashmir themselves to decide their future without external pressure and without Anglo-American interference," of depriving "the people of Kashmir of the right of self-determination." He branded the United Nations representative, Dr. Frank Graham, as an agent of the Pentagon. Finally, he stated that the solution of the Kashmir problem "can be achieved if that status [of Kashmir] is determined by a Constituent Assembly democratically elected by the Kashmiri people."[14]

The pro-Communist *Blitz* characteristically put the responsibility for the United Nations failure "squarely and

[14] S.C.O.R. Seventh Year, 570th meeting, January 17th, 1952, pp. 13-18.

solidly on the shoulders of Frank Graham himself . . . as responsible for the sabotage of a nearly agreed plan of demilitarization." Later it said of Dr. Graham, ". . . behind his renewed efforts lies the brain of wily Churchill and the dollar strength of America, coupled with willing stooging of Pakistan to sabotage the Asian nationalist aspirations vis-à-vis Western imperialist strategy of aggression."[15]

The unexpected and sudden intervention of Malik in the Security Council caused something of a sensation in the circles of the United Nations. Its explanation could be related to the fact that India was in the midst of an election campaign and Malik's statement was meant to help the Indian Communists. It was indirectly addressed to the government of Pakistan as a warning not to seek Anglo-American support. Above all, it was aimed at endorsing the policy of Sheikh Abdullah, who was in Paris at that time and had the opportunity to inform the Soviet representative that "self-determination" and "democracy" were well on the way in Kashmir. Had Malik had a grain of political honesty, he would have admitted that the United States and Britain have for all these years followed exactly the aim for which he pleaded, namely, the right of the Kashmiri people to a free, democratic determination of their own fate.

The Soviet newspapers and the Soviet broadcasts beamed at Central Asia immediately picked up the theme and opened a campaign against the Anglo-American imperialists. The Indian Communist leaders and the Kashmiri politicians developed a well-concerted action.

The Communist leader in Kashmir, Ghulam Sadiq, declared, ". . . the time has come for India to withdraw the Kashmir question from the Security Council . . . [as] the Kashmiris realized that the talk of fair plebiscite was a mere smoke-screen behind which the Anglo-American powers were planning to enslave the Kashmiris. Nothing will suit

[15] *Blitz* (Bombay), January 12, 1952; March 8, 1952.

them better than the façade of trusteeship in Kashmir behind which they can build war bases against our neighbours."[16] Sheikh Abdullah, it must be noted, did not approve of Sadiq's demand to withdraw the case of Kashmir from the United Nations, aware as he was that such was not possible. But, apparently encouraged by Malik's intervention, he hinted about Kashmir independence and the international implications of the problem. In a press interview which he gave upon his return from Paris he declared, ". . . we are going to exercise this right [to decide the future of the country] to the fullest measure and at the earliest opportunity. . . . The feeling abroad now is that this question is not simply a Hindu-Muslim business, but that it contains as its basis high principles of politics. This question received added importance on this occasion as a result of the intervention of the Soviet delegation in the debate after nearly four years of silence." Should the Kashmiri people not ratify the accession to India this would not mean, according to Sheikh Abdullah, "that as a matter of course Kashmir becomes part of Pakistan. . . . It would regain the status which it enjoyed immediately preceding the accession [i.e., independence]. Let us be clear about it."[17] *The Times of India* pointed to this development which may "lead ultimately to an independent Kashmir, which may come in the orbit of influence of India, Pakistan, or the strongest third neighbour, the USSR."[18]

Another Moscow ritual, the Peace Congress, held with such fanfare in various parts of the world, also took place in Kashmir. It was staged in Jammu in September 1952, and expressed in a resolution "grave concern at the manner in which the Kashmir issue has been handled by the United Nations [which] instead of helping [solve] the problem paved [the] way for drawing Kashmir, India and Pakistan

[16] *Delhi Express*, January 1, 1952.
[17] *The Hindu* (Madras), March 26, 1952.
[18] *The Times of India* (Bombay), February 15, 1952.

into the orbit of a third world war. . . . The people of Jammu and Kashmir alone have the right to decide their destiny and no foreign power has the right to intervene in our internal affairs, no matter under what cover they may be operating."[19] Ghulam Sadiq, addressing the Peace Conference, declared, "The Anglo-American bloc does not want peace in the world and it wants to control all the strategic places of the world and Kashmir is one of them."[20]

Another Peace Conference, on a large international scale, met a month later in Peking. The delegate of Pakistan, Pir Sahib of Manki Sharif, and of India, Dr. Saifuddin Kitchlew (who was awarded Stalin's Peace Prize in December 1952), issued a joint statement in which they accused the United Nations of having seriously widened the gulf between India and Pakistan. "The unmistakable purpose of the Anglo-American Powers in the Kashmir dispute is to intensify Indo-Pakistan conflict with a view to making both countries subservient to them," read the declaration. "The situation endangers the sovereignty of both countries and makes them a prey to imperialist demands for war bases and cannon fodder." The statement asked for the right of the Kashmiri people "to determine their future destiny freely on the basis of equality and fairness, without hindrance, fear or favour." It is not without significance that the statement spoke about the future destiny of Kashmir without mentioning whether she would join India or Pakistan. When the declaration was read before the session of the Peking Peace Conference, both leaders "embraced each other to the applause of 400 delegates. . . ."[21]

In December 1952 the Soviet representative at the Security Council, Mr. V. Zorin, picked up again the theme of Anglo-American imperialist policy on Kashmir and pleaded for the right of the Kashmiri people to elect a Constituent

[19] *Tribune* (Ambala), September 9, 1952.
[20] *Delhi Express*, September 8, 1952.
[21] *The Pakistan Times* (Lahore), October 20, 1952.

Assembly and decide freely their fate. He condemned the recommendations of the United Nations as interference in Kashmir's internal affairs and serving the imperialist interests to turn Kashmir into a strategic base.[22]

When the Kashmiris demonstrated in August 1953 against the governmental coup in Srinagar, Bakshi and the Communists launched a series of accusations against the United Nations military observers for their alleged encouragement of the demonstrators and their distribution of money and food among them.

It must therefore be noted that the Delhi agreement of August 20, which took the Kashmir issue at least temporarily out of the hands of the United Nations, unwittingly served the years-long agitation of the Communists. Indeed, the Soviet newspapers welcomed the agreement as a victory over the "Anglo-American imperialist forces."[23]

Following the instruction of its Central Committee, local organizations of the Communist Party of India observed "Kashmir Day" on August 30 and passed resolutions asking for the "immediate expulsion of the UN representatives and other imperialist agents" from Kashmir. The Communist leader in the House of the People, A. K. Gopalan, appealed "for the creation of an atmosphere in Kashmir conducive to the State's final accession to India," and suggested "that all UN observers should be asked to leave Kashmir State before the plebiscite is held." P. Ramamurthy, member of the Politbureau, declared that the party was of the opinion "that the best interests of the people of Kashmir lay in their union with India. That would help strengthen the democratic movement in both countries."[24]

Sadiq accused the United Nations observers "of liaison

[22] S/PV 611, December 23, 1952, pp. 61-64.

[23] *Pravda* (Moscow), August 22, 1953; *New Times* (Moscow), No. 36, September 2, 1953.

[24] *The Statesman* (Calcutta), September 1 and 20, 1953; *The Times of India* (Bombay), September 19, 1953; *The Hindustan Times* (Delhi), September 7, 1953.

activities between pro-Pakistani elements in Kashmir and interested foreign powers outside" and declared that the Kashmir government would refuse the appointment of Fleet Admiral Chester Nimitz as plebiscite administrator, with the implication that he was a "nominee of an imperialist power."[25]

At its third congress in January 1954, the Communist Party of India urged in a resolution the withdrawal of the Kashmir issue from the United Nations, alleging that it was being exploited "to create division between India and Pakistan."

The Zig-Zag Tactics

The peculiar nature of the relations between the central government of India and the government of Kashmir has long presented the Communists with a wonderful opportunity "to fish in troubled waters." They encouraged Sheikh Abdullah in his policy toward possible independence, and yet they wished to be prepared for any other possible solution.

When Abdullah, in the summer of 1952, managed to sign the agreement with Jawaharlal Nehru, which in fact launched him on the road towards independence, the Communist Party of India welcomed the agreement. A. K. Gopalan not only supported the government in its action but also suggested that the Kashmir policy of land reform be applied to the rest of India. The Jammu Communist leader, Dhanwantry, expressed at a public meeting the belief that the future of Kashmir was safe only with India. "In this respect we wholeheartedly support the Nehru Government," he stated, and added that he wished the Kashmir case might be withdrawn from the United Nations.[26] Interestingly enough, he also pleaded for the separation of

[25] *The Hindustan Times* (Delhi), October 26, 1953.
[26] *Ibid.*, August 26, 1952.

Jammu from Kashmir, on the linguistic basis, as he explained.

It seems safe to assume that the Communist Party of India hoped that the privileged position of Kashmir would attract the attention of other Indian states and would lead to a weakening of the political structure of the Republic. In some of them the Communists have considerable strength. Then, too, a request to extend the Kashmir-modeled land reform to the whole of India could be expected to attract additional support. Moreover, the Nehru-Abdullah agreement sharpened the Indo-Pakistani tensions over Kashmir. On the whole, it could not have served the Communists better.

When the crisis in Indo-Kashmir relations reopened in the spring of 1953, the Communists joined the rightist elements in their disruptive activities in Jammu, though in Srinagar they continued to give support to Abdullah. This policy, contradictory as it was, gave them the double benefit of corroding the political structure of the state and at the same time of enjoying the freedom of political agitation. While all public meetings in Jammu were forbidden and illegal gatherings were severely dispersed, the field of politics was open to the Communists. The Democratic Youth League held a three-day convention at Jammu town in May and the Communist leader from India, Professor H. Mukkerji, while criticizing the communalist Praja Parishad, declared that the people's grievances were justified. The party was gaining ground. A correspondent reported that the National Conference "has seemingly made no conscious effort to plant itself securely in Jammu. Instead, organizationally, it has abdicated in favour of the Communists whose bread is buttered by official patronage and whose nest is feathered by discontent. Thus the entire space between the regime and the Parishad is allowed to be tenanted by the Reds."[27]

[27] *Ibid.*, May 23, 1953.

In high politics in Srinagar, the Communists supported Abdullah's drive towards wide autonomy. It can be assumed that they reasoned that it would be a serious setback for them if Kashmir should join Pakistan, where she would be tightly knitted within Islamic society and offer limited possibilities to their policy. But to establish a semi-independent Kashmir with the glittering hope of turning it at an opportune moment into an Outer-Mongolia on the Subcontinent, appeared to be their bold dream. Yet with characteristic opportunism, when Abdullah in his speeches gave the impression that he was about to bring their dream to realization, they suddenly switched to the bandwagon of the winning and pro-Indian Bakshi. Abdullah was jailed and the Communists remained in the government. In November their position was even strengthened; Ghulam Sadiq, the President of the Constituent Assembly, was nominated minister in charge of education, public health, information and broadcasting. Thus in the Kashmir government, three out of five ministers (Ghulam Muhammad Sadiq, Girdari Lal Dogra, the Minister of Finances, and Syed Mir Quasim, the Minister of Revenue) and heads of several important departments are now Communists or fellow-travelers.

It does not appear difficult to interpret the abrupt change in Communist policy in Kashmir. Trained in realistic appraisals of political situations, the Communist leaders held a rather dim view of the possibility of declaring Kashmir's independence at that time—in the presence of the Indian army. More than that, when rumors reached their ever-suspicious ears that the United States was supporting the idea, the very rumor seemed to be enough to convince them that the Abdullah policy was now for them a very risky move—one immediately to be abandoned. Indeed, Abdullah, for six years their protector and protégé, was now branded as a traitor and a lackey of American imperialists.

Joining the chorus of individual speakers who attacked

the alleged intervention of the United States in Kashmir affairs (some of the Indian newspapers did not lag behind in these attacks), the Communist Party of India now expressed in a resolution an emphatic opposition to the idea of an independent Kashmir. It warned against the danger of occupation of the strategic Valley of Kashmir by the American military forces and called upon "the democratic forces of Kashmir and Jammu to save the people from these new designs of imperialists and their conscious supporters and misguided votaries." The resolution also supported a qualified accession of Kashmir to India, declaring, "By limited accession, not only the State is united in friendship with India" but it also retains "its own status of virtual independence within the framework of the Indian Union."[28]

When the Prime Ministers of India and Pakistan confirmed in the Delhi agreement the policy of having a plebiscite in Kashmir, the Communists welcomed the agreement. At first thought this appeared rather strange; for nothing would serve the Communist plans less than a final and peaceful solution of the thorny Kashmir conflict. Such a position might be interpreted as only an attempt to turn necessity into a virtue, but more probably it reflected their hope that the Delhi agreement would not lead to any solution of the conflict, but rather, if not implemented, that it might actually lead to a deadly dangerous deterioration of the relations between India and Pakistan.

International Implications

Seven years ago, in October 1947, the Kashmir conflict began as a purely Indo-Pakistani problem. Eventually both sides agreed to its solution by way of a free plebiscite. They still appear to agree on this democratic procedure. But since the conflict's inception, many things have happened in Kashmir and on the international scene which have taken it out of the realm of local politics and have pro-

[28] *The Times of India* (Bombay), August 1, 1953.

jected it into the field of the global East-West struggle.

It is, of course, utter nonsense to accuse the United States and Great Britain of planning to establish in Kashmir military bases against the Soviet Union and China. If they have had any devious military schemes, "they have been singularly unsuccessful," as Sir Gladwyn Jebb once dryly remarked. Their only interest in Kashmir has been to see the conflict settled peacefully, well aware that such a solution would strengthen their own cause, well aware also that the continuance of the conflict aids the elements of disruption and expansion.

Not everyone concerned with the Kashmir problem has seen the American and British policy in this light, however. Even Nehru, while not questioning their motives and intentions, has often been openly critical of their advice and of what he has called "foreign interference." Sensitive as he is to American policy, he has been, on the other hand, very anxious to avoid any suspicion in Moscow about the situation in Kashmir.

When explaining to the House of the People his critical attitude towards the maintenance of Fleet Admiral Nimitz as plebiscite administrator, Nehru frankly stated, "He was appointed as plebiscite administrator about more than four years ago . . . much has happened in those three or four years. . . . We must try to isolate [the question of Kashmir] from big power politics. . . . It will not be fair to any of the big powers to ask them to supply a representative as a plebiscite administrator, however admirable he may be, because that would be embarrassing and needlessly creating suspicion, not in my mind necessarily, but in some other big power's mind."[29]

The nationality of the plebiscite administrator is, however, only a symbolic illustration of the East-West implications of the Kashmir conflict. Of more serious import were the events of the winter of 1953, which dramatically

[29] From Nehru's speech, September 17, 1953.

revealed the relationship of the problem of Kashmir to the East-West struggle. For whereas India continued to insist with increasing vehemence upon a course of policy independent of the global conflict, it was during this winter that Pakistan initiated a course of action which clearly revealed her willingness to become an active participant in the free world's defense against Communism. It was then that Pakistan opened negotiations with the United States for military assistance; India was vehemently opposed, and inevitably the issue of Kashmir was immediately drawn into this clash of policy.

A meeting of the National Conference passed a resolution protesting against the idea of American military help to Pakistan. Bakshi declared that "America might arm Pakistan or help her in any other way but Kashmir will never form part of Pakistan"; and Sadiq seconded, "Pakistan leaders want to ruin Kashmir but we want to make it clear to them that we are vigilant and shall not allow them to deprive us of our freedom."[30] The Kashmiri leaders renewed the cries that the United States planned to secure bases in Gilgit, and Nehru warned at the press conference that "it is not open [to Pakistan] to do anything on Kashmir territory, least of all to give bases."[31]

Both the United States and Pakistan governments denied the reports about negotiations which would provide for establishment of military bases anywhere in Pakistan, but the news about the envisaged armament of Pakistan with American assistance was sufficient enough to throw another dark shadow on the Kashmir dispute. Already Nehru declared in one of tens of speeches he made against this assistance that the Kashmir problem had been discussed between him and Mohammed Ali in August and an agreement reached "on the basis of a certain situation" but "the

[30] *The Hindu Weekly Review* (Madras), November 30, 1953.
[31] *Indiagram* (The Embassy of India, Washington, D.C.), No. 333, November 18, 1953.

whole context in which those agreements were made will change if military aid comes from America."[32]

In the light of all these international implications, the solution of the Kashmir dispute appears even more complex than ever before, but it also imperatively requires an early settlement.

From Sinkiang and Tibet, Kashmir is exposed to ever-increasing pressure. Its rugged and hilly borders are ideal for infiltration. From the other side it is exposed to the relentless hostility of the Azad and Pakistan governments which will not—in fact cannot—give up their demand for a plebiscite or another satisfactory solution. Should they conceivably attempt to do so, the pressure of their people would forbid it, a pressure which increases with each postponement of the plebiscite, constantly threatening a resumption of hostilities.

These two forces, the Pakistani-Azad and Communist-Chinese, as diametrically opposed as they are to each other, squeeze the unhappy Kashmir between them. Here in the soil of uncertainty, in the darkness of intrigue, in an air heavy with hate and suspicion and fear, the fungi of Communism flourish. Only an impartial plebiscite or other similarly democratic solution to the problem can put an end to the danger of a conflict between India and Pakistan and at the same time restore to Kashmir the possibility of an openly administered democratic life. For should Kashmir, as a result of a just solution, go to Pakistan, she would in all certainty become a full member of Pakistan society; should Kashmir go to India, her government would deal with the subversive activities there in the same fashion that it has done in India. Nothing is worse for Kashmir herself, for Pakistan or for India, than to have the present situation indefinitely prolonged. Only one cause profits from the continuation of the dispute: the cause of Communism.

[32] From Nehru's speech in the House of the People, December 29, 1953.

10. The Double Shadow

THE Kashmir situation, packed as it is with explosive tensions between India and Pakistan and with Communist subversion, constitutes a direct threat to the peace of the Subcontinent and a danger to the peace of the world. A portion of the danger lies in the fact, however, that the government of India refuses to recognize that threat.

When at the beginning of 1954 the question of American military help to Pakistan was publicly debated, Jawaharlal Nehru raised the argument that such help would turn the Subcontinent into a "war area." But the fact is that the Communist ideological dictates and global strategy in political warfare make any region potentially a war area. As to Kashmir, she has been to the Communists one among many theaters of political and military warfare ever since the inception of the conflict. To them a divided Kashmir is another divided Korea, another divided Indo-China, another divided Germany, another divided Austria. If Kashmir were united through democratic process and under democratic rule, the Communist spearhead, aimed as it is today against the Subcontinent, would be blunted, and this area would enter the sphere of the free world. No one realizes these international implications of the Kashmir conflict better than the Communists.

The government of India has pursued a policy independent of the ideological and power struggle between the forces of democracy and of Communism because it does not see the danger to its country in the same way as does the West. Jawaharlal Nehru shares with the West deep convictions on personal freedom, political democracy, and the rule under law. He is equally profoundly convinced that the best way to combat Communism is to combat poverty through economic and social reforms; and he is engaged in a colossal experiment in democracy on the home front. But at the same time he sees no danger to India from without and he is sure that any closer tie with the rest of the free world may only provoke Moscow and Peking, perhaps with disastrous effects on India.

Nehru's attitude toward the Kashmir situation is colored by these beliefs about combating Communism and about the non-aggressive nature of the Soviet and Chinese policies. And because he underestimates the outside threat to India, he does not recognize the utter necessity of settling the Kashmir conflict. Nehru has persisted in this attitude toward Russia for many years. In one of his books he asked himself, "Who might be the aggressor against India?" And he answered, "Soviet Russia is definitely out of the picture so far as aggression goes; she seeks a policy of international peace, and the acquisition of Indian territory would fulfill no want of hers." He considered Soviet foreign policy as "consistently one of peace" and "of fulfilling international obligations and supporting the cause of democracy abroad."[1] One can understand such a judgment made as it was in 1938 against the backdrop of the world scene at that time; nor should such a judgment be used as a yardstick of the wisdom of Nehru's present attitude. But his present reliance on a non-aggressive Soviet foreign policy, against the backdrop of the past fifteen years, is something else again. For, since 1939 many countries—Latvia, Lithuania, Estonia, Poland, East Germany, Hungary, Rumania, Bulgaria, Yugoslavia, Albania, Czechoslovakia, Northern Korea, and China —have been communized in a fashion which does not commend itself to the principles of international peace and to the cause of democracy. In none of them, with the exception perhaps of China, was such communization the result of a spontaneous search on the part of their peoples for a revolutionary solution to their economic and social ills, but, rather, a result of direct political or military Soviet intervention.

So far as her own security is concerned, India does not

[1] Jawaharlal Nehru, *The Unity of India, op.cit.*, pp. 24, 116.

appear to be impressed by this record of Soviet war-time and post-war policy. Her refusal to see the Soviet aspect of the international implications of the Kashmir conflict is a logical outgrowth of her basic assessment of Soviet intentions. One can, however, grasp the full gravity of this conflict only if it is analyzed against the broader background of Communist interest in the Subcontinent. In this connection, a brief survey of Czarist and Soviet policy towards South Asia is revealing and enlightening.

The Lessons of History

The lessons of history caution against hasty conclusions. Indeed, they raise serious doubts as to the practical possibility of a large-scale Soviet invasion of the Subcontinent. Yet, the old Czarist dreams of conquering India indicate at least a traditional desire of the Russian Empire to expand in that direction.

It can be assumed that the British, while ruling in India, were better acquainted with the Czarist threat to the Subcontinent than any other people. There were actually two schools of thought among British statesmen, distinguished members of the Indian Civil Service, and scholars. One proposed to deal with the Russian danger by pursuing a "forward policy"; the other minimized the threat and recommended a policy of cooperation with Czarist Russia and of applying in the border regions of India a strategy of "masterly inactivity." Others even welcomed Russian expansion in Central Asia as a Christian missionary work. But all seemed fully aware of at least the possibility of Russian expansion in Afghanistan, Persia, and China, exposing India to the very real threat of encirclement. The British policy in the nineteenth and the first decade of the twentieth century was directed towards the specific goal of preventing this encirclement. It pushed the direct military control of India towards the North-West Frontier Province in occupying strategic positions; it tried to pacify the restless Pathan tribes. With the Russian danger in mind, the British waged the two Afghan Wars (1839-1842 and 1879-1881), and another in 1919; they helped the Afghan rulers to consolidate their power, with an eye to establishing a solid buffer state between Russia and India; they tried to strengthen, similarly, the hand of the Shahs in Persia and took the southern regions under military control in 1907. They observed with keen interest the developments in autonomous Sinkiang and endeavored to develop commercial contacts with this region. They stationed British Imperial troops in the northern area of the Princely State of Jammu and Kashmir.[2]

There are few original sources which reveal the specific intentions of Czarist policy concerning India, but few would argue that St. Petersburg was unaware of her strategical and economic importance. In 1722, the founder of modern Russia, Peter the Great, after he had reached the Gulf of Astrabad on the Caspian Sea, pointed towards India and was reported to declare ". . . from there [Astrabad] to Balkh and Badakshan with pack-camels is only twelve days' journey and on that road to India no one can interfere with us."[3] He planned also the conquest of Central Asia and ordered one of his commanders, Prince Bekovich, to prepare an expeditionary India-bound force which would penetrate into India from Central Asia.

In 1791, the Empress Catherine studied plans for the invasion of India via Bokhara and Kabul. France under Napoleon and Russia under Czars Paul and Alexander I had at one time common reasons to cast their eyes on

[2] For detailed information, see Archibald R. Colquhoun, *Russia Against India*, Harper and Brothers, New York, 1900. Francis Henry Skrine, *The Expansion of Russia*, Cambridge University Press, 1904. W. E. Baxter, *England and Russia*, Swan Sonnenschein, London, 1885. William Digby, *India for the Indians—and for England*, Talbot Brothers, London, 1885. Demetrius Charles Boulger, *England and Russia in Central Asia*, W. H. Allen, London, 1879.

[3] A. R. Colquhoun, *op.cit.*, pp. 7-8.

India, namely to weaken their common enemy, Great Britain. Paul wrote, "The French Republic and the Emperor of Russia must send a combined force of 70,000 men to the borders of India. . . . The two governments have resolved to unite their forces in order to liberate India from the tyrannical and barbarous yoke of the English." In 1801, he wrote to one of his generals, Orlov, ". . . You will therefore proceed to India. . . . I entrust this expedition entirely to you and your army. . . . This enterprise will cover you with glory, and according to your deserts, you will earn my special good-will. You will acquire riches and treasures, and will affright the enemy in his heart. I send you maps—as many as I have—and remain, your well-wisher, Paul."[4] The maps extended only to Khiva and Oxus, and General Orlov's expedition was withdrawn by Paul's successor, the Czar Alexander.

In 1808, one year after the Tilsit Treaty, Napoleon tried to reestablish the spirit of Russian-French friendship. He made offers to Alexander I which were meant to restore the Czar's confidence in the French Emperor, which had been considerably shattered by his maneuvering in regard to Turkey. He wrote to the Czar, "If an army of 50,000 men with Russians, Frenchmen, and perhaps a few Austrians were to make its way into Asia, through Constantinople, it would not reach the Euphrates without making England tremble. . . . I am ready in Dalmatia; Your Majesty is ready on the Danube. One month after we have made our arrangements, the army might be on the Bosphorus." The Czar reacted to this glittering offer, saying, "When we have settled things in Turkey and India, this will force England to make peace."[5] Napoleon's invasion of Russia

[4] Edward H. Sutherland, *Russian Projects Against India*. Remington and Co., London, 1885, pp. 34, 36, 38.

[5] H. Butterfield, *The Peace Tactics of Napoleon*. Cambridge University Press, 1929, p. 352, as quoted from *Sbornik*, LXXXVIII, 456-458; Louis Fischer, *The Life of Mahatma Gandhi*, Harper and Brothers, New York, in the Notes to Chapter XXII, p. 582, mentions

put an end, however, to the plans of a Russian-French expedition into India.

In the nineteenth century several Czarist generals elaborated plans for the invasion of India. They considered the gradual penetration of Central Asia as a steppingstone to still further advances. General Perovski understood his march to Khiva, in 1839, as the first step to "shake India." General Duhamel presented a project to Czar Nicholas in 1854, and General Khrulev prepared another plan the following year. In 1878, General Skobelev elaborated a detailed invasion of India by three columns, one of which would advance in the direction of Chitral and Kashmir. The project was published in 1883. It considered the idea of an invasion through Kashmir as a militarily feasible operation. This opinion was fully shared by another Russian officer, V. T. Lebedev, who devoted a book to the military aspects of an invasion of India.[6] He described the situation in Kashmir and concluded, ". . . it will be easy to arrange an uprising in Kashmir as the population suffers under the burden of heavy taxes." He emphasized also the strategic importance of Chitral and Gilgit, giving detailed plans for the invasion of these provinces.

The Russian historian, A. E. Sneserev, told Louis Fischer that despite all these plans, "the Czarist Government never looked upon an invasion of India as a serious matter and only permitted the military governors in Turkestan to toy with the idea."[7] This may be true and yet the impressive recurrence of military planning and preparation would suggest that the idea of an invasion of India failed to materialize for reasons other than Russian disinterest. It is more probable that constant interruptions from European sources

---

copying from the Czarist archives in Moscow Napoleon's letters to the Russian emperors Paul and Alexander I.

[6] V. T. Lebedev, *V Indiu*, Voenno-statisticheskii i strategiiskii otcherk. Projekt budushchego pohoda, S. Petersburg, 1898.

[7] Louis Fischer, *The Soviets in World Affairs*. Princeton University Press, 1951, vol. I, p. 420.

postponed serious Russian attention to India. The interruptions were many and successive: Catherine the Great, by war against the Turks for Crimea and by preparations for the division of Poland; Paul and Alexander, by the Napoleonic Wars; Nicholas, by the Crimean War; Alexander II, by the Balkan War, in 1877-1878. As to Central Asia, the Czarist Empire expanded systematically in the second half of the nineteenth century until, in 1891, it reached the Pamirs, the borderland of India.

A similar policy of gradual Czarist penetration was pursued in Sinkiang. Ever since 1870, when the Russians succeeded in consolidating their position in Central Asia, their influence in Sinkiang has been on the increase. This province, never under effective control of the central Chinese government and with access to the Chinese mainland only through Russian territory, became increasingly dependent economically upon trade with Russia. Hard on the heels of commercial privileges in Sinkiang came pressure by the St. Petersburg government for political advantage.

In both areas then, in the Middle East and in Northern China, Czarist policy reflected its traditional interest in expanding towards the Persian Gulf and the Arabian Sea and towards Chinese Turkestan respectively. Inevitably it came into conflict with British positions and interests.

To put an end to this unsettled and dangerous situation, and to free their hands to face the German threat in Europe, the two nations, on August 31, 1907, signed the "Convention between Great Britain and Russia relating to Persia, Afghanistan, and Tibet." Though formulated in cautious terms, the Convention meant, for all practical purposes, the partition of Persia between Russia and Great Britain, the recognition by Russia of Afghanistan to be "en dehors de la sphère de l'influence Russe," with the implication that Afghanistan lay within the British sphere of influence, and the obligation of both Great Britain and Russia to respect the territorial integrity of Tibet, under

Chinese suzerainty, and to abstain from intervening in its internal affairs.[8]

The position of Sinkiang was not mentioned in the Convention. This omission might be due to a feeling on the part of the British that they could afford to overlook Russian economic penetration of the province, satisfied that they had prevented further expansion of Russia in the Middle East and the spreading of her influence in Tibet. That they had principally the security of India in mind appears beyond doubt.

The State of Jammu and Kashmir was like a wedge thrust into Czarist possessions in Central Asia. Its strategic importance was obvious. In 1889, the Maharaja, Sir Partab Singh, was accused of having been in treasonable correspondence with Russia, but the letters he allegedly exchanged with St. Petersburg proved to have been forged.[9] The British Crown, however, though not taking the accusation seriously, did not want to be exposed to any possible risk in view of increased Russian activities in the area of the Pamirs, and consequently established a council to rule over Kashmir. Only in 1905 was the Maharaja reestablished with full powers.

A Double-Barrelled Weapon

World War I and the Bolshevik revolution brought dramatic changes in the nature of traditional British-Russian rivalry in the vast areas of the Middle East and South Asia. Both the war and the revolution gave new impetus to the upsurge of nationalism and anti-foreignism. The Arab countries clamored for the self-rule which had once been promised them but never delivered. Persia and Afghanistan were eager for an opportunity to get rid of Brit-

[8] For the text of the Convention see *British and Foreign State Papers*, 1906-1907, vol. c. Compiled and edited by Richard W. Brant and W. Maycock, London, 1911, pp. 556-559.

[9] William Digby, *Condemned Unheard—the Government of India and H. H. The Maharaja of Kashmir*. London, 1890.

ish influence. The national sentiments of the temporarily established union of the Hindu-Muslim front found an outlet in the Khilaphat movement and the first waves of non-violence and non-cooperation in India. China disintegrated into a maelstrom of fighting war lords. The entire situation was almost tailor-made for a Communist thrust.

If the British had been previously only slightly concerned about the intentions of the Czars toward India and had felt satisfied by her blunting of Russian penetration on her flanks, they became truly alarmed at the new double-barrelled weapon which appeared on the scene of power politics and which fitted so snugly into Russian hands: the ideological weapon of revolting nationalism and Communism. But Soviet Russia was herself in the grip of a civil war, and the Bolshevik government's existence was threatened by the armies of the Whites supported by the Western Allies in the first years of its power. Her principal remedy, therefore, was to weaken Great Britain in the Middle East and Asia. Toward this end the ideological weapon served as a powerful instrument. National sentiments and agitation offered the Soviet leaders a great opportunity.

In one of its first acts, on December 3, 1917, the Council of People's Commissars appealed to the "Muslims of the East, Turks, Arabs and Hindus" to throw off the yoke of imperialism and help the Russian revolution.[10] At the beginning of September 1920, the Third International organized the First Congress of the Peoples of the East in Baku. Delegates of many nationalities and religious groups gathered at this big show, all of them linked together by the common tie of their hatred of England. There were thirteen representatives in Baku from India and one, named Agaria, was elected to the Presidium of the Congress. The Third International was represented by its Chairman, Grig-

[10] *Soviet Documents on Foreign Policy.* Selected and edited by Jane Degras. Oxford University Press, 1951, vol. I, pp. 15-17.

ory Zinoviev, and by Karl Radek. Zinoviev voiced an anxiously awaited sentiment when he addressed the session, saying, ". . . we want to free all nations, all working people, regardless of the color of their skin, regardless of their being white, black or yellow." He had a special word for India, which was "so mercilessly grabbed by the English capital." He appealed to the excited and passionate leaders, "Comrades! Brothers! The time has come when you can begin to organize the forthcoming national holy struggle against the usurpers and oppressors. The Communist International turns today towards the nations of the East and tells them: Brothers! We invite you to a holy war first of all against English imperialism." Radek climaxed his appeal, "Long live a Red East which together with the working Europe creates a new culture under the banner of Communism."[11] These were still the times of bold appeals for a "permanent revolution," and the Baku Congress vibrated with these words. The delegates fell into a delirium of enthusiasm and brought back to their homes the fires of a revolutionary fervor lighted at Baku.

In Persia, the Soviets maneuvered shrewdly to expose British policy. They declared null and void the Russian-British convention of 1907, renounced the extraterritorial rights and various economic privileges in Persia, transferred the Russian assets to the "Persian people," and, after initial complications connected with the Allied intervention in the Russian civil war, withdrew the Red army from Northern Persia. These gestures of magnanimity did not, however, prevent them from attempting to establish a Soviet Republic of Ghilan, in 1920-1921. They gave support to the nationalist and anti-British movement led by Riza Khan, who, however, later disappointed them by establish-

[11] *Pervyi S'ezd Narodov Vostoka.* Baku, 1-8 Sentiabr 1920, Stenografskicheskie otcherti. Izdatel'stvo Komunisticheskogo Internatsionala, 1920, Petrograd, pp. 34, 46, 48, 72.

ing friendly relations with London after he had been crowned Shah towards the end of 1925.

King Amanullah of Afghanistan, who had special reasons for hating the British (they had sentenced him to death during the war), was highly praised in an official communication by Lenin because the Afghan nation was "heroically defending itself against foreign oppressors." In another letter Lenin promised to join Afghanistan in the struggle, "against the most rapacious imperialistic government on earth—Great Britain," and said he was ready to give Afghanistan "military aid against England. . . ."[12] In February 1921, both countries, Persia and Afghanistan, entered into a treaty relationship with the Soviet Union.

In 1921 the flames of Asiatic nationalism momentarily slackened, and the Soviet government's need for imports and for credits from the West prevailed over their policy of openly encouraging revolutions abroad. In a commercial treaty with Britain, signed March 16, 1921, the Soviet government promised to abstain, "from any attempt by military or diplomatic or any other form of action or propaganda to encourage any of the peoples of Asia in any form of hostile action against British interests or the British Empire, especially in India and in the Independent state of Afghanistan."[13]

Despite this official attitude, however, the Soviet government continued to press, secretly, its direction of Communist revolutionary activities on the Subcontinent, supporting organized terrorist groups with money and arms.

The Third International on the Scene

Mahendra Partab, an Indian revolutionary, was in the

[12] Louis Fischer, *op.cit.*, vol. I, pp, 285, 286.

[13] Great Britain, Foreign Office, *Agreement between Great Britain and Russia for the Resumption of Trade and Commerce between the Two Countries* (Cmd 1207), British and Foreign States Papers, vol. cxiv (1921), London, H.M. Stationery Office, 1924, p. 374.

service of the Soviet government as early as the end of 1917. He travelled throughout Central Asia and helped organize revolts in Kazan, Tashkent, Bokhara, and later worked from Kabul. Another Indian revolutionary was Barakatullah Khan.

A nucleus of the future Communist Party of India was created in 1920 in Berlin, a city which appeared to be an ideal place for the illegal activities of political exiles. Moscow was within easy reach, as was London to the West, where British Communists followed with great attention and a helping hand the development in India. Moreover, Germany, stripped as she was of colonies, no longer carried the stigma of imperialism. So it was that in Hamburg, an Indian group led by M. N. Roy published the paper, *The Vanguard of Indian Independence.*

To further the subversion of the Subcontinent, Tashkent was established as a training center for professional revolutionaries and as the seat of an Association of India, and a school was founded at Samarkand in 1920 which was attended by 3,500 "experts," of whom 931 were Hindus.[14] These experts were then sent to India, well provided with money. The Soviet Minister at Kabul, Raskolnikov, gave special attention to the tribesmen in Waziristan and to the situation in the North-West Frontier Province among other things sending arms to the tribesmen.

"The Russian Minister at Tehran has been the most tireless, though not always the most successful, operator in this field [of anti-British activities]. He has housed Indian seditionists within his hospitable walls, and has sped them on their mission to India," stated a British document listing a number of instances of Soviet activities aimed against British rule in India.[15]

[14] J. Castagné, *Les Musulmans et la politique des Soviets en Asie centrale.* Les Indes et Egypte vues de Russie. Editions Ernest Leroux, Paris, 1925, pp. 78-82.

[15] *Correspondence between H.M.'s Government and the Soviet Government.* Cmd 1869, p. 7.

The Third International cherished high hopes about Communist upheavals in India. It established an Islamic and an Indian section to study the situation and to direct revolutionary activities on the Subcontinent. Soviet experts published treatises about the problem, harping particularly on colonial and national issues.[16]

In his address, on November 22, 1919, before the Second All-Russian Congress of the Communist organizations of the nations of the East, Lenin analyzed the political situation in Asia and gave to the delegates detailed instructions on how to spread the flames of the revolution.[17]

In May, 1920, he greeted the Indian Revolutionary Association on the occasion of "the proclamation of the worker-peasant republic" and appealed to the Indian revolutionaries "fighting heroically for their freedom" to maintain the solidarity of the Muslim and non-Muslim elements. "Only then, when the Indian, Chinese, Korean, Japanese, Persian, Turkish workers and peasants stretch out their hands each to the other and march together toward their common goal of liberation, only then will be assured decisive victory over exploiters. Long live free Asia!"[18]

The Second Congress of the Third International, held in Moscow in the summer of 1920, passed an elaborate thesis on "the National and Colonial Questions," presented by Lenin, with a special supplementary statement on China and India.

Stalin was reported to have declared, in June 1921, before the Executive Committee of the Third International, "The general guiding purpose of the Eastern Secretariat [of the Third International] in all its work lies in exerting pressure upon the political authority of the capitalist Powers of

[16] M. P. Pavlovitch-Volonter (Vel'tman), *Voprosy Kolonial'noi Politiki i 3-i Internatsional*, Moskva, 1920. Tivelj, *Puti i Perspektivi Indiiskoi Revoliutsii*. Novyi Vostok, Kniga I, Moskva, 1922.

[17] V. I. Lenin, *Sochinenia*, 4th ed., Gosudarstvennoe izdatel'stvo politicheskoi literaturi, 1950, vol. 30, pp. 130-141.

[18] *Ibid.*, p. 116.

Western Europe through their colonies. . . ." In the Soviet-Afghanistan treaty of February 1921, which in articles 4 and 5 made provisions for establishing Soviet consulates in Eastern Afghanistan, he saw an instrument, ". . . through which the Communist International maintains direct communications further South with British India. . . ." The Communist leader Eliava was able to report on the same occasion, ". . . we are already taking the offensive against foundations of capitalism in India itself."[19]

At the Third Congress of the Comintern, in the summer of 1921, Lenin declared, "[In British India] the revolution grows the more quickly, the more notably stands up the industrial and railroad proletariat on the one side and the more brutal becomes the terror of the English on the other. . . ."[20] In his last article published in *Pravda* on March 4, 1923, he based his conviction of the inevitable victory of Communism over capitalism on the rapid emancipation of the Asiatic nations and concluded, "In the last analysis, the upshot of the struggle will be determined by the fact that Russia, India, China, etc., account for the overwhelming majority of the population of the globe."[21]

The British government protested in several diplomatic notes against these violations of the Trade Agreement of March 16, 1921. The Soviet government rejected the charge and protested against being identified with the Third International. The British brought the exchange of correspondence to a climax when Lord Curzon, on May 2, 1923, sent an ultimatum to Moscow: the situation must be remedied or the Trade Agreement would be cancelled. The Soviet government gave partial satisfaction to London and reiterated its pledge not to interfere with British policy in

[19] A *Selection of Papers dealing with the relations between H.M.'s Government and the Soviet Government*, 1921-1927. Cmd 2895.

[20] Lenin, *op.cit.*, pp. 430-431.

[21] V. I. Lenin, *Selected Works*. Two-volume edition. Lawrence and Wishart, London, 1947, vol. 2, p. 854.

Asia. Then it made the grand gesture: "Further, in view of complaints which have been made," read the official statement, "the Soviet Government undertakes not to support with funds or in any other form persons, or bodies, or agencies, or institutions whose aim is to spread discontent or to foment rebellion in any part of the British Empire . . . and to impress upon its officers and officials the full and continuous observance of these conditions."[22]

This declaration, signed on June 4, 1923, was indeed observed for a little while as the Soviet government recognized the utter necessity of maintaining trade with Britain. Besides, the events in China were promising enough from the Soviet point of view to command Moscow's full attention. Before too long, however, the Soviet government fell from grace and returned to the policy of directing the activities of Indian Communists, much of the work being done through the Colonial Department of the Communist Party of Great Britain. One of its principal weapons was to draw the attention to the Muslims on the Subcontinent to the now autonomous, predominantly Muslim regions of Tadjikistan and Turkestan, declaring, in the words of *Pravda* in May 1925, "The people of Tadjikistan are the outposts of the new culture in the eyes of millions of men who constitute the masses of the Orient and who are of the same origin but who have been so far enchained by imperialism."[23]

In 1926 Soviet hopes for a revolution in South Asia were running high. The Chinese Communists cooperating with the Kuomintang, as had been "advised" by the Soviet representative, Borodin, held key positions in the government. Nikolai Bukharin had the vision of things to come, "In the event of the further victorious advance of the Canton armies, it is not Utopia to assert that a victorious Chinese

[22] Command Paper 2895, p. 24.
[23] *Pravda* (Moscow), May 7, 1925, as quoted in J. Castagné, *op.cit.*, p. 62.

revolution will find an immediate echo in the neighbouring colonial countries—India, Indonesia and Dutch India. All this makes China a mighty center of attraction for the colonial periphery."[24] The vision, however, failed to materialize. Chiang Kai-shek ousted Borodin from China in 1927 and turned against the Communists. But the Moscow-directed Communist activities in India continued.[25]

At the Sixth Congress of the Third International, in the summer of 1928, the revolutionary campaign in the colonial countries was intensified. The Communist parties were called upon to establish strong leadership and to lead the proletariat in a class struggle, not only against the British imperialist rule, but also against the "liberal-national bourgeoisie."[26] M. N. Roy, the first Indian Communist leader, wrote later, after having become their fiercest opponent, "The resolutions of the Communist International regarding India since 1928 were the height of stupidity."[27] The Communists failed completely to realize the popular strength of the All-India National Congress, against which any opposition was bound to be unsuccessful.

The Soviet theoreticians saw in the Indian situation a classical Marxist field for a class struggle. On one side was the foreign capitalist linked with feudal exploitation, on the other the enslaved masses of the Indian proletariat. The bourgeois movement led by the National Congress was, in their view, made ineffectual by its lukewarm attitude toward British rule. They expected a steady strengthening of the proletariat through its open and systematic struggle against both foreign imperialism and the local bourgeois nationalists.[28] "The historic meaning and world-wide significance

[24] Command Paper 2895, p. 47.
[25] Command Papers 2682, 2874.
[26] *Komunisticheskii Internatsional v Dokumentah*, 1919-1932. Ed. Bela Kun. Partiinoe Izdatel'stvo, Moskva, 1933.
[27] M. N. Roy, *The Communist International*. Radical Democratic Party Publication, Bombay, 1943, p. 48.
[28] A. Pronin, *Klassovaia Borba i Konstitutsionnye Reformi Britanskogo Imperializma v Indii*. Moskva, 1934.

of the period 1920 to 1930" lay for them "in the fact that the proletariat has begun the struggle for the hegemony in the national-liberating movement."[29]

Stalin himself, elaborating on his theory of a proletarian revolution breaking off the chains of the imperialist world at its weakest link, hopefully expected, "It is not impossible that this may be in India . . . because there we find a young and militant revolutionary proletariat in alliance with the movement of national liberation."[30]

However, the actual development in India, as elsewhere, was a grave disappointment to the Third International. The leadership, unable to produce satisfactory revolutionary zeal, found the masses unresponsive to its appeals for a class revolution. Consequently, the Seventh Congress of the Comintern, in the summer of 1935, reversed its strategy and called for the creation of Popular Fronts in cooperation with democratic parties. The Indian Communists were severely criticized by the Chinese member of the Presidium of the Executive Committee of the Third International, Wang Ming, for sectarianism and for not having allied themselves with the masses. They were ordered to create a Popular Front with the National Congress and the Socialist Party and enter their ranks.[31]

The Communist Party of India Fails

If the Soviet leadership considered India as an ideal field for a Communist revolution, it must have been thoroughly disappointed by the poor performance of the Indian Communists all through the interwar period. Chiefly responsible for its ineffectiveness was the membership of the party in the years following World War I. It was made up mostly of

[29] A. J. Shtusser, *Marks i Engels ob Indii*. Gosudarstvennoe Izdatel'stvo, Moskva, 1930, p. 7.

[30] Joseph V. Stalin, *Foundations of Leninism*. International Publishers, New York, 1932, p. 34.

[31] *Contre la guerre et le Fascisme: L'Unité*. Résolutions et Décisions. Bureau d'Editions, Paris, 1935, pp. 30-33.

intellectuals suffering from dogmatism, sectarianism, and factionalism. They failed to recognize the strength of a well-knit organization and blind discipline, and they did not follow the duty of "descending" to the masses. Some strikes were organized in 1923 in Bombay, Bengal, and the United Provinces, but the leaders were arrested and put on trial in 1924 (the Cawnpore Conspiracy Case). In 1928 the Communist Party led workers into another strike, and its leaders were again sent behind bars (the Meerut Conspiracy Case). In 1930, a Draft Program of Action asked for a violent overthrow of the Indian government and the establishment of a Soviet government. Four years later, all party organizations were banned and the Communist leadership went underground. The following year the Indian Communists followed Moscow orders and in considerable numbers entered the All-India National Congress, with as many as fifty Communists in leading party positions in 1942.

World War II presented new opportunities to the Indian Communists, but it also presented them (as it did Communists all over the world) with some delicate problems.

Stalin Follows the Czars' Path

After twenty years, the Soviet government was tempted to indulge in the traditional Czarist expansionist dreams in the Middle East and in South Asia. As Napoleon with Czar Paul and Alexander I had contemplated the invasion of India as a deadly blow to their chief enemy, England, so in 1940 Adolf Hitler and Joseph Stalin were, in their thoughts, carving out huge slices of foreign territories for themselves. When Vyacheslav Molotov paid an official visit to Berlin in November 1940, Ribbentrop laid before him the grand plan of the division of the world between Germany, Japan, Italy, and Russia. Russia was offered to look for "possible Soviet aspirations in the direction of British India." In a draft agreement prepared by Ribbentrop, the

Secret Protocol No. 1, paragraph 4, read, "The Soviet Union declares that its territorial aspirations center south of the national territory of the Soviet Union in the direction of the Indian Ocean."[32] Molotov seems not to have been convinced by Ribbentrop's repeated allegations that Great Britain was already beaten on the battlefield. He saw clearly that the German Foreign Minister wished to embroil the Soviet Union in a war against Britain, as Napoleon had a hundred and forty years before. He was more anxious to clear away the misunderstandings which arose out of the interpretation of the now notorious agreements signed by Germany and Russia on the eve and at the beginning of World War II, than to indulge in future dreams of expansion. He was disturbed by German activities in Finland and the Balkans.

Back in Moscow, Molotov became increasingly eager to come to an agreement with Berlin, the more so as there were unmistakably heavy clouds accumulating on the horizon of Soviet-German friendship. So, in the spring of 1941, he proposed to sign the draft agreement, but making such an act conditional upon the clarification of the situation in Finland and Bulgaria. In the final draft agreement, also, reference to the Indian Ocean was to be omitted and it was to read, ". . . the area South of Batum and Baku in the general direction of the Persian Gulf is recognized as the center of the aspirations of the Soviet Union."[33]

The Soviet government thus realistically appraised the situation. It certainly did not wish to estrange Germany, but at the same time it did not wish to provoke Great Britain. And it felt that an eventual occupation of Iran would not necessarily cause open hostilities with anyone. Once the Soviet Union was in possession of the Persian Gulf, however, it believed that it would be able to strike

[32] *Nazi-Soviet Documents, 1939-1941*, edited by R. J. Sontag and J. S. Beddie. Department of State, 1948, pp. 251, 257.

[33] *Ibid.*, p. 259.

from this strategical center in several directions, including India.

It was not through any virtue of Moscow that the agreement was never signed. By spring 1941, the preparations of the German army to attack the Soviet Union were far advanced.

The Party Uses the Opportunity

The Indian Communists did not appear to be disturbed by the policy of cooperation between the motherland of Communism, the Soviet Union, and Nazi Germany. But on June 22, 1941, the day of the German invasion of Russia, the situation changed. Great Britain, and through her, British India, became allies of the Soviet Union. For a few months the Communists were confused, maintaining the rather difficult thesis that British participation in war was imperialist, Soviet participation just and correct. Only when the Japanese opened an all-out attack on South-East Asia did the Communists in India declare the struggle as a people's war and appealed for a maximum war effort.

This was a period of great opportunity for them, the more so as the National Congress leaders were in jail for their anti-war agitation. In July 1942 the Communist leaders were released from prison and the party was recognized again as a legitimate organization. Its ranks grew and its organization was strengthened. Its headquarters were located in Bombay. P. C. Joshi became the Secretary-General. Although it never attracted vast numbers, its membership rose from 2,000 in 1942, 9,000 in 1943, 25,000 in 1944, to 40,000 in 1945. More important was the fact that the character of its membership was no longer predominantly intellectual but was now largely made up of workers and peasants. In 1945, 36 per cent of the party members were peasants, 26 per cent workers, 11 per cent students, and 5 per cent women, the remainder belonging to the intelligentsia. The party became active not only in India but in such Princely

States as Gwalior, Baroda, Travancore, Cochin, Mysore, and Hyderabad.

The party exercised decisive control over the All-India Students Federation, which in 1943 claimed 52,000 members; various women's organizations, with 41,000 members; Children Brigades, with 9,000 members; Friends of the Soviet Union, Progressive Writers Association, India's People's Theatre Association, and above all the All-India Trade Union Congress, which in 1945 had a membership of 432,000 persons and in 1951 claimed a membership of 706,000 workers. Since 1944, increased attention was also given to the organization of peasants. Out of 25 members of the General Council of the All-India Peasant Association—Kisan Sabha—22 were Communists. The party managed to infiltrate the ranks of the National Congress, though its Popular Front program suffered a defeat in 1942 when it changed its attitude towards the war, while the Congress leaders continued their opposition. The Communists made little headway in the Muslim League, except in Punjab.[34]

The policy of the Communist Party of India toward an independent Pakistan was one of vacillation. An enlarged plenum of its Central Committee passed a resolution in September 1942 "On Pakistan and National Unity," in which it rejected the idea of a separate Pakistan. Instead, it asked for a united India composed of a great number of autonomous nationalities: Pathans, Punjabis, Sikhs, Sindhis, Hindustanis, Rajasthanis, Gujerathis, Bengalis, etc., each with the right of secession. When, however, toward the end of the war, the idea of an independent Pakistan was

[34] For more detailed information, see *The Communist Party of India*, Office of Strategic Services, R & A No. 2681, August, 1945; M. R. Masani, "The Communist Party in India," *Pacific Affairs*, Vol. xxiv, No. 1, March 1951, pp. 18-38. Ruth Fischer, "The Indian Communist Party," *Far Eastern Survey*, Vol. xxii, No. 7, June 1953, pp. 79-84. Merrill C. Goodall, "Soviet Policy and India: Some Post-war Trends," *Journal of International Affairs*, vol. viii, No. 1, 1954, pp. 43-51.

approaching the actual final stages, the Indian Communists supported it, envisaging that the withdrawal of the British would create a perfect situation for them to fish in troubled waters. But the Mountbatten Plan of Partition and the statesmanship of the Indian and Pakistani leaders marred these expectations, and the Indian Communists and their Moscow masters did an about-face, charging that partition was an imperialist maneuver and labeled its acceptance by the National Congress as betrayal of the Indian people.[35]

This was the signal for the Indian Communists to revive their program of class struggle and terrorist activities. By the beginning of 1948, their membership had risen to 90,000. Joshi was demoted and replaced by the radical, B. T. Ranadive. Under his leadership, the party organized shock brigades, strikes, and acts of sabotage; villages were raided, houses destroyed, bridges blown up, factories burned, trains attacked, banks robbed, roads barricaded, and busses set on fire. All these activities were perpetrated mainly in Hyderabad and West Bengal.[36] In the Telengana districts of Hyderabad the party succeeded, following the Chinese Communists' example of the 1930's, to form its own government—*patri sarkar*—with its own army. It was reported to comprise some 4,000 villages which were under the administration of "People's Independent Committees." Another Communist stronghold was in the neighboring districts of Andhra in Madras, now a separate state in the Republic of India, and in the eastern state of Tripura.[37]

The government of India and some state governments struck mercilessly against the terrorist activities of the party. Many Communist leaders were arrested, and politically the

[35] *Krizis Kolonialnoi Sistemi.* Izdatel'stvo Akademii Nauk SSSR, Moskva, 1949; see A. M. Diakov study, pp. 87-123. See also *Communist Party of India*, political thesis, adopted at the Second Congress, Calcutta, February 28 to March 6, 1948, pp. 31-33.

[36] *Communist Violence in India.* Issued by the Ministry of Home Affairs, Government of India, 1949.

[37] Karaka, *op.cit.*, pp. 167-169.

strategy of violence proved to be a failure. The Executive Committee was forced once again to reconsider its policy. It decided, following Moscow's order, to return to the idea of a more gradual build-up of strength by allying itself with the peasantry and workers in cooperation with other organizations and parties. The experience of the Chinese Communist Party became an example. Ranadive was politically liquidated in October 1951 and the less radical A. K. Ghosh became the party's Secretary General. Then the party went through a period of crisis, the right and left wing fighting each other. The National Congress and the Socialist Party recaptured the support of workers who, during the war years, had been attracted by the Communist-controlled All-India Trade Unions Congress. Now this organization lost many of its members to the Indian National Trade Union Congress and the socialist Hind Mazdoor Sabha. The party returned to solicitation of members from the ranks of intelligentsia. This policy of a softer approach showed its success in the elections held from November 1951 to February 1952. The party did not put up candidates in all states but rather concentrated its efforts in some. As a result, although they had no remarkable success in the over-all picture (gaining only 6 million, about 5.5 per cent, of all votes, 27 seats out of 497 in the House of the People, and 12 seats in the Council of States), they did achieve considerable local success in Hyderabad, Travancore-Cochin, Madras, Orissa and PEPSU (the Patiala-East Punjab States Union).

In June 1952 Dr. Satyanarain Sinha, a member of the Indian Parliament, spoke out bitterly against the Communist Party of India. He accused it of subversive activities, directed by the Cominform. He spoke with authority—Dr. Sinha had once been a captain in the Soviet army and had worked for the Communist movement. He submitted documents revealing that the Soviet expansionist plans included India and that the Indian party was serving as a fifth column to organize insurrections in India. He asserted that many Indian Communists were being trained in the Cominform centers in Prague and Leipzig, from whence were directed the terrorist activities of the party in India. He specifically charged that the violence in the Telengana districts was actually directed through radio communications from these centers. He warned that government offices, including the Ministry of Defense, were infiltrated by Communists. To prove all his points, Dr. Sinha submitted documents to the Privileges Committee of the Parliament, which, however, has not as yet published the results of its investigation.

At its congress in Madura at the beginning of January 1954 the Communist Party of India re-elected A. K. Ghosh, who had just returned from a six-month stay in Moscow, as its Secretary-General. It confirmed the policy of a united front seeking cooperation of all groups standing for "democracy and peace." It extended support to Nehru's government in its policy of peace and economic reforms. The propaganda value of this resolution was probably thwarted a month later when copies of a secret document were disseminated, according to which the congress reaffirmed the party commitment to armed revolution in India.[38]

The Party in Pakistan

The Communist Party of India, which had functioned since the 1920's for the whole Subcontinent, recognized the consequences of the partition in its own organization only in March 1948, when its offices and organizations were divided into the Communist Party of India and the Communist Party of Pakistan. The party in Pakistan had made small

[38] *The New York Times*, February 2, 1954. For detailed information see Marshall Windmiller, "Indian Communism Today." *Far Eastern Survey*, vol. xxiii, No. 4, April 1954. *Communist Conspiracy in India*. Private proceedings and secret documents of the third congress of the CPI. The Democratic Research Service, Bombay, 1954.

inroads into the Muslim League, but it has been very active, though in a semi-clandestine way, in West Punjab, particularly in Lahore, Sind, and East Pakistan. It controls the Pakistan Federation of Trade Unions, which though small numerically is well organized. It uses for its own purposes the Association of Progressive Workers of Pakistan and the Pakistan-Soviet Cultural Association. It is very active among students. The Communist leaders, Syed Sajjad Zaheer, the Secretary General of the Party, and Faiz Ahmed Faiz, an influential intellectual and poet, were involved in a military plot which was intended to establish, with help from "a certain foreign country," a Communist government in Pakistan. The plot was discovered in March 1951, and the two Communist leaders were sentenced to four years in prison in January 1953.

Throughout 1953 Communist prospects in Pakistan were brighter than at any time before. A severe economic crisis, caused by food shortage and a fall in commodity prices on world markets, has made the Communists' work easier. The elections in East Pakistan in March 1954 not only brought a crushing defeat to the Muslim League and victory to the United Front, but they also demonstrated Communist strength. According to some estimates, up to 70 out of 309 seats of the Assembly went to Communist or pro-Communist candidates.[39] Strikes and political disorders which followed the elections and which cost several hundreds of lives were, the governmental circles claimed, instigated by Communist elements. The Communist party was banned, first in East Pakistan (July 5) and then in all other provinces (July 24). The government also imposed restrictions on the movement of Soviet diplomats.

All in all, the Communist parties of India and Pakistan may not as yet represent any immediate danger, but the economic situation and the appallingly low standard of liv-

[39] See Richard L. Park, "East Bengal: Pakistan's Troubled Province." *Far Eastern Survey*, vol. xxiii, No. 5, May 1954.

ing, which for some years to come cannot be appreciably improved even by the best government, offer to the Communists a favorable field for their operations. Thus it is that although the threat may yet be somewhat remote, all observers agree that the situation is no cause for comfort, the more so as it must not be considered separately from what is happening on the other side of the border, in Soviet Central Asia, in Sinkiang and Tibet.

On the Borders of India

The last Soviet Five Year Plan, as scanty as is reliable information about it, did reveal plans for a concentration of capital investment and the construction of railroads in Central Asia. The Kuznetsk industrial area has been connected with the Uzbekistan and Kazakhstan Republics close to the Sinkiang province. What may be considered as a normal and legitimate activity for the development of the economic potentialities of these isolated regions may likewise carry serious strategic implications concerning Communist policy in South Asia.

The Soviets have always given great attention to the happenings in Sinkiang. Soon after World War I they entered the path of penetration opened by the Czars in the second half of the nineteenth century by helping various war-lords fight each other for the control of Sinkiang. In 1933 they even sent Soviet soldiers into the country. They established good trade with Kashgar, the capital. The consular representation was not interrupted even in the period when diplomatic relations between the Soviet Union and China were severed, between 1927 and 1932.

Soviet activity in Sinkiang has been greatly intensified since the victory of the Communists in China. At the beginning of 1950 groups of Soviet officers, instructors, technicians, and economic experts were reported to have arrived in the Kashgar area to explore the possibility of exploiting its considerable resources of iron, oil, tin, lead, coal, copper, wolfram, and gold. They set up a number of joint Soviet-Chinese companies for that purpose and organized the construction of airfields on the edge of the Sinkiang-Kashmir-Soviet border. Kashgar was being developed as a major military base. An atomic energy plant or a test site was reported to be constructed in Sinkiang and the atomic scientist, Bruno Pontecorvo, was believed working there. A railway across Sinkiang, connecting Soviet Turkestan with Central China, has been under construction. In 1952 one million Chinese were ordered to move to the province. In the fall of 1953 the Chinese government refused to accord recognition to the Consulate General of India and Pakistan at Kashgar, with the explanation that Sinkiang was closed territory and, as such, no foreign mission could be permitted to function there.

Developments in Tibet appear to be even more serious. According to reliable intelligence reports, in the summer of 1950 (even before the Chinese conquest of this largely unknown country), groups of Soviet experts in the guise of Buddhist pilgrims infiltrated Western Tibet to survey the area of Lakes Manasarowar and Rakas for the construction of airfields. They found the area strategically ideal; from there, planes passing through the valleys could easily reach Delhi. The lakes offer good bases for seaplanes and Lake Rakas freezes solidly in the long winter months to offer a good landing field. The agricultural nature of the region would permit the feeding of a great number of people without the necessity of supplies from the outside. Vast resources of raw materials hitherto unknown appear to be there, among them, uranium, northeast of Lake Manasarowar.

There is a constant influx of military equipment to Western Tibet, and some 20,000 Chinese soldiers, mainly stationed along the Indian border, are there at the moment, the final aim being 200,000 soldiers. Mao Tse-tung declared in November 1952 that it was his government's aim to raise the Tibetan population from its present two or three millions to ten millions. In February 1953 an increased military build-up was reported from Tibet, as was intensive construction by slave labor of an airfield in the vicinity of Lhasa, and another at Lharingo in Eastern Tibet. Three big military roads are under construction across Tibet; one from Sinkiang to Rudok, in Northwestern Tibet, along the Kashmir border, is completed. The other part will follow the old caravan route to Lhasa. All this is taking place close to the India-Nepal-Tibet 850-mile border—the McMahon Line—which, though demarcated in 1914, was never accepted by China.[40] "The Tibetan merchants say that Chinese military maps in Lhasa show Sikkim, Bhutan and Kashmir's northernmost province of Ladakh as part of Tibet. . . . Chinese officers and men are attending special classes in Hindi, Urdu, and Nepalese in a military school set up in a garden house . . . in Lhasa."[41]

On the other side of the boundary is the Kingdom of Nepal, the isolated Princely States, Sikkim and Bhutan, and Communist-ridden Assam; their strategic position obviously is rather precarious. The long boundaries are open to invasion via a number of caravan routes. The old dream of an impregnable Himalayan barrier has been dispelled by modern weapons and modern warfare. The population on the Indian side shares with the Tibetans the affinity of a common Buddhist religion; and in the north, from Sinkiang over Soviet Turkestan to Afghanistan, stretches a belt of Muslims, cherishing the same religious beliefs as the Muslims on the Subcontinent. They are mostly tribesmen, capable of the most formidable guerrilla warfare. The country is ideal for such a war, and a common religion is the best pretext for ideological infiltration.

[40] See Robert Trumbull, *The New York Times*, November 22, 23, 24, 1950 and December 28, 1953; Reuter's Report in *The New York Times*, February 3, 1953.
[41] *Civil & Military Gazette* (Lahore), February 24, 1953.

It is true that so far India has not been exposed to any open diplomatic or military pressure from the Soviet Union or China, although in the latter case the occupation of Tibet caused some apprehension in New Delhi. Most probably the Soviet government has considered it advantageous to its over-all program of disintegrating the solidarity of the free world to cultivate for the time being Indian friendship; and the Chinese government has been preoccupied by the paramount need of solidifying its position at home. Also, both governments concentrated their expansionist efforts in other directions, in Korea and Indo-China. Rightly, a political friend of Nehru remarked at a closed meeting in the winter of 1951 to a group of students of international affairs, "We realize that as long as you Americans keep the Chinese Communists busy in Korea, we do not feel their pressure in Burma."

Speaking at the celebration of the thirty-second anniversary of the October Revolution, G. Malenkov considered it important to remind the world of Lenin's prediction "that the outcome of the world struggle between capitalism and communism depended in the long run on the fact that Russia, India and China comprised the gigantic majority of the population being drawn with exceptional rapidity into a struggle for its liberation." To Malenkov, "The victory of the Chinese democracy has opened a new page in the history, not only of the Chinese people, but of all the peoples in Asia oppressed by the imperialists.[42] Some competent students of the Soviet Union have been of the opinion that Malenkov had then given expression to his convictions on the importance of Asia overriding, at least for the time being, the importance of Europe. Certainly, the experience of the last five years would tend to support the notion that Soviet emphasis is on Asia. Faced with the necessity of consolidating its conquests in Eastern and Central Europe and with the growing active defense of NATO,

[42] *The New York Times*, November 7, 1949.

the Soviet Union is increasingly turning its attention toward the power vacuum of Asia.

Expansionist powers have always moved into militarily undefended spaces, and it is no reflection on the fighting spirit of the Indian and Pakistani forces to state that they would be no match for the combined strength of a Chinese and Soviet onslaught, facilitated, as it would be, from within by the disruptive activities of the Communist fifth column and the almost paralyzing hostility that now exists between India and Pakistan. Indeed, one does not need to think in terms of an open attack, but rather in terms of spasmodic infiltration and the subjugation of exposed areas close to the Soviet-Chinese boundaries.

Should such a threatening situation arise, any hope that India and Pakistan under the circumstances of the Kashmir tensions would help each other borders on illusion. Rather, one might fear, any weakening of the internal or international position of one power would be viewed by the other with feelings of relief, if not satisfaction. And yet it appears so obvious that any such attitude ignores the lessons of modern history.

How many European nations have expended their energies in petty quarrels with each other over fragments of territory and thus, their eyes fixed on today's annoyances, have neither seen nor been able to resist the real threat that eventually engulfed them? Still another lesson of history needs to be read. How many of these nations thought to buy peace by being neutral, by sitting on the fence. How many sought "peace in our time" through appeasement? Can any doubt that all who did, and with them the whole world, paid for their errors in the excruciating currency of war? Such is the melancholic warning of history.

Pakistan appears to have accepted the evidence of our times, as dreary as it may be, that democratic countries can survive the manifold Soviet and Chinese expansionist designs only if they are united and militarily strong. She requested military assistance from the United States and is ready to do her share in the defense of the exposed area of South Asia and the Middle East. India, on the other hand, professes not to see the imminence of any Communist threat. For her Prime Minister "it is not easy to imagine even any aggression . . . from that great country China. . . ." He insists that if India finds "it comfortable to sit on the fence, we will continue to sit on the fence."[43] Not only therefore, has India rejected even the idea of military help from any country, but she has also expressed great alarm over Pakistan's policy. Jawaharlal Nehru has declared on numerous occasions that military assistance to Pakistan from the United States "will disturb, without fail, the entire balance of powers"; "the cold war will come right up to our borders"; "the whole country [of Pakistan] becomes a [military] base"; "it is a step not only toward war, but a step which will bring war right to our doors"; it "is likely to create conditions which facilitate and encourage aggression"; it causes "insecurity, uncertainty and instability"; it is calculated to "help spread the climate of war." Such condemnations, as harsh as they are, are understandable, if we remember that they come from a statesman who is not disturbed by present-day Communist policy and who is so deeply convinced that he serves the peace of his country best by keeping it aloof from commitments to the collective cause of security. Recently Nehru went even a step further in his foreign policy by recommending to the world certain principles which would, in his opinion, assure peaceful coexistence of the Communist and democratic camps.

Toward the end of June 1954, on the occasion of the visit to India of Chou En-lai, the Prime Minister and Foreign Minister of the People's Republic of China, Nehru and his guest subscribed in a joint communiqué to the principles

[43] *Indiagram* (Embassy of India, Washington, D.C.), No. 403, March 3, 1954; *The New York Times*, February 11, 1954.

of mutual respect of territorial integrity, non-aggression and non-interference to guide relations between India and China. The two Prime Ministers expressed belief that these principles, if applied in international relations generally, "would form a solid foundation for peace and security."[44]

As one reads this estimable enunciation of principles which in theory commend themselves to the conduct of foreign affairs of any country, one is reminded that the Soviet Union solemnly pledged before, during and after World War II, to every one of its neighbors that it would respect these very same principles. It should also be remembered that it violated each and every one as the opportunity arose. This policy has become indeed a pattern of conquest for totalitarian regimes, and for their neighbor states a pattern of doom. For one by one, as the small states embraced the false hope of security through agreements with powerful dictatorships, their only real hope for security, that of lasting solidarity with powerful democracies, was shattered. This pattern of conquest is all too recent and all too familiar to give any ring of reliability to similar proposals, coming from a nation with the record of Communist China. The State of Jammu and Kashmir, its boundaries with China undefined, its administration exposed to Communist subversion, may yet become an agonizing testing ground for China's respect for principles of territorial integrity, non-aggression and non-interference.

Kashmir may have started as a local issue between India and Pakistan, and Prime Minister Nehru may now thoroughly dislike what he considers improper foreign intervention in the dispute. However, the truth of the matter is that today because of the constant, unjustifiable postponement of the solution of the conflict, the Kashmir problem has played havoc with the crucial relations between India and Pakistan and it has been irretrievably thrust onto the scene

[44] *The New York Times*, June 29, 1954.

of world politics. Without question it has contributed materially to the dangerous and, under the circumstances, almost inevitable estrangement in the orientation of their foreign policies. Kashmir has become a veritable powder keg for the whole of Asia.

Whatever the future may have in store, the free world shares with India and Pakistan not only common ideals but also common responsibility for the fate of democracy and it awaits with trepidation the solution of the Kashmir problem. Its own security may depend on such a settlement. Even as Jawaharlal Nehru, in the interests of his own country's peace and security, feels justified, and rightly, to be actively concerned with the international implications of the problems of faraway Korea, South Africa, Sudan, Tunisia, Morocco, and Kenya, so do other countries share, for the same compelling reasons, an equal interest in the final solution of the vexing question of Kashmir.

The once distant home of the fabulous Maharaja, where gay beds of tulips border the flowing fountains of the gardens of Shalimar, has become by the mutations of modern times a grim threat to the peace of a free society. As long as this is true, the free world cannot but remain concerned with the problems and the people of Nehru's ancestral home.

11. From Default to War

OVER eleven years have passed since this record of the continuing problem of Kashmir was written. Time has proved to be no healer. Instead, the record of this decade has been a dreary succession of continuing crises between the two great powers of the Subcontinent, crises which involved not only the peace, the freedom, and the security of the six hundred million people of this area but that of the entire world as well. Eventually, perhaps inevitably, the continuing tension flared into armed conflict, and for a period of six weeks late last summer the world watched with intense anxiety as the armies of India and Pakistan engaged in furious fighting. Yet, for a variety of reasons, both sides were responsive to the desperate demands of the United Nations Security Council that fighting cease, and the two nations moved back a little from the brink of total war. Once again there exists a tenuous and uneasy armistice that is far removed from a state of peace. The problem remains unresolved; for the peoples of the world there is still grave "danger in Kashmir."

The record of this last decade which culminated in the explosion of last summer deserves investigation. It is not an epilogue. It is a continuation (with added complications) of the old story.

An examination reveals that the problems are no less complex, no less difficult, no more promising of solution than they were in 1954. Political and social change within the disputed territory has made the situation there more dangerous. United States foreign policy, in continuing pursuit of the goodwill and cooperation of both principal parties, India and Pakistan, has been involved, and by no means the least important factor of this involvement was the shipping of arms to each nation for purposes of "defence against aggression," arms which were heavily employed in last summer's fighting. The interests of the Soviet Union have had their influence, but these have been overshadowed by the unexpected acceleration of Chinese involvement in this area and the even less expected breach between the two great Communist powers.

It has been a decade of fruitless negotiation, bilateral and multilateral, both involving and without the involvement of the United Nations. It has been a decade, not of accommodation, but of a toughening of attitudes, of growing irreconcilability. It has been a decade which has led, as could have been expected, to war and to a tragic diversion of the all too scarce resources of these two nations to such acts of war, rather than to the welfare of their people and to the building of politically and economically viable states.

Bilateral Negotiations

It will be remembered that the Prime Ministers of India and Pakistan met in the summer of 1953 and reached an agreement on negotiating preliminary issues, with an understanding that a plebiscite administrator would be appointed by the end of April 1954. The agreement ignored the United Nations and its representative, Frank Graham, who was left with no choice but to stand idly by. Nevertheless, the principle of deciding the fate of Kashmir by way of a plebiscite was reaffirmed.

Despite this agreement, however, it was another two years before bilateral negotiations were resumed, when Prime Ministers Nehru and Mohammed Ali met in May 1955. At this time a new idea was officially injected into the picture: a division of the State of Jammu and Kashmir. Pakistan suggested that she keep the northern and western areas with additional territory from the district of Riasi and a part of Punch's district, then held by India. The future of the Valley of Kashmir, the principal prize of the dispute, was to be decided by a plebiscite conducted under international supervision. On appearance at least, this was a new approach, because Pakistan officially suggested for the first time the possibility of a partial division of the country. It was, however, largely a bargaining gesture: Pakistan knew in advance that India was not vitally interested in the territory which was already under Pakistani jurisdiction, knew as well that India would not expose the Vale to the uncertainty of a democratic vote.

India rejected Pakistan's proposition, suggesting instead that the *status quo* be maintained along the cease-fire line and that the fate of the Vale be placed in the hands of a newly elected Constituent Assembly. As such an election, in a one-party state and without an adequate international guarantee, would bear little resemblance to democratic processes, the Indian gesture was given less than sympathetic consideration by Pakistan.

An official *communiqué*, couched in innocuous terms, covered the failure of these bilateral efforts, although it did promise a continuation of the negotiations.[1] Nevertheless, it should be noted that India had at least conceded the idea of an election of one kind or another in the Vale. It is possible that further probing from Pakistan might have yielded some assurances from India regarding the processes of such an election.

Fulfillment of the promise was delayed another five long years, however. Pakistan domestically entered an uneasy period of political turmoil and changing governments, a condition not finally stabilized until the reins were taken over by the strong-willed Marshal Mohammed Ayub Khan. None of the governments, however, modified the Pakistani position on Kashmir; indeed, none of them dared consider a major change, as it would have been negated by popular opposition.

In the meantime, Indo-Pakistani relations further deteriorated in other ways. Pakistan continued to receive

[1] *New York Times*, May 15, 19, 1955.

American military aid, despite repeated criticism and warnings from the Indian government. At the same time, India, which was herself cherishing the growing friendship of the Soviet Union and China, was viewed with equal suspicion by Pakistan.

Impressed in all probability by President Ayub Khan's firmness, Nehru paid a five-day visit to Pakistan in September 1960. The two leaders reached an agreement on a number of minor problems, but not on Kashmir.

In January 1962 President Kennedy suggested that Eugene R. Black serve as a mediator of this dispute, as he had assisted both countries in the past in negotiating an agreement on the division of the waters of the Indus River. Pakistan was willing to accept his good offices, but India argued that the dispute should be solved through direct bilateral negotiations.

Then, in the following fall, an overpowering event did bring the two countries to the conference table: China invaded India. The United States and Great Britain capitalized on India's desperate need for military assistance and one can assume that they exercised a friendly pressure on Nehru to reach an agreement on Kashmir. Little is known about the mission of Averell Harriman, Assistant Secretary of State for Political Affairs, and Duncan Sandys, British Secretary for the Commonwealth Relations, except that it was accompanied by wide publicity, an environment not conducive to the delicate processes of successful persuasion. Neither Pakistan nor India was anxious to resume the negotiations. The latter dreaded the thought of discussions under the pressure of a national crisis, while the former, probably viewing her opponent's predicament with some satisfaction, would not be too anxious to negotiate away whatever gain the current situation gave her and her position on Kashmir. Finally, however, both parties did agree to meet.

From the end of December 1962 until May 1963, the

representatives of India and Pakistan held six sessions, or as they were called, rounds. At the outset they reached an understanding that unless the talks led to an agreement they would be purely exploratory and without prejudice to the original positions of the two nations, and this is exactly what happened after the six rounds were brought to a close. Nevertheless, even the noncommittal nature of the meetings provided some insights about the trend of thought on both sides, indicating (as they possibly still do) directions for a future plan of action.

Pakistan opened the negotiations by asking for a plebiscite in accordance with the UNCIP resolutions. As could have been anticipated, India only reiterated what Nehru had told the world on several previous occasions, namely that circumstances had changed since 1949 and that a plebiscite was no longer feasible. One could not expect to have the political and economic arguments of a plebiscite campaign separated from the religious aspects; religious considerations, in India's view, should be entirely eliminated; ergo, a plebiscite was impossible. India also rejected the idea of a plebiscite limited to the Valley of Kashmir, and, instead, proposed a practical, "political" solution: partition.

Pakistan was not unwilling to consider such a straightforward step—which represented a radical departure from her past position. However, she insisted that such a settlement keep in mind the composition of the population, exigencies of defense, allocation of rivers, and so on. In addition, Pakistan was willing to accommodate India's current and hopefully temporary needs in the Vale and Ladakh as related to the latter's defense against China.

While Pakistan's position was motivated by religious affinity and economic considerations, with primary focus on the Vale, India's stand was based on the opposite aspect of the situation, with an eye to keeping the Vale as the jewel of the entire area. India urged a realistic solution which would take into account geographical and administrative considerations without disturbing the life and welfare of the people involved. This meant, in fact, partition along the cease-fire line, with some minor adjustments.

On one occasion Pakistan proposed to have the Vale isolated and put under neutral control, with the provision that after a given length of time a vote of the population would be taken. India refused. However, India did revive an old idea of signing a No War agreement with Pakistan, further proposing disengagement of military forces in and around Kashmir. It was now the turn of Pakistan to refuse. Nor would Pakistan agree with what she considered to be a "mathematical" proposition according to which she would have more than 34,000 square miles of the State and India would keep less than one-half of the whole area (taking into consideration that China was in occupation of 12,000 to 14,000 square miles of the State's territory).[2]

After five months of fruitless discussion both parties reverted to their original position. A precious opportunity had been lost; both sides apparently had failed to keep in mind the paramount need for cooperation under the shadow of mounting Chinese aggression. Nor did Pakistan make discussions any easier when, in March 1963, she concluded negotiations with China regarding their mutual boundaries with the State of Jammu and Kashmir. India had protested in vain, justifiably accusing Pakistan of disposing of a territory which was in dispute. Pakistan explained that the agreement with China provided for reopening negotiations on the boundaries after the settlement of the Kashmir dispute. Only if the area became definitively a part of Pakistan would the boundary agreement remain in force. India was not impressed with the explanation.

Early in May 1963 the American Secretary of State, Dean

[2] This brief survey of the six rounds is based on various Indian, Pakistani, and other sources.

Rusk, and Duncan Sandys were in Delhi, offering their services for a settlement of the dispute. This time the Indian government, contrary to its policy in the past, expressed a willingness to cooperate, and it was Pakistan, seeking clarification of the various aspects of this procedure before accepting the mediation offer, that thwarted this attempt.

Finally, in August 1963, Nehru stated that "there [was] no question of . . . considering any proposals for internationalising or division of the Valley, or joint control of Kashmir, and the like." He closed the door to further negotiations by declaring, "The concessions which we offered to Pakistan are no longer open, and they must be treated as withdrawn."[3]

The two governments did not meet again around a conference table; the next encounter was on the battlefield.

The United Nations' Failure

As the internal situation in Kashmir changed, and as that country moved closer and closer to India, the Security Council, either out of apathy or with acknowledged helplessness, did nothing. Then, after a four-year interval, it reopened the issue at the request of Pakistan. Kashmir had adopted a new Constitution and India was about to ratify Kashmir's accession.

The Security Council first confirmed its previous position in a resolution to the effect that any action taken by the Kashmiri authorities "would not constitute a disposition of the State in accordance" with the principle of plebiscite; the resolution was carried by ten votes, with the abstention of the Soviet Union.[4]

The Pakistani Foreign Minister, Malik Firoz Khan Noon, asked the Security Council to "call upon India to refrain

[3] *Kashmir.* Prime Minister Nehru's statement in Parliament, August 13, 1963. Information Service of India, p. 7.
[4] S/3779 of January 24, 1957.

from accepting the change envisaged by the new Constitution" and then restated Pakistan's old demand for a withdrawal of troops from Kashmir and an early induction into office of the Plebiscite Administrator. In addition, he introduced a new concept, asking for an immediate introduction of a United Nations' force into the area.[5]

The Indian representative, V. K. Krishna Menon, emphatically rejected the Pakistani proposals. In a speech extending over three sessions he took the position that Kashmir's accession was valid and final, that the Kashmiri people had expressed their desires in the elections of October 1951, and that these elections ended India's obligations in the matter of a plebiscite—a plebiscite to which India had never actually been committed by a binding treaty. Moreover, he went on, once the merger of Kashmir with India was consummated, it could not be revoked, because the Indian Constitution did not recognize the right of secession. To strengthen Krishna Menon's position, India, on Republic Day, January 26, confirmed Kashmir's accession.

Then, in the middle of February, the Security Council voted on another resolution; it requested the President of the Council, Gunnar V. Jarring, "to examine with the governments of India and Pakistan proposals which, in his opinion, were likely to contribute to the achievement of demilitarization or to the establishment of other conditions for progress towards the settlement of the dispute, having regard to . . . the proposal for the use of temporary United Nations force. . . ."[6]

Even this oblique reference to a United Nations force brought the Soviet delegate to his feet; he immediately vetoed the resolution. Even before this, however, Prime Minister Nehru had already stated that his country would not tolerate the stationing of foreign troops on "its soil."

[5] S/PV 761 of January 16, 1957, p. 36.
[6] S/3787 of February 14, 1957.

Confronted with the Soviet veto, the Security Council a few days later adopted a milder resolution, this time with Soviet abstention, requesting Mr. Jarring to go to the Sub-continent and to "examine . . . any proposals which, in his opinion, were likely to contribute towards the settlement of the dispute . . . ," with due regard, however, "to the previous resolutions of the Security Council and of the United Nations Commission for India and Pakistan."[7]

Mr. Jarring's report makes it clear that his experiences in India and Pakistan did not differ from those of his predecessors. He first explored the hindrances to a full implementation of the UNCIP resolutions. The Indian government told him that Part I of the UNCIP resolution of August 13, 1948, in particular sections B and E (see Appendix II), had not been implemented by Pakistan; it was, therefore, premature to discuss Parts II and III and the subsequent resolution of January 5, 1949. India also felt aggrieved that the Security Council had not expressed itself on the question of Pakistan's aggression against Kashmir and India. She requested that Pakistan "vacate the aggression" before India's commitments to demilitarize Kashmir reached an operative stage. Pakistan, however, insisted that Part I of the resolution had been implemented and that steps should be taken to implement Part II.

Mr. Jarring then suggested that the problem be submitted to an arbitrator who would not only decide whether Part I was or was not implemented, but who would also, in case of a negative finding, indicate to the parties in dispute the measures which should be taken for full implementation. After a given time limit, the arbitrator would determine whether his recommendations had been followed and whether Part I had been implemented.

As Mr. Jarring reported, Pakistan accepted his suggestion "after a certain hesitation." But India did not consider an arbitration appropriate because "such a procedure would be

[7] S/3793 of February 21, 1957.

313

inconsistent with the sovereignty of the State of Jammu and Kashmir and rights and obligations of the Union of India in respect of this territory." Arbitration might also be interpreted as implying that Pakistan had a *locus standi* in the Kashmir dispute.

Jarring ended his report with a polite note that his "examination of the situation . . . would indicate that, despite the present deadlock, both parties [were] still desirous of finding a solution to the problem."[8] In fact, however, the report only confirmed the persistence of old issues, old problems, and old arguments with no new hopes.

The Security Council discussed Jarring's report during several sessions in the autumn of 1957. It tried to approach the problem in a more resolute manner. But after the Soviet Union had indicated its opposition, a mild resolution was adopted, requesting the United Nations Representative for India and Pakistan, Dr. Frank P. Graham, to make such recommendations as he saw fit to the parties concerned on the implementation of the UNCIP resolutions and a peaceful settlement of the dispute.[9]

So after five years of incredible frustration, the unhappy Dr. Graham found himself once more requested to resume the thankless job of mediation. Older in age but with the same burning dedication to the causes of peace, freedom, and justice that had characterized his entire life, he embarked once more upon a pilgrimage to the Subcontinent.

Graham's report, the sixth in a long series, though largely a reiteration of a now familiar story, did indicate however some possibility of escape from the entangled web of claims and counterclaims regarding interpretations of past resolutions.[10] Acutely aware of past difficulties in persuading India and Pakistan to withdraw their forces from the State of Jammu and Kashmir, Graham's mission concentrated

[8] S/3821 of April 29, 1957.
[9] S/3922 of December 2, 1957.
[10] S/3984 of March 28, 1958.

primarily on this very problem. Equally aware of the changing local conditions, he linked the question of the withdrawal of Pakistani forces to the vexing problem of subsequent administration of the evacuated territory.

Dr. Graham's succinct report contained five recommendations of which the third and fifth formed the essence of his approach. He suggested a prompt study, under his auspices, of the methods of administering the territory which would be evacuated by the Pakistani troops. He recommended further that consideration be given to the possibility of stationing a United Nations force on the Pakistani territory bordering the State of Jammu and Kashmir, following the withdrawal of Pakistani troops. He also proposed that a conference between the Prime Ministers of India and Pakistan be held under his auspices in the spring of 1958, or at the earliest possible time.

This was both a modest and a bold proposition. It was modest in the sense that a study of administrative methods for the evacuated territory—before the Pakistani withdrawal—was merely a substitution for such terms as "surveillance" and "local authorities" used in the 1948 UNCIP resolution, which were vague and by 1958 possibly inapplicable.

The proposition was bold in that Dr. Graham introduced the idea of stationing a United Nations force on Pakistani territory to insure the withdrawal of the Pakistani troops and to alleviate India's concern over their possible return to the Pakistani part of the State.[11] In proposing an early conference between the Prime Ministers of the two countries, Dr. Graham wished also to follow the time-tested wisdom that there would be no shooting as long as the conflicting sides were talking to each other.

Pakistan accepted Dr. Graham's recommendations in principle; India rejected them. Once again she blamed both

---

[11] The author suggested this idea in 1954; see p. 197.

Pakistan and the United Nations for failure to implement Part I of the UNCIP resolution of August 13, 1948. India also felt that an acceptance of his proposals would imply that Pakistan had not violated previous undertakings and that she was not engaged in an illegal occupation of Indian territory. India stated that she would "consider it as highly improper and indeed an unfriendly act to promote a suggestion which would involve stationing of foreign troops in a neighboring sovereign State. . . ," but she acknowledged that such a decision could be made only by Pakistan. She could not accept the idea of a conference because it would "place the aggressor and the aggressed on the same footing."

Dr. Graham's report concluded with a lofty expression of faith in the creative capacities of mankind but, significantly, contained no recommendations to the Security Council as to further steps it might consider.

The position taken by the two countries requires a brief comment, though by this time it may appear rather redundant. Pakistan, eager to proceed toward a plebiscite in Kashmir, was ready to accept a temporary limitation on her national sovereignty; she was aware that she had nothing to fear except a vigorous protest from her powerful neighbors, the Soviet Union and China.

India's objection, on the other hand, regarding the failure to implement Part I of the UNCIP resolution, was, to say the least, highly debatable since, over the years, both parties may be considered guilty to this charge. Nor can one sustain her legal argument about Pakistan's illegal possession of Indian territory because not only the Azad Kashmir, the area in question, but the whole State of Jammu and Kashmir was neither Pakistani nor Indian territory in terms of international law. Furthermore, India had accepted this position when she acquiesced in the United Nations resolutions and agreed to have the fate of Kashmir decided by an internationally-supervised plebiscite. Even when she finally resigned herself to the possibility of the United Nations sending a force into the area, India probably counted on a Soviet veto to prevent such a move.

Such attitudes and arguments were to be expected and understood in the light of the ten-year history of the case. What is difficult to comprehend, however, is the position taken by the United Nations. The Security Council did not even consider Dr. Graham's report! Frustrated by past experiences, it probably did not see any hope in his recommendations. Yet, they seemed to be worth trying. Had the Soviet Union vetoed a resolution which called for the sending of a United Nations force to Pakistan, as in all probability it would have, the Kashmir issue could then have been transferred to the General Assembly. In all likelihood, the General Assembly would have approved such a policy with a substantial majority. The presence of troops on the Pakistani-Kashmir border would have facilitated the Pakistani withdrawal and placed on India additional pressure to withdraw the bulk of her army from her part of Kashmir.

In this way, UN presence in the area would have made the tragic conflict in the summer of 1965 unlikely, perhaps even averting it. However, as the conditions in South and Central Asia changed, so disappeared this avenue of resolving the Kashmir problem. It would seem apparent, therefore, that the United Nations committed a grave error in March 1958 when it ignored Dr. Graham's recommendations. Seven years later it was forced to consider the problem in the face of compelling circumstances: a war between India and Pakistan over Kashmir.

Over the years, letters from the governments of India and Pakistan continued to reach the Security Council, each accusing the other of violations of the United Nations resolutions and raising alarming warnings about the aggravation of the situation. The Security Council met on several dates in February, April, May, and June 1962 to hear

Pakistan's new proposals and India's rejections. Another Soviet veto killed a UN resolution to bring India and Pakistan again together for negotiations.[12]

Then the Security Council met again in February and May 1964 at the request of Pakistan, who protested against steps which were to complete Kashmir's integration into India. This was at the time when the sacred hair of Mohammed had been reported stolen from a shrine near Srinagar. Muslim demonstrations in Kashmir were suppressed, and Indo-Pakistani relations were dangerously strained. Pakistan's warning went beyond the usual scope of protests when her representative ominously stated that unless UN procedures were capable of halting India's dangerous policy, "the people of Azad Kashmir and Pakistan may, in desperation, turn to other measures."[13] The warnings went unheeded, and as the Security Council meetings continued to be inconclusive, the abyss between India and Pakistan widened.

Internal Changes

It would be a mistake to assume that the situation in Kashmir itself remained unchanged while the Security Council, its representatives, and the governments of India and Pakistan tried over a period of seventeen years to settle its future.

While Sheikh Mohammed Abdullah was indefinitely detained in prison, his successor, Ghulam Mohammed Bakshi, worked at the problem of bringing Kashmir closer to India. Although he permitted the nominal existence of such political groups as the Praja Socialists, the Plebiscite Front, and the Kashmir Political Conference, he arrested, released, and rearrested their leaders at will, according to the demands of the moment. Public meetings were likewise

[12] S/5134 of June 22, 1962.
[13] *United Nations Review*, Vol. 11, No. 3, March 1964, p. 5.

banned. As a result of these actions, however, the National Conference, the backbone organization of Bakshi's power, steadily lost popular support.

It should be noted, also, that Kashmir had proved to be an enormous economic liability for India. It was reported that in the first six years alone after the Maharaja's declaration of accession, the Indian government invested in Kashmir about $100,000,000, built some 500 primary schools, constructed a tunnel under the Banihal Pass, widened and improved the only surface road linking Jammu with Srinagar, and built a hydro-electric plant.[14] As Chinese-Indian tensions turned the Valley of Kashmir into a strategic base for the defense of distant outposts in Ladakh, the heavy investment in Kashmir was presumably accelerated. India's attachment to Kashmir, originally based on emotional, political, and prestige considerations, was now intensified by economic and military commitments.

The process of integration was, therefore, accelerated. On November 17, 1956, the one-party Kashmir Constituent Assembly, "elected" in 1951, adopted a new Constitution, declaring the State to be an integral part of India. It included provisions for a parliamentary government with a Head of State (Sadar-i-Riyasat) elected by the Legislative Assembly and recognized by the President of India. It also provided for a process for amending the Constitution, although it excluded the possibility of any change in the relationship between the State and India.

In the elections for the Legislative Assembly, held in March 1957, Bakshi's National Conference won 68 seats, of which 38 were unopposed, and Praja Parishad, representing Hindus in Jammu, won 5 seats; in addition, an independent candidate and a former untouchable from India were elected.

In spite of this resounding victory, troubles were in store for Bakshi. It had been reported on various occasions that

[14] *New York Times*, July 28, 30, 1955.

Communist fellow travellers had gained increasing influence in the Kashmiri government, particularly in the Departments of Education and Health, Finance, and Home Affairs. Friendly relations between India and the Soviet Union, as well as Nehru's resolute policy toward the Communist Party of India, served as an encouragement to Bakshi to "clip the wings" of the Kashmiri radicals, led by Ghulam Mohammad Sadiq. Already in June 1956, Bakshi had stripped him of a key position, the Ministry of Information, by taking it under his own direct control. Then, in July 1957, soon after Bakshi returned from a visit with Nehru, four alleged leftists, Sadiq, Girdari Lal Dogra, Syed Mir Quasim, and Durga Parshad Dhar, were dismissed from the Kashmiri government. In an interview Dogra and Quasim denied that they were Communists but added with seeming naïveté that they were "not opposed to communism or any other ism." Sadiq could not be reached for comment.[15]

In August 1963, however, Bakshi himself was replaced by another National Conference leader, Kwaja Shamsuddin, in what appeared to be part of a general reorganization of the Indian government at various levels. Then, one year later, in September, Bakshi was arrested on charges of corruption, other criminal charges, and suspicion of endangering public peace and security. Before his arrest, however, he fostered a violent clash with Sheikh Abdullah's followers and was apparently able to bring about a split in the ranks of the National Conference.

No special effort, however, was required to speed up such a development. The population grew restless, as was evidenced by frequent street demonstrations organized by opposition leaders. In January 1964, as the result of an event which was certain to inflame the emotions of the devout Muslims in Kashmir, the atmosphere exploded. A sacred

[15] *New York Times*, July 27, 1957.

relic, a hair of Prophet Mohammed which had been safeguarded for three hundred years in a silver and glass tube
behind a locked door in Hazratbal Mosque near Srinagar,
vanished. Some knowledgeable persons believe that the theft
was engineered by a politically conscious Muslim who
hoped for just such a violent reaction by the population as
would bring "the forgotten nation" of Kashmir and its fate
to the attention of the world. The reaction did come.
Thousands of Muslims marched in the streets, and rioting
broke out in Srinagar. Five days later, the relic was found,
but processions of protest continued. These protests had a
significance beyond the events themselves, for they evidenced a profound change in the centuries-old political
lethargy and submissiveness of the Kashmiri people.

Shamsuddin was compelled to resign in February and
was replaced by none other than Sadiq, who immediately
promised to continue the process of integrating Kashmir
into India.

In fact, however, little was needed to complete the
process of integration. In January 1960, the Delhi Agreement, which had preserved some prerogatives of sovereignty
for the State of Jammu and Kashmir, was drastically
changed. The jurisdiction of India's Supreme Court was
now extended to Kashmir, reducing the status of its High
Court to that of similar courts within India. The only re-
striction still imposed upon the President, who was given
the right to appoint the judges of the Kashmir High Court,
was first to consult with the Head of State. In some other
respects, however, Kashmir still enjoyed a unique status.
Its Legislative Assembly, for example, still was to delegate
to the Indian Parliament ten representatives, while other
states of the Union of India elected its members directly.
In addition, Kashmir continued to have its own Constitution.

To adjust the party organization to the constitutional
developments, the All-India National Congress amended its

statutes in January 1965 and established a state organization in Jammu and Kashmir, which until then had been the principal domain of the Congress's affiliate, the All-Jammu and Kashmir National Conference. Sadiq, head of the party in Jammu and Kashmir, proposed the dissolution of his party and invited its members to join the State organization of the National Congress party.

At the same time, two more articles of India's Constitution were extended to Kashmir. Accordingly, the President of India had the right to take over the administration of the State in case of a collapse of the constitutional machinery, and the Indian Parliament could promulgate laws for Kashmir during such a period of crisis.

To complete this process of integration and to deprive the State of the last formal vestige of constitutional individuality, the Kashmir Legislative Assembly in April 1965 approved a bill according to which (in order to conform with the other Indian States) the title of the Head of State was changed to that of Governor, and that of the Prime Minister or Head of Government to Chief Minister. It was subsequently reported that it was this legislative step which triggered the developments which led to armed conflict between India and Pakistan.

Azad Kashmir, it should be noted, also underwent similar developments. Though its government maintained legally a considerable measure of autonomy, in fact, and for political reasons, its political and economic development became increasingly dependent upon decisions of the government of Pakistan.

All these changes, on both sides of the cease-fire line, had repercussions in the chambers of the United Nations. The governments of India and Pakistan protested in letters and oral presentations against these developments which ran counter to the Security Council's and the UNCIP's resolutions, but diplomatic démarches could hardly affect the trends which had been so facilitated by years of inaction on the part of the United Nations.[16]

Taming of the Lion

As Kashmir was being brought step by step into the constitutional and political fabric of India, as the issue of its future was lying dormant at the closed door of the Security Council, and as bilateral negotiations failed to resolve the dispute, Mohammed Sheikh Abdullah spent his years in prison. The man whom the Kashmiris had called *Sher-E-Kashmir*, the "Lion of Kashmir," for having courageously led the first rebellion in 1941 against the Maharaja, seemed all but forgotten. He had been arrested in August 1953 but never brought to trial. Then, on January 8, 1958, he was suddenly released, probably through the intervention of his old-time friend, Jawaharlal Nehru.

If Nehru anticipated that his political companion of more than two decades would resume working for the union of Kashmir with India as he had before his arrest, he was to be disappointed. Quite the opposite took place.

Five years in detention must have caused a complete change of political heart, for no more had Abdullah exchanged his prison clothes for a civilian suit than he went from one town to another making inflammatory speeches before enthusiastic audiences. True, he suggested the necessity for a mutual understanding between India and Pakistan on the Kashmir issue, but his radical speeches did little to contribute to the essential prerequisite to such an understanding. In summary, Abdullah pressed the following arguments: that Mr. Nehru had no business speaking on behalf of Kashmir; furthermore, the State's accession to India had lost its validity after his dismissal and detention

[16] S/3939, S/3943, S/3981, S/4217, S/4242, S/4238, S/5437, S/5504, S/5454, S/6114, S/6218.

in August 1953. Bakshi could "shout from the top of the Banihal Pass that Kashmir's accession to India [was] final and irrevocable," but his government was composed of "goondas, opportunists and thieves." Abdullah had not betrayed India, India had betrayed him. She had discriminated against Kashmiri Moslems in the army and the militia, refused to give them jobs, and established an intelligence service in Srinagar to bribe and corrupt officials. He demanded a termination of Kashmir's constitutional relationship with India and a plebiscite, at the same time ruling out the possibility of an independent Kashmir, which, according to him, could not exist by itself. Most of the members of the Kashmir Constituent Assembly "were forced to accept the Constitution, and only the people of Kashmir had the right to decide about their future."[17]

Obviously, the "Lion of Kashmir" had not lost any of his old political fire and oratory during his years of imprisonment, but it is no wonder that by May 1958 he found himself back in jail, charged with an attempt to overthrow the government. He was to spend another six years in custody.

On April 8, 1964, Sheikh Abdullah was released again after the court acquitted him of a charge of conspiracy. It was reported that he was set free to relieve India of embarrassing pressures. Political agitation in Kashmir, particularly after the theft of Mohammed's hair, was indicative of the extent and intensity of discontent of the populace; communal violence had broken out in East India and Pakistan; and, on the international scene, India was worried about a growing isolation from African and Asian nations because of the Kashmir problem.[18]

This time, discretion seems to have prevailed over Abdullah's political valor, and though he resumed his de-

[17] *Asian Recorder,* January 11-17, 1958, pp. 1850-1852, January 18-24, 1958, p. 1860; *New York Times,* January 11, 14, 1958.
[18] *New York Times,* April 9, 1964.

mand for the right of self-determination, he declined to propose any specific solution of the Kashmir problem before discussing it with Nehru, whom he still called his "dearest comrade and colleague." He now conceded that Kashmir had acceded to India in matters of defense, external affairs, and communications, but that she had not surrendered her residual sovereignty; final accession would depend on the result of a plebiscite. In his opinion the people of Kashmir would not oppose any solution that would be mutually acceptable to India and Pakistan, the friendship of both of whom was absolutely essential to Kashmir's future. He suggested a negotiated settlement in case some people believed that a plebiscite would cause troubles, and added that a solution must be found "that [did] not harm the honor of India or of Pakistan but that [would be] in [Kashmir's] interest." He was then closeted in meetings with Nehru that lasted four days. It was reported that he had suggested to Nehru and other Indian statesmen the idea of a condominium of India and Pakistan over Kashmir and that the Indian Prime Minister had shown some sympathy for it.

Abdullah then went to Pakistan, which he had never visited before. He rejected publicly the position that Kashmir's accession to India was irrevocable, but he also stressed that Kashmir's salvation lay in friendship between India and Pakistan. "I come here with faith," he stated, "that I will succeed. There is no question of my failing. They realize in India that the time has come to solve this problem."[19]

As he met with Prime Minister Nehru and President Ayub Khan, he was impressed, he reported, "by the intense desire of them both to settle the much vexed question of Kashmir by mutual discussion and negotiation." He continued, "At my insistence Pandit Nehru and President

[19] *Asian Recorder*, April 29-May 5, 1964, pp. 5797, 5798, July 29-August 4, 1964, p. 5951; *New York Times*, April 10, May 3, 10, 1964.

Ayub Khan agreed to meet together to settle this long outstanding matter."[20]

The two statesmen who had the power and respect of all concerned to give it another try never met. A sorrowful event had befallen India and, indeed, the whole free world: Jawaharlal Nehru was dead.

The man who had dedicated his long life to the service of his beloved India was gone. He had seen his country, whose national struggle he led along with his teacher, Mahatma Gandhi, emerge from the shadow of colonialism to the brightness of independence; through a process of democratic education he had cemented its heterogeneous components into a politically conscious entity; he had exercised a profound influence upon the shaky world scene, leading India along the path of nonalignment. But his emotional attachment to Kashmir, the country of his ancestors, had lured him away from a peaceful solution to this particular problem. If Abdullah had hoped that Nehru could still reverse his position, he had now lost that influence in his efforts to resolve the Kashmir dispute, for Nehru's successors did not appear anxious to resume direct negotiations with Pakistan.

At the beginning of 1965 Sheikh Abdullah went abroad to plead his country's case before other sympathetic nations. In March he appeared in Cairo and appealed to the Afro-Asian countries for support. It was reported that he planned for the issue to be brought before the Afro-Asian Conference in Algiers, which was in the process of preparation.

Then Abdullah, apparently with the encouragement of Pakistan, gambled—and lost. According to Peking radio, he met Chou En-lai in Algiers and let it be known that the Chinese Premier had invited him to visit the People's Republic of China, which, Chou assured him, had "always

[20] *Foreign Affairs*, April 1965, Vol. 43, No. 3, p. 533.

supported the Kashmir people's right of self-determination."

Quite understandably, Prime Minister Shastri took a "most serious view" of Abdullah's contacts with India's enemy, which implied that the latter had "condoned Chinese aggression" against India. Pakistan's Foreign Minister, Zulfikar Ali Bhutto, rushed to encourage Abdullah in this obvious disregard for the elementary rules of diplomacy and announced that Pakistan was prepared to give him a passport to visit China.[21]

India did not intend passively to watch this political game. One month later, on April 30, Abdullah was re-arrested and detained in Madras. Once again the Lion of Kashmir was separated from his country and from contacts with the outside world.

Before this new imprisonment he revealed some insights on the developments which had led to his downfall in 1953. He published in the April 1965 issue of *Foreign Affairs* an article in which he first recapitulated the history of the Kashmir conflict, emphasizing Nehru's repeated statements about India's obligation to let the people of Kashmir decide by way of a plebiscite their own fate. Then he disclosed that the leaders of the National Conference, dismayed by the suffering of their nation, had held several meetings in May and June of 1953 to wrestle with the problem. They considered various alternatives: an over-all plebiscite; independence of the whole State; independence with an India-Pakistan joint control of foreign affairs; or an adjusted Dixon plan of partition with a plebiscite in the Vale of Kashmir, combined with the possibility of its independence.[22] Noticeably enough, the leaders' scheme did not mention the alternative of union with India, even though for the previous five years all had expressed the view that the accession of Kashmir was final.

The solidarity of the National Conference leaders did

[21] *New York Times*, April 2, 3, May 9, 1965.
[22] *Foreign Affairs*, Vol. 43, No. 3, pp. 533-34.

not last long. Abdullah was accused of treason and thrown in prison in August 1953, while most of his political friends remained in the newly formed government and confirmed the allegiance to India. Since then, the government has been reshuffled several times, leading on every occasion to further splits in the party leadership, until today as these lines are written, in January 1966, it has reached a state of complete disarray.

Abdullah, far from his native land and after eleven years of imprisonment, still remains the only man who commands the popular support of the Kashmiris, as he still is, in their minds and hearts, the "Lion of Kashmir." Meanwhile, his son, Tariq Abdullah, keeps his father's name alive in the international councils; he is a member of Pakistan's delegation to the United Nations.

Whatever the future brings, Sheikh Abdullah can hardly be ignored in any peaceful solution of the grave problem of Kashmir. He has a magnetic hold over his people; he did not cut all his ties with India; and he did win the respect of Pakistan.

International Changes

In 1954 the United States inaugurated a policy of building up, through SEATO and CENTO (originally the Baghdad Pact), the resistance of the vulnerable areas of South-East Asia and the Middle East to Communist aggression. Pandit Nehru repeatedly raised his voice against these alliances, which, according to him, were drawing the Kashmir issue into the realm of the Cold War. He differed with the United States on almost every problem of world tensions, while at the same time following his own policy of non-alignment he moved closer to the Soviet Union and the People's Republic of China. In addition, he feared that American weapons supplied to Pakistan might be used against India and not for the purpose of defense against Communism.

Nehru saw his policy of neutrality collapse when China invaded India in the autumn of 1962 and advanced further into a part of Ladakh, an area belonging to the State of Jammu and Kashmir, and Nehru's successors saw his fears justified when Pakistan in September 1965 used American-made tanks and jets in action against India in a war over Kashmir. Neither of these traumatic experiences helped to bring the Kashmir dispute closer to a solution.

In March 1956 Nehru had warned that "the American military aid to Pakistan and Pakistan's membership in military pacts . . . has destroyed the roots and foundations of the plebiscite proposal in Kashmir."[23] Then he proceeded to negate the United Nations' resolutions, first by integrating Kashmir step by step with India and finally by openly rejecting the idea of a plebiscite. He received official support for this policy from the Soviet Union and for a while seemed to have tacit approval from India's other "friend," China.

Toward the end of 1955 Nikolai Bulganin and Nikita Khrushchev made their memorable swing through South and South-East Asia. On the way home, at the invitation of the titular Head of the State of Jammu and Kashmir, they stopped in Srinagar, although the visit could not have been arranged, of course, without the approval of the Indian government. Their statements went well beyond the position taken previously by the Soviet representative at the United Nations, and they pleased not only the local dignitaries, gathered in Srinagar, but also the statesmen in Delhi. Khrushchev first acknowledged that the future of Kashmir should be "decided by the people themselves," but then he added that they "had already decided" to join India. He was also critical of Pakistan and condemned in particular the Baghdad Pact.[24] In his report to the Supreme Soviet, Bulganin accused the Western powers of worsening

[23] *Asian Recorder*, March 24-30, 1956, Vol. 1, No. 65, p. 746.
[24] *New York Times*, December 11, 1955.

the Kashmir problem for military and political purposes under the pretext of giving help to Pakistan. He confirmed Soviet support for India's policy on Kashmir because it was in accord with the interests of consolidating peace in Asia.[25]

For years the Soviet Union had abstained from voting when a resolution on Kashmir was submitted before the Security Council, but in 1955 it took a clear-cut position in favor of India. When, on later occasions the Security Council again discussed the problem, the Soviet Union twice vetoed the Council's contemplated action. The United States, on the other hand, consistently voted together with many other delegations for the numerous resolutions which were acceptable to Pakistan and criticized or rejected by India. Naturally enough, this trend only fanned the flames of the smouldering relations between India and Pakistan, whose views on basic concepts of peace in Kashmir differed so materially.

In the American concept of defense of South and South-East Asia and of the Middle East, Pakistan was to be a pivotal state. Generous American military and economic assistance to Pakistan was meant to fortify the warm relations between the two countries, and the United States' position on Kashmir, which was in keeping with her traditional stand on the question of national self-determination, appeared only to solidify this friendship. However, as the world has experienced all too often, alliances all too frequently produce fruits of questionable value. Self-centered national interest still remains the primary motivation in the conduct of foreign policy, and the Pakistani-American alliance did not prove to be an exception.

As the Soviet Union took a position openly in favor of India on the Kashmir issue, Pakistan began to complain through various channels about the lack of more resolute support from the United States. Even though the Council of SEATO, in its *communiqué* of March 8, 1956, con-

[25] *Ibid.*, December 28, 1955.

demned the Soviet statements on Kashmir and gave support to the United Nations resolutions,[26] Pakistan considered this step ineffective. However, the situation did not end with gentle warnings; Pakistan began slowly to re-evaluate her orientation in foreign policy. Since the Bandung Conference, in April 1955, when Chou En-lai and Mohammed Ali, the Prime Minister of Pakistan, exchanged complimentary statements, Peking had waited patiently behind the scene of American-Pakistani amity for a propitious moment to extend its hand of cooperation to Pakistan. It "had realized the value of Pakistan's friendship long before it was revealed in the 1960's."[27] A policy of *rapprochement* with Pakistan would lead to an isolation of India, strengthen China's security on her borders, alleviate the fears of her own Muslim minority, and, last but not least, weaken the American position in South Asia.[28]

Nevertheless, toward the end of 1956, when Prime Minister H. S. Suhrawardy was on an official visit in China, he still was to be embarrassed by Chou En-lai's statement that the partition of the Subcontinent was an "unfortunate result of British imperialism's policy of divide and rule."[29] This had been the Indian position in 1947, and the Kashmir problem would not have arisen, of course, had the Subcontinent not been partitioned.

Nor could Pakistan be pleased with a statement made a few weeks later by Chou En-lai in Colombo that India and Pakistan should seek a peaceful solution of the Kashmir question by themselves and that China did not favor sending United Nations' forces to Kashmir.[30] After all, this was

[26] *Ibid.*, March 9, 1956.
[27] Madeleine Albright, "Pakistani-Chinese Relations, 1960's." An unpublished paper, School of Advanced International Studies, Johns Hopkins University, 1963; pp. 10-11.
[28] *Ibid.*, pp. 23-26.
[29] *New York Times*, December 10, 1956.
[30] *Survey of China Mainland Press*. No. 1467, February 11, 1957, p. 34.

also India's position, while Pakistan was ready to accept a United Nations force.

Though important official visits were exchanged between Peking and Karachi, and trade relations slightly improved, China's patience continued to be taxed by Pakistan's faithful adherence to her Western allies. After Marshal Ayub Khan came to power, the Pakistani-American friendship seemed to have acquired a new, fresh dimension. Fully aware of the Communist threat, he even suggested, toward the end of 1959, a plan for joint defense of India and Pakistan, expecting that such a sweeping proposal would not only pave the way to the solution of the Kashmir problem but might also strengthen the Subcontinent's military posture against Chinese threats. The idea was rejected by India, who saw in it an attempt to foment discord between India and China, and her reply only reaffirmed her claim on Kashmir.

Pakistan did not need to sow seeds of dissension between China and India. Their two governments had exchanged confidential notes for several years on the question of common boundaries, and the Chinese occupation of Tibet had brought the mutual tensions into the open. By 1960 Indo-Chinese relations were strained to the point of border clashes.

Simultaneously with these developments, the American-Pakistani friendship was exposed to new tests. President Ayub did not make any secret of his discontent that Washington was taking Pakistan's loyalty for granted. He began to enlarge his nation's group of friends, including the Communist countries.

China's patience with Pakistan's pro-Western policy now paid off. As she faced a critical struggle with the Soviet Union for influence in Asia, and as Moscow was committed to a policy of giving support to India both in the question of Chinese-Indian tension and of Kashmir, Pakistan's growing disillusionment with the United States presented a remarkable opportunity to move toward gaining Pakistan's friendship.

Pakistan was ready for some such development. As early as March 1961 she secretly suggested to China that her boundary with Pakistan's part of Kashmir should be demarcated. Negotiations opened in the spring of 1962, and India was not slow to protest.

Then, in the autumn of 1962, Chinese armies penetrated further into Ladakh and the frontier areas of India and inflicted a humiliating defeat upon the Indian armed forces. India was in desperate need of military and political help.

Considering the fifteen years of tense relations between India and Pakistan and in particular their intense feelings on Kashmir, it is extremely difficult to pass judgment on the policy which Pakistan and India adopted toward each other at this moment of supreme Indian crisis. Some statesmen analyzing the Pakistani position and aware of the inescapable interdependence of the two countries in the ultimate defense of their national existence, would have seen that a spirit of understanding was ultimately the wisest course, pinning their hopes on an equally enlightened reaction from New Delhi. Others would have used the opportunity to take advantage of India's dramatically demonstrated weakness.

On the Indian side, some would have seen in the clash in the Himalayan mountains a propitious moment for settling the fate of the region at their foothills, the Vale of Kashmir, and of reinforcing the position of the Subcontinent against the common threat from Communist China. Others would have refused, in spite of all dangers, to submit to pressures in time of national peril.

At any rate, the attitude which Pakistan and India assumed was not calculated to bring them closer together; on the contrary, it only further aggravated their mutual bitterness.

Feelings were running high in Pakistan during the Indo-

Chinese war. Newspapers and demonstrators in streets not only expressed small concern for India but rather gave vent to their bitterness. They insisted that this was the moment for settling the Kashmir problem. The official position was more cautious. Friendly letters were exchanged between Nehru and Ayub, but there was no evidence of intent on the part of the Pakistani government to alleviate India's predicament. It reportedly declined the Western powers' suggestion to refrain from pressing the Kashmir issue during the Indo-Chinese war. On the other hand, it did assure them that it would not move militarily against India. President Ayub, at an emergency session of the National Assembly, declared that Pakistan was being threatened both by international Communism and Hindu imperialism but that the Indian threat was the more pressing. He stated that the Kashmir question could be solved either by war or by negotiations and that he favored the latter course.

Ayub also used the opportunity to de-emphasize Pakistan's ties with SEATO and CENTO, which in his opinion had become less effective, and stressed that Pakistan would not hesitate to leave the two defense organizations if they proved to be inimical to the country's interest.[31]

Pakistan's Foreign Minister Mohammed Ali went further. He stated that "there [was] no eternal friendship in international relations and there [was] no eternal enmity. As situations change, enemies can become friends and friends can become enemies." To help identify Pakistan's new friends, he praised Chou En-lai for his "act of statesmanship" by offering a cease-fire in the Chinese-Indian war. Another governmental speaker, Zulfikar Ali Bhutto, then the Minister of Industries, eulogized China even further by saying, "There are no conditions to our friendship with China. Friendship with the Chinese people is fundamental."[32] He appeared not to remember the recent

[31] *New York Times*, November 6, 7, 22, 1962.
[32] *Ibid.*, November 23, 27, 1962.

past when Nehru had viewed Indian friendship with China as equally fundamental.

In a secret speech before the National Assembly President Ayub Khan stressed that there was no understanding between Pakistan and China regarding the latter's military operations against India. He did not consider such operations as a large-scale invasion but rather as a serious border clash which had been, in fact, provoked by India—a view taken at that time also by some prominent American military experts. He took a stand against an armed action in Kashmir and emphasized the urgency of channelling Pakistan's resources into economic projects and not into a war. Pakistan also declined to sign a pact of non-aggression with China. However, to rub Indian wounds somewhat more raw, during the Indo-Chinese war Pakistan finalized negotiations with China on the delimitation of the boundary with the Pakistani part of the State of Jammu and Kashmir. One wonders what would have been the reaction of the Pakistanis had the Indians disposed of the Indian part of the State, the international status of which was still in dispute. However, the political reactions of India aside, Pakistan thus weakened her own legal position on Kashmir by having negotiated with an outside power about a state, the fate of which she had insisted (with the United Nations' approval) was yet to be decided by way of a plebiscite.

The Western world was, of course, alarmed by the Chinese aggression against India and by the lack of Indian preparedness to face it. As has been related, Averell Harriman and Duncan Sandys rushed to the Subcontinent to investigate India's military needs and to attempt a *rapprochement* between India and Pakistan. Even though the two representatives received an assurance from India that military aid would not be used against Pakistan, President Ayub Khan expressed grave disappointment over this development, convinced as he was that the Indians would "not use that force against the Chinese. In the end they will use it against us, and our friends are doing it."[33]

The Anglo-American presentations did produce an agreement between the governments of India and Pakistan to renew their efforts to resolve their outstanding differences on Kashmir so that the two countries could "live side by side in peace and friendship." They decided to start discussions at an early date "with the object of reaching an honorable and equitable settlement."[34]

The six rounds that followed this agreement did not, as we have seen, lead to any settlement; if anything, the experience of the war with China and the Pakistani attitude had only produced further deterioration in Indo-Pakistani relations.

The crisis also resulted in a regrouping of international forces. The American and British assistance to India opened an avenue to closer friendship with New Delhi, but their alliance with Pakistan suffered a severe shock in spite of their ardent desire to maintain it. Meanwhile, the Soviet Union sided with India without, however, endangering the process of improving relations with Pakistan. But Pakistan, still professing friendship for the West, continued to move closer to China. The two countries signed a trade agreement, a civil aeronautics agreement (providing for an exchange of commercial flights), a cultural exchange agreement, and a boundary agreement and exchanged official visits at top level. When Chou En-lai and the Foreign Minister of Communist China, Chen Yi, visited Pakistan for six days in February 1964, they moved away from their former position on the Kashmir question, which had been vague expressions in favor of India, to an official endorsement of Pakistan's demand for a plebiscite.[35] The game of

[33] *Pakistan News Digest*, December 15, 1962.
[34] *Asian Recorder*, December 24-31, 1962, pp. 4957-4958.
[35] *Ibid.*, March 18-24, 1964, p. 5729.

power politics had been thrown into the open; its results were not yet clear.

The War

Even as bilateral negotiations between India and Pakistan continued to reveal their barrenness, and even as the United Nations continued its exercises in frustration, the changing conditions in and around both South Asia and the disputed territory itself brought the conflict to new levels of precariousness.

Within the disputed area, the Kashmiris, long molded into submissiveness by their history of oppression under Maharaja rule, had begun to find a new spirit since the release of Sheikh Abdullah from prison in 1958. They protested on several occasions against the measures which were meant to complete the integration of their country with India. They found a political channel for the expression of their feelings in the Kashmir Plebiscite Front, which largely represented Abdullah's following, and some other small groups of opposition.

By 1965, also, the 500-mile cease-fire line supervised by some forty-five United Nations military observers had become more of a fire line than an area for peaceful contacts. Border violations had occurred in the past, but they had been rare and in most cases the result of misunderstandings among local civilians. From the beginning of 1965, however, shots were exchanged between regular Pakistani and Indian soldiers, and accusations of almost daily violations on the cease-fire line were being registered with the United Nations. In May, one battalion of Indian troops crossed the cease-fire line near Kargil and occupied several posts in the area, accusing Pakistan of interference with the traffic moving from Srinagar to Ladakh, an area exposed to Chinese pressure. The Indians subsequently withdrew the unit upon receiving assurance from U Thant that a United Nations military observers' team would be installed on both sides of the cease-fire line.

Then, unexpectedly, that same spring a local war flared up between India and Pakistan for the disputed region, Rann of Cutch. Though peace was established toward the end of June, the direct confrontation of the armed forces of the two countries further embittered their relations and led to additional tensions in Kashmir.

In May Sheikh Abdullah's internment was followed by widespread riots and arrests. The atmosphere was charged with emotional and political dynamite, ready to explode at the slightest provocation.

During the summer the drama moved toward a calamitous denouement, and by August reports began to flood the world press about a growing crisis in Kashmir.

Conflicting reports and a lack of authentic documents prevent an accurate reconstruction of events. One is limited in such a brief survey to the presentation of a composite picture as it was painted by both sides.

On August 5, according to an official Indian announcement, a considerable infiltration into Kashmir had taken place, two sabotage parties, trained and equipped in Pakistan, had crossed the cease-fire line, and, further, Pakistani troops had been firing continuously across this line in the previous few days. The reported figure of 1,000 infiltrators soon rose to 4,000. Pakistan denied the statements and asserted that the Kashmiris had risen in revolt against Indian rule. Kashmir's Chief Minister Sadiq issued a warning that if Pakistan did not stop sending infiltrators, India would march into the Pakistani territory. This intention was confirmed a few days later in a public statement by the Prime Minister of India, Lal Bahadur Shastri. A spokesman for the Azad Kashmir government, in return, threatened to send its troops across the cease-fire line if the

Indian authorities attempted to crush the freedom movement.

On September 3 the Secretary-General of the United Nations presented to the Security Council a report on the violations of the cease-fire line during the period beginning August 5, basing it primarily on the information submitted by General Robert H. Nimmo, the head of the UN observers.[36] The report stated that in the first five months of 1965 both sides had submitted a total of 2,231 complaints charging violations of the cease-fire line; of these, 377 violations were confirmed by the military observers, 218 of these having been committed by Pakistan and 159 by India. Beginning August 5, however, the number and intensity of violations increased, and, as "General Nimmo has indicated" to the Secretary-General, they "were to a considerable extent in subsequent days in the form of armed men, generally not in uniform, crossing the CFL from the Pakistan side for the purpose of armed action on the Indian side." This was a conclusion "reached by General Nimmo." In addition, a heavy and prolonged artillery fire from Pakistan across the line took place on August 15, 16, 19, 26, and 28. There was an exchange of artillery fire on August 14 and Indian artillery fire on August 25.

On August 15 the Indian troops reoccupied the Pakistani positions in the Kargil area and, as of August 24, the Pakistani armed elements were still in occupation of Indian positions in the Punch area. The same day the Indian troops occupied and retained positions in the Tithwal area, and on August 27 and 28 their artillery shelled the Pakistani area north of Punch and crossed the cease-fire line in the Uri-Bedori area. In a few days these local violations developed into an all-out war.

An annotated list of incidents, covering the period between August 5 and 30, was submitted by General Nimmo,

[36] S/6651 of September 3, 1965.

a list which was "by no means complete" because the grossly under-staffed group of United Nations military observers was unable to investigate all complaints. However, the list supports the Indian accusation that the violations immediately preceding the crisis were largely initiated by Pakistan: of the 23 incidents which were investigated, 19 occurred on the Indian side of the cease-fire line, 4 on the Pakistani side. In the case of infiltrators' activities inside the Indian part of Kashmir, General Nimmo's report cautiously "presumed" or "believed" that the infiltrators had crossed the cease-fire line from the Pakistani side.

What followed was a case example of an escalation from limited hostilities to a full-scale war. Casualties on both sides increased, as did bellicose spirits. Military logistics led to the expansion of the conflict beyond the Kashmir area as both Indian and Pakistani forces crossed their mutual boundaries in attempts to occupy strategic points and weaken or isolate the fighting in Kashmir. In addition, both sides engaged their air force, the Pakistanis using American-supplied F-86 and F-104 jets, which by agreement with the American government they were theoretically committed to use only in defense against a Communist attack. As September opened, India and Pakistan were mutually gripped in a major war. U Thant's pleas to end the conflict were unheeded.

Both governments tried to justify their actions by explanations which were frequently questionable or misleading. President Ayub Khan spoke in a broadcast[37] about popular revolt and freedom fighters in Kashmir, without mentioning infiltrators, but confirming in a general way Pakistan's pledge to support the people of Kashmir in their struggle for self-determination. However, there were no disinterested observers who reported an uprising, even though there was general agreement among knowledgeable

[37] *Press Release*, No. 27, September 1, 1965. Embassy of Pakistan, Washington, D.C.

340

people about the state of widespread unrest and growing tension in the Vale of Kashmir. Selig Harrison, for instance, reported that during a tour of Kashmir in July he found the sentiments of the people almost solidly hostile to the Indian rule and that only the presence of twelve Indian army brigades kept the movement for self-determination contained.[38]

By the same token, it was clouding the issue when Prime Minister Shastri declared[39] that there had been three elections since 1949 in the State of Jammu and Kashmir, which now was part of India, a state whose Constitution guaranteed civil rights, freedom of worship, and free elections.

At long last, on September 4, the Security Council entered the picture. In its resolution, adopted unanimously, it called upon the governments of India and Pakistan for an immediate cease-fire and for a withdrawal of armed personnel to the respective sides of the cease-fire line; it further requested the Secretary-General to report within three days on the implementation of the resolution.[40]

U Thant's pilgrimage to the Subcontinent ran into expected obstacles. The Pakistani government was reported to have refused a cease-fire which would not provide for a plebiscite in Kashmir. The Indian government stated with equal resoluteness that Kashmir was an integral part of India and that the infiltration had become a key issue. India's insistence on the necessity prior to a cease-fire to find a way to prevent a repetition of such infiltrations was indicative of her determination to hold onto certain strategic areas in the Azad Kashmir territory.

Having heard the Secretary-General's report, the Security Council on September 6 unanimously passed another resolution repeating its appeal for cessation of hostilities and

[38] *Washington Post*, August 14, 1965.
[39] *The All-India Congress Committee Economic Review*, Vol. 17, No. 7, September 15, 1965.
[40] S/RES/209 of September 4, 1965.

requesting the Secretary-General to take "all measures possible" to strengthen the United Nations observers' team. It also decided to keep "the issue under urgent and continuous review."[41]

Meanwhile, a few factors appeared which facilitated immensely the United Nations' resolute action for peace. The Soviet Union and the United States took an identical position on the conflict; the United States and Great Britain discontinued giving assistance to both belligerents; world public opinion was pressing for peace; and last but not least, the war was quickly and inexorably sapping the limited supplies of India's and Pakistan's arsenals.

On September 20 the Security Council carried a rigorous resolution; it was supported by all its members, with Jordan's abstention. The resolution first commended the Secretary-General "for his unrelenting efforts"—an unusual recognition and tribute to his services. Then it simply but firmly demanded a cease-fire in three days, "September 22, 1965 at 0700 hours GMT," and a "subsequent withdrawal of all armed personnel back to the positions" held by both governments on August 5, when the attacks began. It also decided to consider as soon as the preceding demands were met "what steps could be taken to assist towards a settlement of the political problem underlying the present conflict."[42]

Both governments complied with the resolution; on the following day the guns were silenced, at least for a few hours, and the whole world took a deep breath as a major conflagration was averted.

The six weeks of war had been accompanied by a significant re-grouping of forces which reflected the change in the relations of the big powers toward India and Pakistan. The American government assumed a policy of "studied neutrality," and though one might assume that hectic

[41] S/RES/210 of September 6, 1965.
[42] S/RES/211 of September 20, 1965.

diplomatic activities went on behind the scene, it gave strong support to the United Nations' peace efforts. Its most telling influence on the situation was its suspension, on September 7, of deliveries of military equipment to both India and Pakistan. When one week later President Ayub Khan appealed to President Johnson to use his enormous influence to bring about a settlement of the Kashmir conflict, indicating at the same time that the plebiscite was a negotiable question, he in all probability intended to offset the conspicuous support of Communist China for Pakistan and, also, to capitalize on the long-standing American friendship for his country. The Administration's impartiality in the conflict, however, was not diminished by this appeal. Its new, cordial relations with India were too valuable to be easily sacrificed, particularly when the United States was embarrassed by the Pakistanis' extensive use of American-made tanks and airplanes. As distasteful as Ayub's invitation to the United States to play a decisive role in Asian affairs must have been to China, President Johnson nevertheless refused to capitalize on the situation and politely declined the invitation. He suggested that the route to peace should be through the United Nations.

Great Britain took a similar attitude, although she was later accused of partiality in favor of Pakistan and the relations between her and India became strained.

Over the past few years the free world on several critical occasions has profited from Chinese-Soviet hostility. Here also it reaped some important benefits during the Indian-Pakistani war. The Soviet Union, who since 1955 had taken a pro-Indian position in the Kashmir conflict and whose relations with Pakistan had been, until recently, unsettled, now appealed several times to both countries to stop fighting. The USSR offered its good offices and invited Prime Minister Shastri and President Ayub Khan to meet in Russia. In this respect, the Soviet government went beyond the diplomatic moves of the American Administration, although its basic policy in the United Nations coincided generally with the American and British attitude. This was, indeed, a rare occurrence; it undoubtedly paved the way to the unanimously-approved actions of the Security Council.

The Soviet Union had a special reason to press for an end in the Indo-Pakistani war. In the conflict between Moscow and Peking the latter exploited ruthlessly any opportunity to spread armed struggle in every area of the globe, just at a time when the Soviet Union was learning to act with some sense of responsibility to avoid the danger of a nuclear catastrophe. A prolonged war between India and Pakistan would have given China a most welcome pretext to interfere, regardless of the consequences. Thus the Soviet threat of a decade ago seemed to have subsided, but in its place was the new threat of Chinese aggressiveness and subversive designs.

Communist China, indeed, took a reckless attitude during the war, encouraging Pakistan and placing India, her former friend, under exasperating pressure. At the beginning of September her Foreign Minister, Chen Yi, stated in Karachi that China supported the "just action by Pakistan to repel the Indian armed provocation"[43] in Kashmir. A few days later the Chinese government issued an ominous protest against an alleged Indian aggression along the Chinese border. Then on September 17 Peking gave India a three-day ultimatum to dismantle the fortifications between Sikkim and Tibet, to stop immediately all intrusions, and to pledge to refrain from any raids across the boundary, or else India would "bear full responsibility for all the grave consequences."[44] The Chinese government added that it would always support Kashmir's right to self-determination, emphasizing once more its approval of Pakistan's position.

Even before the Chinese ultimatum the United States had warned China not to interfere in the Indo-Pakistani

[43] *New York Times*, September 5, 1965.
[44] *Times* (London), September 18, 1965.

conflict. Peking now extended the ultimatum by another three days, until September 22, but refused the Indian offer for a joint investigation of the military situation on the Sikkim-Tibet border. Then, one day before the ultimatum expired and when it was evident that India and Pakistan would comply with the Security Council's resolution to stop fighting, the Chinese government blithely announced that the Indian forces had fled and that the Chinese army was in complete control of the disputed military installations. India denied the statement.

The Pakistani Foreign Minister, Bhutto, later acknowledged with satisfaction that China's ultimatum had played a "decisive" role in forcing the United Nations to link a settlement of the Kashmir problem with the cease-fire. While he admitted at a press conference in Rawalpindi that there might have been "some synchronization" in the actions of the two nations, he also stressed that China acted on her own as each country pursued "its own vital objectives independently of each other."[45]

The acceptance of the Security Council's demand for a cease-fire brought the major fighting to a halt, although the prospects for a settlement remained grim. The cease-fire was almost daily violated by shooting, and both sides continued to ignore a renewed demand "promptly to withdraw all armed personnel as necessary steps in the full implementation of the resolution of 20 September."[46] In defiance of this demand, they made public their intention to remain in possession of the areas which they had occupied during the war, Pakistan having advanced beyond the Kashmir cease-fire line and into the Indian territory of Rajasthan and India having penetrated into Azad Kashmir and Pakistan's territory near Sialkot, Lahore, and across the Rajasthan border. President Ayub Khan even warned that the cease-fire would remain in force only as long as he could see that

[45] *Washington Post*, October 7, 1965.
[46] S/RES/214 of September 27, 1965.

the United Nations was making progress toward an honorable solution of the Kashmir dispute.[47] His Foreign Minister Bhutto, on September 22 issued what sounded like an ultimatum to the Security Council when he declared "This is the last chance for the Security Council to put all its force, all its energy, all its moral responsibility behind a fair and equitable and honorable solution of the Jammu and Kashmir dispute." If the Security Council should not avail itself of "this last chance . . . Pakistan will have to leave the United Nations." He continued, "We shall give the United Nations a time-limit. Within a certain period of time [reportedly January 1, 1966], if the Security Council is not able to act in accordance with the responsibility placed upon it . . . Pakistan will have to withdraw from the United Nations."[48]

Bhutto made an eloquent plea before the General Assembly, in which he was convincingly critical of the Security Council's policy on the Kashmir issue, and served a slightly milder notice that Pakistan "might have to withdraw from this Organization"[49] should it further delay its settlement. He also used the opportunity to express thanks to Iran and Turkey for the help they gave to Pakistan in her hour of peril. In addition, he acknowledged the "full moral support" from "our great neighbor to the north, the People's Republic of China," addressed "a special word of thanks" to Indonesia, and paid "lasting tribute to the President of Indonesia," adding that the bonds that bind the nations of Pakistan and Indonesia "have been tempered by this crisis and have become stronger than steel."[50] Bhutto renewed the proposal for withdrawing Indian and Pakistani troops and for sending in a United Nations force as a preliminary step to a plebiscite.

[47] *Times* (London), September 23, 1965.
[48] S/PV 1244 of September 22, 1965.
[49] A/PV 1339 of September 28, 1965, p. 67.
[50] *Ibid.*, pp. 48-50, 51.

If the two Pakistani statesmen by these pronouncements meant to exercise pressure on all parties directly concerned with the issue, the impact of their diplomacy was not immediately apparent.

India demonstrated equal resoluteness in her position. Prime Minister Shastri stated that he would not budge from the stand he had taken on the basic issue of Kashmir and that there was no case for any further exercise of the right of self-determination of the Kashmiri people. The Minister of Education, M. C. Chagla, indicating the willingness of the Indian government to meet with President Ayub Khan, nevertheless declared that "Kashmir [was] a closed chapter. We are not going to vacillate on this."[51] In an identical vein the Foreign Minister of India, Sardar Swaran Singh, declared before the General Assembly of the United Nations, that "legally, constitutionally, morally, and on the basis of the will of the people, the State of Jammu and Kashmir [was] an integral part of the Indian Union." Stressing that the future of Kashmir was not negotiable, he added, "This is a position on which India takes her stand and will continue to do so."[52]

As these and other statements were made, the Kashmiri people, the focus of the calamity of Indo-Pakistani hostilities, did not remain silent. A number of opposition groups, which had been underground, now raised their voices and, demonstrating in the streets, demanded freedom. Such groupings as the Kashmir Political Conference, the Awami Action Committee, and the Plebiscite Front, were joined by young men, many of them students, who demanded resolute action, criticizing the generation of older leaders for softness and the failure of the Gandhi-tailored policy of non-violence.[53]

With the beginning of 1966 a ray of hope, faint as it

[51] *Times of India*, September 25, 1965.
[52] *New York Times*, October 13, 1965.
[53] *Ibid.*, October 19, 1965.

347

was, enlightened somewhat the somber scene of Indo-Pakistani relations. Responding to repeated invitations of the Soviet government, President Ayub Khan and Prime Minister Shastri met at the beginning of January in Tashkent. With the Chairman, Alexei Kosygin, limiting at first his role to that of the affable host, the opening contacts between the two statesmen yielded few results. President Ayub insisted on negotiating the Kashmir issue as the principal problem in the Indo-Pakistani relations, while Prime Minister Shastri refused, subsequently making the concession that Kashmir could be discussed but not negotiated. Kosygin, aware of the harm that would result from the complete failure of this confrontation not only to prospects for peace in South Asia but also to the prestige of the Soviet Union (in particular vis-à-vis Communist China), appears in the last critical moment to have extended his original function of host to one of a forceful though unofficial mediator.

The intervention produced some gratifying though partial results. On January 10, Shastri and Ayub signed a declaration, which has since become known as the Tashkent Agreement.[54] Accordingly, they resolved to restore "normal and peaceful relations" and reaffirmed "their obligation under the Charter not to have recourse to force and to settle their disputes through peaceful means." As to Kashmir, "it was against this background that Jammu and Kashmir was discussed, and each of the sides set forth its respective position." They also agreed to withdraw "all armed personnel not later than February 25, 1966, to the positions they held prior to August 5, 1965" and base their relations "on the principle of non-interference in the internal affairs of each other." They further consented to encourage propaganda promoting friendly relations and to meet at various levels on matters of mutual concern.

[54] *Ibid.*, January 11, 1966.

The Tashkent Agreement, some parts of which carry the imprint of hasty drafting, was dramatically reinforced when Prime Minister Shastri died suddenly from a heart attack only a few hours after its signing.

The Agreement unquestionably signified a marked step forward in that it provided for the withdrawal of Pakistani and Indian forces behind the cease-fire line, established in January 1949, a withdrawal demanded also, though unheeded, by the Security Council resolution of September 20, 1965. India failed to gain Pakistan's signature to a No War declaration though both parties confirmed their obligation, stipulated by the United Nations Charter, not to use force in settling their disputes. Pakistan, on the other hand, was confined merely to discussing the Kashmir issue which, moreover, might be eliminated in the future from further discussions because the signatories of the Tashkent declaration agreed not to interfere in mutual internal affairs—and India, we know, has repeatedly insisted that Kashmir is indeed a part of the state of India. As Pakistan is certain to bring the issue of Kashmir to the conference tables, either in the U.N. or in relations with India, this part of the Agreement is equally certain to be interpreted in different ways and to cause additional frictions. As important as is the Tashkent Agreement in the attempt to bring Indo-Pakistani relations under manageable control, it did not advance the solution of the Kashmir conflict.

The Soviet role in Tashkent, however, resulted in a new advantage. The Soviet government, now in the role of peacemaker, must not only assume some responsibility for the implementation of the Agreement, but it is also at least informally committed to a more impartial attitude toward the solution of the Kashmir conflict.

One could assume that Pakistan would reopen the issue before the Security Council soon after the withdrawal of the troops because its resolution of September 20 decided to consider steps which would aid in a settlement of the problems underlying the conflict. If the Soviet position draws closer to that of the United States and Great Britain, a new though still rather narrow path may open to a solution of the dispute. In spite of the détente brought about by the Tashkent Agreement the situation continues to harbor grave dangers of another explosion, calling categorically for wisdom and restraint not only by both parties at issue but also on the part of all peace-loving nations, and from the U.S. a renewed and resolute search for a satisfactory solution.

What Next?

A few paragraphs under the same title were written on this subject in the first edition of the book (pp. 196-197). It was not difficult to suggest at that time, in 1954, a course of further action which might believably lead to a peaceful solution of the Kashmir dispute.

At that time the resolutions of the Security Council and of the UNCIP were not yet rusty with disuse and outmoded in method. India then continued to accept her international obligation to permit a plebiscite in Kashmir under United Nations supervision. At that time Kashmir had not become so clearly a theatre of the Cold War, and China's active role in the politics of South Asia was more a threat than a reality. The implementation of the United Nations' resolutions had hinged on such seemingly manageable problems as the procedure for the demilitarization of the State of Jammu and Kashmir.

However, with the passage of eleven years profound changes have taken place, changes that increase tremendously the problems of a solution to the Kashmir crisis. For example, the government of India has now repudiated publicly and repeatedly its commitment to a plebiscite. Such unilateral declarations relieve her in no way of her legal and moral pledge, but they do make far more difficult, in the light of an inflated emotional engagement of her populace, any relaxation of this point of view.

On the international scene, India now faces for an indefinite period, as she did not in 1954, a Chinese threat which makes the demilitarization of Ladakh and the Vale of Kashmir, one of the basic prerequisites for the plebiscite, almost impossible. The Indo-Pakistani war over Kashmir has now intensified mutual grief and bitterness beyond the point of speedy reconciliation. All in all, therefore, much of the original procedure designed in 1948 for the solution of the Kashmir conflict, and still pertinent in 1954, may now be outdated by these overpowering events.

Yet, certain factors stand out in the seventeen-year history of the conflict as immutable guidelines for any new effort.

1. The people of Kashmir have made it unmistakably known that they insist on being heard. Whatever may be their wishes about their future, they must be ascertained directly or through their legitimate, popular representatives. This does not necessarily mean the government of the State, for the current government has now been compromised by its identification with the government of India and the rising opposition of the Kashmiris. The National Conference, ever since Sheikh Abdullah's imprisonment in 1953, has steadily lost the support and the confidence of the Kashmir people. Whatever process is used, however, the will of the people of Kashmir cannot be ignored, just as the wishes of scores of African nations—some of which are smaller and even less developed—could not be bypassed in the decades when nationalism and self-determination were sweeping across continents.

2. The accession of the State of Jammu and Kashmir to India cannot be considered as valid by canons of international law.

3. The issue itself cannot be sidetracked. The history of the case has made it clear that time has only aggravated, not

healed, the conflict; that neither the Pakistanis nor the Kashmiris will accept the *status quo* as a solution. A prolonged neglect on the part of the participants would most certainly turn against their own fundamental interests, their national security, indeed perhaps their national existence.

4. No high hope should be entertained that bilateral negotiations will lead to a settlement. They took place on several occasions during the past years and produced no results. With the cruel experience of bloodletting last September, the resumption of bilateral efforts is beyond useful consideration. The Soviet intervention at the Tashkent meeting lends further strength to this observation. Even if Pakistan and India agreed in due course to meet, all the evidence of the accumulated past points to the conclusion that such negotiations would only prolong the agony.

5. The United Nations has a principal responsibility to seek a solution not only as the chief international agency for maintenance and enforcement of peace but also as an organ which was asked by India and Pakistan to intervene in the conflict and which has committed its prestige and authority to its solution through numerous resolutions. In terms of its future, it cannot tolerate a prolonged flaunting of its decisions without dissipating completely its influence. In this light, a possible fresh start should take into careful consideration at least the spirit of the original resolutions of the Security Council and the UNCIP, which were and still are the only legal foundations for a settlement of the conflict.

If these and other factors are kept in mind, an equitable and honorable solution of the Kashmir conflict may yet be found. The procedures and processes would matter little, whether by mediation, arbitration on individual nonpolitical aspects of the dispute, or through the engagement of the International Court of Justice. Varied solutions, acceptable to all parties directly concerned, could then be reached, whether accession to India or Pakistan, independence, partition, or condominium.

As profound as is the crevasse between India and Pakistan, now in 1966 as a result of another major bloodletting, this very experience—made more fearful by the significance of the Chinese threats to India—may yet, as a painful twist of history, serve as the compelling reason, overriding all secondary considerations, why they may now accept a solution of the Kashmir dispute and open an avenue to friendly, cooperative relations. One cannot abstain from expressing the feeling that with the human suffering of the war, with China threatening from across the Himalayas and with the hopes of India and Pakistan for the future of their peoples wasted in profitless war, their responsible statesmen may have had second thoughts about the dubious advantage of being in charge of the defense of the faraway reaches of the State of Jammu and Kashmir. Therein may yet be found a clue to a solution of the conflict. If it is not achieved, India and Pakistan, indeed the whole free world may reap the harvest of shortsightedness and indecision of unpredictable dimensions.

Appendices, Bibliography, and Index

Appendix I

Resolution of the Security Council of April 21, 1948:

The Security Council,

Having considered the complaint of the Government of India concerning the dispute over the State of Jammu and Kashmir;

Having heard the representative of India in support of that complaint and the reply and counter-complaints of the representative of Pakistan;

Being strongly of the opinion that the early restoration of peace and order in Jammu and Kashmir is essential and that India and Pakistan should do their utmost to bring about a cessation of all fighting;

Noting with satisfaction that both India and Pakistan desire that the question of the accession of Jammu and Kashmir to India or Pakistan should be decided through the democratic method of a free and impartial plebiscite;

Considering that the continuation of the dispute is likely to endanger international peace and security,

Reaffirms the Council's resolution of 17 January;

Resolves that the membership of the Commission established by the resolution of the Council of 20 January 1948, shall be increased to five and shall include in addition to the membership mentioned in that resolution, representatives of . . . and . . . and that if the membership of the Commission has not been completed within ten days from the date of the adoption of this resolution the President of the Council may designate such other Member or Members of the United Nations as are required to complete the membership of five;

Instructs the Commission to proceed at once to the Indian Subcontinent and there place its good offices and mediation at the disposal of the Governments of India and Pakistan with a view to facilitating the taking of the necessary measures, both with respect to the restoration of peace and order and to the holding of a plebiscite, by the two Governments, acting in co-operation with one another and with the Commission, and further instructs the Commission to keep the Council informed of the action taken under the resolution, and to this end,

Recommends to the Governments of India and Pakistan the following measures as those which in the opinion of the Council are appropriate to bring about a cessation of the fighting and to create proper conditions for a free and impartial plebiscite to decide whether the State of Jammu and Kashmir is to accede to India or Pakistan.

A. RESTORATION OF PEACE AND ORDER

1. The Government of Pakistan should undertake to use its best endeavours:

(a) to secure the withdrawal from the State of Jammu and Kashmir of tribesmen and Pakistani nationals not normally resident therein who have entered the State for the purpose of fighting and to prevent any intrusion into the State of such elements and any furnishing of material aid to those fighting in the State;

(b) To make known to all concerned that the measures indicated in this and the following paragraphs provide full freedom to all subjects of the State, regardless of creed, caste, or party, to express their views and to vote on the question of the accession of the State, and that therefore they should co-operate in the maintenance of peace and order.

2. The Government of India should:

(a) When it is established to the satisfaction of the Commission set up in accordance with the Council's resolution of 20 January that the tribesmen are withdrawing and that arrangements for the cessation of the fighting have become effective, put into operation in consultation with the Commission a plan for withdrawing their own forces from

Jammu and Kashmir and reducing them progressively to the minimum strength required for the support of the civil power in the maintenance of law and order:

(b) Make known that the withdrawal is taking place in stages and announce the completion of each stage;

(c) When the Indian forces shall have been reduced to the minimum strength mentioned in (a) above, arrange in consultation with the Commission for the stationing of the remaining forces to be carried out in accordance with the following principles:

(i) That the presence of troops should not afford any intimidation or appearance of intimidation to the inhabitants of the State;

(ii) That as small a number as possible should be retained in forward areas;

(iii) That any reserve of troops which may be included in the total strength should be located within their present base area.

3. The Government of India should agree that until such time as the Plebiscite Administration referred to below finds it necessary to exercise the powers of direction and supervision over the State forces and police provided for in paragraph 8, they will be held in areas to be agreed upon with the Plebiscite Administrator.

4. After the plan referred to in paragraph 2(a) above has been put into operation, personnel recruited locally in each district should so far as possible be utilized for the re-establishment and maintenance of law and order with due regard to protection of minorities, subject to such additional requirements as may be specified by the Plebiscite Administration referred to in paragraph 7.

5. If these local forces should be found to be inadequate, the Commission, subject to the agreement of both the Government of India and the Government of Pakistan, should arrange for the use of such forces of either Dominion as it deems effective for the purpose of pacification.

B. PLEBISCITE

6. The Government of India should undertake to ensure that the Government of the State invite the major political groups to designate responsible representatives to share equitably and fully in the conduct of the administration at the Ministerial level, while the plebiscite is being prepared and carried out.

7. The Government of India should undertake that there will be established in Jammu and Kashmir a Plebiscite Administration to hold a plebiscite as soon as possible on the question of the accession of the State to India or Pakistan.

8. The Government of India should undertake that there will be delegated by the State to the Plebiscite Administration such powers as the latter considers necessary for holding a fair and impartial plebiscite including, for that purpose only, the direction and supervision of the State forces and police.

9. The Government of India should, at the request of the Plebiscite Administration, make available from the Indian forces such assistance as the Plebiscite Administration may require for the performance of its functions.

10. (a) The Government of India should agree that a nominee of the Secretary-General of the United Nations will be appointed to be the Plebiscite Administrator;

(b) The Plebiscite Administrator, acting as an officer of the State of Jammu and Kashmir, should have authority to nominate his assistants and other subordinates and to draft regulations governing the plebiscite. Such nominees should be formally appointed and such draft regulations should be formally promulgated by the State of Jammu and Kashmir;

(c) The Government of India should undertake that the Government of Jammu and Kashmir will appoint fully qualified persons nominated by the Plebiscite Administrator to act as special magistrates within the State judicial system to hear cases which in the opinion of the Plebiscite Administrator have a serious bearing on the preparation for and the conduct of a free and impartial plebiscite;

(d) The terms of service of the Administrator should form the subject of a separate negotiation between the Secretary-General of the United Nations and the Government of India. The Administrator should fix the terms of service for his assistants and subordinates;

(e) The Administrator should have the right to communicate directly with the Government of the State and with the Commission of the Security Council and, through the Commission, with the Security Council, with the Governments of India and Pakistan and with their representatives with the Commission. It would be his duty to bring to the notice of any or all of the foregoing (as he in his discretion may decide) any circumstances arising which may tend, in his opinion, to interfere with the freedom of the plebiscite.

11. The Government of India should undertake to prevent, and to give full support to the Administrator and his staff in preventing, any threat, coercion or intimidation, bribery or other undue influence on the voters in the plebiscite, and the Government of India should publicly announce and should cause the Government of the State to announce this undertaking as an international obligation binding on all public authorities and officials in Jammu and Kashmir.

12. The Government of India should themselves and through the Government of the State declare and make known that all subjects of the State of Jammu and Kashmir, regardless of creed, caste or party, will be safe and free in expressing their views and in voting on the question of the accession of the State and that there will be freedom of the Press, speech and assembly and freedom of travel in the State, including freedom of lawful entry and exit.

13. The Government of India should use and should ensure that the Government of the State also use their best endeavours to effect the withdrawal from the State of all Indian nationals other than those who are normally resident therein or who on or since 15 August 1947 have entered it for a lawful purpose.

14. The Government of India should ensure that the Government of the State release all political prisoners and take all possible steps so that:

(a) All citizens of the State who have left it on account of disturbances are invited, and are free, to return to their homes and to exercise their rights as such citizens;

(b) There is no victimization;

(c) Minorities in all parts of the State are accorded adequate protection.

15. The Commission of the Security Council should at the end of the plebiscite certify to the Council whether the plebiscite has or has not been really free and impartial.

C. GENERAL PROVISIONS

16. The Governments of India and Pakistan should each be invited to nominate a representative to be attached to the Commission for such assistance as it may require in the performance of its task.

17. The Commission should establish in Jammu and Kashmir such observers as it may require of any of the proceedings in pursuance of the measures indicated in the foregoing paragraphs.

18. The Security Council Commission should carry out the tasks assigned to it herein.

Appendix II

Resolution of the Commission of August 13, 1948:

The United Nations Commission for India and Pakistan,
Having given careful consideration to the points of view

expressed by the representatives of India and Pakistan regarding the situation in the State of Jammu and Kashmir, and

Being of the opinion that the prompt cessation of hostilities and the correction of conditions the continuance of which is likely to endanger international peace and security are essential to implementation of its endeavours to assist the Governments of India and Pakistan in effecting a final settlement of the situation,

Resolves to submit simultaneously to the Governments of India and Pakistan the following proposal:

PART I

Cease-fire order

A. The Governments of India and Pakistan agree that their respective High Commands will issue separately and simultaneously a cease-fire order to apply to all forces under their control in the State of Jammu and Kashmir as of the earliest practicable date or dates to be mutually agreed upon within four days after these proposals have been accepted by both Governments.

B. The High Commands of the Indian and Pakistani forces agree to refrain from taking any measures that might augment the military potential of the forces under their control in the State of Jammu and Kashmir.

(For the purpose of these proposals forces under their control shall be considered to include all forces, organized and unorganized, fighting or participating in hostilities on their respective sides.)

C. The Commanders-in-Chief of the forces of India and Pakistan shall promptly confer regarding any necessary local changes in present dispositions which may facilitate the cease-fire.

D. In its discretion and as the Commission may find practicable, the Commission will appoint military observers who, under the authority of the Commission and with the co-operation of both Commands, will supervise the observance of the cease-fire order.

E. The Government of India and the Government of Pakistan agree to appeal to their respective peoples to assist in creating and maintaining an atmosphere favourable to the promotion of further negotiations.

PART II

Truce agreement

Simultaneously with the acceptance of the proposal for the immediate cessation of hostilities as outlined in Part I, both Governments accept the following principles as a basis for the formulation of a truce agreement, the details of which shall be worked out in discussion between their representatives and the Commission.

A.

1. As the presence of troops of Pakistan in the territory of the State of Jammu and Kashmir constitutes a material change in the situation since it was represented by the Government of Pakistan before the Security Council, the Government of Pakistan agrees to withdraw its troops from that State.

2. The Government of Pakistan will use its best endeavour to secure the withdrawal from the State of Jammu and Kashmir of tribesmen and Pakistani nationals not normally resident therein who have entered the State for the purpose of fighting.

3. Pending a final solution, the territory evacuated by the Pakistani troops will be administered by the local authorities under the surveillance of the Commission.

B.

1. When the Commission shall have notified the Government of India that the tribesmen and Pakistani nationals

referred to in Part II, A, 2 hereof have withdrawn, thereby terminating the situation which was represented by the Government of India to the Security Council as having occasioned the presence of Indian forces in the State of Jammu and Kashmir, and further, that the Pakistani forces are being withdrawn from the State of Jammu and Kashmir, the Government of India agrees to begin to withdraw the bulk of its forces from that State in stages to be agreed upon with the Commission.

2. Pending the acceptance of the conditions for a final settlement of the situation in the State of Jammu and Kashmir, the Indian Government will maintain within the lines existing at the moment of the cease-fire the minimum strength of its forces which in agreement with the Commission are considered necessary to assist local authorities in the observance of law and order. The Commission will have observers stationed where it deems necessary.

3. The Government of India will undertake to ensure that the Government of the State of Jammu and Kashmir will take all measures within its power to make it publicly known that peace, law and order will be safeguarded and that all human and political rights will be guaranteed.

C.

1. Upon signature, the full text of the truce agreement or a communiqué containing the principles thereof as agreed upon between the two Governments and the Commission, will be made public.

PART III

The Government of India and the Government of Pakistan reaffirm their wish that the future status of the State of Jammu and Kashmir shall be determined in accordance with the will of the people and to that end, upon acceptance of the truce agreement, both Governments agree to enter into consultations with the Commission to determine fair and equitable conditions whereby such free expression will be assured.

Appendix III

Resolution of the Commission of January 5, 1949:

The United Nations Commission for India and Pakistan,

Having received from the Governments of India and Pakistan, in communications dated 23 December and 25 December 1948, respectively, their acceptance of the following principles which are supplementary to the Commission's Resolution of 13 August 1948:

1. The question of the accession of the State of Jammu and Kashmir to India or Pakistan will be decided through the democratic method of a free and impartial plebiscite;

2. A plebiscite will be held when it shall be found by the Commission that the cease-fire and truce arrangements set forth in Parts I and II of the Commission's resolution of 13 August 1948 have been carried out and arrangements for the plebiscite have been completed;

3. (a) The Secretary-General of the United Nations will, in agreement with the Commission, nominate a Plebiscite Administrator who shall be a personality of high international standing and commanding general confidence. He will be formally appointed to office by the Government of Jammu and Kashmir.

(b) The Plebiscite Administrator shall derive from the State of Jammu and Kashmir the powers he considers necessary for organizing and conducting the plebiscite and for ensuring the freedom and impartiality of the plebiscite.

(c) The Plebiscite Administrator shall have authority to appoint such staff of assistants and observers as he may require.

4. (a) After implementation of Parts I and II of the Commission's resolution of 13 August 1948, and when the Commission is satisfied that peaceful conditions have been restored in the State, the Commission and the Plebiscite Administrator will determine, in consultation with the Government of India, the final disposal of Indian and State armed forces, such disposal to be with due regard to the security of the State and the freedom of the plebiscite.

(b) As regards the territory referred to in A.2 of Part II of the resolution of 13 August, final disposal of the armed forces in that territory will be determined by the Commission and the Plebiscite Administrator in consultation with the local authorities.

5. All civil and military authorities within the State and the principal political elements of the State will be required to co-operate with the Plebiscite Administrator in the preparation for and the holding of the plebiscite.

6. (a) All citizens of the State who have left it on account of the disturbances will be invited and be free to return and to exercise all their rights as such citizens. For the purpose of facilitating repatriation there shall be appointed two Commissions, one composed of nominees of India and the other of nominees of Pakistan. The Commission shall operate under the direction of the Plebiscite Administrator. The Governments of India and Pakistan and all authorities within the State of Jammu and Kashmir will collaborate with the Plebiscite Administrator in putting this provision into effect.

(b) All persons (other than citizens of the State) who on or since 15 August 1947 have entered it for other than lawful purpose, shall be required to leave the State.

7. All authorities within the State of Jammu and Kashmir will undertake to ensure, in collaboration with the Plebiscite Administrator, that:

(a) There is no threat, coercion or intimidation, bribery or other undue influence on the voters in the plebiscite;

(b) No restrictions are placed on legitimate political activity throughout the State. All subjects of the State, regardless of creed, caste or party, shall be safe and free in expressing their views and in voting on the question of the accession of the State to India or Pakistan. There shall be freedom of the press, speech and assembly and freedom of travel in the State, including freedom of lawful entry and exit;

(c) All political prisoners are released;

(d) Minorities in all parts of the State are accorded adequate protection; and

(e) There is no victimization.

8. The Plebiscite Administrator may refer to the United Nations Commission for India and Pakistan problems on which he may require assistance, and the Commission may in its discretion call upon the Plebiscite Administrator to carry out on its behalf any of the responsibilities with which it has been entrusted;

9. At the conclusion of the plebiscite, the Plebiscite Administrator shall report the result thereof to the Commission and to the Government of Jammu and Kashmir. The Commission shall then certify to the Security Council whether the plebiscite has or has not been free and impartial;

10. Upon the signature of the truce agreement the details of the foregoing proposals will be elaborated in the consultations envisaged in Part III of the Commission's resolution of 13 August 1948. The Plebiscite Administrator will be fully associated in these consultations;

Commends the Governments of India and Pakistan for their prompt action in ordering a cease-fire to take effect from one minute before midnight of 1 January 1949, pursuant to the agreement arrived at as provided for by the Commission's resolution of 13 August 1948; and

Resolves to return in the immediate future to the Sub-continent to discharge the responsibilities imposed upon it by the resolution of 13 August 1948 and by the foregoing principles.

Appendix IV

Resolution of the Security Council of March 14, 1950:

The Security Council,

Having received and noted the reports of the United Nations Commission for India and Pakistan, established by the resolutions of 20 January and 21 April 1948

Having also received and noted the report of General A. G. L. McNaughton on the outcome of his discussion with the representatives of India and Pakistan which were initiated in pursuance of the decision taken by the Security Council on 17 December 1949

Commending the Governments of India and Pakistan for their statesmanlike action in reaching the agreements embodied in the United Nations Commission's resolutions of 13 August 1948 and 5 January 1949 for a cease-fire, for the demilitarization of the State of Jammu and Kashmir and for the determination of its final disposition in accordance with the will of the people through the democratic method of a free and impartial plebiscite and commending the parties in particular for their action in partially implementing these resolutions by

(1) The Cessation of hostilities effected 1 January 1949;

(2) The establishment of a cease-fire line on 27 July, and

(3) The agreement that Fleet Admiral Chester W. Nimitz shall be Plebiscite Administrator,

Considering that the resolution of the outstanding difficulties should be based upon the substantial measure of agreement on fundamental principles already reached, and that steps should be taken forthwith for the demilitarization of the State and for the expeditious determination of its future in accordance with the freely expressed will of the inhabitants,

1. Calls upon the Governments of India and Pakistan to make immediate arrangements without prejudice to their rights or claims and with due regard to the requirements of law and order, to prepare and execute within a period of five months from the date of this resolution a programme of demilitarization on the basis of the principles of paragraph 2 of General McNaughton's proposal or of such modifications of those principles as may be mutually agreed;

2. Decides to appoint a United Nations Representative for the following purposes who shall have authority to perform his functions in such place or places as he may deem appropriate:

(a) To assist in the preparation and to supervise the implementation of the programme of demilitarization referred to above and to interpret the agreements reached by the parties for demilitarization,

(b) To place himself at the disposal of the Governments of India and Pakistan and to place before these Governments or the Security Council any suggestions which, in his opinion, are likely to contribute to the expeditious and enduring solution of the dispute which has arisen between the two Governments in regard to the State of Jammu and Kashmir,

(c) To exercise all of the powers and responsibilities devolving upon the United Nations Commission by reason of existing resolutions of the Security Council and by reason of the agreement of the parties embodied in the resolutions of the United Nations Commission of 13 August 1948 and 5 January 1949,

(d) To arrange at the appropriate stage of demilitarization for the assumption by the Plebiscite Administrator of the functions assigned to the latter under agreements made between the parties,

(e) To report to the Security Council as he may consider necessary submitting his conclusions and any recommendations which he may desire to make;

3. Requests the two Governments to take all necessary precautions to ensure that their agreements regarding the cease-fire shall continue to be faithfully observed, and calls upon them to take all possible measures to ensure the creation and maintenance of an atmosphere favourable to the promotion of further negotiations;

4. Extends its best thanks to the members of the United Nations Commission for India and Pakistan and to General A. G. L. McNaughton for their arduous and fruitful labours;

5. Agrees that the United Nations Commission for India and Pakistan shall be terminated, and decides that this shall take place one month after both parties have informed the United Nations Representative of their acceptance of the transfer to him of the powers and responsibilities of the United Nations Commission referred to in paragraph 2 (c) above.

Appendix V

Resolution of the Security Council of March 30, 1951:

Having received and noted the report of Sir Owen Dixon, the United Nations Representative for India and Pakistan, on his mission initiated by the Security Council resolution of 14 March 1950;

Observing that the Governments of India and Pakistan have accepted the provisions of the United Nations Commission for India and Pakistan resolutions of 13 August 1948 and 5 January 1949 and of the Security Council resolution of 14 March 1950, and have re-affirmed their desire that the future of the State of Jammu and Kashmir shall be decided through the democratic method of a free and impartial plebiscite conducted under the auspices of the United Nations;

Observing that on 27 October 1950 the General Council of the "All Jammu and Kashmir National Conference" adopted a resolution recommending the convening of a Constituent Assembly for the purpose of determining the "future shape and affiliations of the State of Jammu and Kashmir"; observing further from statements of responsible authorities that action is proposed to convene such a Constituent Assembly and that the area from which such a Constituent Assembly would be elected is only a part of the whole territory of Jammu and Kashmir;

Reminding the Governments and Authorities concerned of the principle embodied in the Security Council resolutions of 21 April 1948, 3 June 1948 and 14 March 1950 and the United Nations Commission for India and Pakistan resolutions of 13 August 1948 and 5 January 1949, that the final disposition of the State of Jammu and Kashmir will be made in accordance with the will of the people expressed through the democratic method of a free and impartial plebiscite conducted under the auspices of the United Nations;

Affirming that the convening of a Constituent Assembly as recommended by the General Council of the "All Jammu and Kashmir National Conference," and any action that Assembly might attempt to take to determine the future shape and affiliation of the entire State or any part thereof would not constitute a disposition of the State in accordance with the above principle;

Declaring its belief that it is the duty of the Security Council in carrying out its primary responsibility for the maintenance of international peace and security to aid the parties to reach an amicable solution of the Kashmir dispute and that a prompt settlement of this dispute is of vital importance to the maintenance of international peace and security;

Observing from Sir Owen Dixon's report that the main points of difference preventing agreement between the parties were:

(a) The procedure for and the extent of demilitarization of the State preparatory to the holding of a plebiscite, and

(b) The degree of control over the exercise of the functions of government in the State necessary to ensure a free and fair plebiscite;

The Security Council,

1. Accepts, in compliance with his request, Sir Owen Dixon's resignation and expresses its gratitude to Sir Owen for the great ability and devotion with which he carried out his mission;

2. Decides to appoint a United Nations Representative for India and Pakistan in succession to Sir Owen Dixon;

3. Instructs the United Nations Representative to proceed to the Sub-continent and, after consulation with the Governments of India and Pakistan, to effect the demilitarization of the State of Jammu and Kashmir on the basis of the United Nations Commission for India and Pakistan resolutions of 13 August 1948 and 5 January 1949;

4. Calls upon the parties to co-operate with the United Nations Representative to the fullest degree in effecting the demilitarization of the State of Jammu and Kashmir;

5. Instructs the United Nations Representative to report to the Security Council within three months from the date of his arrival on the Sub-continent. If, at the time of this report, he has not effected demilitarization in accordance with paragraph 3 above, or obtained the agreement of the parties to a plan for effecting such demilitarization, the United Nations Representative shall report to the Security Council those points of difference between the parties in regard to the interpretation and execution of the agreed resolutions of 13 August 1948 and 5 January 1949

which he considers must be resolved to enable such demilitarization to be carried out;

6. Calls upon the parties, in the event of their discussions with the United Nations Representative failing in his opinion to result in full agreement, to accept arbitration upon all outstanding points of difference reported by the United Nations Representative in accordance with paragraph 5 above; such arbitration to be carried out by an Arbitrator, or a panel of Arbitrators, to be appointed by the President of the International Court of Justice after consultation with the parties;

7. Decides that the Military Observer group shall continue to supervise the cease-fire in the State;

8. Requests the Governments of India and Pakistan to ensure that their agreement regarding the cease-fire shall continue to be faithfully observed and calls upon them to take all possible measures to ensure the creation and maintenance of an atmosphere favourable to the promotion of further negotiations and to refrain from any action likely to prejudice a just and peaceful settlement;

9. Requests the Secretary-General to provide the United Nations Representative for India and Pakistan with such services and facilities as may be necessary in carrying out the terms of this resolution.

Selected Bibliography

Ambedkar, *Pakistan or Partition of India* (Bombay: Thacker and Company, 1945)

Archer, J. C., *The Sikhs* (Princeton: Princeton University Press, 1946)

Barton, Sir William, *The Princes of India* (London: Nisbet & Co., 1934)

Bazaz, Prem Nath, *Truth about Kashmir* (The Kashmir Democratic Union, 1950)

Bourke-White, Margaret, *Halfway to Freedom* (New York: Simon and Schuster, 1949)

Bowles, Chester, *Ambassador's Report* (New York: Harper & Brothers, 1953)

Brailsford, H. N., *Subject India* (New York: John Day, 1943)

Brecher, Michael, *The Struggle for Kashmir* (New York: Oxford University Press, 1953)

Brown, W. Norman, *The United States and India and Pakistan* (Cambridge: Harvard University Press, 1953)

The Cambridge History of India. Ed. by Sir Wolseley Haig. Vol. III, Chapter XII, The Kingdom of Kashmir (New York: The Macmillan Company, 1928)

Campbell-Johnson, Alan, *Mission with Mountbatten* (New York: E. P. Dutton & Co., Inc., 1953)

Colquhoun, Archibald R., *Russia against India* (New York: Harper & Brothers, 1900)

Coupland, R., *The Cripps Mission* (London: Oxford University Press, 1942)

———, *The Indian Problem* (London: Oxford University Press, 1944)

Curran, Jr., J. A., *Militant Hinduism in Indian Politics, A Study of the R.S.S.* (New York: Institute of Pacific Relations, 1951)

Davis, Kingsley, *Population of India and Pakistan* (Princeton: Princeton University Press, 1951)

Diver, Maud, *Royal India* (New York: D. Appleton-Century, 1942)

Dutt, R. Palme, *India Today* (Bombay: People's Publishing House Ltd., 1949)

Fischer, Louis, *The Life of Mahatma Gandhi* (New York: Harper & Brothers, 1950)

India, Pakistan, Ceylon. Edited by W. Norman Brown (Ithaca, N.Y.: Cornell University Press, 1951)

Jones, George E., *Tumult in India* (New York: Dodd, Mead & Co., 1948)

Karaka, D. F., *Betrayal in India* (London: Victor Gollancz, 1950)

375

Bibliography

* Krishen, Rajbans, *Kashmir and the Conspiracy against Peace* (Bombay: People's Publishing House Ltd., 1951)

Lawrence, Sir Walter R., *The India We Served* (New York: Houghton Mifflin, 1929)

——, *The Valley of Kashmir* (London: Oxford University Press, 1895)

Letters of Iqbal to Jinnah (Lahore: Kashmiri Bazaar)

Mellor, Andrew, *India Since Partition* (New York: Frederick A. Praeger, 1951)

De Montmorency, Sir Geoffrey, *The Indian States and Indian Federation* (Cambridge University Press, 1942)

Moreland, W. H., and Chatterjee, A. C., *A Short History of India*, Second Edition (New York: Longmans, Green and Company, 1945)

Motwani, Kewal, *India: A Synthesis of Cultures* (Bombay: Thacker & Company, 1947)

Muehl, John Fr., *Interview with India* (New York: John Day, 1950)

Nehru, Jawaharlal, *Autobiography* (London: The Bodley Head, 1949)

——, *The Unity of India* (New York: The John Day Company, 1946)

——, *The Unity of India* (New York: The John Day Company, 1942)

Pakistan, The Heart of Asia. Speeches by Liaquat Ali Khan (Cambridge: Harvard University Press, 1950)

Parkin, Raleigh, *India Today* (New York: John Day, 1946)

Prasad, Beni, *India Hindu-Muslim Questions* (London: George Allen & Unwin, 1946)

Prasad, Rajendra, *India Divided* (Bombay: Hind Kitabs, 1947)

Rajput, A. B., *Muslim League Yesterday and Today* (Lahore: Muhammad Ashraf)

Raman, T. A., *Report on India* (London: Oxford University Press, 1943)

Rawlinson, H. G., *India. A Short Cultural History* (New York: D. Appleton-Century, 1938)

Saiyid, M. H., *Mohammad Ali Jinnah: A Political Study* (Lahore: Ashraf Press, 1945)

Sinha, Dr. Sachchidananda, *Kashmir: "The Playground of Asia"* (Allahabad, 1943)

Skrine, Francis Henry, *The Expansion of Russia* (Cambridge University Press, 1904)

Smith, Vincent H., *The Oxford History of India* (London: Oxford University Press, 1923)

Smith, Wilfred C., *Modern Islam in India*, Second Edition (London: Victor Gollancz, 1946)

376

Smith, William Roy, *Nationalism and Reform in India* (New Haven: Yale University Press, 1938)

Some Recent Speeches and Writings of Mr. Jinnah. Col. and Ed. by Jamil-ud-Dinahmad (Lahore: Kasmiri Bazar, 1942)

Spear, Percival, *India, Pakistan and the West* (New York: Oxford University Press, 1949)

Sufi, G. M. D., *Islamic Culture in Kashmir* (Simla: The Army Press, 1925)

————, *Kashīr, Being a History of Kashmir*. Two volumes (Lahore: The University of Punjab, 1948)

Symonds, Richard, *The Making of Pakistan* (London: Faber and Faber, 1950)

Thompson, Edward, *The Making of the Indian Princes* (London: Oxford University Press, 1943)

Time Only to Look Forward. Speeches of Rear Admiral the Earl Mountbatten of Burma (London: Nicholas Kaye, 1949)

The Tuzuk-I-Jahangiri or Memoirs of Jahangir. Translated by A. Rogers, Edited by H. Beveridge. Two volumes (London: Royal Asiatic Society, 1914)

Vairanapillai, M. S., *Are We Two Nations?* (Lahore: Herbert Milton Williams, 1946)

Wallbank, T. Walker, *India in the New Era* (Chicago: Scott, Foresman, 1951)

Younghusband, Sir Francis E., *Kashmir* (London: A. and C. Black, 1909)

Documents and Pamphlets

Published by:

THE GOVERNMENT OF INDIA:

Aitchison, C. U., *A Collection of Treaties, Engagements, and Sanads Relating to India and Neighbouring Countries.* Vol. XII. (Calcutta: Government of India Central Publication Branch, 1931)

Documents Regarding Kashmir. (Washington, D.C.: Government of India Information Services)

Government of India. *White Paper on Jammu and Kashmir*

Indian Muslim Leaders on Kashmir. (New York: The India Delegation to the United Nations)

Twelve Months of War in Kashmir. (Washington, D.C.: Government of India Information Services)

THE GOVERNMENT OF PAKISTAN:

The Background of the Kashmir Problem.

India's Threat to Pakistan. Correspondence Between the Prime

Bibliography

Ministers of Pakistan and India 15th July-11th August, 1951. White Paper

India's War Propaganda Against Pakistan. White Paper. Government of Pakistan. (Ministry of the Interior, Information and Broadcasting)

Inside Kashmir. (Lahore: Printed by the Superintendent, Government Printing, West Punjab, 1948)

Kashmir Before Accession. (Lahore: Printed by the Superintendent, (Government Printing, West Punjab, 1948)

Khan, Sardar Mohammad Ibrahim. *Kashmir and the United Nations.*

No War Declaration and Canal Waters Dispute. (Correspondence Between The Prime Ministers of Pakistan and India) (Superintendent, Government Printing and Stationery, Sind Karachi)

The Story of Kashmir.

THE GOVERNMENT OF THE STATE OF JAMMU AND KASHMIR:

Abdullah, Sheikh Mohammad, *Jammu and Kashmir* (1947-1950)

Abolition of Hereditary Rule in Kashmir. (Background based on speech made by Hon. Sheikh Mohammed Abdullah, 1952)

Administration Report of the Jammu and Kashmir State for S. 2002. (13 April 1945 to 12 April 1946.) (Jammu: The Ranbir Government Press, 1947)

Administration Report of the Jammu and Kashmir State for S. 2006. (13 April 1949 to 12 April 1950.) (Jammu: The Ranbir Government Press, 1952)

Bedi, B. P. L., and Bedi, Freda, *Sheikh Abdullah, His Life and Ideals.*

Beg, Mirza Mohammad Afzal, *On the Way to Golden Harvests. Agricultural Reforms in Kashmir.* (Jammu: Land Reforms Officer, Jammu and Kashmir Government)

Census of India, 1941. Vol. xxii: Jammu and Kashmir (Jammu: The Ranbir Government Press, 1943)

Elections to Jammu and Kashmir Constituent Assembly. (Jammu and Kashmir: Ministry of Information and Broadcasting)

4 Years. (Issued by: Ministry of Information and Broadcasting, Jammu and Kashmir. The Caxton Press, New Delhi)

5 Years. (Issued by: Ministry of Information and Broadcasting, Jammu and Kashmir. The Caxton Press, New Delhi, 1953)

How They See Us: How They Saw Us. (Jammu and Kashmir: Ministry of Information and Broadcasting)

Jammu and Kashmir Constituent Assembly. *Opening Address by The Hon'ble Sheikh Mohammed Abdullah.* (Srinagar, 1951)

Bibliography

The Jammu and Kashmir Constitution Act No. XIV, of S. 1996. (1939 A.D.)

Jammu and Kashmir 1947-1950. An account of activities of first three years of Sheikh Abdullah's Government. (Jammu: Ranbir Government Press, 1951)

Jammu and Kashmir Today. (Published by the Ministry of Information and Broadcasting, Jammu and Kashmir)

Kashmir (August 7 to September 17, 1953). (New Delhi: Current Affairs Publications)

Kashmir's Journey to Freedom. (A rapid survey of political events in Jammu and Kashmir since 1931.) (Published by: J. N. Zutski for the Jammu and Kashmir National Conference)

Land Reforms. (Land Reforms Officer, Jammu and Kashmir State)

New Kashmir. With an Introduction by Sheikh Md. Abdullah (New Delhi: Kashmir Bureau of Information)

On the Road to New Kashmir. (Srinagar: Ministry of Information and Broadcasting)

Report of the Inquiry Committee Appointed to Examine the Working of Land Reforms, Price Control, etc. (Jammu: The Ranbir Government Press, 1953)

Towards Solvency. (Published by the Land Reforms Officer, Jammu and Kashmir Government)

Index

Index

Index

Goodall, M. C., 292 n.

Gopalan, A. K., Indian Communist leader, favors accession to India, 264; on Delhi agreement of July 1952, 265

Gracey, General Sir Douglas D., 87; justifies Pakistani military intervention, 138-139

Graeffe, Egbert, member of UNCIP for Belgium, 119 n.

Graeffe, Harry, alternate member of UNCIP for Belgium, 119 n.

Graham, Frank P., UN mediator, 178; reaction in Kashmir to appointment of, 182; proposals made by, 185-187; five reports to Security Council, 185; methods of mediation pursued by, 188-189; Soviet accusation of, 260

Grand Mufti of Jerusalem, 183

Great Britain, relationship with Princely States, 14, 46; tribesmen and policy of, 74, 137; and Security Council resolution of April 21, 1948, 111; Pakistan critical of, 113, 184; the Kashmir conflict and attitude of, 176, 177; Nehru critical of, 182; accused of imperialist policy in Kashmir, 257, 258; and solution of Kashmir conflict, 269; and Czarist policy toward India, 274 ff; signs Convention with Russia in 1907, 278; establishes Council in Kashmir, 279; and Baku congress, 281; and Soviet policy in Middle East, 281 ff; signs commercial treaty with Soviet Union in 1921, 282; Soviet subversion denounced by, 283, 285

Greece, India points to analogy of, 106

Gulab Singh, Maharaja, 13, 15

Gulmarg, 241

Gurdaspur, 62

Gurkhas, in the Maharaja army, 54

Gwalior, Princely State, 292

Haight, R. K., 94-95

Hall, Rear Admiral J. T. S., 86

Hamdard (Srinagar), 20, 22

Hammarskjold, Dag, 164

Hari Singh Bahadur, Maharaja Sir, 16

health services, in Azad territory, 201-202; and New Kashmir, 205; in Ladakh, 229

Hedgewar, Dr. K. B., founder of RSS, 52

Hertz, Frederick, on nationalism, 30

Himalayas, 8, 299

Hind Mazdoor Sabha, 294

Hindu, The (Madras), 182 n., 189 n., 190 n., 207 n., 222 n., 223 n., 227 n., 230 n., 233 n., 235 n., 262 n.

Hindu Mahasabha party, supports Praja Parishad agitation, 234; calls off agitation, 237

Hindu-Muslim relations, history of, 25 ff; Kashmir's role in, 42-43; and riots preceding and following Partition, 48-50, 52-54, 72; riots in Punjab, 64; riots in Kashmir, 68; and Abdullah's appeal for unity, 71; and tribal invasion, 77; and bloodshed in Kashmir, 92; and Gandhi, 107; riots in February 1950, 166; and proposed arbitration of disputes, 179; and Lenin's appeal for unity in, 284

Hindus, in Kashmir, 6, 8, 13; in Jammu, 8; and conversion to Islam, 11, 13, 28; and their privileged position, 16, 240;

Index